NEW FRONTIERS
IN INTERNATIONAL
COMMUNICATION THEORY

Communication, Media, and Politics

Series Editor
Robert E. Denton, Jr., Virginia Tech

This series features a broad range of work dealing with the role and function of communication in the realm of politics, broadly defined. Including general academic books, monographs, and texts for use in graduate and advanced undergraduate courses, the series will encompass humanistic, critical, historical, and empirical studies in political communication in the United States. Primary subject areas include campaigns and elections, media, and political institutions. *Communication, Media, and Politics* books will be of interest to students, teachers, and scholars of political communication from the disciplines of communication, rhetorical studies, political science, journalism, and political sociology.

Titles in the Series

Forthcoming

NEW FRONTIERS IN INTERNATIONAL COMMUNICATION THEORY

Edited by
Mehdi Semati

ROWMAN & LITTLEFIELD PUBLISHERS, INC.
Lanham • Boulder • New York • Toronto • Oxford

ROWMAN & LITTLEFIELD PUBLISHERS, INC.

Published in the United States of America
by Rowman & Littlefield Publishers, Inc.
A wholly owned subsidary of The Rowman & Littlefield Publishing Group, Inc.
4501 Forbes Boulevard, Suite 200, Lanham, Maryland 20706
www.rowmanlittlefield.com

PO Box 317, Oxford OX2 9RU, UK

British Library Cataloguing in Publication Information Available

Library of Congress Cataloging-in-Publication Data

Semati, Mehdi.
  New frontiers in international communication theory / edited by Mehdi Semati.
    p. cm. — (Communication, media, and politics)
  Includes bibliographical references and index.
  ISBN 0-7425-3018-3 (alk. paper) — ISBN 0-7425-3019-1 (pbk. : alk.
paper)
  1. Communication, International. I. Title. II. Series.
P96.I5 S46 2004
302.2'01—dc22

                                                        2003024472

∞™ The paper used in this publication meets the minimum requirements of American
National Standard for Information Sciences—Permanence of Paper for Printed Library
Materials, ANSI/NISO Z39.48-1992.

In loving memory of my niece, Sarina Semati,
whose smiles in a life all too short
made this world a more beautiful place

Contents

Acknowledgments

I WROTE MY FIRST PAPER as an undergraduate student for an international communication class at the University of Kentucky-Lexington. The course was
taught by Professor Milton Shatzer, and the term paper was entitled "Cultural
Imperialism." It was an audacious attempt. Although the paper was beautifully
typed, Dr. Shatzer didn't think much of it. I could tell by the grade he gave it. I
found that paper recently. I now see why Dr. Shatzer, as generous as he was, did
not think I was going to win an award. Fifteen years later, this volume is an attempt to answer some of the questions I tried to raise in that paper.

A number of people deserve recognition for their teaching and support
over those years. I want to thank Milton Shatzer and Tom Lindlof for their
teaching and for the scholarship (the cash prize saved my neck). I would like
to thank Michael Porter for his guidance and charm, Pam Benoit for being
demanding, Bill Benoit and Michael Kramer for getting me interested in reading in their fields. Charlie Shepherdson made Derrida, Lacan, Foucault, Kris-
teva, and Irigaray fun. For those amazing seminars, for making research a
great teaching tool, and for being Charlie, thank you.

I also want to thank colleagues at Michigan Technological University, espe-
cially Jennifer Daryl Slack, for taking me in and giving me continued support.
The incredible Patty Sotirin has been a true friend and a remarkable mentor.
She has given me countless constructive criticisms and thoughtful guidance.
Thanks for the coffee shop talks too. Thanks to the Conjunctures group for in-
tellectual stimulation, to Yahya Kamalipour and Mark Borzi for their support.

I should not forget to thank those anonymous reviewers who provided substantive and substantial feedback, and to everyone at Rowman & Littlefield,

especially Brenda Hadenfeldt and Bob Denton Jr., for their professionalism. Finally, I want to thank the contributors to this book for sharing their work.

A few other individuals, call them crazy, have remained my friends throughout the years: Joe and Sheila Lebrato in Dubai, Kelly Mitchell in Missouri, Stephanie Kaiser in Germany, Nasser Arafati, Nader Arafati, and Cyrille Habert, from a long list of people in France. Above all, Philippe Ohanian, despite all my efforts to deter him from doing so, has remained my best friend. I could not have done it without you and your family (add Sabrina Bartoletti, the gem). I cannot thank you enough. To all my friends in Paris, *Merci*, and I will add: Mehdi *n'est pas à la maison!*

A nomad needs the support of a loving family. Thanks to Faezeh for putting up with me lovingly, and to Susan and Masoud for locking the door that night. More than anything else, the loving support from my parents, and from Hadi, Abbas, Nazee, Sara, and their families, has been the constant factor in my life. Without them, I am lost. Thank you for being there.

Introduction

New Frontiers in International Communication

Mehdi Semati

INTERNATIONAL COMMUNICATION is increasingly indispensable in a world where increased interdependency, interconnectivity, proximity, and international/intercultural contact have become the order of the day. Matters of politics, commerce, culture, security, and health, to name the obvious, are linked to forces that are at once internal to local contexts and responsive to external pressures. International communication is a complex and critical force within and among these contexts and pressures. At this explosive juncture of world history, politics, and economics, it behooves us to attend more acutely to our conceptualizations of international communication and the traditions and trajectories of the scholarly field that investigates them.

This volume has a twofold purpose: first, to refigure the problematics that configure the field of international communication studies and, second, to move conceptually beyond the limits of extant formulations, approaches, and trajectories—to chart new frontiers of inquiry. These purposes beg the preliminary and contested issues of designating and delimiting international communication as a discrete field of study. I would like to address these issues briefly before introducing the chapters to follow.

The claim that international communication is a "field" is neither straightforward nor uncontested. If I say "field" of inquiry, it is because international communication is not a discipline (Mowlana 1996). Indeed, the eclecticism of international communication studies both denies any unmuddled disciplinary identity and invites identity contestations and crises. The disciplinary stakes in the field are multiple: various aspects of international communication technologies, forms, and structures have been addressed by other disciplines (e.g., international relations, sociology, political science). Little wonder that international communication as a field of study shares in the disciplinary identity crisis that historically has plagued communication studies more generally as well as the pernicious longing for academic legitimacy that often fuels ambitions among communication scholars for disciplinary status.[1]

Furthermore, designating international communication as a "field" embroils us in arguments over definitions and parameters. In an article entitled "Defining International Communication as a Field," Stevenson (1992) noted wryly that "it's hard to define, but you know it when you see it" (543). Of course, knowing and seeing are always already framed by disciplinary allegiances and theoretical commitments. For example, Mowlana (1996, 1998), one of the pioneers in the field, keeps his sights on contributions by scholars from international relations while Stevenson (1994) is especially cognizant of the role of journalism scholarship. More in tune with the developments in the social scientific approach to "mass communication," Hur (1982) views the field as "international mass communication." These variations attest to the complexity of international communication as a field of study and the futility of defining the field within any particular disciplinary or paradigmatic perspective.[2]

The claim I wish to make by designating international communication as a "field" is that, following Peters's (1993, 132) argument for communication studies more generally, international communication studies is a mode of "organizing inquiry." Here a field is a topic field rather than a discipline field (133). This conception of the "field" of international communication is more fluid and dynamic than most definitional projects might allow. The advantage of such a conception is that we can think "organizing" as an ongoing process, allowing us to continually redraw the contours of the field. It is in such a spirit that I introduce and reorganize some of the constitutive topics of international communication.

Clustering Topics of Inquiry in/as International Communication

The wide range of issues studied in international communication textbooks, journals, and classes may be grouped in a list of topics that intimate the expansiveness of the field's empirical concerns.[3] These entries are not mutually exclusive or exhaustive, but they do draw a picture that shows the dynamic conceptual and empirical contours of the field.[4]

- Communication and development (development communication)
- Technology transfer (e.g., diffusion of innovation)
- Development journalism
- Modernization theory
- Dependency theories

- Nation, nationalism, and national cultural
- State, nation-state, and sovereignty
- International relations and communication
- Global communicative access (e.g., new world information order, new world information and communication order)
- Cultural imperialism
- Media imperialism
- Transnational corporations, transnational media corporations
- International organizations and communication (e.g., UN, UNESCO)
- International television and radio broadcasting
- Broadcasting and propaganda (e.g., Radio Free Europe, Radio Liberty)
- Theories of the press (e.g., *Four Theories* of the press model)
- Free flow of information
- International traffic in media content (e.g., international market in film and television programs)
- Global news flow
- International news agencies
- Transborder data flow
- International (tele)communication technology (e.g., satellite technologies)
- International (tele)communication policy and regulation (e.g., International Telecommunications Union)
- Cross-cultural media reception studies
- Globalization

These topics in different combinations make up different clusters of issues that either share empirical roots or address common structural concerns and might provide focus points for a variety of courses and research projects. We may say, for example, that the following cluster of topics has development or modernization as a central problematic or as the structuring element.

Development/Modernization Cluster

- Communication and development (development communication)
- Technology transfer (e.g., diffusion of innovation)
- Development journalism
- Dependency theories

To take another example, we may group the following topics under the cluster of journalism in the arena of international relations.

Journalism in the International Arena Cluster

- Theories of the press (e.g., *Four Theories* of the press model)
- International news agencies

- Free flow of information
- Global news flow

The following topics would make up a telecommunication cluster.

Telecommunication Cluster

- Transborder data flow
- International telecommunication technology (e.g., satellite technologies)
- International telecommunication policy and regulation (e.g., International Telecommunications Union)
- International television and radio broadcasting

Or we may reorganize the topics to form a cluster in culture and international communication.

Culture and International Communication Cluster

- Nation, nationalism, and national cultural
- Cultural imperialism
- Media imperialism
- International traffic in media content (e.g., international market in film and television programs)
- Cross-cultural media reception studies

As already mentioned, these clusters are not mutually exclusive. For example, we may select some entries from the journalism cluster and add them to others to form a differently focused cluster.

Global Media Access Cluster

- Global communicative access (e.g., new world information order, new world information and communication order)
- International traffic in media content (e.g., international market in film and television programs)
- International news agencies
- Free flow of information
- Global news flow
- International news agencies

Another cluster may be formed around geopolitics and communication.

Geopolitics and Communication

- International relations and communication

- State, nation-state, sovereignty, and communication
- Nation, national identity, national cultural, and media
- Broadcasting and propaganda (e.g., Radio Free Europe, Radio Liberty)
- International organizations and communication (e.g., UN, UNESCO)

These clusters of issues and topics offer one way to engage with the field as a mode of organizing inquiry.[5] Another way is to write the history of the field as a narrative of the logics and modalities that have organized scholarly inquiry into international communication. For example, among the organizing forces critical to the formation of the field were geopolitical relations and economic logics. In the aftermath of World War II, and in the context of the Cold War, prominent American social scientists were funded (often through unacknowledged government subsidies) to research specific topics of interest in line with broader U.S. geopolitical objectives. Therefore, the selection of these topics was not politically disinterested or historically accidental. The creation of the Center for International Studies at Massachusetts Institute of Technology during the Cold War is an example of the academic activities that took place in such a context (Simpson 1993; Mowlana 1996). "Modernization theory" and "development communication," perspectives that continue to be influential, are among the intellectual and theoretical frameworks in the history of the field that are difecult to explain outside of this geopolitical context (see Samarajiva 1985; Simpson 1994; Thussu 2000). In short, a comprehensive mapping of the field must account for various (temporal and topical) organizing dynamics and logics and the contexts in which they operate. The following section develops a circumscribed narrative of the concepts and contexts that have organized international communication as a field of inquiry.

U.S. Communication Research as an Organizing Context

Exploring the conceptions, logics, and contexts that have organized scholarly inquiry into international communication is one way of writing the history of the field. Given the specification of international communication as a mode of organizing inquiry, there can be no definitive history since the contexts and contours of the field are dynamic and contestable. There are competing views of the way theoretical and conceptual constituents may be grouped and organized (e.g., Sreberny 2000; Boyd-Barrett 1998). Nonetheless, it is important to situate the emergence of the field within larger geopolitical, economic, cultural, theoretical, and conceptual contexts (Mody and Lee 2002; McDowell 2002; Rogers and Hart 2002). Any attempt to refigure the "frontiers" of international communication must acknowledge the various (temporal and topical) organizing dynamics and logics that have shaped the field and the contexts within which they operate. While I remain suspicious of linear narratives and their teleological presuppositions, I wish to highlight the juncture of forces and contexts that constituted early communication research in the United States as particularly significant for understanding the emergence of international communication as a recognizable field.

Early propaganda studies of World War I and similar studies in World War II provided some of the political-conceptual grounds for international communication studies. Development and modernization theories took off in the 1950s and continued in the 1960s (the decade in which the field of international communication started to undergo institutionalization in the United States). Marxist and neo-Marxist perspectives on imperialism and dependency, which gained prominence in the 1970s, provided an alternative to the development paradigm. In the 1980s, while British cultural studies influenced some of the arguments in the field in one direction, the remnants of the development paradigm formed the "telecommunication for development" tradition (McDowell 2002) in another direction. In the 1990s (and up to the present moment), the international communication field has been preoccupied with the empirical and theoretical implications of globalization.

Among the most prominent contributions to the early propaganda studies was Lasswell's *Propaganda Technique in the World War* (1927). The tone and direction of much communication research to come was formulated in this text by a founding question: "Who says what to whom via what channels with what effect?" This question invoked a specific conception of communication and mobilized a tradition of research that dominated the field of communication as such in the United States. It is not insignificant that much of the research by many of the founding figures in U.S. communication studies (Harold Lasswell, Paul Lazarsfeld, Wilbur Schramm, Daniel Lerner, Hadley Cantril, Ithiel de Sol Pool, among others) was military-related U.S. government-subsidized research in psychological warfare and propaganda. As Simpson (1993, 1994) demonstrates, research centers such as Cantril's Institute for International Social Research at Princeton, Lazarsfeld's Bureau of Applied Social Research at Columbia University, and Pool's Center for International Studies at MIT were among the communication research centers that "grew up as de facto adjuncts of government psychological warfare programs" (Simpson 1993, 316). Simpson's view is that "it is unlikely that mass communication research could have emerged in anything like its present form without constant transfusion of money for the leading lights in the field from U.S. military, intelligence, and propaganda agencies" (316). In short, one of the earliest research traditions in communication that shaped the emergence of international communication studies was related to U.S. international affairs and conduct.[6]

In the aftermath of World War II, and in the context of the Cold War, prominent American social scientists continued to be funded (often through unacknowledged government subsidies) to research specific topics of interest in line with the broader geopolitical objectives of the United States. The selection of these research topics—many of which still predominate in international communication studies—was not politically disinterested or historically accidental. The establishment of the Center for International Studies at MIT is an example of Cold War–related academic activity (Simpson 1993; Mowlana 1996). Not surprisingly, it was during this time that the institutionalization of international communication studies gained momentum. There are intellectual and theoretical frameworks in the history of the field that cannot be explained coherently outside this historical-geopolitical context, notably the still influential and historically significant "development communication" perspective or "modernization theory" and four theories of the press model (Samarajiva 1985; Simpson 1994; Thussu 2000; Nerone 1995). The four theories of the press model was conceived in an enormously influential book by Siebert, Peterson, and Schramm, *Four Theories of the Press* (1956). Examples of major work that contributed to the dominance of this paradigm included Lerner, *The Passing of Traditional Society: Modernizing the Middle East* (1958); Everett Rogers, *Diffusion of Innovation* (1962); and Schramm, *Mass Media and National Development: The Role of Information in the Developing Countries* (1964).

It is hard to overstate the importance of the development or modernization framework for the field of international communication. In the first place, it guided much of the theorizing and the research at the time. Additionally, it was against this perspective that many Marxist and neo-Marxist dependency theories directed their arguments. Some of the chief reasons for the emergence of this paradigm and its popularity among academics and policymakers include the formation of newly independent states after decolonization; the success of the Marshall Plan in the reconstruction of Europe during the aftermath of World War II; the experience of economic growth in the Western nations following industrialization; the dominance of quantitative research in the social scientific tradition; the founding of the United Nations and its related agencies (engaged in activities impacting all aspects of life—economic, educational, cultural, and so on—in the nation-states); the establishment of the U.S. Agency for International Development; liberal/capitalist ideology as a political and intellectual framework; the interest of the United States, the Soviet Union, and Europe in the study of "other" parts of the world; the influence of the United States in bringing the less industrialized countries into the dominant capitalist social and economic system; the spread of communism as a political ideology and the onset of the Cold War (Singhal and Sthapitanonda 1996; Mowlana 1998; Mowlana and Wilson 1990). In the postwar environment, the modernization perspective provided the theoretical language for

U.S. foreign policy and its Cold War ideological confrontations. It also provided the theoretical framework for most of the studies concerned with international communication conducted in the United States (Mowlana 1998).

The modernization perspective divided the world into "traditional" and "developed" (i.e., "Western-like") societies. The goal of development in this perspective was to facilitate the transformation of a society from a traditional to a developed state in a unidirectional and irreversible movement. Here exposure to media was viewed as a step in the process of development. For Lerner (1958), the media realized a "magic multiplier" effect with tremendous power for social mobilization and development. Mass media were seen as both an index of social change and the agent of socialization. Rogers (1962) studied the process of adopting new technologies in a given social system and the changes that were brought about as a result. Schramm (1964) studied social change and mass media in terms of changes in individuals in a social system. Ultimately, these studies were, in one form or another, interested in a mode of social change unwittingly rooted in U.S. perspectives and interests.

The modernization perspective was criticized for, among other things, its ethnocentric worldview and its neglect of external factors for "underdevelopment." An alternative to the worldview espoused by modernization theory was advanced by dependency theories, which framed development processes in the perspective of the developing nations. Dependency theorists, often writing in different shades of neo-Marxism sought to explain the structural conditions in which development in some parts of the globe was conditioned or structured by underdevelopment in others. They argued that the countries of the south were kept in a state of "dependent development" as the transnational corporations, through the policies adopted by their northern governments, dominated the world market in various arenas, including communication and media industries (e.g., Schiller 1969; Amin 1976; Tunstall 1977; Mattelart 1979).[7]

Two major developments in the field grew out of this context: the embracing of the movement advocating the new world information and communication order (NWICO) and the conceptualization of cultural imperialism, one of the most persistent lines of argument in the field of international communication. Global communicative access was first formally demanded in the new international information order at the conference of the nonaligned countries held in Algiers in 1973. Supplementing calls by the Third World for a new international economic order, the proponents of NWICO recognized massive disparity in access to the means of international communication and in the one-way flow of information (from north to south). The United Nations Educational, Scientific, and Cultural Organization (UNESCO) took up the ambitious call for restructuring world communication systems. A very ideologically charged debate ensued during which opponents of NWICO framed the call as an attempt by the Third World countries at press regulation and censorship instead of seeing it as an attempt to address global inequities in the realm of communication (Roach 1987; Preston, Herman, and Schiller 1989; Gerbner, Mowlana, and Nordenstreng 1993).

The cultural imperialism thesis, sometimes viewed as distinct from media imperialism, belongs to the tradition of critical discourse that emerged out of the sociopolitical upheavals of the 1960s in many parts of the world. The proponents of this thesis have put forth various arguments in the domain of international culture and communication: the media have been viewed as the ideological arm of multinational corporations, promoting and extending capitalist forms of social and economic organization; the media promote the culture of capitalism; the dominant Western media spread Western cultural values and norms; global communication technologies in the hands of multinational corporations threaten the cultural sovereignty of the dominated nations; the multinational media corporations contribute to a homogenization of national cultures and identities (Schiller 1976; Schiller and Nordenstreng 1979; Boyd-Barrett 1977; Lee 1980). As one would expect from any conceptual edifice with such wide-ranging appeal and application, the cultural imperialism thesis has been regularly assessed, contested, and reassessed (e.g., Fejes 1981; Tomlinson 1991; Golding and Harris 1997; Boyd-Barrett 1998).[8] That the cultural imperialism thesis has enjoyed popularity and longevity in the face of its equally enduring theoretical critique is, I would argue, a reflection of the perennial need for a *critical* enterprise capable of addressing persistent structural asymmetry in the area of global communication that cannot be explained away by a tedious "active audience" line of argument (Schiller 1991).

The notion of an active audience was a preoccupation of the 1980s, the decade in which cultural studies (and sometimes "postmodernism") began to exert influence in certain areas of international communication. One of the issues the cultural imperialism thesis raised was the "dumping" (the one-way flow) of cultural products into the south.[9] Critics of the cultural imperialism thesis found a weak spot in its catalog of charges by focusing on what local audiences might make of cultural imports. These critics found evidence for their position in both the traditional approaches to communication (e.g., Katz and Liebes 1986) and in the emerging field of cultural studies (Hall 1980; Morley 1980; Ang 1985).[10] Studies from both approaches suggested that popular audiences resist manipulation, find their own indigenous values reinforced in the encounter with mediated cultural imports, and hold the "pleasure of the text" to be more important than the ideological content of the "text."

This line of thinking was associated with the "interpretative" turn in the social sciences, building on reception studies and the rise of qualitative methodology.[11] Critics charged that this model of audience resistance addressed only a fraction of the structural asymmetry in world communication systems. Further, researchers in the radical tradition of mass communication studies rejected optimistic and rosy scenarios based on the limited notion of an active audience, seeing such developments as politically disabling (Schiller 1991; Curran 1990). Later, even within cultural studies the excessively celebratory treatment of popular culture, as allegedly exemplified by the work of Fiske (1987), was rejected (Morris 1990; Morley 1997). Both in Europe and in the United States, interpretive researchers were charged with "revisionism." For example, Curran (1990) questioned the contribution of revisionist arguments to the extent that they sought, according to Curran, to reinvent the wheel.[12] An issue of a U.S. journal, *Critical Studies in Mass Communication* (June 1990), entitled "Reading Recent Revisionism," reflected the range of views on revisionism. In some instances it became an indictment of "American cultural studies" (Budd, Entman, and Steinman 1990). Others saw revisionists' contribution as a repetition of the past, characterizing interpretive media models as merely previous models like "uses and gratifications" dressed up in a new language (Evans 1990).[13]

Some of these debates became wrapped into issues of globalization, localism, global capitalism, the dissipation of the nation-state, and other empirical and theoretical concerns. During the 1990s, the question of "globalization" became a pressing issue across various fields of inquiry, including communication and media studies, as well as international communication (e.g., Mohammadi 1997; Golding and Harris 1997; Sreberny-Mohammadi et al. 1997; Boyd-Barrett and Rantanen 1998). Keeping in mind the lessons and the limitations of globalization debates, we must look to new scholarly frontiers to maintain the organizing vitality of international communication as a field.

Exploring New Frontiers in International Communication Theory and Research

In a volume entitled *Beyond Cultural Imperialism: Globalization, Communication, and the New International Order*, the editors charge that international communication has lost its eclectic and expansive scope: "Our focus on communications and media issues led us to the surprising observation that this most international and interdisciplinary of fields of study had become curiously insular in its approach." Moreover, "while exciting and vital debates about the nature of changes in international politics and social dynamics were attracting the attention of other intellectual and political fields, communication scholars were increasingly, and unproductively, becoming self-enclosed in their own ever more introspective dialogues" (Golding and Harris 1997, 2). I encourage readers to attend to the chapters in this book to remedy such insularity.

Taken together, the chapters in this volume endeavor to achieve several objectives. First, they reexamine and reformulate persistent problematics of the field. Second, they advance the field of international communication beyond political economy and the established sociological spheres by assuming interdisciplinary perspectives (communication, history, political theory, international relations, and cultural studies). Third, they reexamine and explore established and new tools and models of inquiry for research in international communication and media studies. Fourth, they challenge the field by addressing phenomena not previously considered appropriate or relevant (e.g., cyber terrorism, transnational genome debates, Islamism). An introduction outlines the context for the arguments in each part. It also explains the logic and justification for the selection and organization of the chapters included in this book.

Earlier I argued that international communication studies is best understood as a "field," that is, as a mode of organizing inquiry. Such a conceptualization permits more fluid and dynamic mappings of the constitutive elements that make up the internal history of the field. This project contributes to such a history by examining the empirical concerns of the field, which in turn allows for a conceptual inventory that sheds light on present configurations. Such a project enables us to see the past in order to envision a different future.

In concluding my introduction to the chapters in *New Frontiers in International Communication Theory*, I wish to reflect on what is invoked by the notion of frontiers. The idea of frontiers in the first place conjures up the image of borderlines and demarcated territories. As such, some of the objectives of this volume are self-reflexive: who we are and what we do in international communication is an object of analysis (such tasks also involve, by necessity, temporal considerations). Moreover, frontiers invite transgressions that disrupt prior views and organize alternative understandings. In exploring new frontiers, we are invariably involved in reorganizing the inquiries that make up the contours of the field from inside out. Additionally, frontiers, much like distant horizons, invoke the leading edge, the beyond. As such, some of our objectives are future-oriented: we seek to move conceptually and methodologically beyond existing formulations, approaches, and trajectories. In all of these ways, this volume hopes to advance international communication into new frontiers of inquiry.

Notes

1. Some have argued that even communication studies in general, which is a larger organized institutional domain, is not a discipline given the wild diversity of the issues it covers (e.g., Rogers and Chaffee 1993). The special issues of *Journal of Communication* devoted to "ferment in the field" in 1983 and a decade later attest to the fact that communication has been inflicted with an identity crisis that reemerges every now and then. The longing for disciplinary status might be a vestige of the past, one in

which disciplinarity in social sciences was an indication of legitimacy in the process of replacing older forms of knowledge and authority (Peters 1993).

2. Thomas Kuhn popularized the notion of a transdisciplinary "paradigm" in his celebrated book, *The Structure of Scientific Revolutions* (1970). The philosophical debates over this conception, its impact on the field of communication studies, and its hold on the politics of scholarly inquiry are beyond the scope of this discussion. Strikingly, the same circularity that plagued the notion of paradigm is a dilemma that confronts those who would define international communication. What is a paradigm? That in which the scientific community believes. Who is a scientific community? Those who subscribe to a paradigm. Similarly, what is international communication? The focus of inquiry of a particular community of scholars. Who is this community of scholars? Those who study international communication. However, not all circularities are, as Kuhn would say, vicious.

3. A different area of study called "intercultural communication" addresses *interpersonal* communication between individuals from unlike cultures. See Rogers 1999 for an exploration of the division between "mass" and "interpersonal" communication in the field as a whole.

4. These topics are distilled from a variety of sources, including Boyd-Barrett 1977, 1998; Schiller 1969; Frederick 1993; Gerbner and Siefert 1984; Gerbner, Mowlana, and Nordenstreng 1993; Gross 1995; Hachten 1999; Head 1985; Hamelink 1984, 1994; Martin and Hiebert 1990; Mattelart 1979; McPhail 1987; Mohammadi 1997; Mowlana and Wilson 1990; Fortner 1993; Merrill 1995; Mowlana 1996, 1998; Nordenstreng and Schiller 1993; Preston, Herman, and Schiller 1989; Schiller 1976; Tunstall 1977; Schiller 1991; Schramm 1964; Stevenson 1994; Tomlinson 1991; Golding and Harris 1997.

5. I have not addressed, for example, the intellectual history of the field, although that story too is critical for an adequate understanding of international communication as a field of inquiry.

6. This issue complicates the received view that international communication is a "subfield" of communication. In this context, communication appears to be an offspring of international communication and not the other way around.

7. For a review of some recent views on development communication, see the special issue of *Communication Theory* 11, no. 4 (2001).

8. For an alternative to the cultural imperialism thesis, see Straubhaar 1991.

9. This does not mean Europe would be immune from such an "invasion." Even a casual observer on a European trip would notice the abundance of new and old Hollywood products (e.g., films, soap operas, sitcoms, music).

10. See Tomlinson 1991 for a book-length discussion of cultural imperialism and its critique.

11. In this context, Tom Lindlof's book *Natural Audiences* (1987) remains an important contribution. The Scandinavian contribution in the area of reception studies is another important contribution.

12. Curran's (1990) essay is a much more ambitious attempt than is often acknowledged. In my view, its theoretical reach and historical scope deserve to be discussed in a way that is beyond the scope of this introduction.

13. Questions of active audiences, qualitative methodology, and interpretive media research have often become occasion for questioning cultural studies. See, for instance, these special issues of *Critical Studies in Mass Communication* 2, no. 3 (1988); 6, no. 4 (1989); and 7, no. 2 (1990). My objective here is not to address cultural studies and/or its institutionalization. Rather, I want to chart the trajectories along which international communication comes into contact with other intellectual and disciplinary formations.

References

Amin, S. 1976. *Accumulation on a world scale: A critique of the theory of underdevelopment.* New York: Monthly Review Press.

Ang, I. 1985. *Watching Dallas: Soap opera and the melodramatic imagination.* London: Methuen.

———. 1996. *Living room wars: Rethinking media audiences for a postmodern world.* London: Routledge.

Boyd-Barrett, O. 1977. "Media imperialism: Towards an international framework for the analysis of media systems." In J. Curran, M. Gurevitch, and J. Woollacott, eds., *Mass communication and society,* 116–35. London: Arnold.

———. 1998. "Media imperialism reformulated." In D. Thussu, ed., *Electronic empires: Global media and local resistance,* 157–76. London: Arnold.

Boyd-Barrett, O., and T. Rantanen, eds. 1998. *The globalization of news.* Thousand Oaks, Calif.: Sage.

Braman, S. 2002. "A pandemonic age: The future of international communication theory and research." In W. Gudykunst and B. Mody, eds., *Handbook of international and intercultural communication,* 399–413. 2d ed. Thousand Oaks, Calif.: Sage.

Budd, M., R. Entman, and C. Steinman. 1990. The affirmative character of U.S. cultural studies. *Critical Studies in Mass Communication* 7, no. 2: 168–84.

Curran, J. 1990. The new revisionism in mass communication research: A reappraisal. *European Journal of Communication* 5, no. 2–3: 135–64.

Evans, W. 1990. The interpretive turn in media research: Innovation, iteration, or illusion? *Critical Studies in Mass Communication* 7, no. 2: 147–68.

Fejes, F. 1981. Media imperialism: An assessment. *Media, Culture, and Society* 3, no. 3: 281–89.

Fiske, John. 1987. *Television culture.* New York: Routledge.

Fortner, R. 1993. *International communication: History, conflict, and control of the global metropolis.* Belmont, Calif.: Wadsworth.

Frederick, H. 1993. *Global communication and international relations.* New York: Harcourt Brace.

Gerbner, G., Mowlana, H., and Nordenstreng, K., eds. 1993. *The global media debate: Its rise and renewal.* Norwood, N.J.: Ablex.

Gerbner, G., and Siefert, M., eds. 1984. *World communications: A handbook.* New York: Longman.

Golding, P., and Harris, P. 1997. Introduction to P. Golding and P. Harris, eds., *Beyond cultural imperialism: Globalization, communication, and the new international order*, 1–9. Thousand Oaks, Calif.: Sage.

Gross, L., ed. 1995. *The international world of electronic media.* New York: McGraw-Hill.

Hachten, W. 1999. *The world news prism: Changing media of international communication.* 5th ed. Ames: Iowa State University Press.

Hall, S. 1980. "Encoding/decoding." In S. Hall, D. Hobson, A. Lowe, and P. Willis, eds., *Culture, media, language,* 128–38. London: Hutchinson.

Hamelink, C. 1984. *Transnational data flow in the information age.* Lund, Sweden: Studentlitterateur AB, Chartwell-Bratt.

———. 1994. *The politics of world communication.* Thousand Oaks, Calif.: Sage.

Head, S. 1985. *World broadcasting system: A comparative Analysis.* Belmont, Calif.: Wadsworth.

Hur, K. 1982. "International mass communication research: A critical review of theory and methods." In M. Burgoon, ed., *Communication Yearbook 6,* 531–54. Beverly Hills, Calif.: Sage.

Katz, E., and T. Liebes. 1986. "Mutual aid in the decoding of Dallas: Preliminary notes from a cross-cultural study." In P. Drummond and R. Paterson, eds., *Television in transition,* 187–98. London: BFI.

Kuhn, T. 1970. *The structure of scientific revolutions.* 2d ed. Chicago: University of Chicago Press.

Lasswell, H. 1927. *Propaganda technique in the world war.* New York: Knopf.

Lee, C.-C. 1980. *Media imperialism reconsidered: The homogenizing of television culture.* London: Sage.

Lerner, D. 1958. *The passing of traditional society: Modernizing the Middle East.* New York: Free Press.

Lindlof, T., ed. 1987. *Natural audiences.* Norwood, N.J.: Ablex.

Martin, J., and R. Hiebert, eds. 1990. *Current issues in international communication.* New York: Longman.

Mattelart, A. 1979. *Multinational corporations and the control of culture.* Atlantic Heights, N.J.: Humanities.

McDowell, S. 2002. "Theory and research in international communication: A historical and institutional account." In W. Gudykunst and B. Mody, eds., *Handbook of international and intercultural communication,* 295–308. 2d ed. Thousand Oaks, Calif.: Sage.

McPhail, T. 1987. *Electronic colonialism: The future of international broadcasting and communication.* Thousand Oaks, Calif.: Sage.

Merrill, J. 1995. *Global journalism: Survey of international communication.* 3d ed. New York: Longman.

Mody, B., and A. Lee. 2002. "Differing traditions of research on international media influence." In W. Gudykunst and B. Mody, eds., *Handbook of international and intercultural communication,* 381–98. 2d ed. Thousand Oaks, Calif.: Sage.

Mohammadi, A., ed. 1997. *International communication and globalization.* Thousand Oaks, Calif.: Sage.

Morley, D. 1980. *The "nationwide" audience: Structure and decoding.* London: BFI.

———. 1997. "Theoretical orthodoxies: Textualism, constructivism, and the 'new ethnography' in cultural studies." In M. Ferguson and P. Golding, eds., *Cultural studies in question,* 121–37. Thousand Oaks, Calif.: Sage.

Morris, M. 1990. Banality in cultural studies. In P. Mellencamp, ed., *Logics of Television: Essays in Cultural Criticism,* 14–43. Bloomington: Indiana University Press.

Mowlana, H. 1996. *Global communication in transition: The end of diversity?* Thousand Oaks, Calif.: Sage.

———. 1998. *Global information and world communication.* 2d ed. Thousand Oaks, Calif.: Sage.

Mowlana, H., and Wilson, L. 1990. *The passing of modernity: Communication and the transformation of society.* New York: Longman.

Nerone, J., ed. 1995. *Last rights: Revisiting four theories of the press.* Urbana: University of Illinois Press.

Nordenstreng, K., and H. Schiller, eds. 1993. *Beyond national sovereignty: International communications in the 1990s.* Norwood, N.J.: Ablex.

Peters, J. 1993. Genealogical notes on "the field." *Journal of Communication* 43, no. 4: 132–39.

Preston, W., Herman, E. and Schiller, H. 1989. *Hope and folly: The United States and UNESCO, 1945–1985.* Minneapolis: University of Minnesota Press.

Roach, C. 1987. The U.S. position on the new world informational and communication order. *Journal of Communication* 37, no. 4: 36–51.

Rogers, E. 1962. *The diffusion of innovations.* Glencoe, Ill.: Free Press.

———. 1999. Anatomy of the two subdisciplines of communication study. *Human Communication Research* 25, no. 4: 618-631.

Rogers, E., and S. Chaffee. 1993. The past and the future of communication study: Convergence or divergence? *Journal of Communication* 43, no. 4: 125–31.

Rogers, E., and W. Hart. 2002. The histories of intercultural, international, and development communication. In W. Gudykunst and B. Mody, eds., *Handbook of international and intercultural communication,* 1–18. 2d ed. Thousand Oaks, Calif.: Sage.

Samarajiva, R. 1985. Tainted origins of development communication. *Communicator,* April-July: 5–9.

Schiller, H. 1969. *Mass communication and American empire.* New York: Beacon.

———. 1976. *Communication and cultural domination.* New York: International Arts and Sciences Press.

———. 1991. Not yet the post-imperialist era. *Critical Studies in Mass Communication* 8, no. 1: 13–28.

Schiller, H., and Nordenstreng, K. 1979. *National sovereignty and international communication.* Norwood, N.J.: Ablex.

Schramm, W. 1964. *Mass communication and national development: The role of information in the developing country.* Stanford, Calif.: Stanford University Press.

Siebert, F. S., Peterson, T, and Schramm, W. 1956. *Four theories of the press: The authoritarian, libertarian, social responsibility, and Soviet communist concepts of what the press should be and do.* Urbana: University of Illinois Press.

Simpson, C. 1993. "U.S. mass communication research, counterinsurgency, and scientific 'reality.'" In W. Solomon and R. McChesney, eds., *Ruthless criticism: New perspectives in U.S. communication history*, 313–48. Minneapolis: University of Minnesota Press.

———. 1994. *Science of coercion: Communication research and psychological warfare, 1645–1960.* New York: Oxford University Press.

Singhal, A., and Sthapitanonda, P. 1996. The role of communication in development: Lessons learned from a critique of the dominant, dependency, and alternative paradigms. *Journal of Development Communication* 1, no. 7: 10–25.

Sreberny, A. 2000. The global and the local in international communications. In J. Curran and M. Gurevitch, eds., *Mass communication and society*, 93–119. 3d ed. London: Arnold.

Sreberny-Mohammadi, A., Winseck, D., McKenna, J., and Boyd-Barrett, O., eds. 1997. *Media in global context: A reader.* London: Arnold.

Stevenson, R. 1992. Defining international communication as a field. *Journalism Quarterly* 69, no. 3: 543–53.

———. 1994. *Global communication in the twenty-first century.* New York: Longman.

Straubhaar, J. 1991. Beyond media imperialism: Asymmetrical interdependence and cultural proximity. *Critical Studies in Mass Communication* 8, no. 1: 29–59.

Thussu, D. 2000. *International communication: Continuity and change.* London: Arnold.

Tomlinson, J. 1991. *Cultural imperialism: A critical introduction.* Baltimore: Johns Hopkins University Press.

Tunstall, J. 1977. *The media are American.* London: Constable.

I

RETHINKING PROBLEMATICS IN INTERNATIONAL COMMUNICATION

Mehdi Semati

T HE FIRST PART OF THE BOOK, entitled "Rethinking Problematics in International Communication," addresses some foundational concepts and longstanding problematics in the field of international communication. These studies make up the bulk of the field. A convenient way of organizing these concepts and problematics as they structure part I is to list the major empirical and theoretical terms that occur: four theories of the press, development paradigm, and diffusion of innovation, which is a major component of the development paradigm. Arguably, the empirical issues and the conceptual problematics that lie behind this short list provide the major impetus for the organization and for the direction of the field in its main historical trajectory. The first part argues that by rethinking these problematics we are able to surpass the limits that confine much of our thinking in the field.

Among the first things I learned as an undergraduate student with an interest in international communication in the late 1980s was the four theories of the press model. It was taught as a tool for studying international media systems. This model and the book in which it was articulated have been wildly popular as pedagogy tools in communication and journalism. Even though it is almost a half-century old, this model continues to influence our habits of thought in studying international media. Chapter 1 analyzes the history and the influence of *Four Theories of the Press*. The other three chapters in part I interrogate the development paradigm and its constituent elements.

In chapter 1, communication historian John Nerone analyzes a long-standing model that became a de facto framework for "comparative analysis" in studying international media systems. Nerone shows to what extent the "four theories of the press" as an "explanatory" framework was a product of the Cold War environment and the American academic setting in that era. His analysis shows the significance and the impact of the four theories on the discipline of communication and media studies in general, particularly its remarkable parochialism. He also addresses the book as an index of the interaction among media scholarship, communication pedagogy, and politics. Beyond the history and the substance of its contribution, he is interested in the popularity and the durability of this model as well as the inability of the field to surpass it. He unpacks the reasons for its popularity and durability. Moreover, he shows its major shortcomings on empirical and theoretical grounds. His critique of the four theories outlines its flaws and points toward the need for new, more complex frameworks for comparative studies that are free of ethnocentric underpinnings.

Development perspective, as I argue in the book introduction, has been a major component of the field of international communication. This perspective launched the inaugurating moment in the institutionalization of the field of international communication, as we understand it today. Many of its principles continue to be the guiding force for international organizations, regional entities, and states. Furthermore, many of the alternative perspectives that are currently debated are the outcomes of various research projects that have engaged this perspective. In sum, it is difficult to exaggerate the importance of this perspective to the field of international communication.

Sujatha Sosale's chapter is a comprehensive and theoretical treatment of development as a *discourse*, a critical genealogy of the concept in the sense Foucault deployed it. Amin Alhassan examines the development literature in order to interrogate the role of the postcolonial state and the postcolonial nation-state in this perspective. By focusing on "e-health care" as a technological apparatus that is caught up in the global diffusion of medical services, discourses, and solutions, John Erni examines the constituent elements of what would be called diffusion of innovation in the development paradigm. His analysis, however, demonstrates the benefits of moving beyond the confines of the established approaches.

In chapter 2, Sujatha Sosale offers a critical genealogy of the development perspective as *discourse*, including the framework and parameters in which development communication dialogue, policy, and practice have occurred. Her chapter covers not only development but also the discursive structures in which development and postdevelopment conceptual constellations have been intelligible. In doing so, she goes beyond the exiting literature in that her approach addresses, on the one hand, technology, economics, and culture as constitutive elements of a discourse of communication and development, and, on the other hand, other positions and perspectives expressed along with and in response to the discourse of development (e.g., modernization, dependency, postdependency, cultural imperialism, participatory communication). Among the strengths of this chapter is the alternative framework that Sosale advances, one that is informed by the insights of critical cultural studies and poststructuralist theories and offers a more nuanced theoretical vocabulary for addressing the empirical and the conceptual elements that make up the development paradigm. In sum, she steps outside the frameworks in which "communication and development" has been debated for the last five decades in order to explain how this concept has been produced and elevated to the status of a "master signifier."

In chapter 3, Amin Alhassan addresses the role of the postcolonial state and the postcolonial nation-state in the context of development literature. He contends that much of this literature, whether supportive or critical, lacks an adequate theory of the state. His analysis shows that the view of the state by the proponents of the development paradigm has been more a product of their political orientation than their analysis of the agency of local institutions and actors (e.g., the state apparatus). Moreover, in his discussion of Ghana and its colonial experience, he argues that in order to obtain legitimacy the state has had to reconstitute the colonial ideals of modernization under the auspices of nation building. What is interesting in his argument is the extent to which globalization exerts a different set of demands on the state. Mechanisms of capture and control demanded in an earlier era are now eclipsed by demands that require "adjustments" in nation-building mechanisms to allow the maneuvers of global capital.

In the final chapter of part I, John Erni achieves, among other things, two major objectives for our purposes in rethinking frontiers. First, he rethinks "health communication" by expanding its frontiers beyond the national context and considering it in global terms. Second, he unsettles the frontiers of international communication by addressing global health communication as a problematic it cannot afford to ignore insofar as viral dynamics and immune responses do not recognize geographical and political borders. In doing so, he addresses the diffusion of technologies, a persistent theme of development communication, in a new context (e.g., "e-health care" as a new information technology issue). Importantly, he engages his object of analysis with a new theoretical vocabulary and a critical perspective. His critical humanism, informed by the insights of cultural studies and international communication, is well suited for addressing the globalized condition empirically. His perspective is particularly valuable in that his argument is cognizant of the need for a new approach to the cultural and political dimensions of international health, one that contributes to, as he puts it, "a sense of political consciousness" about matters of life and death.

1

Four Theories of the Press in Hindsight: Reflections on a Popular Model

John Nerone

IN THE UNITED STATES AND ELSEWHERE in the westernizing world, no framework of understanding international media has been more influential in communication education than the *Four Theories* (Siebert, Peterson, and Schramm 1956) model. Now half a century old and unmistakably dated, it provides an elegant and easily applied grid for classifying media systems under four headings—authoritarian, libertarian, social responsibility, and Soviet communist—meant to characterize the dominant theory within that system. So appealing is its form that even its harshest critics instinctively retain the form while revising the content—offering six or eight theories of the press. Its usefulness as a teaching tool is matched by its sweep and moral vision. It invites scholars and students to picture the world in terms of good guys and bad guys. It translates the moral vision of World War II—the war against fascism—into a timeless struggle between authoritarian and libertarian press systems. Apparently neutral in its presentation, it nevertheless covertly urges the libertarian position. Apparently clear and even superficial in its construction, the model nevertheless makes profound and sometimes confused theoretical moves.

The extraordinary appeal of *Four Theories* is worth exploring. In this chapter, I will address some of the issues surrounding the history and impact of *Four Theories* and offer some thoughts on the book as an index of the relationship between communication education, media scholarship, and political affairs. The career of *Four Theories* is an opportune object for analysis. Its genesis and substance can be simply recounted; its popularity and durability require some puzzling out. If it was initially popular because of its immediate context, then one would have expected it to have aged poorly, as all timely texts do. More puzzling still is the inability of scholars to replace it. Surely the changed times should produce an equally eloquent successor or substitute.

The Authors and Argument of *Four Theories*

Four Theories came about by accident, more or less. Wilbur Schramm, a leading thinker and institution builder in the emergent field of communication, had some money left over from a grant he received from the National Council of Churches to do a report on "responsibility" in mass communication. He ran into Ted Peterson, then an assistant journalism professor working on his dissertation, at the water cooler and asked him if he'd be interested in writing a chapter of a book he had in mind. The two of them then chatted up Fred Siebert, who had just finished his magisterial history *Freedom of the Press in England, 1476–1776* (1952). Having agreed to write the book, they met once, hammered out the conceptual schema, divvied up the chapters, and went to writing.

The book came together quickly, almost effortlessly. The three authors knew each other well and had worked together on other projects. Moreover, they shared an informal training in both journalism education and in the World War II war effort.

Siebert, the oldest of the three, had worked on newspapers and was trained in law at Illinois in the 1920s. On graduation, he joined the journalism faculty and became very active in both journalism education and the legal concerns of the industry. He worked as counsel for the Illinois Press Association, the National Editorial Association, and the Inland Daily Press Association, and filed an amicus brief on behalf of Colonel McCormick of the *Chicago Tribune* in the case of *Near v. Minnesota* (1931). He was equally active as a journalism educator, serving as president of the American Association of Schools and Departments of Journalism and helping to found the American Council on Education for Journalism.

Siebert's contribution to *Four Theories* was the most significant. Not only did he author two of the four chapters; he also anticipated the overall structure of the book in his earlier work, enumerating models of press–government relations quite similar to those later codified in *Four Theories*. Siebert also recruited Ted Peterson from Kansas State and was Peterson's teacher and dissertation adviser.

Wilbur Schramm had been trained in literature and, as a writer, won the O. Henry Prize and helped found the Iowa Writer's Workshop. At Iowa, he became associated with educational psychologist George Stoddard, who shaped Schramm's subsequent career. During World War II, Stoddard joined the Office of War Information (OWI) and brought Schramm in to work with poet Archibald MacLeish in the OWI Office of Facts and Figures. He went from there back to Iowa, where he was appointed director of the School of Journalism. In 1947, Stoddard became president of the University of Illinois and recruited Schramm to oversee the campus's various communication units, including the University of Illinois Press, and to head the newly established Institute of Communications Research. He commenced building the field of communication research by hosting a series of conferences that produced classic scholarly collections—*Mass Communications* (1949) and the *Process and Effects of Mass Communication* (1954). Less well known than his field-building work was his continuing involvement in military and quasi-military initiatives. *Process and Effects* was supported by the United States Information Agency (USIA). More remarkably, as a key figure in "psychological warfare" efforts during the Korean War, he coauthored (with John Riley) *The Reds Take a City* (1951), a nightmare imagining of what would happen in Seoul under communist rule (McEnany 1988). One of the classics of Cold War pop lit, and based on field research in Korea funded by the air force, it was translated and distributed throughout the Far East and Europe at government expense (Simpson 1994, 63–64). He consulted on psychological warfare for the air force, the State Department, the Army Operations Research Office, the Defense Department, and the USIA, and chaired the defense secretary's advisory board on "specialized warfare" (Guback 1995). Simpson (1994, 108, 168–89) contends that Schramm's more specifically academic oeuvre has the same psy ops intentions and inspirations, and the same sources of funding, particularly *The Process and Effects of Mass Communication* (1952). Even if *Four Theories* was something of an afterthought to these other projects, his contribution to the book was deeply rooted in work funded by the various U.S. Cold War agencies.

Their work expresses the common sense of a generation of scholars in the emerging field of communication and in the U.S. academy generally, which came of age in the Depression and World War II and experienced the tragedy and triumph of capitalism and liberalism. Their faith in a reformist libertarianism—the overall message of *Four Theories*—could remain unstated because they thought it went without saying. But it is the foundation for the schema the book explicitly presents.

Four Theories offers a schema of philosophies as categories for understanding media systems. Each philosophy in the schema is defined by four components: a notion of "man," a notion of the "state or society," a notion of knowledge, and a notion of truth. The book identifies four such philosophies: authoritarianism, libertarianism, the social responsibility theory, and Soviet communism. Each theory gets a chapter. Siebert wrote the chapters on authoritarianism and libertarianism from his research for *Freedom of the Press in*

England, 1476–1776: The Rise and Decline of Government Controls (1952), a classic book that remains an authoritative and nuanced treatment. These chapters extend Siebert's narrative of English history by augmentation; he adds mentions of other mostly European and American thinkers and political figures. The social responsibility theory is the subject of Ted Peterson's chapter. Peterson, who also authored the definitive history, *Magazines in the Twentieth Century* (1956), concentrated on the work of the Hutchins Commission and its reception; his chapter remains useful and even wise. The final chapter, by Wilbur Schramm, dealing with the Soviet communist theory, must have seemed silly to many in the 1950s, and it certainly seems silly now. Schramm's involvements in field building (he ranks as the most institutionally effective founder of academic communication research in the United States) now overshadow his political and military involvements, but his *Four Theories* work suggests that the two are better viewed as complementary and mutually reinforcing.

Each of the four theories is easily summarized. In the authoritarian theory, "man" is incomplete without the state or society, which is the really real actor in history. Knowledge is difficult, either revealed to a few or knowable only by the wise and educated through complex scientific operations. Truth is absolute—or, on the other hand, can be completely manipulated, as in Hitler's Germany. The libertarian theory, by contrast, sees truth as relative, and the state or society as contrivances of individuals, who exist before collectivities and design them for their convenience. In the authoritarian theory, information and expression must be controlled; in the libertarian theory, regulation is neither legitimate nor useful. The social responsibility theory is a modification of the libertarian theory. It acknowledges that, in the twentieth century, the media have grown too large and powerful, the world too complicated, and the people too vulnerable to allow media owners to pursue private agendas; at the same time, it denies the state the authority to supervise the media and therefore relies on media owners to police themselves. The Soviet communist theory, a modern variant of authoritarianism, justifies state control of the media system under an intellectual vanguard as a way of dispelling false ideologies and promoting revolutionary consciousness. Just as the social responsibility theory accepts the basic premises of the libertarian theory, though, the Soviet communist theory accepts the premises of authoritarianism and produces similar practices.

The Place of the Four Theories in Communication Scholarship

The book instantly became widely influential as a teaching tool. It has remained a steady seller, with net sales to date of 84,995 copies by 2001 (it is the University of Illinois Press's all-time nonfiction best-selling book) and still selling between 500 and 700 a year. Translation rights were licensed for a Japanese edition in 1958, an Indonesian edition in 1981, a Malaysian edition in 1987, and a Russian edition in 1996, and editions are also available in several other languages. Moreover, summaries of *Four Theories* are featured at the top of many of the textbooks in the field and its subfields. Even though all the authors have now passed on, the book itself achieved a second life with the collapse of the Soviet Union. Ironically, at a point when most Western academics had begun to think of it as a dinosaur of the Cold War era, Eastern European journalists, casting about for tools for thinking about their newly achieved independence from state control, found the *Four Theories* approach congenial. Kaarle Nordenstreng remarks that it has been translated into more languages than any other textbook in the field of journalism and mass communication (1997, 97).

Its international standing is attested to by the fact that its critique has been international too. In collections and textbooks on international communication, it is often the first thing the authors mention: the initial template for theory construction, or the original sin that establishes the field. Curran and Park offer a pointed example of the latter:

> Perhaps the most striking feature about this book, in retrospect, is how little its talented authors felt they needed to know. They display some knowledge of the American and Russian media, and of the American Colonial and early English press, but little about any other media system. They got round their evident lack of comparative expertise by advancing a convenient, idealist argument. Media systems, they claimed, reflect the prevailing philosophy and political system of the society in which they operate. To understand the international media system, it is necessary merely to identify "the philosophical and political rationales or theories which lie behind the different kinds of press we have in the world today." In their account, these rationales were written almost entirely by Western theorists. By implication, the world's communication system could be laid bare by studying their thought.
> . . . Why this book was taken so seriously is now something of a mystery. The explanation is probably that it drew upon a Cold War view of the world widely endorsed in the West, and seemed therefore authoritative. (2000, 4)

Although correct in both their assessment of lack of "comparative expertise" in *Four Theories* and its involvement in the politics and policies of the Cold War, Curran and Park might note other reasons why the book was taken seriously. One, as I've already suggested, was its elegance as a teaching tool, which was grounded in the apparent clarity of its schema. Another, of more interest to scholars, is the serious call it sounds to ground media study in philosophy. Although *Four Theories* did not properly answer this call—its philosophizing was crude in most regards—it is still a call worth heeding, and it is the dimension of the book that authorized its international reception. It makes it more profound as well as more portable than competing traditions of media analysis grounded in comparative media systems and media law. Media law tends to remain grounded in the traditions of its host countries. It doesn't travel well. Scholars in the United States, for instance, have tended to think of freedom of the press mostly in terms of the First Amendment, and journalism educators universally agree that that tradition is unique, that no other country has quite the same understanding of freedom of the press, no matter how devoted it is to freedom of the press as a value. First Amendment scholarship has produced an overwhelmingly negative notion of freedom of the press. It consists entirely of noninterference by the government. Few of the world's national traditions are so limited to negative liberty.

Media law in the United States, as well as constitutional theory generally, has trouble conceptualizing entities larger than an individual and smaller than the state. In the language of U.S. labor law, for instance, all labor rights have to be cast as the individual rights of workers; the word "union" is surprisingly rare because collectivities cannot be rights bearing. The extraordinary suppleness of U.S. laws regarding corporations springs from the same failure: corporations have rights as "fictional persons," and so are endowed with many freedoms, few responsibilities, and, unlike real persons, no mortality. Like labor law and corporate law, media law has trouble conceptualizing the press as a collectivity or an institution, rather than as an individual. Although common sense dictates, and any person you talk to understands, that the press is not an individual, and that freedom of the press is not the same thing as the individual right to free expression, the language of U.S. constitutional law lacks the capacity to think that way.

By comparison, the "philosophical" approach of *Four Theories* offers more purchase for critical thinking. The *Four Theories* framework takes the insights of media law scholarship and incorporates them into an expansive map of all sorts of ways of thinking about the press. So the First Amendment tradition, for example, becomes in *Four Theories* an exemplar of "the libertarian theory." It assumes a position neighboring the "social responsibility theory," often treated as an entering wedge for authoritarianism by First Amendment scholars (Helle 1995).

The comparative systems approach has an opposite structural shortcoming— where media law is too narrow and rigid, the comparative media systems approach is too expansive and therefore has trouble achieving closure. No matter how dedicated or conscientious, any collection on the media systems of various regions or countries will always be incomplete and uneven. The simple problem is that the approach insinuates but cannot provide the categorical elegance and clarity of *Four Theories*. Failing that, it might try to provide encyclopedic knowledge, but how can it succeed? The messiness of the approach is unavoidable and reflects the messiness of the world.

Ironically, one might argue that *Four Theories* bears the closest resemblance to the traditions that revile it the most. It aims for the sweep, depth, and moral or political gravity that critics of media imperialism, advocates of dependency theory, and commentators on globalization claim. It seeks in the same way to provide both a globally convincing framework for understanding historical developments and a compelling set of normative principles.

Why so much praise at a time when most scholars think a burial is more in order? I intend only to point out that the intellectual work that *Four Theories* would devote itself to, somewhere east of law and west of systems, is work worth doing, work that its critics are often engaged in. This is not to excuse the shortcomings of the project.

Historical and Theoretical Weaknesses of the Four Theories Schema

However much one admires the aims and elegance of the *Four Theories* approach, its many omissions and its apparently unconscious incorporation of liberal ideology must be acknowledged. It is, as critics have charged, a remarkably provincial cosmopolite. Composed at a time when the United States could simultaneously straddle and ignore the world, it innocently blinks away the phantoms that stalk its cozy mansion.

Although *Four Theories* sought to overcome the provincial boundaries of much of its day's thinking about the press, it did this in part by imposing an Anglo-American schema on the world. One might compare it with the internationalism that produced the Universal Declaration of Human Rights (Glendon 2001). The Universal Declaration exemplifies a truly international and sincerely philosophical approach to issues of freedom. Its principal architects were P. C. Chang, the delegate from China who had earned a doctorate under John Dewey at Columbia, and Charles Malik from Lebanon, who had studied philosophy under Alfred North Whitehead and Martin Heidegger. The drafting committee was chaired by Eleanor Roosevelt. In the drafting process, every available catalog of rights from any national tradition was studied. The final result is both a summary of every bill of rights and a theoretically coherent architecture of rights.

The Universal Declaration departs from the classical liberal tradition of thinking about rights by asserting a connection between the standard negative liberties of late-eighteenth-century declarations and positive liberties—social and economic rights—enshrined by later social welfare regimes. In the thinking of the declaration, rights like freedom of the press are built on the foundation of social and economic rights, like the right to a livelihood.

Needless to say, this unification of negative and positive freedoms has not resonated with Anglo-American understandings of rights. Despite some glamorous exceptions—Franklin Roosevelt's Four Freedoms, for instance—rights thinking in the United States has usually viewed social welfare initiatives as inimical to rather than constitutive of negative liberties. Movements like welfare rights and affirmative action have always had to swim against a powerful mainstream.

The impact of the declaration in the United States was also dampened by the advent of the Cold War. The liberal internationalism of the World War II coalition, along with the rapprochement with the Soviet Union, gave way to a more chauvinistic internationalism that saw many aspects of what the rest of the world called rights as simply communistic. Nowhere is this habit more apparent than in the reaction of U.S. politicians and media to the MacBride Commission report, which was understood as a movement to censor free media and license journalists, and which in turn led to charges of politicization and corruption at UNESCO and the eventual withdrawal of the United States and Britain from that organization. The MacBride Commission's report simply extended the thinking of the Universal Declaration to the problems of the media (International Commission for the Study of Communication Problems 1980). The end of the Cold War, which one might have hoped would eased U.S. paranoia, so far has only strengthened this tendency.

Oddly, in *Four Theories* the Universal Declaration goes unmentioned. A critic would suspect that this is not an accidental omission: *Four Theories* clearly does not see social welfare as constitutive of a regime of liberty. And so it has trouble making theoretical space for something like the MacBride Commission's recommendations.

The closest *Four Theories* came to the Universal Declaration was its treatment of the Hutchins Commission (Commission on Freedom of the Press 1947). Funded by media mogul Henry Luce, the Hutchins Commission assembled a cast of thinkers with impressive credentials and performed its work through intense discussion and investigation. Ultimately its recommendations deviated sharply from the agenda of its backers and provoked a stern counterreaction from the press, which saw its call for responsibility to be a harbinger of the kind of government control that had characterized many New Deal initiatives. The treatment of the work of the Hutchins Commission, in the chapter entitled "The Social Responsibility Theory," by Ted Peterson, is lucid and sympathetic. Had the book ever gone through a revision, one might have hoped that Peterson would have extended this chapter to embrace international movements.

The absence of serious treatment of international thinking on rights is emblematic of the more fundamental philosophical failings of *Four Theories*.

Over the years, the schema has generated a hearty corps of critics who have pointed out a wide variety of lapses.

Some of the complaints are fairly obvious. To some, four is too few, and the framework should be augmented by adding some others—development communication, for instance, or non-Soviet socialist models. For others, four is too many. There are really only two theories of the press, the libertarian (with a social democratic variant) and the authoritarian (with a communist variant), and these theories describe exactly the relationship of the press to the government. Either the press is independent of the government or it is a branch of the government.

These reasonable arguments seem to miss the deeper point. What is it that you're counting? It's not merely the relationship of the press to the government, but also the rationale or set of principles behind it. This leads to a more complicated issue—not the problem with *Four,* but the problem with *Theories.*

What is a theory of the press? In *Four Theories,* the question is never really answered because it is never explicitly addressed. The book assumes that the answer is obvious, and much of the commentary on it does the same. But in fact the book uses the term "theory" in a very haphazard manner. Look first at the four theories the book describes. Libertarianism is a historically grounded ideological movement, and as such deserves to be called a theory. Soviet communism is a well-articulated system of governance, and deserves to be called a theory, but of a different sort. The social responsibility theory is in essence a professional ideology; it is a theory in a decidedly different register. The authoritarian theory isn't really a theory at all but a set of practices. Moreover, states professing libertarian values employ authoritarian practices all the time, and it is not at all clear that the libertarian professions make a damned bit of difference.

If that is so, then a communication theory is not the same sort of thing as a communication system. *Four Theories* is ill-applied to the study of comparative media systems. Because these theories are really all different kinds of creatures, it is possible for any number of them to coexist in any given system. In the present-day U.S. media system, for instance, the prevailing legal ideology is libertarian, but the government employs many authoritarian practices (prepublication censorship of intelligence community publications, postal rate regulations, differential taxing structures for various institutions, libel and defamation laws, incitement and sedition laws, time and place regulations, hostile environment regulations, and a vast propaganda machine that includes media outlets of every sort), and the community of professional journalists adheres to a modified social responsibility model of practice (Kovach and Rosenstiel 2001).

The authors of *Four Theories* clearly believe that, in any system, only one theory can be dominant or ascendant, even though another one might be rising as the dominant one falls. Although the theories seem airtight philosophically, they are not so historically. And that is itself a deep problem—*Four Theories* never declares that it is history or philosophy, and blithely assumes that it can be both.

This conflation of history and theory is the source of the book's philosophical incoherence as well as its ideological impact. The chapter on authoritarian theory is the best example. Siebert argues that the authoritarian theory considers the individual subordinate to the society or the state, and that it considers knowledge the province of an elite, and truth absolute. He grounds this theory in history by citing thinkers like Plato, Hegel, and Hobbes and leaders like the pope and Adolf Hitler. Did any of these figures really espouse Siebert's version of the authoritarian theory? Certainly Hobbes shared a view of human nature with his antagonist, the "libertarian" theorist John Locke. Certainly Hitler, the author of the "Big Lie" theory of propaganda, did not consider truth absolute. Certainly the popes dissent from the worship of the state that one finds in Hegel. Certainly Plato's celebration of Socrates' martyrdom to truth constitutes a rebuttal to the authoritarian theory that Siebert and others derive from his *Republic* and *Laws*. And certainly no authoritarian government really needs a theory to inspire its actions. On close examination, the "theory" part of each of the categories will deconstruct, even when the category is theoretically self-conscious.

Why is it that readers have instinctively recognized the authoritarian theory as an existing thing? Because, I think, they do not recognize themselves as authoritarian. A classic constructed other, the textbook authoritarian exists everywhere and nowhere as the fevered expression of what we reject. In this way, its philosophical failure supports its ideological success.

Keeping the Faith

Can a bogeyman be a good tool for thinking? One might argue yes, that constructed others like the authoritarian theory are invaluable and inescapable features of especially professional discourse. On balance, a journalist who has internalized the lessons of *Four Theories* will be dedicated to a particular model of democratic communication—vigilant of concentrations of power, quick in the defense of the right to know and the right to free expression, always hostile to censorship but always mindful of the professional's responsibilities to the public. The solidity of this faith will necessarily rest on the suppression of guilty knowledge, however—the fact that responsibility can be exercised only by those with power—power that reporters lack but owners command; the fact that censorship can be exercised by units other than governments; the fact that concentrations of power exist in the private sector and shield themselves from scrutiny with the same negative liberties that reporters claim in their sparring with governments; the fact that freedom of expression presumes that one has a voice, which in turn presumes a whole sociology of expression. Better not to think about these things, perhaps, if you want to be a good reporter.

Sophistication costs. There is a boldness to the theory of *Four Theories* that we sophisticates can never hope to emulate. We can never hope to convince ourselves that our theories come out of history and not out of our heads. We can never hope to convince ourselves to believe that the way things happen corresponds to the ideas in people's heads. In other words, we will never be able to believe that the history of freedom of the press is properly a history of ideas—the animating spirit behind *Four Theories*. Altschull (1984) is convincing when he argues that this is really a story about power, and that any communication system will work in service to the concentrations of power in its society. Would that it were not so. If ideas really mattered, then those of us who live for ideas would have something important to do.

The very real business of the authors of *Four Theories* in the world—the many "defense" activities of Schramm, Siebert's many dealings with the legal affairs of the media industry—show that their intellectual practice was anything but ivory tower. The present generation of communication educators and media scholars is ambitious of such involvement but rarely accomplishes it. In our academic lifespan, the separation between the academy and the world has widened as the academic view of the world has sharpened. Perhaps this detachment is the price we pay for clarity of vision and purity of motive.

In its passion for ideas as well as in its boldness and simplicity *Four Theories* was very much a creature of its age. It breathes a kind of optimism that its authors, comfortable with their worldview and confident of its success, clearly felt on behalf of the world, freedom, and civilization. To the critics in us, this optimism is unjustifiable; to the politicians in us, it is pernicious. Cynically, we expect such bromides to suds up on the surface after history has moved through great agitations, then gradually pop of their own fatigue. The agitations of the mid-twentieth century are now over. As new agitations begin, we await the next lather.

References

Altschull, J. H. 1984. *Agents of power: The role of the news media in human affairs*. New York: Longman.

Commission on Freedom of the Press. 1947. *A free and responsible press*. Chicago: University of Chicago Press.

Curran, J., and Park, M.-J. 2000. "Beyond globalization theory." In J. Curran and M.-J. Park, eds., *De-westernizing media studies*, 3–18. New York: Routledge.

Glendon, M. 2001. *A world made new: Eleanor Roosevelt and the Universal Declaration of Human Rights*. New York: Random House.

Guback, T. 1995. "The historical moment of Four Theories." In J. Nerone, ed., *Last rights: Revisiting four theories of the press*, 7–16. Urbana: University of Illinois Press.

Helle, S. 1995. "'Positive freedom' as the 'entering wedge.'" In Nerone et al., eds., *Last rights: Revisiting four theories of the press*, 90–98. Urbana: University of Illinois Press.

International Commission for the Study of Communication Problems. 1980. *Many voices, one world: Communication and society, today and tomorrow: Towards a new more just and more efficient world information and communication order*. New York: Unipub.

Kovach, B., and Rosenstiel, T. 2001. *The elements of journalism: What newspeople should know and the public should expect*. New York: Crown.

McEnany, E. G. 1988. Wilbur Schramm 1907–1987: Roots of the past, seeds of the present. *Journal of Communication* 38, no. 4: 109–22.

Nordenstreng, K. 1997. "Beyond the four theories of the press." In Servaes, J., and Lie, R., eds., *Media and politics in transition: Cultural identity in the age of globalization*, 97–125. Leuven: Acco.

Peterson, T. 1956. *Magazines in the twentieth century*. Urbana: University of Illinois Press.

Riley, J. W., and Schramm, W. 1951. *The Reds take a city: The communist occupation of Seoul, with eyewitness accounts*. New Brunswick, N.J.: Rutgers University Press.

Schramm, W. 1949. *Mass communication*. Urbana: University of Illinois Press.

———. 1954. *The process and effects of mass communication*. Urbana: University of Illinois Press.

Siebert, F. S. 1952. *Freedom of the press in England, 1476-17766: The rise and decline of government controls*. Urbana: University of Illinois Press.

Siebert, F. S., Peterson, T, and Schramm, W. 1956. *Four theories of the press: The authoritarian, libertarian, social responsibility and Soviet communist concepts of what the press should be and do*. Urbana: University of Illinois Press.

Simpson, C. 1994. *Science of coercion: Communication research and psychological warfare, 1945-1960*. New York: Oxford University Press.

2

Toward a Critical Genealogy of Communication, Development, and Social Change

Sujatha Sosale

IT IS ALMOST CUSTOMARY NOW TO study development and the role of communication in development from certain standard theoretical perspectives such as modernization, dependency, and postdevelopment perspectives. At various historical junctures, each of these perspectives has offered a wealth of explanations and/or prescriptions for "development," an ideology that has generated a way of thinking about the world in two broad categories—of advanced and backward nations. The framework and parameters in which development communication dialogue, policy, and practice take place is the discourse of development that works to articulate an ideology that has been normalized in the international vocabulary.

My concern in this chapter is to attempt to step outside the frameworks in which communication and development have been debated for the better part of the past four to five decades or so and to understand how this concept has been produced and elevated to the status of, in Žižek's (1993) term, a "master signifier" by examining the historical trajectory of communication and development as a discourse. To this end, I suggest an alternative framework located at the intersection of critical cultural studies and poststructuralism. This framework is mindful of the critique posed by postcolonial scholars such as Spivak, who acknowledge the global applicability of these theories, but question the absence of the constitutive role of empire and the colony in the study of discourses emerging from these theoretical traditions. For example, Slater cites Spivak's objection to Foucault's Eurocentric, or more closely, Francocentric archaeological foci that have prevented a "reading of the broader narratives of imperialism. . . . To buy a self-contained version of the west is to ignore its production by the imperialist project" (Spivak, cited in Slater 1992). Studying the discourse of communication and development calls for an engagement with an enterprise that has been frequently characterized as an extension of colonialism, and as a phenomenon set squarely in the international arena.

I draw the notion of centering power that is distilled in the concepts of ideology and hegemony from critical cultural studies. The impermanent nature of language, meanings, and the continuous contestation of signifiers that is associated with the poststructuralist perspective enable us to grasp and account for the multiple discursive strands that have contributed to the discourse of communication and development. According to Melkote and Steeves, the "epistemological plurality" characteristic of poststructuralist perspectives expands considerably our understanding of the discourse of communication and development (Melkote and Steeves 2001, 335). The proposed alternative framework helps explain the establishment of modern communications and modern development as an arbitrary yardstick of the ultimate quality of life for about three-fourths of the world's population. It also helps us understand the resultant implications for considering communication more as an expressive cultural practice—be it through traditional or vernacular modern modes and channels—rather than as a tool integrated into the disciplining power of development.

Increasingly, scholars have problematized communication and development from various perspectives such as participatory communication (Huesca 2001; Jacobson and Kolluri 1999; Servaes 1998), indigenous media (Michaels 1993), citizens' media (Rodriguez 2001a), humanitarian journalism and communication (Shah 1996; Teheranian 1999a), human rights and communication (Servaes 1998), feminist perspectives, and spiritually oriented and world religions–derived standpoints on communication and social change (Rodriguez 2001a; Steeves 2001; Teheranian 1999b). These recent works and their precursors signal a paradigm shift in thinking about communication and development. In part, this chapter participates in the conversation that animates this paradigm shift. Theoretically, the integration of postmodern and poststructuralist thought and their critique of the metanarratives of development and social change have been considered in recent works (see, e.g., Teheranian 1999a; Shah 1997 for excellent summaries, and Jacobson 1996 for a critical analysis of these new theoretical approaches and their critique of the metanarrative of development). However, the project at hand differs from these works in that it contributes to two relatively unexplored areas. First, it extends the above-mentioned summary works by examining the roles of technology, economics, and culture as constitutive elements of a discourse of communication and development. To this end, the chapter attempts to provide an account of the *mechanisms* through which the major reference points for organizing knowledge about societies in the international arena from communication perspectives have emerged. This vein of scholarship in international communication is yet to be fully developed. Second, it accounts for the positions and perspectives articulated in parallel with and in response to the development discourse. These positions and perspectives have come into their own as reflexive and ethical dialectic responses to mainstream notions of communication and development. I attempt to cast these new voices as a collective "other" that is integral to the notion of discourse as a whole (Derrida 1986). This "other" details the power/knowledge nexus that informs our understandings of a world order.

The ensuing section on the framework begins with a general introduction of four concepts—centering (of communication and development in the collective imaginary of populations and governments), multiple discursive configurations (modernization and dependency as examples of a metrocentric version of development), ambiguity (that explains fissures and ruptures in the dominant discourse), and the margins (or the "other"). As this framework is developed, both extra-discursive (institutional, contextual) and textual elements are considered. Each of the concepts is treated more extensively in separate sections. I conclude with a brief note on the importance and implications of such a framework and analysis for an area that has long defined international communication—communication, development, and social change.

The analysis in this chapter traverses a range of works, both well-known and lesser known, and a time frame of about six decades to map a critical genealogy of communication, development, and social change. The development of the framework does not necessarily coincide chronologically with the history of communication and development. I move across the time frame to demonstrate the ways in which the discourse sustained by taking into consideration the seemingly dispersed and fragmented theories and practical efforts at various times that nevertheless constitute the larger discourse.

The modernization paradigm in particular offers openings for a deconstructive reading of communication and development, some of which are available in the corpus of works on this subject. We are still in the grip of this paradigm in many parts of the world. The race to catch up with information technology (IT) industries in the West as is apparent in India (Chakravartty 2001), and Malaysia (Jackson and Mosco 1999) has recently been cited as a case in point. These works enable us to infer that this is not as much a race to catch up with the postmodern West as the technologized (read modernized) West. Given that this paradigm's interpellatory power persists, modernization continues to serve as one of the important reference points for the analysis that follows.

Mapping a Critical Genealogy of
Communication, Development, and Social Change

A productive way to think about the idea of communication and development for social change established over the past half century or so is to cast it as a historical dialectic. This idea has acquired the gravity and magnitude of a discourse, an entity that embodies the power to confer meanings by establishing classifications of what Hall has expressed elsewhere as social intelligibility. Tracing the discourse would involve paying close attention simultaneously to what Young, in his reading of Foucault's method, explains as "'critical' analysis (which examines the functions of exclusion)" and "'genealogical' analysis (which examines the formation of discourses)" (Young 1981, 49). Drawing broadly from critical cultural studies and poststructuralism, I develop a framework to map a "critical genealogy" of communication and development. Doty (1996) introduced the term "critical genealogy" to define her project on representations of north–south relations. The term encapsulates the critical perspective associated with concepts of ideology and hegemony as well as the Foucaultian approach to discourse through genealogy. Specifically, the term "critical" refers to problematizing centralized forms of power manifested in meanings, institutions, and practices. In using the term "genealogy," I refer to a historical approach to studying communication and development as a discourse. The genealogy is mapped by examining what Escobar (1999), in explaining the relevance of Foucault for development studies, has termed "nondiscursive practices." Nondiscursive practices include social, economic, and institutional factors. Genealogy, following Foucault, calls for considering power that organizes discourse as socially dispersed, rather than socially centered. Nevertheless, a "structured, relational totality" (Doty 1996, 6) is evident in this dispersal of power, and the resultant discourse comes to define a specific reality. This totality, however, does not imply discursive closure; it is a particular reality that is at least temporarily fixed (and therefore lived as such) and continually contested. The multifarious practices of development have, over time, produced a knowledge that has come to define a "truth" about the status of societies and cultures. Such a framework points to the persistence of the development enterprise as well as the equally persistent alternate modes of understanding and acting for social change.

There are two parts to the analytical framework developed here. The first consists of mapping a "unity of fields" that identifies a discourse (Foucault 1972). For instance, Melkote and Steeves (2001) have identified disciplinary efforts in anthropology, religion, sociology, political science, and so on, that have contributed to the creation of a unity of fields that can be identified as development. The second part involves a deconstruction of this unity of fields and, in a sense, constituting the discourse through its "other." Three concepts—centering, multiple discursive configurations, and ambiguity—are central to the task of mapping a unity of fields that constitutes the discourse of communication and development. Establishing a particular set of meanings and practices that determine expectations and set criteria for evaluating societies demonstrates the work of power in *centering* meanings and naturalizing them in the social imaginary. In this sense, I read a making of the center that is communication and development. Firmly established development indicators such as production and/or use of advanced media technologies for evaluating a society, for instance, articulate the formation of a center. *Multiple discursive configurations* point to contradictory and overlapping discourses within a larger discourse in that they "share a common locus" (Foucault 1972, 152). The techno-social discourse of modernization and the economic discourse of dependency are two contradictory discourses sharing a common locus at the intersection of development and capitalism. Operational theories such as modernization and critical responses such as dependency or participatory approaches have not occurred in a linear fashion, as Wilkins and Mody (2001) remind us. Instead, they are both dialogic and parallel activities that form various discursive strands. A "critical genealogy" approach would problematize the taken-for-grantedness, or naturalized assumptions, parameters, and practices that have accumulated over a period of time and that now constitute a dominant knowledge about communication and development.

Ambiguity is inherent in discursive formations in that it is impossible to achieve discursive closure on any ruling idea. The concept of ambiguity allows for both contestation and negotiation, acts equally constitutive of a discourse as is centering. In fact, the tension between centering and contestation, evident in ambiguity, is at the heart of discourse. Ambiguity compels us to consider communication and development more as a floating signifier, to use Laclau and Mouffe's term (1985), than as a master signifier. Efforts to dislodge the master signifier create oppositional (as Cuba, Tanzania, and China delinked from the development project) or negotiatory meanings and actions (e.g., vernacular versions of modernity and attendant adaptations of modern communication systems and technologies that might take place on an everyday basis in various parts of the world), demonstrating the limits of the discourse while simultaneously opening up possibilities for new and perhaps more effective modes of social change.

The second part of the proposed analytical framework takes into account the exclusionary practice of discourse. I draw from Derrida's notion of deconstruction for this part of the framework. Thus if the idea of communication and development is entrenched in the speech and action of Third World (a term that continues in use today) governments and development agencies, it is at the expense of a possibility whereby the culture and practice of communication need not be connected to "development" in the established sense of the term. Deconstructing key ideas helps identify and articulate the presence of an "other"; this "other" is a collective other that encompasses subaltern viewpoints and negotiatory attempts of various stripes to produce alternate routes to social change. Finally, I address trends that are now being identified as characteristic of a postdevelopment era; these so-called trends may not all be recent or purely contemporary, but they have emerged vigorously in recent years to problematize the discourse of communication and development.

Centering: Constructing the Master Signifier

From the media and modernization era in the 1950s and the 1960s through the diffusion programs based on agricultural communication models in the United States in the 1970s, to the debates on journalism's role in development through the 1980s, the sense of having no way to proceed except in the direction of development (i.e., moving toward Western social, institutional, and cultural arrangements) directed much international aid and interaction among countries. In official, state, and diplomatic rhetoric, both the various media and planned acts of communication became instruments charged with the function of changing backward and traditional societies to modern, developed ones. Development itself underwent many shifts in definition and approaches, from exogenous aid to self-reliance, from capital-intensive economic activity to labor-intensive economic activity, and from eradicating tradition to working within frameworks of indigenous cultures (Jayaweera 1987). The central thread tying together all these changes was the idea that development was a state reached by some nations, which had to be reached by others; development, as the master signifier, established a norm that strove to preclude thinking about societies that might fall outside its purview as equally legitimate and viable social systems.

Using Castoriadis's concept of the social imaginary signification, Tomlinson (1991) identified a space that development has come to occupy in the modern mind and life practices. Neither "real" nor "rational," the social imaginary signification is a seat of power, like the "concept of God" around which is developed representations and practices. As we know, signification involves choice, a selection and legitimization of meanings to "make sense of" concepts and phenomena. Thus modernization, for example, legitimizes technology, "rational" thinking (according to certain historical experiences and resultant definitions), control over nature, and so on; what is left out is an alternate way of living that Esteva (1992) has termed noncomparable, where life without the latest information technologies or metropolitan centers might be very real and very possible. This is not to imply a certain romanticizing of tradition, culture, and rural, pastoral modes of living, but to emphasize that *a* certain way of life was seen as *the* only possible way of life, one that the world would ignore at its (collective) peril.

Modernization has, in Tipps's estimation, "evoke[d] vague and generalized images" that emerged from "social changes wrought by industrialization" (1973, 199). The mystique of this promise of the future of an ideal society, just beyond the reach of most of the world (and arguably all societies), is continually conjured up in the imagination. This ideal society does not appear to have a definite holistic and tangible form (beyond owning a television set or tasting a soft drink), but has become a desirable goal among sufficiently large populations to claim a central place in the collective imaginary. Esteva sums up the amorphous yet ubiquitous presence of the concept of modern development as follows: "Development occupies the centre of an incredibly powerful semantic constellation . . . even though it lacks, on its own, any precise denotation, it is firmly seated in the popular intellectual perception" (1992, 8–10).

The centered idea of development produced practically universal social effects. In the mid-twentieth century, the concept of modernization informed economic, political, social, cultural, and psychological spheres of life. In many instances, modernization projects emerged from post–World War II U.S. foreign policy decisions. It formed the wellspring from which states and international agencies drew their meanings and defined their activities. In this context, Mowlana and Wilson see modernity (often interchanged with modernization and development in the communication and development literature) as "a form of occidental rationalism which required the creation of an economy, secularization, and the development of the nation-state in small- and large-scale communities" (Mowlana and Wilson 1990, xii). International conditions today are testimony to the centering of this rationalism. The significance of the economy is evident in postmodern global capitalism, and some hold that states continue to modernize in what is, to the advanced industrial nations, a postmodern era.

A sense of totality in meanings, practices, institutions, and rules emerges from this center. The discourse of development has thus facilitated a dominant way of mapping, classifying, and knowing the world. Ferguson has conceptualized development as "an interpretive grid" through which the world is made or rendered "real" (Ferguson 1990, p. xiii). Thus development, and communication and development, have come to occupy a central place in the social imaginary and divide the world into advanced and backward nations.

Multiple Discursive Configurations: The Techno-Social and the Economic

Communication and development emerged as a larger discourse consisting of various discursive strands that work to keep the ruling concept of development in place. It is neither possible nor useful to identify a single dominant idea of communication and development. The discursive strands encompass a unity of fields such as technological, social, economic, institutional, cultural, and so on. Escobar claims that creating this unity involved "creating ... a field of force that produces and reproduces 'development' through every single one of its practices and which, in doing so, systematically relates fields of knowledge and spheres of power" (Escobar 1987, 130). The result is the process of "developmentization" in which many actors and institutions participate and, in the process, construct multiple discourses that share a common locus. Far from being a neat assemblage waiting to be identified, the emergent sense of totality is a continually contested yet (at least) temporarily fixed discourse. Since techno-social and economic configurations dominate the discourse of communication and development, they merit closer examination.

The Techno-Social

Modernization theory best exemplifies the techno-social discourse integral to communication and development. President Woodrow Wilson's pronouncement that the "benefits of scientific advances and industrial progress" (Esteva 1992, 6) should serve all nations is often cited as the official signal for putting into motion an elaborate worldwide development machinery and setting standards for industrialization and technologization of societies. Industrialization came to define what Esteva explains as "the terminal stage of a unilinear way of social evolution" (Esteva 1992, 8–9).

Reading a dialogic relationship between two scholars' works sheds light on the constituent elements of the techno-social discourse. Wallerstein (1995) identifies two discourses of modernity—the modernity of technology and the modernity of liberation. Freedom from the arbitrariness of calamity represented the "triumph of humanity over nature," enabled by the modernity of technology. Release from the arbitrary use of power signified for Wallerstein the "triumph of humanity over itself," or the modernity of liberation. Together these discourses exist oppositionally, and this clash represents the essential contradiction of the modern world system (Wallerstein 1995, 472). Where Wallerstein saw the two discourses of technology and liberation as oppositional, political scientist and communication scholar Pool envisioned one as the outcome of the other. In Pool's (1990) analysis, the free flow of communications technologies and data, both symbols of development, would ultimately empower individuals in all societies with the knowledge available through these technologies. Communication technology breaks "communities with contiguity," communities bounded by (and therefore constrained by) lines of the state, regional bloc, and other geopolitical divides (Pool 1990). In making a passionate case for the creation of less hierarchical, more horizontal power distribution through the use of communication technologies and international data flow, Pool implied that the modernity of liberation could indeed be an outcome of the modernity of technology.

For Lerner, considered one of the fathers of modernization theory in communication, modernity represented a "behavioral system" and a "comprehensive interlocking of lifeways" (Lerner 1958, viii). He explained this behavioral system through an elaborate psychological profile of the "transitional man" preparing for a modernized (re)location in geography and lifestyle. The technologies and the use of modern communications media would enable the move into transition and create the mind-set necessary for the complete modernization of the "traditional" individual. Media would serve as "magic multipliers" in transitioning premodern peoples from members of agrarian and feudal societies into informed citizens of a modern democratic social order similar to that of many developed countries (i.e., a capitalistic democracy). Hence persuasion, mass media, and what Melkote and Steeves term "the climate of acceptance" came to define development activity through communication (Melkote and Steeves 2001, 66).

Other approaches to understanding the techno-social configuration of communication and development include the concepts of time and space, both of which have been breached and redefined by media technologies and related media practices. Shah (1996) has analyzed the spatio-temporal organization of the concept of "modern" in relation to development journalism. Development enthusiasts first had the task of changing the concept of time in the premodern mind-set. Shah observed that often, change involved the investment of value in concepts such as the future, punctuality, and long-term planning. Another rearrangement in temporal thinking involved the assumption that Third World histories were similar to those of the First World nations, and hence a similar path, albeit speeded up, toward the present of the West was a natural and inevitable course of history for the rest of the world. Shah's (1996) observation is particularly helpful here. Spatially, the ideas of tribe or village would have to expand to the concept of nation in the social imaginary of the developing societies. In this context, development news would provide desirable images of progress and, more importantly, "direct people toward modernization by depicting images of rational decision making, efficient social organization, and technological sophistication" that modernization promised (Shah 1996, 148).

The Economic

Economics, on the whole, has been given prime position in the discourse of development. Esteva has argued that economic activity was isolated from the social (of which it used to be a part) and subsequently formed the center around which universal understandings of development and underdevelopment were constructed. The idea of "scarcity" formed the origin for economics and, from here on, related notions of underdevelopment and the market as deliverer from scarcity acquired currency of such magnitude that thinking beyond the economic to envisage a different world order continues to present a major challenge (Esteva 1992). It is interesting to note that the idea of "development journalism" was coined in 1968 in conjunction with a training program for economics reporting (Lent and Vilanilam 1977; Ogan 1982). Righter observes, "its [development journalism's] successes alerted governments to the importance of economic and social reporting," where prioritizing economic reporting pointed to the instrumental and functional value of developmental journalism in serving the goals of (economic) development (Righter, cited in Ogan 1982, 8).

Dependency theory, the economics-based critical response to modernization theory, was fundamentally a critique of the promotion of capitalism on a world scale, implicit in early modernization's advocacy for a Western version of democracy (what Escobar has termed elsewhere as developmentized democracy, and which we can also interpret as capitalism-based development). The international capitalist economy constituted the primary focus of dependency theory. The detrimental effect of exogenously induced capitalism "preclude[d] the materialization of the classic conditions of growth" (Baran; cited in Randall and Theobald 1985, 105). This statement implies that the classic conditions of growth (as delineated in Western economic history) would be possible to achieve endogenously. Critics of the dominant discourse of development, such as Esteva and Escobar, attribute the link of capital and "growth" to the discourse of development established by industrialized societies.

Dependency theory in the domain of information and communication appears in works by Hamelink, Schiller, and Mattelart, among others. Hamelink translated data and information (serving as raw material or finished product) into economic and manufacturing terms and demonstrated the impact of economic activity of the transnational corporations (TNCs) in the information domain on developing regions. Crucial data needed for allocative decisions in national contexts (i.e., information as national resource) were appropriated by TNCs in the interest of profit. Information and communication technologies, then, play a critical role in the accumulation process fundamental to capitalism. Information from satellites provided TNCs with data on natural resources in various countries and regions (Hamelink 1984). Such information rendered many Third World countries hosting TNCs vulnerable since it was not always readily available to decision makers in these countries. Thus the "media-data convergence," as Pavlic and Hamelink (1985) have termed it, points to the ways in which communication has been subsumed under economics. With the advent of the third communication revolution (or the digital revolution), multimedia convergence in conjunction with media-data convergence has reenergized capitalistic domination in the global information domain (Gunaratne 2001; includes a detailed analysis of support technology density, the dominance of the core, and the reinstitution of the world systems paradigm).

Both modernization and dependency share a common origin—the philosophy of modernity and the economics of capitalism. As Shohat and Stam point out, though dependency "rejected the Eurocentric premises of 'modernization,'" its Marxian origins made it "metrocentric" (Shohat and Stam 1994, 17–18), and according to dependency theorists, the Third World could exercise little agency in the face of capitalism. The concept of ambiguity suggests that agency is continually exercised, demonstrating that interstitial spaces or fissures are part of the topography of a dominant ideology, and that it is through these fissures that it is constantly challenged.

Ambiguity

Negotiation with the modernization discourse and the resultant meanings and understandings of development are particularly illustrative of the unstable nature of discourse explained by the concept of ambiguity. In the context of their study on communication and development in a Korean village, Kincaid and Yum (1976) understood the "process of development and modernization" to emerge contextually from a multiplicity of lived realities, rather than as a prescription emerging from a center. Exogenous intervention does not guarantee quick social change; what is needed for developing societies, according to them, is a longer time frame, perhaps similar to the protracted and painful social change that occurred during the industrialization of Europe. For Kincaid and Yum, communication for solving local problems ("to gather, transform, and create new information to solve social . . . problems," 82–83) far exceeded the importance placed on communication for economic development alone. They held that solutions to local problems within local contexts would eventually result in sustained economic growth. Kincaid and Yum's negotiation with the dominant discourse pertains to the process of communication; however, the results (a modern mediatized society) would coincide with the criteria of an exogenously prescribed modern society.

Critics like Inayatullah argue that the experiences of other (here, Western) societies offer valuable lessons for the developing world, but that these lessons would be of little use if the meaning of development were not subjected to localized understandings, since development is "a process of moving from what [a society] is to what it aspires to be" (Inayatullah 1976, 241). Fundamentally, Inayatullah calls for an exchange of development models in a nonhierarchical manner; the term "exchange" suggests a two-way flow where multiple development experiences at various points in history need to be legitimated, instead of valorizing and pursuing a predetermined path to a single dominant state of development.

Ambiguity in discourse is apparent in the cracks and fissures caused by continuous contestation and negotiation of the dominant knowledge. Identifying these fissures leads us to inquire into the politics of the discursive production of communication and development, as to how the "other" emerges in deconstructive readings of the dominant discourse. As Gupta reminds us, the discourse of development is "enunciated from multiple positions." These positions are not always obvious and are often situated in the fissures that constantly work to erode the dominant project of development (Gupta 1998, 43).

Constituting Communication and Development through Its Other

The process of identifying a discourse entails consideration of what to include and what to exclude from a body of knowledge. White describes the process of identifying a discourse as "a matter of trying to *mark out* . . . [an] area, *define* its contours, *identify* the elements in its field, [and] *discern* the kinds of relationships that obtain among them" (White 1978, 1). The term "developmentization" describes the processes by which the discourse of development marked out and defined its space (Escobar 1995). We understand the operation of power in the discourse of communication and development by attempting to articulate its "other." This "other" constitutes a collection of marginalized meanings and practices of development.

Deconstruction as a mode of analysis enables a critical examination of discourse where it is only possible to understand more comprehensively (and politically) the expressed when the unsaid is accounted for. According to Bass, this means that "every totality . . . can be shown to be founded on that which it excludes" (Bass 1978, xvi). Specifically, Derrida's concept of *différance* encompasses two terms—"difference" (between the signifier and that which the signifier overcomes to establish itself as the dominant) and "deferral" (which indicates an indefinite delay in the signifier reaching its ultimate goal—the object it is supposed to mean). Doty has translated the concept effectively in her study on constructions of international hierarchy—the difference, in development discourse, is evident in dichotomies such as First World/Third World, modern/traditional, progressive/backward, and so on. The deferral is embedded in the signifier "development"—it is a state of affairs that is always "yet to come" for the Third World, or a location to which the Third World seems to be perpetually striving to arrive (Doty 1991). To arrive at a critical genealogy of communication and development, therefore, a double reading of both the articulated and its *différance* is needed.

Young observes that the study of the sign should address "the absence of everything from which it is differentiated" (Young 1981, 15). It is this absence that scholars have increasingly attempted to address in the domains of theory and practice in communication, development, and social change. I attempt to articulate this "absence" in three ways. I begin with deconstructive readings of early prescriptions for media and language and new conventions for new media technologies that were gradually being adopted worldwide in the mid-twentieth century. I then look at some works that address the origins and the meaning of "development," assumptions about social structures, the definition of "news" in the development context, and journalistic practice. Finally, I locate recent historical accounts and theoretical advances as a dialectic response to the dominant notions of communication, development, and social change. These recent accounts and advances articulate and position the theory and practice of development and communication in general from non-metrocentric standpoints. The series of examples that follow demonstrate possible deconstructive readings of positions and perspectives in communication and development. The examples also include existing works that perform this task but have not been cast explicitly in the framework of the "other." However, a detailed analysis of any single aspect of the discourse lies beyond the scope of this chapter.

New Media Technologies and Language Conventions

If the definition of technology were to include professional knowledge (the division in the literature includes hardware, software, and training or knowledge transfer), observations made in the 1960s during the heyday of the modernization paradigm relating to the discourse of the modernity of technology (Wallerstein 1995) compel a deconstructive reading. According to sociologist Passin (1963), the first step toward developing a modern communication system included the creation of a parallel "modern" language. He observed that part of the bottleneck to practicing "effective" journalism was the prevalent linguistic schizophrenia (as Todorov has termed elsewhere) in countries like

India and some African countries. Passin reasoned that as a result, a Sene-galese politician campaigned in French in a predominantly Woloff-speaking country, or that the Hindi press catered to a narrow audience in the multilin-gual environment in India. Although Passin's observation of the linguistic problem in these countries is true, it poses certain problems. For one, the states in developing regions could take exception to creating a new national language to suit modern media technologies and demands on grounds that it would invade and displace traditional languages (the cultural imperialism thesis). For another, a new language would involve creating literate publics to consume media fare produced in the new language, no mean task considering that literacy with existing languages is a gargantuan challenge that developing regions continue to meet.

Establishing appropriate new conventions for new communication situa-tions created by modern mass media technologies is another prescriptive area to be considered for deconstructive reading. It has been pointed out that In-dian government officials were reluctant to use "low Hindi" in their All India Radio (AIR) broadcasts intended for national reach (Pool 1963). While this critique is valid from a class standpoint considering the barely literate small village audiences, it is nevertheless embedded in the discourse of the moder-nity of technology. Hence AIR broadcasts were seen as lacking a language ap-propriate to the intended use of the technology as a mass medium. Nandy's (1992) historical inquiry into the colonial origins of technology, society, and culture enables a counterreading of Pool's critique. Nandy observed that the European colonizers' discourse melded the "superiority of science" and the "craft status" of technology. This resulted in the blending and naturalizing of the ideas of scientific objectivity, rationality, and Western technology as a jus-tification for Western domination. This merging of the categories has carried over to the development discourse. Nandy's observation could provide a dif-ferent understanding of the use of "high Hindi" broadcasts on AIR. Radio, then a relatively new mass medium in India, could have been viewed for the most part as a scientific invention first, and given a culture-specific exalted status in keeping with the "superiority of science" over the "craft status" of the technology. This perception could have influenced the use of a specific stra-tum of language for the radio broadcasts. Thus a culture of science that is dif-ferent from the one engendered by the modernity of technology could inter-act in unexpected ways with modern communication technologies to produce effects that do not fit a universal definition of an appropriate professional lin-guistic code for modern media.

In addition to a common modern language, Passin saw a definite need for developing objective journalistic practices. Journalists in transitional societies (a term that continues to apply to about three-fourths of the world) were required to shed political commitment and don the cloak of neutral observation of events, in keeping with the practice of journalism in developed countries, particularly in the United States (many European nations have a history of politically affiliated or partisan presses). In transitional societies, political alignment has formed an integral part of journalistic practice, particularly at certain historical junctures. For example, the Indian press has a history of a declared nationalistic press under British rule. In the aftermath of colonial rule, though largely directed by Western professional ideology, the press continued to (critically) follow state development projects. Hence journalists' deliberate use of vernacular languages and their overt political commitment could be read as an "other" of a universal set of journalistic norms and conventions.

"Development," Social Structure, and Social Change

The origins of the term "development" in its modern usage in international studies is attributed to President Truman's speech on January 20, 1949, in which he separated development from its obverse condition, underdevelopment (Esteva 1992; Illich 1992; Escobar 1995). Esteva traces the evolution of the term "development" to Darwin and his work on a universal theory of human evolution. In this context, "developed" is seen as adult, more evolved, and in general holds a more superior connotation to the term "underdeveloped." In a rare attribution to the origins of the term "development" to a non-Western source, communications scholar Mowlana and coauthor Wilson traced the term's origins to the fourteenth-century Islamic social thinker Ibn Khaldun, who referred to "the development of human societies in space and time" (Mowlana and Wilson 1990, 9)—a general definition in which the development of a society can be best understood in its own historical context. This historical legacy is not recognized in the modern discourse of development.

In his critique of the "theoretical orthodoxy" informing communication and development in the 1970s, Golding (1974) observed that theories of differentiation of social systems—complex modern social systems about which the mass media would inform and educate the public—assumed that structural arrangements of traditional societies were far simpler than those in modern societies. He has pointed out that such assumptions disregarded the sophisticated social structures that existed in many premodern and preindustrial societies. On the issue of aid for development, Golding, among others, has critiqued exogenously induced change from which modernization theorists believed that values, resources, technology, and knowledge had to be imported to effect social change in preindustrial societies. Two readings obtain from Golding's critique—first, that preindustrial societies are capable of using their own resources to reach the level of modernization of the economically powerful countries, and, second, that other social, political, cultural, and economic changes can be effected through use of either indigenous or a combination of local and nonlocal resources (the predominant practice today).

Journalistic Practice and Definitions of News

One of the problems cited in relation to development news is the professional demands and institutional settings that hinder effective development reporting. Ogan and Fair (1984) cite Schramm and Atwood's study of news in Asia, where the nature of news flow (from wire services to the editor's desk) does not allow the editor sufficient time to recognize patterns of events and piece them together as development news for the public. Additionally, the definition of news itself sets the bounds for reporting development—"News is timely. It is a change in something; it can be dated and specified" (Ogan and Fair 1984, 174). This universal definition of news marginalizes other possible meanings for the term "news." For example, "change in something" takes into account immediate and fragmentary change; documenting development as changing conditions would involve considering the "other"—the possibility of change as more long term than the dominant definition of news recognizes, or the deemphasis of the time/duration factor, which has no room in the mainstream definition of news. Similarly, the idea of "timely," in keeping with change, could be reinterpreted to expand the time frame for longer-term change. Involvement and critique (viewed as political journalistic practice) would enable the reporter to include long-term change and reinterpret the idea of "timely" to mean the necessity of capturing the beginnings and closures of successful social change programs of any nature, and to effect timely critiques of failing projects of "emancipation" (Shah 1996). Thus, as Gunaratne (1998) has pointed out, development journalism attempted to go past "traditional news values."

The Nonmetrocentric

Emergent alternative histories of communication studies in general, and specific approaches to development communication in particular, now point to ways of seeing the communicative act in development contexts from perspectives that are a critical response to metrocentric approaches outlined in this chapter under the mechanism of centering. These responses have twin roots—in intellectual concerns for ethical practice and in the lived development experiences of grassroots communities. The wealth of empirical studies in the area of participatory communication denotes a disengagement with traditional approaches to development sponsored by the state and development agencies (that continues on a more systemic level). These works document the move to diffuse power from specific loci to the more general public, the intended recipient of development programs. It is in this diffusion that an "other" is now being articulated (Wilkins and Mody 2001). This "new" approach can be identified, in Steeves's (2001) term, as nonmaterial, a stark contrast to earlier approaches to social change measurable in the material growth in capital, technology, infrastructure, and so on. For example, approaches to development based on liberation theology in Brazil (latest synoptic works include Rodriguez 2001a, 2001b; Steeves 2001) encompass participatory and feminist perspectives, where acts such as "nam[ing] the social world" (Rodriguez and Murphy 1997, 32) and calls for changing the fundamental social structures with gender equity and balance as social goals become integral to development questions. These questions are embedded in grassroots and everyday experiences of peoples in developing regions, rather than ones usually arrived at on a national level that are framed dominantly in the language of economic growth and technologization of developing societies.

Conclusion

Recent intellectual and activist developments in this era of globalization may, at least on the surface, suggest a "moving on" from concerns about development to questions raised by the process of globalization. Globalization is bringing about an increasing divide in the already divided and hierarchized international arena, but this is not the object of study here. Rather, this chapter attempts to account for recent history in a more comprehensive way, and a historically oriented project allows us to consider what Dean (1994) describes as "our changing historical sense," thus giving perspective to our practices in the present. In the case of communication, development, and social change, the discourse is far from achieving closure. Deliberations about the construction of this discourse thus continue to be germane.

My purpose in this chapter was to explore a framework, a critical genealogy, to understand the processes by which the discourse of communication, development, and social change interpellates peoples, determines national agendas, and defines social change. A critical genealogy thus requires consideration of a historical span in the formation of the discourse, simultaneously with an account of the multiple marginalized positions and practices. The benefits of such a framework lie in its ability to account for the operation of power to create and govern knowledges about social systems and communicative cultures and practices as both processual and dialectic. To this end, the chapter has drawn broadly from theoretical legacies of critical cultural studies and post-structuralism, and has ranged over several key and not-so-prominent works to trace an enduring discourse. In the process, I attempt to bring to the fore the disciplining power of dominant modes of understanding communication, development, and social change in the study of international communication.

References

Bass, A. 1978. Translator's introduction to J. Derrida. In *Writing and difference*, ix–xx. Chicago: University of Chicago Press.

Chakravartty, P. 2001. Flexible citizens and the Internet: The global politics of local hi-tech development in India. *Emergences* 11, no. 1: 69–88.

Dean, M. 1994. *Critical and effective histories: Foucault's methods and historical sociology.* London: Routledge.

Derrida, J. 1986. "Différance." In M. C. Taylor, ed., *Deconstruction in context: Literature and philosophy*, 396–420. Chicago: University of Chicago Press.

Doty, R. L. 1991. The social construction of contemporary international hierarchy. Ph.D. diss., University of Minnesota.

———. 1996. *Imperial encounters: The politics of representation in north–south relations.* Minneapolis: University of Minnesota Press.

Escobar, A. 1987. Power and visibility: The invention and management of development in the Third World. Ph.D. diss., University of California.

———. 1995. *Encountering development: The making and unmaking of the Third World.* Princeton, N.J.: Princeton University Press.

———. 1999. "Discourse and power in development: Michel Foucault and the relevance of his work to the Third World." In J. Servaes and T. Jacobson, eds., *Theoretical approaches to participatory communication*, 309–36. Creskill, N.J.: Hampton.

Esteva, G. 1992. "Development." In W. Sachs, ed., *The development dictionary: A guide to knowledge as power*, 6–25. London: Zed.

Ferguson, J. 1990. *The anti-politics machine: "Development," depoliticization, and bureaucratic power in Lesotho.* Cambridge: Cambridge University Press.

Foucault, M. 1972. *The archaeology of knowledge and the discourse on language.* New York: Pantheon.

Golding, P. 1974. Media use in national development: A critique of a theoretical orthodoxy. *Journal of Communication* 24: 39–53.

Gunaratne, S. 1998. "Old wine in a new bottle: Public journalism, developmental journalism, and social responsibility." In M. E. Roloff, ed., *Communication Yearbook 21.* Thousand Oaks, Calif.: Sage.

———. 2001. "Convergence: Informatization, world system, and developing countries." In W. B. Gudykunst, ed., *Communication Yearbook 25.* Mahwah, N.J.: Erlbaum.

Gupta, A. 1998. *Postcolonial developments: Agriculture in the making of modern India.* Durham, N.C.: Duke University Press.

Hamelink, C. 1984. *Transnational data flow in the information age.* Lund, Sweden: Studentlitterateur AB, Chartwell-Bratt.

Huesca, R. 2001. Tracing the history of participatory communication approaches to development: A critical appraisal. Paper presented at the annual conference of the International Communication Association, May, Washington, D.C.

Illich, I. 1992. Needs. In W. Sachs, ed., *The development dictionary: A guide to knowledge as power,* 88–101. London: Zed.

Inayatullah, C. 1976. "Western, Asian, or global models of development: The effect of the transference of models on the development of Asian societies." In W. Schramm and D. Lerner, eds., *Communication and change: The last ten years—and the next,* 57–59. Honolulu: University of Hawaii Press.

Jackson, J., and Mosco, V. 1999. The political economy of new technological spaces: Malaysia's multimedia super corridor. *Journal of International Communication* 6, no. 1: 23–40.

Jacobson, T. 1996. "Development communication theory in the 'wake' of positivism." In J. Servaes, T. L. Jacobson, and S. W. White, eds., *Participatory communication for social change.* New Delhi: Sage.

Jacobson, T., and S. Kolluri. 1999. "Participatory communication as communicative action." In J. Servaes and T. Jacobson, eds., *Theoretical approaches to participatory communication,* 265–80. Creskill, N.J.: Hampton.

Jayaweera, N. 1987. "Rethinking development communication: A holistic view." In N. Jayaweera and S. Amunugama, eds., *Rethinking development communication.* Singapore: Kefford.

Kincaid, L., and Yum, J. O. 1976. "The needle and the axe: Communication and development in a Korean village." In W. Schramm and D. Lerner, eds., *Communication and change: The last ten years—and the next,* 83–97. Honolulu: University of Hawaii Press.

Laclau, E., and Mouffe, C. 1985. *Hegemony and socialist strategy: Towards a radical democratic politics.* London: Verso.

Lent, J., and Vilanilam, J. 1977. *The use of development news: Case studies of India, Malaysia, Ghana, and Thailand.* Singapore: Asian Mass Communication Research and Information Centre.

Lerner, D. 1958. *The passing of traditional society: Modernizing the Middle East.* Glencoe, Ill: Free Press.

Melkote, S., and Steeves, L. 2001. *Communication for development in the Third World.* 2d ed. New Delhi: Sage.

Michaels, E. 1993. *Bad aboriginal art: Tradition, media, and technological horizons.* Minneapolis: University of Minnesota Press.

Mowlana, H., and Wilson, L. 1990. *The passing of modernity: Communication and the transformation of society.* New York: Longman.

Nandy, A. 1992. *Traditions, tyranny, and utopias: Essays in the politics of awareness.* Delhi: Oxford University Press.

Ogan, C. 1982. Development journalism/communication: The status of a concept. *Gazette: International Journal of Mass Communication Studies* 29: 3–13.

Ogan, C., and Fair, J. E. 1984. A little good news: The treatment of development news in selected Third World newspapers. *Gazette* 33: 173–91.

Passin, H. 1963. "Writer and journalist in the transitional society." In L.W. Pye, ed., *Communication and political development.* Princeton, N.J.: Princeton University Press.

Pavlic, B., and Hamelink, C. 1985. *The new international economic order: Links between economics and communication.* Paris: UNESCO.

Pool, I. 1963. "The mass media and politics in the modernization process." In L. W. Pye, ed., *Communication and political development.* Princeton, N.J.: Princeton University Press.

———. 1990. *Technologies without boundaries: On telecommunications in a global age.* Edited by Eli Noam. Cambridge, Mass.: Harvard University Press.

Randall, V., and Theobald, R. 1985. *Political change and underdevelopment: A critical introduction to Third World politics.* Durham, N.C.: Duke University Press.

Rodriguez, C. 2001a. *Fissures in the mediascape: An international study of citizens' media.* Creskill, N.J.: Hampton.

———. 2001b. Shattering butterflies and amazons: Symbolic constructions of women in Colombian development perspective. *Communication Theory* 11, no. 4: 472–94.

Rodriguez, C., and Murphy, P. 1997. The study of communication and culture in Latin America: From laggards and the oppressed to resistance and hybrid cultures. *Journal of International Communication* 4, no. 2: 24–45.

Servaes, J. 1998. Human rights, participatory communication, and cultural freedom in a global perspective. *Journal of International Communication* 5, no. 1–2: 122–33.

Shah, H. 1996. Modernization, marginalization, and emancipation: Toward a normative model of journalism and national development. *Communication Theory* 6: 143–56.

———. 1997. Continuities and discontinuities in communication and development research since 1958. *Journal of International Communication* 4, no. 2: 3–23.

Shohat, E., and Stam, R. 1994. *Unthinking Eurocentrism: Multiculturalism and the media.* London: Routledge.

Slater, D. 1992. "Theories of Development and the Politics of the Postmodern: Exploring a Border Zone." In J. N. Pieterse, ed., *Emancipations modern and postmodern.* London: Sage.

Steeves, L. 2001. Liberation, feminism, and development communication. *Communication Theory* 11, no. 4: 397–414.

Teheranian, M. 1999a. *Global communication and world politics: Domination, development, and discourse.* Boulder: Lynne Rienner.

———. 1999b. "Where is the new world order? At the end of history or a clash of civilizations?" In R. C. Vincent, K. Nordenstreng, and M. Traber, eds., *Towards equity in global communication: MacBride update.* Creskill, N.J.: Hampton.

Tipps, D. 1973. Modernization theory and the comparative studies of societies: A critical perspective. *Comparative Studies in Society and History* 15: 199–226.

Tomlinson, J. 1991. *Cultural imperialism: An introduction.* Baltimore: Johns Hopkins University Press.

Wallerstein, I. 1995. The end of what modernity? *Theory and Society* 24: 471–88.

White, H. 1978. *Tropics of discourse: Essays in cultural criticism.* Baltimore: Johns Hopkins University Press.

Wilkins, K. G., and Mody, B. 2001. Reshaping development communication: Developing communication and communicating development. *Communication Theory* 11, 4: 385–96.

Young, R. 1981. "Introduction to Michel Foucault: The order of discourse." In *Untying the text: A post-structuralist reader.* Boston: Routledge & Kegan Paul.

Žižek, S. 1993. *Tarrying with the negative: Kant, Hegel, and the critique of ideology.* Durham, N.C.: Duke University Press.

3

Communication and the Postcolonial Nation-State: A New Political Economic Research Agenda

Amin Alhassan

The state may have exhausted much of its progressive role in the industrial world, where the welfare state has been nearly completed or according to some interest groups even overdone so that it should be rolled back, with the civil society and the so-called third sector assuming a greater role in the management of society. But the developing countries are far from ready for this. In these countries it is mainly the state that can ensure that poverty and inequality can be seriously treated, and counting on the civil society or NGOs would be largely wishful thinking.

—Nordenstreng 2001, 160

A BLIND SPOT IN THE MAINSTREAM literature on international and development communication is a lack of an interrogation of the *postcolonial state* in particular and the *postcolonial nation-state* as a whole as significant actors in the local scene. While the effects of the global and international activities of communication industries are said to have significant consequences on the postcolonial societies, local actors are often read as either collaborators or helpless and hapless participants in the drama of international cultural traffic. This chapter examines the *state* and *nation* in the *postcolony* as significant conceptual categories that must be treated as institutional actors, each of whose agency is shaped by both local and international pressures as well as the fact of their historical trajectory. Drawing on specific instances of African experience will draw attention to some of the historical circumstances that still shape the direction of communication and development in developing countries, much of which appears to have been overlooked in earlier approaches to questions of development and communication.

Conceptually, the term "postcolonial" is quite popular in Third World scholarship and is concerned with issues of identity and culture on a global level. Ella Shohat (1992, 101) defines it as "a designation for critical discourses which thematize issues emerging from colonial relations and their aftermath, covering a long historical span (including the present)." Such a definition already resolves the superficial understanding of postcolonial as meaning a period after colonialism. Conceptually, postcoloniality is concerned with the social transformations that result from the colonial encounter and that is today manifested as the postcolonial nation-state. Introducing this concept into development communication will help overcome the tendency to treat the modernization process as a postindependence phenomenon. Treating the postcolonial as a social formation (and as a conjuncture) is fruitful because of the ability to interrogate the onset of modernization as predating the development planning practices of the nation-state in Africa. Consequently, we can conceptualize the postcolonial state as an institution that may not be so distinct from its colonial ancestry. As Stuart Hall points out, political independence did not necessarily mean that the colonial values vanished from the scene. In many ways, life under independence "is characterized by the persistence of many of the effects of colonialism" (Hall 1996, 248). We can then examine the communication and development practices of both the colonial and postcolonial states as part of the same process of modernization, even if they have differing agendas. For the sake of convenience, I sometimes refer to the postcolonial nation-state as the postcolony (Mbembe 2001). I do not mean to suggest that the society under discussion is not measuring up to the designation "nation-state," even if the designation "developing country" suggests that the postcolonial nation-state is in the process of becoming.

The Slighted Postcolonial State

The postcolonial state projects itself as a developmentalist one because of the distributive task in the making of a nation out of different groups. Its adoption of the modernizing technologies of communication has been geared at this objective (Martin-Barbero 1993, 165). This is the basis of much of the postcolonial state's interest in communication and development activities. Yet a review of the existing literature on development communication shows an absence of a theory of the state. The first generation of scholarship, led by Lerner (1958) and Schramm (1964) through dependency theory and latter-day multiplicity paradigm theorists such as Servaes (1999), has discussed the state as if its constitutive agency does not count. References to the constitutive action of the state occur by default and not explicitly. Take, for instance,

Schramm's (1964) comprehensive discussion of on the role of communication in the development of postcolonial nation-states. One gets the feeling that he is discussing the development of acephalous societies and not nation-states. When he discusses the "development process" he focuses on the liberal economic theories of development and economic planning. The nature of the planners is not mentioned by Schramm (1964, 20ff.). The "developer" or phrases such as "mobilizing human resources requires" (33) take the place of admitting that there is a political institution that directs development. Schramm prefers to give more attention to technocrats, such as when he builds on David McCleland's theory of "need achievement" or relies on an anthropologist such as Margaret Mead to elaborate on how the development process must be executed. When Schramm (1964, 246–71) finally offers his fifteen-point recommendations, he starts them with "a developing country should . . ." Yet the apex of local power that must carry out his recommendation is left out.

Lerner's book *The Passing of Traditional Society* (1958) was not about Africa but focused on the development of former colonies that became nation-states. It was about modernizing the Middle East into the Western divide of what became known as the bipolar world of Washington and Moscow. The book established its place in the classics of development communication because of its pioneering effort in looking at how to modernize what were considered "traditional" societies. Thus a search for a theory of state in modernization and development through communication may as well start from this book. Apart from this justification for expecting a theory of state from Lerner, Samarajiwa's (1987) revelation that the ten-year research project that culminated in the book actually benefited from state largess warrants us to put a higher premium on our expectation. The state being referred to here is the U.S. government, through the Voice of America. In addition, Lerner's project actually had a case-by-case study of various Middle East countries.

Unlike Schramm's later work, Lerner does bother with the subject of local state's agency in the constitution of modernization. But he reads this in a troubling way. That is as the personal feats of individual leaders and not the state as a machinery of power with distributive ability that responds to the various social forces that it represents. Imagine, for instance, when he writes:

> We begin with Turkey as the area's most impressive example of modernization—impressive in that it has steadily evolved, along the lines laid down by a revolutionary dictatorship over three decades ago. Ataturk's genius as a social planner was to see "economic development" within a comprehensive behavioral matrix. To raise industrial production, Ataturk began by simplifying the national language separating religion, installing schools, building roads, creating cities. (Lerner 1958, 105)

The story goes on to personalize the gamut of innovations that the state of Turkey carried out. We have to grant Lerner the credit for the details he provides to show the constitutive action of the state in modernization. Researching an area that was just at the heels of decolonization, he provides us with perceptive commentary that is suggestive of the anatomy of the postcolonial state. "The very concept of a Syrian elite requires qualification" Lerner writes, "The native elite did not exercise sustained authoritative power" (270). He says that "the French played the classic game of divisiveness. Every internal minority—linguistic, ethnic, regional, religious or nomadic—was encouraged to develop in its own case" (271). Beyond this descriptive enterprise, however, Lerner offers us no theory of the state in communication and development of postcolonial societies.

Both pioneers of communication and development are not particularly interested in the local dynamics of developmental state but do not hesitate to credit UNESCO as a development actor. Such an attitude to the state can be understood from the political orientation of their work. They have a liberal view of development that tends to think of the state in a very limited sense or when it comes to the state in the developing countries, they see it as dictatorships, undemocratic or just plain weak states. The history of the state, its colonial parentage and how power is reproduced within the postcolonial context as the embodiment of the state apparatus is simply unappealing to them. The development enterprise, for them, can be understood in terms of economic and psychological theories of change within the logic of the market. But what we are sure of is that such a comprehensive program of development through the transfer of technology that Schramm and Lerner suggest cannot be carried out by market forces without a local state.

If the defining texts such as Schramm's and Lerner's neglected the state dimension in the nexus of development, social change, and technological transfer, they set the pace and paradigm for later generations of communication researchers. Not even their ideological opponents, whose writings are visibly influenced by the leftist radicalism of Marxism, neo-Marxism, and dependista, as well as the realism of living in the postcolony, would bother about a theory of the state. By this I am referring to anthologies such as *Rethinking Development Communication* edited by Jayaweera and Amunugama (1987), *Communication in Development* edited by Casmir (1991), and the monograph by Melkote (1991), *Communication for Development in the Third World*. These are books no undergraduate or graduate student in a standard development communication program will be allowed to miss. And most of the contributions in these books are discussing the development of former colonies and/or the programs of postcolonial states. In Casmir's volume, for instance, more than half of the contributors discuss national policy programs and outcomes.

Yet the state is always assumed to be unproblematic. International communication literature that falls under this omission of the state includes founding texts of the cultural imperialism thesis, including Nordenstreng and Schiller (1979, 1993), Schiller (1976), and the MacBride Report (1980).

After these four decades of oversight, one would expect a change of attitude. But recent additions to the literature tend to be on the same paradigm of neglect of the postcolonial state, while ironically discussing the very business of that state. Two books are worth noting at this stage, *Communication for Development: One World Multiple Cultures* (1999) by Jan Servaes and *Theoretical Approaches to Participatory Communication* (1999) edited by Jacobson and Servaes. The former concentrates on policy and development but neglects the anatomy of the key institutional actor. Jan Servaes is a communication scholar who has insisted on the revision of the previous two schools of thought. He argues that paradigms, as used in communication and development studies, "as frames of meaning" do not necessarily come and go. Rather, new paradigms are generated out of previous ones. In this light, the dependency approach should be seen as enriching the previous dominant paradigm through its criticism (Servaes 1999, 5–7). Elsewhere he states, "Most scholars agree that communication and development as a distinct discipline emerged after World War II, and they usually point out two paradigms: modernization and growth versus dependency and underdevelopment. I perceive a new perspective in terms of a new paradigm. This new paradigm, which can be broadly described as multiplicity in one world, is gradually emerging but still in the process of formation" (Servaes 1991, 52). This statement from Servaes, an advocate of the multiplicity paradigm, summarizes the circumstances surrounding the emergence of the paradigm. It can be said that it was due to the disappointing results from decades of development efforts guided by modernization theory and the lack of a comprehensive policy guidelines from the dependistas that led to the rethinking of a more participatory, open-minded, and all-embracing paradigm.

A guidepost for this evolving paradigm is empowering people at the grass roots by involving them at all stages of any project. This implies that any communication system must be dialogic, interactive, and sustained (Servaes 1991, 32–35). The communication system must be participatory so that local perceptions, attitudes, values, and knowledge are fully taken into consideration in the design of any development project. The involvement of the people must be substantive at all levels. Such a Freirean formulation is quite attractive and seems to offer a normative solution to the high-rise posture of the previous paradigms by insisting on the relevance of local agency. Servaes (1999, 140) therefore calls for the adoption of the *right to communicate* as the ideals of any policy practice that is based on the multiplicity paradigm. Who will carry out this policy prescription? It is a question he does not answer. By default, the assumption is that the state, as the main policymaker within the nation-state, is listening. But you have to wait until you read his take on the state: "Fundamental here is the other vision of the role of the authorities in the processes of social change. Unlike the confidence in and respect for the role of the state, which characterized the modernization and dependency paradigms, the multiplicity paradigm has a rather reserved attitude towards the authorities. Policies therefore should be built on the more selective participation strategies of dissociation and association" (Servaes 1999, 140).

We have to read Servaes here in perspective. First he rightly pointed out the limitation of the previous paradigms, and how the elite of developing country has a contradictory posture of disinterest in democratization at home but demand democratization internationally. Thus he damns these previous paradigms and the complicity of the state (1999, 119–43). And drawing from the radical pedagogy of the Brazilian scholar Paulo Freire, he calls for a more participatory approach. Here lies the strength of his formulation. But even Freire himself did not have this dissociative attitude toward authority. For Freire (1974, 21), the process of liberation is not aimed at bracketing out the oppressor but transforming the relation between the oppressed and the oppressor. The state is considered oppressive and elitist. No matter how participatory a development enterprise is intended, it will be strategically naive to disengage from the state. Freire (1974, 30) points out that the implementation of his dialogical pedagogy "requires political power and the oppressed have none." Thus Freire's dialogic setup acknowledges the relevance of the state as an unavoidable institution.[1] The state is the most well-organized institution, with the legitimate authority of making comprehensive national policy. It also has the monopoly of conferring legitimacy on all other institutions and the deployment of national economic resources. In addition, it has the legitimacy and monopoly over the use of violence. With all this resources, why will we shun the state? Strategically it is defeatist. What we need is not a damnation of the state but an analytical focus on the state.

What I am trying to point out is that there seem to be, what I will call, following Dallas Smythe's phrase, a blind spot of a theory of the state in development communication. Obviously there is an explanation for this oversight. The very apparent one is the Marxist influence with its disinterest in the "nation-state" as a legitimate object of analysis. In the dependista school, for example, which is predominantly neo-Marxist in orientation, the tendency has been to think of local problems of poverty and underdevelopment within the global political economic framework of imperialism. Such a posture has led to this theoretical blind spot. The influence it has had on previous attempts at understanding policy practices in development such as some of the references stated above is that they fail to take seriously "the constitutive role of the state" Mosco (1996, 250).

Recently Nordenstreng (2001) offered an appealing justification for the neglect of the dimension of the state in international communication, especially the cultural imperialism school. His justification places the blind spot into context. He admitted that the nation-state, contrary to the rhetoric of the globalization cheerleaders, "continues to matter both in global reality and in studies about it, while at the same time the state as a concept remains shamefully underanalyzed; and, hence there is a burning need to rethink the field" (Nordenstreng 2001, 155). Such an admission coming from someone at the forefront of the cultural imperialism thesis in communication studies should be taken seriously. How could such an omission be tolerated for three decades of discourse on cultural imperialism? Some of the defining texts such as the Nordenstreng and Schiller (1979, 1993) edited volumes on national sovereignty and international communication were blind on conceptual clarifications on the nation-state, democracy, citizenship, and sovereignty. Nordenstreng offers an explanation for this limitation that is worth quoting at length:

> The idea of media imperialism, with the notion of information sovereignty as an integral part of it, was a paradigm that was badly needed at that stage of understanding the world of communications. Seen from the angle of history of ideas, one may even say that it was a necessary step in the continuous intellectual project of understanding the world. Like all paradigms that convert sensitive social realities into scientific and/or political narratives, media imperialism and its cousin, the New World Information and Communication Order (NWICO), were turned into mantras serving political agitation rather than scientific analysis. (Nordenstreng 2001, 155)

After this self-criticism, he underlines the relevance of the state in national development in the developing countries and criticizes the tendency of the day to argue for market solutions to what is undoubtedly a state responsibility. Such a rethinking of the state in modernization injects fresh directions to the field.

The neglect of the power dynamics that shape the constitutive role of the state has probably resulted into what appears to be policymakers' consistent neglect of research findings. Cees Hamelink captured the spirit of this attitude well: "The problem seems to lie in the relationship between research and policy making. Over the past 20–30 years policy makers have paid insufficient attention to research results. All the studies that have been done so far on the relationship between social research and actual policy making show that in the majority of cases, policy makers on various levels totally neglect research.

They do not want to be bothered by it or even read it" (IPDC 1985, 26). Hamelink was contributing to a round table discussion of policymakers and experts convened by the University of Tampere on behalf of UNESCO on communication and development activities.

The problem is not that actors in the communication policy circles deliberately snub the results of hardworking researchers. Conversely, the researchers have been snubbing the various pressures that impact on the state in its constitutive role in development. Restated, communication research has never accorded due regard to the state's subjectivity as constituted by its trajectory as a colonial apparatus and later an agent in development in a postcolonial conjuncture. We may have to ask whose ideas shape policy direction? Is policy responding to the demand for leadership in development from the people in the postcolony or it is busily living up to the expectation of certain powerful interest groups whose interest is anything but the development concerns that researchers have been working to illuminate? These questions suggest that instead of taking the developmentalist state for its word (that its main business is nation building through development), or think of it as some superstructure in the hands of some all powerful ruling class, we interrogate the very practices of policy actors as human agents who make choices. These questions call for a recovery of the past to trace the itinerary of the formation of the state. It is only then that we will know what institution we are dealing with and how we can work to make sure that the findings of development communication research resonate with the needs of a developmentalist state.

Colonial and Postcolonial Continuities

In slighting the institutional characteristics of the postcolonial state, international communication scholarship took an ahistorical approach to the question of development in the postcolony. But a review of the history of the state in the colony suggests that development, as the business of the state, was not a postcolonial invention. For instance, the British colonial authorities expanded the role of the colonial state from just maintaining law and order to facilitate colonial exploitation to include "development planning" (Lee 1967; Escobar 1995). The colonial state in much of Africa had started courting the growing native middle class with the idea that it was engaging in development and modernization through the scientific application of knowledge to local social problems. Poverty had already been problematized and the idea of "development officers" had already been born in the colonies. The rhetoric of "improving standards of living" in the colonies was already a subject of administrative phraseology and attention in the 1940s (Lee 1967, 78).

The Colonial Development and Welfare Act of 1940 inaugurated in colonies such as Gold Coast (Ghana) the idea of social reform, transformation of society through the provision of welfare services including education and modern health facilities. "Good government meant that official classes accepted full responsibility for development schemes, neither more nor less" (Lee 1967, 13). The anticolonial movement within the British Labor Party and the activism of British families that had investments in the colonies contributed in the revision of colonial policy with the idea that the colonies needed development. Lee (1967, 6) explains that the 1940 act "established the principle that the British tax payer had a duty to make direct contribution towards the development of the colonial peoples." The empire had succeeded in convincing the British taxpayer to fund the modernization of the colonies so that the British class of colonial investors would continue to milk the resources of the colonies. Here is a double-edged sword: using public resources from the metropolis to enhance the process of imperialist accumulation. This period thus marks the beginning of an ideology-christened development, which uses public resources under the pretext of pursuing humanist goals but in reality aims at facilitating private business interests. Development had acquired a new meaning: a rhetorical gesture of conditioning certain social forces.

Between 1940 and 1955, the belief that modern technology held the answers to the development needs of the colonies was the conventional wisdom in Britain. The extension of modern medicine, mechanized methods of food production, and modern means of communication including telecommunication were already considered important requirements for the colonies (Lee 1967, 32). The recognition that the colonies were underdeveloped by British standards was already the accepted norm among colonial administrators and their work therefore included helping out to raise living standards.

In light of this, we have to take seriously Luke's (1990) argument that modernization and development were the latest sophistication in imperialist idiom. He points out that "colonialism" and "westernization," which were used to justify the domination of the colonies, became dated after World War II. A new vocabulary, including "modernization" and "development," had to be produced to replace the discredited equivalents. "Elements such as modernization and modernity can be readily detected in any nation and they do not need to be associated with any single culture or political regime in order to have meaning; hence they are more difficult to rebel against or to reject as 'foreign.' By the same token, the modernizationists can appear to be more progressive and respectful of cultural traditions by advocating the *modernization* rather than the *Westernization* of the developing world" (Luke 1990, 222).

In the transition from the colony to the postcolony, nothing much revolutionary occurred apart from the deracialization of the state apparatus. The very colonial ideas of modernization and development as the business of the state were simply amplified within the rubric of nation-building in order to purchase legitimacy. Mahmood Mamdani's penetrating analysis of the obstacles to democratization in contemporary postcolonial Africa probably offers the most comprehensive and articulate new reading of the legacy of colonialism and the state in Africa. One of his questions centers on the level to which the structure of power in contemporary Africa embodied in the state is shaped by its colonial ancestry rather than the anticolonial revolt that ostensibly brought it into being (Mamdani 1996, 7). Answering such a question will surely help explain the contemporary nature of the state and its relations to the nation as a key agent in its constitution in much of Africa. For it is evident that the postcolonial state operates in the shadow of its colonial heritage.

In retrospect, the nation-state in Africa can be seen as a discursive product. A discourse in which the emerging black elite took advantage of their commonality of skin color, and in some cases ethnicity with the native masses, to continue a job that was earlier performed by the colonist. In this discursive project, the symbolizing codes of blackness and ethnicity were relied on in domesticating difference between what used to be the citizen and the subject in the colony and protectorate, respectively. In the process of nation formation through anticolonialism, power reproduced itself by exaggerating racial difference and denied the existence of an oppressed majority defined by ethnicity, class, and location.

In making an intervention into the development problems of former colonized societies, communication researchers, from this perspective, are in a better position to understand various local actors and how they respond to development initiatives. Is the citizen/subject divide still evident in these new nation-states? How are they reflected in the policy preferences that the local state initiate in the name of development? What is the mythic purchase of development as a device to ameliorate contending social forces in the postcolony? These are questions that should be part of the problematic of communication researchers because four decades are not enough time for the state to evolve and metamorphose into a totally new institution unlike its colonial ancestry.

Probably the first opportunity to interrogate the postcolonial state was at the height of the debates on the new world information and communication order in the 1970s and 1980s at UNESCO. Following the spread of new communication technologies, especially the first generation of transborder data flow technologies, the near monopoly situation in global news gathering by only five news agencies, the increasing domination of American films worldwide, and the corresponding decline in the reach of developing country-owned media, developing countries under the banner of non-aligned movement launched a campaign to demand a more democratic communication order (Nordenstreng 1984). What was ironic about the demands of the developing countries was their disinterest in democratization of communication at the national level, while expecting the West, the United States in particular, to yield to their demand for global democratization (Servaes 1999, 138). How do we make sense of this paradox in communication policy? The answer lies not necessarily in illegitimacy of U.S. dominance, but in the heritage of the postcolonial state. The elite of the developing countries had acquired an institution that was deracialized but not democratized and acquired legitimacy through the rhetoric of development and not democracy. The idea that democracy was a luxury that could wait for the serious business of development to be accomplished seems to have been the creed of all black African leaders who led their countries to independence. This thinking went unchallenged even at the international levels until the 1980s as if the two ideals, democracy and development, can be separated. This self-serving abuse of development communication practice, however, found opposition from radical development journalism advocates (Domatob and Hall 1983; Shah 1999).

So far we have seen how the colonial state invented development as a way of accommodating various pressures. It tried to change its face so as to ensure continuous colonial relationship. But by doing that, it redefined the constitutive role of the state and sowed the seed of what today is championed by the postcolonial state as development planning. Colonialism was no doubt an economic project of accumulation by the British Empire, and thus other humanist projects such as development were not the main concern. But there were possibilities of individual and group pressures that resulted in the restructuring of the economic project to include the political project of a developmentalist state. The subject of the peculiarity of this developmentalist state has become pertinent in view of the current liberal impatience with the state in Africa, Asia, and Latin America. The push for the privatization of many aspects of the developing economies including their telecom and broadcasting sectors contained in structural adjustment programs backed by the World Bank and the IMF portends the death of the developmentalist state, so to speak. The understanding of development as a deliberate effort by the state, contra market rules, to democratize the material conditions for a participatory civil life is now more or less being jettisoned in favor of Darwinian theater of free market.

The Postcolonial State under Global Economic Fundamentalism

In the past two decades most of the countries of sub-Saharan Africa have, in one way or another, gone to the World Bank and the International Monetary Fund (IMF) to request their involvement in the management of their economies. This has resulted in the implementation of what has become known as structural adjustment programs (SAP): a package of policy prescriptions that a country must follow in order to qualify for World Bank and IMF loans and help them make debt repayments on the older debts owed to commercial banks, governments, and the World Bank. SAPs are designed for individual countries that approach these two financial institutions for assistance, but the common guiding principles and features, which characterize the prescriptions so far handed out to all adjusting developing countries, include export-led growth, privatization and liberalization, and the efficiency of the free market. SAPs generally require countries to peg their currencies against the U.S. dollar (which invariably means devaluation), lift import and export restrictions; balance their budgets and not overspend; and remove price controls and state subsidies (Sarris and Shams 1991; Brydon and Legge 1996; Hadjimichael et al. 1996). Based on these policy prescriptions, communication industries are affected on two grounds: liberalization and privatization in the case of state-owned telecommunications broadcasting and press organizations, and the removal of subsidies to the public service broadcasting corporation resulting in their increasing commercialization.

In Ghana, for instance, while SAP was launched in 1983, it took the Provisional National Defense Council (PNDC) government almost a decade to venture into the delicate affair of selling state-owned enterprises to the private sector. In 1992 the government took the bold decision to start its privatization scheme (Hadjimichael et al. 1996, 41). The gold mines, hotels, and factories were the first to go. It took another two years for the communication sector to come under divestiture. The reluctance was probably an indication that the government was politically uncomfortable to relinquish its monopoly of the telecom and broadcasting industries.

At independence in 1957, and immediately after, Ghana was held up as a model African nation-state, a paragon of black nationalism, what Africans were capable of achieving when left alone. But by the 1970s and 1980s, the country experienced unprecedented economic decline leading to the launching of SAP as a solution. And after about a decade of faithfully implementing SAP, Ghana was once again cited as a model. This time, though, not a model of a black nation under self-rule, but a model of a developing country that had successfully adjusted its economy to become a "significant cog in the wheel of globalization" (Brydon and Legge 1996, 1). In retrospect, for Ghana, as for most of the other African countries that were to follow, SAP marked their latest and final baptism into globalization, or more precisely, economic globalization. In political economic terms, therefore, SAP refers to the extensive commodification of all aspects of life in the postcolony by applying the rules of market valorization to sectors of the national economy that were hitherto thought to be outside the domain of the market in the grand project of nation building. These sectors include health, education, mass communication, local government, and utility services.

As if these drastic changes are not enough, a new World Bank/IMF policy initiative in 1996 toward the debt problems of developing countries has been the establishment of Heavily Indebted Poor Countries Initiative (HIPC). At the conceptual level, this new coinage, HIPC, is now used to describe about 90 percent of sub-Saharan African countries. In the words of the president of the World Bank, James D. Wolfensohn, it is designed to help developing countries to deal "with debt in a comprehensive way to give countries the possibility of exiting from unsustainable debt. It is very good news for the poor of the world."[2] At the wider political economic level, it means the postcolonial state's declaration of financial insolvency and ultimate bankruptcy. The program requires that qualifying countries apply to be admitted to the status of HIPC. Between 1996 and 2001, the response was overwhelming.[3] Countries that qualify for HIPC status will have their debt canceled, bought, or the cost of debt servicing absorbed by a special HIPC trust fund to enable the state to undertake, in the words of the World Bank, a "sustained implementation of integrated poverty reduction and economic reform programs."[4] But in return, the postcolonial state acquires the status of a financially bankrupt institution. This is a troubling development that cannot be ignored by development communication researchers. Not only is it shifting to a preference for market-led development with SAP and HIPC, the postcolonial state as we have known it, is undergoing some fundamental changes.

The implementation of SAP and HIPC means that the postcolonial state as an apparatus for development in much of sub-Saharan Africa has been in retreat, even as it continues to found its legitimacy on the rhetoric of development and nation building. While this contradiction works itself out, the market acquires a hegemonic status, resulting in commodification as the rule of the game. In this new game, communication and communication infrastructure as a "public service" in the process of development is shifting to communication as a commodity in a free market. The wider implications of SAP and HIPC suggest that communication researchers interested in developments in postcolonial nation-states in Africa avoid a ghettoization of their research focus and widen their scope to include economic policy issues that have consequences on national development. For instance, a study on the increasing commodification of communication cannot avoid the general question of commodification of other sectors such as health, public utilities, and education.

Mosco (1996, 143–44) defines commodification as "the process of turning use values into exchange values, of transforming products whose value is determined by their ability to meet individual and social needs into products whose value is set by what they can bring in the marketplace." Such a Marxist political economic approach to commodification, which is conceptually more useful than commercialization, allows us then to interrogate the dominance of the rhetoric of free market and cost-based pricing of public services and programs that characterize contemporary policy practices. The postcolonial nation-state, so it seems, has abandoned the rhetoric of use value for the rhetoric of exchange value through its privatization policies. Thus economic fundamentalism has triumphed over the nationalist imperative in which modernization and development resonated with the humanist project of sharing the national cake based on collective need.

If it is the liberal thinking that the market can democratize the material conditions for civil society, which the postcolonial nation formation promised, while the postcolonial state apes the practice of the postwelfare state (e.g., in Europe and North America), then we should remember that it took the welfare state several decades of a program of democratizing resources before it started going into retreat. Even as nineteenth- and twentieth-century America and Europe appreciated all that the market had to offer, they bracketed it out in the development planning of communication infrastructure. Nordenstreng (2000, 29) points out that the European welfare program was "a way to materialize democracy." After proving the needed baseline infrastructure, including well-established transport, telecom, and media infrastructure and fair tariffs for telecom, well-endowed educational infrastructure for the industrial production of the needed human resources, the welfare state may be ready to retreat and allow market forces to keep the balance in civil society–state relations (and even then, that is debatable). But when after only four decades the developmentalist state is being dismantled without achieving the promises it made to the people to entice them to join in the formation of the imagined community of nation-state, there is much to worry about.

Notes

1. Freire suffered unlawfully in the hands of the Brazilian state in 1964, when he was imprisoned for seventy days and later forced into exile (see Richard Shaull, foreword to Freire 1974). Thus his personal experience would lead him not to slight the state.
2. www.worldbank.org/hipc/about/hipcbr/hipcbr.htm.

3. www.worldbank.org/hipc/progress-to-date/status_table_Sep03.pdf.
4. www.worldbank.org/hipc/about/hipcbr/hipcbr.htm.

References

Brydon, Lynne, and Karen Legge. 1996. *Adjusting Society: The World Bank, the IMF, and Ghana.* London: Tauris Academic Studies.

Casmir, Fred L. 1991. *Communication in Development.* Norwood, N.J: Ablex.

Constantine, Stephen. 1984. *The Making of the British Colonial Development Policy, 1914–1940.* London: Frank Cass.

Domatob, Jerry Komia, and Stephen William Hall. 1983. Development Journalism in Black Africa. *Gazette: International Journal of Mass Communication Studies* 31: 9–33.

Escobar, Arturo. 1995. *Encountering Development: The Making and Unmaking of the Third World.* Princeton, N.J.: Princeton University Press.

Freire, Paulo. 1974. *Pedagogy of the Oppressed.* New York: Penguin.

Hadjimichael, Michael T., Michael Nowak, Robert Sharer, and Amor Tahari. 1996. *Adjustment for Growth: The African Experience.* Washington, D.C.: IMF.

Hall, Stuart. 1996. "When Was 'the Post-Colonial'? Thinking at the Limit." In Iain Chambers and Lidia Curti, eds., *The Post-Colonial Question: Common Skies, Divided Horizons.* London: Routledge.

Ingham, Barbara. 1987. "Colonialism and the Economy of the Gold Coast, 1919–1945." In Barbara Ingham and Colin Simmons, eds., *Development Studies and Colonial Policy.* London: Frank Cass.

IPDC. 1985. *Two Seminars on IPDC.* Finland: University of Tampere, Department of Journalism and Mass Communication.

Jacobson, Thomas, and Jan Servaes. 1999. *Theoretical Approaches to Participatory Communication.* Cresskill, N.J.: Hampton.

Jayaweera, Neville, and Sarath Amunugama, eds. 1987. *Rethinking Development Communication.* Singapore: AMIC.

Lee, J. M. 1967. *Colonial Development and Good Government.* Oxford: Oxford University Press.

Lerner, Daniel. 1958. *The Passing of Traditional Society: Modernizing the Middle East.* New York: Free Press.

Lerner, Daniel, and Herbert Schiller, eds. 1980. Review of Kaarle Nordenstreng, *National Sovereignty and International Communication: A Reader (1979). Public Opinion Quarterly* 44, no. 1: 137–38.

Luke, Timothy W. 1990. *Social Theory and Modernity: Critique, Dissent, and Revolution.* Newbury Park, Calif.: Sage.

Mamdani, Mahmood. 1996. *Citizen and Subject: Contemporary Africa and the Legacy of Late Colonialism.* Princeton, N.J.: Princeton University Press.

Many Voices, One World: Communication and Society Today and Tomorrow. 1980. MacBride Report. Paris: UNESCO Press.

Martin-Barbero, Jesus. 1993. *Communication, Culture, and Hegemony: From Media to Mediation.* London: Sage.

Mbembe, Achille. 2001. *On the Postcolony.* Berkeley: University of California Press.

Melkote, Srinavas R. 1991. *Communication for Development in the Third World: Theory and Practice.* New Delhi: Sage.

Mosco, Vincent. 1996. *The Political Economy of Communication: Rethinking and Renewal.* London: Sage.

Nordenstreng, Kaarle. 1984. *The Mass Media Declaration of UNESCO.* Norwood, N.J.: Ablex.

———. 2000. "Media and Democracy: What Is Really Required?" In Jan van Cuilenburg and Richard van der Wurff, eds., *Media and Open Societies: Cultural, Economic, and Policy Foundations for Media Openness and Diversity in East and West.* Amsterdam: Het Spinhuis.

———. 2001. Epilogue to Nancy Morris and Silvio Waisbord, eds., *Media and Globalization: Why the State Matters.* Lanham, Md.: Rowman & Littlefield.

Nordenstreng, Kaarle, and Herbert I. Schiller. 1979. *National Sovereignty and International Communication.* Norwood, N.J.: Ablex.

———. 1993. *Beyond National Sovereignty and International Communication in the 1990s.* Norwood, N.J.: Ablex.

Samarajiwa, Rohan. 1987. "The Murky Beginnings of the Communication and Development Field: Voice of America and 'the Passing of Traditional Society.'" In Neville Jayaweera and Sarath Amunugama, eds., *Rethinking Development Communication.* Singapore: AMIC.

Sarris, Alexander, and Hadi Shams. 1991. *Ghana ender Structural Adjustment: The Impact on Agriculture and the Rural Poor.* New York: IFAD.

Schiller, Herbert I. 1976. *Communication and Cultural Domination.* White Plains, N.Y.: International Arts and Sciences Press.

Schramm, Wilbur. 1964. *Mass Media and National Development: The Role of Information in the Developing Countries.* Paris: UNESCO/Stanford University Press.

Servaes, Jan. 1991. "Towards a New Perspective for Communication and Development." In Fred Casmir, ed., *Communication in Development.* Norwood, N.J.: Ablex.

———. 1999. *Communication for Development: One World, Multiple Cultures.* Cresskill, N.J.: Hampton.

Servaes, Jan, and Randy Arnst. 1999. "Principles of Participatory Communication Research: Its Strengths and Weaknesses?" In Thomas Jacobson and Jan Servaes, eds., *Theoretical Approaches to Participatory Communication.* Cresskill, N.J.: IAMCR/Hampton.

Shah, Hermant. 1999. "Emancipation from Modernization: Development Journalism and New Social Movements." In Richard C. Vincent, Kaarle Nordenstreng, and Michael Traber, eds., *Towards Equity in Global Communication: MacBride Update.* Cresskill, N.J.: Hampton.

Shohat, Ella. 1992. Notes on the postcolonial. *Social Text* 31–32: 99–113.

4

Global AIDS, IT, and Critical Humanism: Reframing International Health Communication

John Nguyet Erni

There are no technological silver bullets to solve the crisis of health care. . . .
Without consideration to the political and policy context of health care systems, technological change will . . . follow the path of least resistance, aggra-
vating instead of alleviating old problems, and creating some new ones.

—Alexander and Stafford 1998, 197

At the end of the day, theory is another word for intelligence.

—Treichler 1999, 2

As THESE EPIGRAPHS SUGGEST, the challenge in the field of international
health communication lies in a proper and rigorous conceptualization
of a focused problem: health-related information technology. What is its
status in the ongoing reality of international health politics and policy systems? In what ways has it been privileged and celebrated as the conduit for a
virtualizing health care delivery? What are the practical implications of a
transportable flow of digital health care for patients, in domestic as well as international contexts? How is it possible to influence the context of medical information flow, the apparently intractable political, economic, organizational,
and cultural constraints that disable rather than facilitate information to work
for patients and physicians? The challenge also lies in the double meaning of
"intelligence" whose valences reside in two distinct but often antagonistic
fields: informatics versus critical humanism. It is to these issues that this chap-

ter turns, with the hope of rebuilding the theoretical and political scaffolding of international health communication. Throughout the chapter, the global AIDS crisis is discussed both as the research context of this meditation and as a heuristic device—an allegory—to rehearse an argument about the significance of a critical humanistic imagination for international health communication.

At the outset, a conceptual field clarification is in order regarding the term "international health communication." The term signals two subdisciplinary formations: international communication studies with a focus on health care and health communication studies with an attention to international problems. For the former, the attention to issues of health care within the field of international communication has strengthened the field by giving it a vital focus. Since, according to Robert Stevenson (1996), "as an area of study, international communication has no identifiable substance, body of theory, or specific research methods, only geography" (181), a focus on health care has offered this same area at least two fertile research possibilities. First, within the framework of development or modernization theory typically deployed in international communication studies (Lerner 1958; Rogers 1962; Schramm 1964), the focus on health has enabled an investigation of the notion of "expertise" in the historical chain of action within nation-building projects and cross-national exchanges. Indeed, the central problems for investigation here have been about the performance of professional expertise in shaping national public health policies and in more concrete delivery of health care within the physician-industry-patient nexus. Second, for those researchers who advocate a critical approach to modernization theory, the focus on health offers them a window to study the political economy of uneven health care in developing countries.

As for the field of health communication, its concern with the geographical dispersion of health messages has been severely limited to the national context. Research in the field has concentrated on interpersonal, organizational, and mass-mediated aspects of health care and health campaigns, with the goal of using research findings to interact with federal health agencies (Atkin and Marshall 1996). Geography, and its attendant sociocultural and political dimensions, is considered primarily along webs of human behavior (such as social learning and reasoned action in individuals' "healthy" or "risky" choices; e.g., Ray and Donohew 1989) and organizational behavior (such as social advocacy and marketing of health messages; e.g., Maibach and Parrott 1995). However, as health information systems become increasingly transnational, which facilitates a rapid transportation of health data and more broadly of the (controversial) practice of telemedicine, health communication researchers have been slow in reorienting their scope of research and theoretical conceptualization of a health information system that has gone well beyond national borders. The global AIDS crisis presents a unique opportunity to both fields of researchers—international communication and health communication. This crisis presents a conjuncture that illuminates the need for cross-fertilizing these two fields, especially at the level of transnational public health practices, where questions about professional expertise, uneven development, transportability of health care campaigns, and so on, can be investigated.

World E-Health: A Cultural Studies Perspective

Jonathan Mann, founding director of the World Health Organization Global Program on AIDS, who tragically died in an air crash in 1998, spoke in many different occasions about three primary features of the AIDS epidemic, features that I believe are both empirically descriptive of world public health and theoretically relevant to international health communication studies.

1. No country or community within a country has halted spread of the virus once infections have begun locally; consequently the major impacts of the pandemic are yet to come;
2. HIV is spreading—sometimes at a very rapid pace—to new communities or subgroups that were previously untouched by the pandemic; HIV has demonstrated its ability to cross all borders be they social, cultural, linguistic, geographic, economic, or political;
3. The global pandemic is a composite of a complex of local epidemics; the spread of HIV may be different from one locale to another depending on the profile of risk spread at different rates (sometimes dramatically so) among the various subgroups in most local settings.

This much is clear, in general terms: to conceptualize public health in a global scale means acknowledging that diseases are not always fully knowable, that they deeply intersect with areas of social and cultural life well beyond viral dynamics and immune responses, and that they require us to think about the global dynamics of health in the multiple "locals" (Keane 1998).

Intervention efforts have entailed remolding the meaning of globalization in the context of an epidemic. Gro Harlem Bruntland, the current director-general of the World Health Organization, has remarked, "Increasing globalization is opening up new opportunities for growth and progress and the potential for worldwide sharing of knowledge and expertise. But the benefits are not adequately felt in the health and social sector in many countries and globalization has brought new and critical threats to global health. In our global society, there is no health sanctuary" (Bruntland 1998). Ironically, globalization, which is usually celebrated as the triumph of advanced modernity, seems to be illuminating and *producing* the gaps, breaks, and fractures in the attempt to deliver world health. More than twenty years into the epidemic (if dated from the first cases in the United States), one of the enduring lessons we have learned about global AIDS is that there are two parallel pandemics: a pandemic of the infection of the body in a worldwide scale, and a pandemic of the infection of the cultural meanings of the human body that have repeatedly turned up and mushroomed especially at the cracks of globalization. The epidemic of meaning, the wild proliferation of cultural ideas, languages, and images about the epidemic, accompanies the viral spread of HIV around the globe (Treichler 1999).

The significance of this duality cannot be underestimated: cultural meanings, once multiplied and distributed over vast distance, can gather a real force with evident consequences in shaping prevention campaigns, health policies, immigration policies, the politics of testing, the politics of the dispensation of drugs around the world, and so on. Globalization is the very field where the immaterial takes on a special material force. At a more local level, scientific interventions, such as testing and risk prevention, must often pass through cultural lenses that promote or obscure a certain way to look at, say, sex work, drug use, racial and ethnic prejudice, and so on.

In articulating diseases as both scientific and cultural, interventionist and interpretive, empirical and symbolic, pathogenic and sociopolitical, we reposition international health research around *questions of cultural politics and critical humanism*. This means, at the very least, developing strategies that not only promote research which integrates the two sides, but research that, when necessary, is capable of showing the contradictions between the two sides. It forces us to ask how science can sometimes obscure the concrete work that needs to be done in nonscientific ways. The needle exchange program in the United States is a good example of how the behavioral model of surveillance of individual actions has consistently obstructed the efforts of local organizing based on a community model of survival rather than an individual model of behavioral modification (Bayer 1989). More importantly, an orientation toward cultural politics and critical humanism means taking seriously the competing symbolic and practical meanings of health, illness, and healing in the global "epidemic of meanings" alluded to above. At one level, faith in modern medicine often clashes with conviction in traditional forms of healing. At another level, even different branches of biomedicine define diseases differently, according to different models of analysis and sets of assumptions used in research. For instance, epidemiology and tropical medicine are closely related but divergent subfields (Patton 1998). While epidemiology relies on a vectoral logic to assess the spread of epidemics, tropical medicine utilizes the logic of geographical separation (between the tropics and the nontropics, for instance).

Whereas epidemiology works by securing an image of traveling bodies, tropical medicine is much more keen on envisioning an image of disease colonies that are indicatively marked as the Third World. In addition, epidemiologists strive to look for vaccines within an overall preventative framework, but researchers in tropical medicine tend to look for ways to contain diseases.

Take patients' relationship to medical information as an example. In developing countries, the possibility for patients to develop a meaningful relationship to increasingly abundant but abstract medical information may depend on seeing and understanding the consequences resulting from the switching of one logic to another. For instance, health ministries in developing countries tend to operate on the U.S. epidemiology model, while international collaborative research bodies often function within a tropical medicine model. When confronting, say, online medical information, patients need to learn to discern these overlapping frameworks out of which "information" is produced. When contrasting, and sometimes competing, meanings collide—a situation that the Web makes notorious—online e-health may be more alienating than helpful. Put in another way, "information" is only useful when it is about "meaning." "Information networking" in international health communication thus refers to meaning creation, appropriation, deployment, and distribution. No amount of money or technological know-how can sufficiently benefit those in need of medical information, until we critically grasp the politics of knowledge creation, maintenance, and circulation. In the following section, I take "information networking" in international public health as a focal point of discussion. I shall offer a critical analysis through a set of questions pertinent to a cultural studies of the subject:

- What counts as "medical information," especially in information-poor countries?
- To what extent is "information" found in medical databases and other knowledge-based medical informatics meaningful to physicians and patients across developing countries and within the urban-rural division of a country?
- What are the implications for the emergence of a proprietary medical informatics industry—which is mostly based in industrialized countries— for users in the developing world?

Transnational Health Informatics: A Cultural Inventory

Costs of health care, labor force structures, patient–physician interactions, comparative health care management, the overall quality and meaningfulness of care: these are some of the crucial areas that are being profoundly affected today by reengineering initiatives privileging the rapid adoption of information, communication, and knowledge-based systems in health care around the world. On the eve of the first U.N. General Assembly of the new millennium in 2000, U.N. Secretary-General Kofi Annan pleaded for a global "moral commitment" to "end poverty and inequality, improve education, increase security, reduce HIV/AIDS and protect the planet" (India: Annan announces 2000). In the charter for development that Annan laid out, he strongly favored the role of IT in fighting poverty and promoting global human development. Among his planned initiatives were the development of a network of 10,000 online sites to provide tailored medical information and resources to hospitals and other health care facilities throughout the developing world. A high-level international office reminiscent of the peace corps was also on his mind, which he dubbed "UNITEs" (U.N. Information Technology Service). UNITEs would summon a consortium of high-tech volunteer corps and dispatch them around the world to help train groups in developing countries in the uses and opportunities of IT. From the purview of Annan's U.N. office, IT was then positioned as the conduit that would bridge the gaping hole left by globalization, the disjuncture between the flourishing global market and the malnourished local societies. More specifically, moral commitment on the part of nation-states and voluntarism on the part of the IT generation were called up to jostle for space in the information highway that had long commodified "information." However utopian they may be, these initiatives cast a spotlight on where globalization projects are bankrupting civil societies around the world. They enable a humanist discourse that simultaneously illuminates the ruins left behind by the aggressive footmarks of globalization and resubjects the agents of globalization to help clean up the mess, so to speak. This humanist discourse thus advances on a politics of negotiation from within the belly of the (technological) beast.

A critical assessment of global informatics may therefore take the form of an inventory, an analytical cataloging, of the technological, social, cultural, and political opportunities and problems of health care IT. This is the approach that I shall take in the following.

Retheorizing the Digital Divide

Everywhere in the developing world, especially in their urban centers, we see a highly paradoxical situation with respect to the access and uses of IT. Countries that boast rapid integration of IT, telecommunication, and satellite facilities realize their unstoppable failure to provide universal access to their own people. Thousands of kilometers of optical fiber cable manage to bypass subsistence areas, such as urban slums, not to mention rural areas. Digital-ready, high-tech telecommunication offices, which are uplinked to what Arjun Appadurai (1996) calls international financescape and technoscape, are found side by side with computerless schools and telephoneless slum neighborhoods and subdistricts. In information-poor Africa, for instance, which has a population of 700 million, fewer than 1 million people had access to the Internet in 1998, and of this number 80 percent lived in South Africa. Among the other 20 percent the ratio of people who had access to the Internet to those who did not is 1:5,000, whereas in the United States or Europe the ratio was 1:6 (Lown et al. 1998). The United Nations Development Program (2000) reports, "There are more [Internet] hosts in New York than in continental Africa; more hosts in Finland than in Latin America and the Caribbean; and notwithstanding the remarkable progress in the application of [information and communication technologies] in India, many of its villages still lack a working telephone." In reports that suggest that "help is on the way," in which dramatic increases in Internet access are being expected in poor countries, the reality is that most beneficiaries will be from urban areas.

In countries where rapid modernization has been taking place for one to two decades or so, such as Thailand, Malaysia, or Tanzania, the problem is particularly egregious. In those countries, the issue of service costs catalyzes the aggravation because providers tend to favor users in metro areas and penalize those in faraway towns. Yet urban-based rapid integration of IT has produced economic loss by ignoring services to rural regions. As the director of the National Electronics and Computer Technology Centre in Thailand puts it:

> There has not been real interest on the part of the state, not to mention the private sector, to invest in basic telephone service to the outer rural and remote villages. There has been little or no clear focus at all on the role of telecommunications in promoting rural development efforts. However, it is also true that, line on line, the *indirect economic return* from rural telephone service (or more precisely, the savings from the economic loss incurred by not having telephone services) is much larger than the direct revenue generated by a city line. In addition, there are numerous other unquantifiable but clearly identifiable social benefits that may be derived from it as well. (Thajchayapong 1996)

This statement was made just before the Asian economic meltdown in 1997, in which Thailand's economy was the first to crumble. Amid the smoldering ashes, many theories and observations have been made to explain its causes, and many point to the unevenness of domestic development in the countries concerned. Globalization wreaks havoc at the local level, bifurcating the local internal economy, long before it causes trouble at the regional and then global level. That globalization in the form of a rapid expansion of e-health is eroding health care is particularly shocking because informatization was supposed to be the solution to improve care.

It would be naive to equate access with knowledge. One is no less informed by being denied access than by being technology-illiterate (not to mention language-illiterate). In developing countries, the chronic condition of an uneven informatization of their populace in schools has deepened the social divisions of class, gender, and ethnicity. While common usage of the computer for relatively simple tasks (such as e-mailing and chatting) may be communally acquired among friends, specialist technical literacy and proficiency that is required for building an IT workforce is quite a lot more difficult to come by. Yet for those who are IT literate and proficient, the manic drive toward globalization within developing countries has created a complex, *politically charged* environment for this so-called elite class.

Viewed as a type of economic capital, the access and knowledge of IT possessed by the information-elite class has brought about a serious resource competition between the state and the private sector. From the perspective of the state, its very embracing of globalization through informatization has indeed led to a weakening of state power, since it consistently observes a "brain drain" of IT professionals to the private sector. This situation is particularly severe in the health field. Since many national health systems in developing countries have not yet followed the path of many developed countries to deregulate or privatize the health sector, they have found it difficult to retain qualified medical staff with IT proficiency from taking more lucrative positions in the private sector (Bin Mansor 1996, 41; Thajchayapong 1996, 24). As a result, health ministries in these countries have found it difficult to embark on ambitious national IT-related plans. Here, the well-recognized problem of a weakened national sovereignty due to globalization takes the form of an internal impotency of the state in the face of domestic market forces.

More importantly, when viewed as a type of social and cultural capital, the access and knowledge of IT possessed by the information-elite class has caused a social division reminiscent of an older aristocratic society. Where print literacy once divided society, IT literacy deepens those historical divisions. Between the "IT-rich" and the "IT-poor" has sprung a renewed social hierarchy. An air of exclusivity often accompanies the possession of IT literacy; we cannot expect it to be any different from the undemocratic potential that various other forms of literacies have carried throughout the path to modernization, particularly in developing countries. In matters of health, one's experience with technologically mediated medical information can have an effect on one's imagination about health and healing, depending on the sense of social empowerment (or the denial of it) one has in encountering that information. When, typically, that medical information is imported from the West with the highest concentration of medical informatics, the encounter may produce more alienation than comfort, more uncertainty than confidence. One's course of treatment, knowledge, and decision-making power—in short, one's survivability—can partly be related to a wholly *nonmedical* social hierarchy.

The worn-out phrase "digital divide" thus remains a useful overarching framework in which further elaborations of differences and hierarchies can be observed. Those differences are, in short, urban–rural, consumption–production, public sector–private sector, high literacy–low literacy. Moreover, they are the result of the varied consequences of localization, comparison, and globalization of IT knowledge in developing countries. Kofi Annan's call for a "moral commitment" on the part of nation-states and volunteerism on the part of the young IT generation, points toward an effort to salvage the disappearing notion of civil society as a result of globalization. In view of the first item in our present inventory of the cultural politics of IT, civil society is by no means a simple object of virtue.

In and Out of the Radar Screen

A librarian in the World Health Organization library recounts a story about the Albert Cook Medical Library at Makerere, Kampala, Uganda (quoted in Lown et al. 1998). In the 1960s, she said, the library boasted over 2,500 medical volumes and journal subscriptions. It was one of the largest, most impressive libraries in East Africa. However, due to a lack of sustainability, by the late 1990s, the library received fewer than forty medical journals. For many years, the Albert Cook and other libraries received no new books, had no new computers, no access to databases. A similar story was told about the Nairobi University Medical School Library in Kenya, which received only twenty journal titles in 1998 compared with three hundred to which it subscribed ten years earlier. However, no mention was made in this story as to where the journals originated from, whose research was published and indexed in them, what languages they used, and so on. In other words, questions about Western hegemony in the production and circulation of medical knowledge are as relevant to these libraries in Africa in so-called good times as they are in bad times. The realization that the disappearing books and journals in those libraries has to do with the electronic transformation of print information into databases, nonetheless, cannot obscure questions of academic hegemony in the biomedical field.

In deciphering information from medical databases, patients often need to decide if the information is relevant to their situation. Guesswork about generalizability is not only necessary; it is often the only reading strategy. As Tessa Edejer (2000) puts it, "There is an insidious problem associated with the availability and visibility of health research from developing countries, particularly in printed media and its electronic counterparts" (798). For instance, Medline, an indexing service for published medical research, routinely excludes research reports from developing countries. Edejer points out that

> western indexing services cover some 3000 journals, of which 98% are from the developed world. The whole of Latin America accounted for 0.39% of the total number of articles referenced by Medline in 1996, down from a "high" of 2.03% in 1966. Because only a small number of journals from developing countries are indexed by Medline, research from these countries is almost invisible. Thus, for example in the 1994 Science Citation Index articles from Singapore accounted for 0.18% of the total compared with 30.8% for the United States, 7.2% for Germany, and 8.2% for Japan. (798; see also Sundram 1998)

In attempting to remedy this situation, alternative means of information exchange were attempted, such as services by ExtraMED and ExtraSCI (Zielinski 1995). Yet they were reportedly available on CD-ROM distribution only, thus limiting accessibility. In addition, many medical researchers in regions of the developing world are establishing networks for the exchange of health information. Interestingly though, sites such as the African Journals Online or the Bioline International were launched through servers located in the West (e.g., in the United Kingdom or the United States; see Godlee et al. 2000). In addition, in order to be indexed at all, entries must be posted in English. Governmental or nongovernmental public service organizations or health workers in the village health center have to act as local intermediaries (Edejer 2000, 799). But do they necessarily possess the skills to handle, say, data standards, nomenclature issues, issues of platform independence and interdependence? Clearly, the burden goes well beyond languages differences and translation needs.

Even as more and more researchers in developing countries learn how to post their work directly on their own Web sites, their visibility is still dependent on reliable portal or search engines. The problem of invisibility is complex, rooted in uneven availability of research funding for research conducted outside of the Western "radar screen." At the same time, it is linked to gatekeeping practices of the biomedical publishing companies. This lack is particularly frustrating for those who want to access locally relevant information and compare it with that of other countries, regions, medical systems, and culturally specific health belief systems.

Privacy versus Connectivity: Cultural Choices?

In 1992, while in the hospital for brain surgery, the former tennis star Arthur Ashe received the overwhelming news that he was HIV positive. Wishing to maintain his and his family's privacy, and well aware of the prejudice and paranoia that was often associated with the disease during its first years of existence, he kept his condition secret with the help of close friends and trusted medical advisers. However, the story was somehow leaked to the press. Because of pressure from a national newspaper that was indicating it had on good record that he had AIDS, Ashe elected to make his condition known to the world in a press conference on April 8, 1992. In another instance, an insurance claims officer took her teenage daughter to work one day and left her in front of a computer terminal to keep her occupied. By chance, the daughter was able to access a database of patients who had been diagnosed with any number of illnesses. Concocting a game, she proceeded to call several names on the database, pretending to be a provider. She told one patient that he had contracted AIDS. The patient committed suicide before he could be reached. Today, anyone who has visited a doctor can experience a profoundly unsettling feeling that her medical record might be leaked, sold, accessed by accident, or used by others to make employment, nuptial, or other decisions.

Privacy concerns were a point of tension in health care well before the current era of informatization. Laws and regulations have been continuously enacted to ensure confidentiality of patient medical records. It is important to understand the nature of privacy concern, and where it emerges, in the entire integrated IT system for health care. The system is typically divided into two main areas: the operational area for the health care system concerned, and the clinical and disease management area (Anderson 2000). In the operational area, information such as basic billing, accounting applications, or orders for laboratory tests has limited interface with outside applications or networks. Hospital operations and finances are generally only of interest to relevant stakeholders. It is in the clinical and disease management area of the health care IT system where privacy issues emerge. The system sets out to amass a representational profile of patients through charting, recording, processing, and retrieving their medical information. Disease management can thus be enacted around the meticulous detailing of the patients' medical history, risk history, and treatment history. The global AIDS crisis has set forth a serious challenge to this normative conception of disease management. Particularly in Western countries but increasingly so in other modernizing countries, patient advocacy and activist groups have demanded privacy and confidentiality in the face of violations that people with AIDS have had to endure. They have demanded the protection of observable, systematic patient information that is either stored in a databank or transferable from one place to another.

That health and illness are conditions in which the boundaries of privacy must be carefully drawn, dovetails with the Enlightenment conception of the individual self. The almost spiritual quality of this self is preserved when a legally defined ethics of privacy and personal autonomy is put in place (Allen 1996; Wellman 1997). I am suggesting that privacy is a code and concept of conduct that is rather specific to (Western) neoliberal societies. Jeffrey Reiman (1997) calls it "critical moral liberalism," in which "privacy, intimacy, and personhood" are upheld. It is, of course, the same societies that sounded the first alarm about the destructive potential of technology and commerce to individual privacy (and by implication to the integrity of the self as an independent, self-contained totality). Generally speaking, industrialized nations have been more concerned with privacy issues than have developing countries. In the area of health care, the twin factors that transform modern health—technologization and commercialization—have indeed been the underlying reasons for careful legal interventions to protect health-related privacy. Civil liberty organizations in the United States, for instance, regularly conduct polls that show the growing concern of U.S. citizens for the privacy of their medical information (Krause 2000, 173). The former secretary of the Department of Health and Human Services, Donna Shalala, has stated emphatically:

> Every day, our private health information is being shared, collected, analyzed and stored with fewer federal safeguards than our video store records. Let me be frank. The way we protect the privacy of our medical records right now is erratic at best—dangerous at worst. (quoted in Krause 2000, 172)

Federal regulations in many countries have been enacted based on observed violations by informational and commercial vendors (especially insurance companies). Heightened interest in patient rights has rendered the right to information as a privacy right. The restoration of the Enlightenment conception of the self is made possible when the "right to information" and the "right to privacy" conjoin.

Ironically though, new privacy regulations in the health care industry have returned to the IT sector for developing technological security measures such as message encryption, access authentication, and detection of corrupted messages or unauthorized activities. The focus on privacy therefore has not led to a serious questioning of the social value of information technology. Meanwhile, savvy commercial enterprises have launched new "privacy products" to the market, most notably individualized portable "smart cards." Smart-card technology encodes a patient's biographical information, health status information, and history of medications and other health services sought (Walker 1995). Individual "ownership" of one's health information—literally in one's hand or pocket—gives the impression of privacy, even "empowerment."

In HIV/AIDS, privacy and confidentiality are deeply political and economic issues. For industrialized countries, entrenched liberal values in the court system and well beyond it have made privacy violations a serious social and legal offence. HIV testing has been the one ground where continuous and creative efforts have been made to secure privacy for people with AIDS. But in many developing countries, where small-scale insurance companies are encouraged by the state to provide coverage for the emerging middle class, the local legal community has found it difficult to negotiate a balance between protecting corporate interest and protecting the liberal value of privacy. In the name of commercial survival in a growing but shaky economy, and for reasons of alleged fraud committed by patients, insurance companies in developing countries have been adamant in obtaining detailed medical records from patients seeking coverage, particularly HIV-related information. For instance, insurance companies in Jamaica are demanding that laboratories properly check on the identification of persons taking HIV tests, noting that fraudulent misrepresentation by patients could end up wrecking the industry (Ministry 2002). An insurance executive argues that anonymous testing may lead to patients cheating the system by, for instance, asking someone else to take the test for an individual with previous illness and suspicion of HIV infection. The insurance executive remarks, "This is why we thoroughly investigate persons who die within two years after signing up life insurance policies. If we find that they were not truthful in their medical declarations then we are not obligated to pay the claims" (quoted in Ministry 2002).

Not only are privacy concerns—as formulated in First World economic and philosophical contexts—a fuzzy area in state and legal arenas in the developing countries, they are usually not the most urgent concern for patients either. Whereas most American online health information seekers have stayed away from using e-mail to seek help from doctors due to privacy concerns—a recent survey showed only 9 percent of Americans have exchanged e-mails with their doctors—many users of the Internet in developing countries have relied on e-mail, electronic bulletin boards, newsgroups, or discussion areas to obtain and share medical information. While anonymity is still important, connectivity is a much more important concern. It would be misleading to suggest that patients in developing countries disregard privacy and confidentiality. It would also be presumptuous to assert that philosophical imaginations outside the West necessarily deemphasize the notion of individual selfhood. It would be Orientalist, for instance, to imagine Asian cultures as "collective," "sharing cultures." In their rational use and application of health care IT, privacy is relatively less urgent than the need to combat the extremely isolating experience of illness, especially a serious, taboo illness such as AIDS. In the absence of an open atmosphere to reveal one's illness in small communities or villages where one lives, a computer connection to sources of knowledge, conversation, and compassion is often the only space where help and support can be obtained. But someone in a small community or village would be lucky to have a computer at all. Connectivity is a preferred choice in relation to privacy *only* in the context of rare resources and indigenous prejudice in local communities. If there is any "anthropological" basis to this relation, it resides in the community-based modes of human interaction seen among groups affected by HIV/AIDS (e.g., Altman 1994; Patton 1994). Writing about women's organizing around AIDS in Thailand, for instance, I made a related observation:

> Today, the single most important form of organizing does not lie in well-organized, institutionalized bodies but in women's informal groups. Research on informal communities of women sharing street-smartness, self-care information, medically related planning skills, and relationally based support remains scarce. Yet the social power that women experience in such communities can combat the erosion of women's status in the social structure. It is particularly important that this kind of informal connection be linked to effective institutions in order to generate spaces for both information acquisition and the sharing of life skills and self-esteem. (Erni 1998, 246)

In the present discussion, this mode of informal organizing can be seen as generating a sociality—a social technology in Foucault's sense—that complements the mode of online connectivity mentioned above. Interestingly, informal human support groups are in this way more and less than Internet-enhanced support. Human support groups combat feelings of isolation and alienation, but they also limit interaction to the local level. Connectivity to online health information and discussion groups, in contrast, provides a platform for a more global kind of connection. We must not assume that in the context of the developing countries, the need to connect makes the need to privacy disappear. It is entirely possible that official notions of privacy as enshrined in the law are less resonant and less of a pressing imperative to patients in the developing world, than, say, their regular habits of anonymity already popularized by common Internet use.

Other important transformations brought by informatization of health care in the international context that lie beyond the scope of this discussion include the structures and functions of labor in the health sector and the political economy of informatics for health e-commerce being set up around the world. A new class of information brokers has emerged to commodify health care at domestic and international markets. Meanwhile, more traditional forms of health care labor (such as nursing) are increasingly subjected to mechanization in the workplace. IT systems in hospitals, for instance, are increasingly being used for staff monitoring, through which the staff's practice of care is increasingly being measured and quantified according to a new logic of "productivity" (Alexander and Stafford 1998, 207–8). This situation goes well beyond switching from human interaction to interaction with the computer; it ushers forth an entirely new orientation to the time and space of health care, flexibilizing and automating "productivity." This transformation is associated with one more critical issue that comes to mind: the practice of telemedicine that wholly operates on a flexible time/space reorientation of medical care. Although I do not have space to explore these concerns in this chapter, I hope by mentioning them here to suggest additional questions for further thoughtful analyses by others.

Conclusion

An existing, and growing, online service has challenged dominant tendencies and political economic forms of power in the global health field, and has done so from what I have called a critical humanist perspective. It is a service that is acutely aware of, and wants to do something about, the undemocratic details of the global digital divide, the Euro American–centered nature of online health information, and the nationalism in the developing countries' desire to informatize their health care systems. "SatelLife" is a global information and communications network for health workers around the world. Its general secretary, John Mullaney (1996), states the reason for establishing SatelLife:

> Unfortunately, in the area of telecommunications, the lessons of the past are being ignored. The emphasis—by the multi-laterals and by developing world governments—is on the latest, hottest technology, regardless of whether the system is appropriate, affordable, or sustainable. . . . While there are hundreds of World Wide Web sites containing information on cancer or heart diseases, there exist very few sources of information on diseases like leprosy, malaria, or cholera that have major consequences outside of the industrialized West. Even sites that deal with tropical diseases are often cursory and unhelpful to clinicians dealing with the disease in hospitals and clinics in the field. . . . Like the big, expensive tertiary care facilities funded by World Bank and others, direct, high-speed Internet access is a national status symbol. But, as the World Bank itself concluded in a report . . . the tertiary care facilities increased in costs without increasing quality of care.

SatelLife serves a relatively small number of health care workers (about 4,000) but its service covers over twenty-five countries, the majority of which are poor. Through Healthnet, SatelLife's global communication and information network, it asks health care workers in each country to identify their own country's health information needs. It uses cost-effective, reliable satellite technologies (low earth orbit). It endeavors to include electronic medical databases that have not been indexed in major net services. It also holds comprehensive archives of professionally moderated discussions on HIV/AIDS and STDs. In short, SatelLife is an attractive alternative to the dominant systems of healthcare IT because of its challenge to the politics of extravagance in the field.

In this chapter, I called for a reorientation of international health communication to attend to the cultural politics of health from a critical humanist perspective. I do not believe this is an entirely new orientation for either international communication or health communication studies. Nonetheless, I stress the need for researchers in these fields not to take "health" and the "international" for granted. In the amazing development of health informatics systems around the world today, we must note the politics of how the body is newly medicalized in a profoundly dispersed and dispersing manner. We must also note the politics of how "e-health care" has often become high-profile, high-tech projects used to showcase nationalism and transnational corporate might. We may be witnessing the emergence of a *logic of connective incompatibility* in the international health field. Governments around the world are pushing for sophisticatedly wired societies; but they are not facilitating the transfer and adoption of meaningful health information to their populations. Technological erudition is being deemed useful to produce national pride precisely after the realization that forces of globalization are eroding national autonomy and sovereignty. Wired but potentially meaningless, connected but along lines of the digital divide, accessible but with no guarantee of decipherability, health care IT promises to be a challenging contemporary condition in which we strive to look for help in health matters around the world. A critical humanist perspective, such as that embedded in the purpose of SatelLife, is aimed at producing a cautionary critique of this condition.

Critical humanism is not a grand doctrine that rests on some experiential foundation. Critical humanism, as it is used in this chapter, is just a mode of thinking through the real confluence of forces—experiential as well as political—in order to make sense of how and where to struggle for clarity and a sense of political consciousness about significant things in the world. "Information networking," as it is used in international health communication, is thus not actually descriptive. Rather, it is distributive, normative, and polarizing. Therefore, I take "information networking" as both a modern fact in an information age and an underlying theoretical model and image for understanding how Third World AIDS, and other health problems, can be understood in the context of a global distribution of capital, policies, ideologies, and technologies. The vision that this conjures is both anarchic and democratizing, and it emphasizes rights of access to information as well as dynamics of power. Moreover, we must think of "information networking" as "meaning networking." Information is useless, no matter how vast and how quickly it travels, if it is not meaningful to the user. Consistently, then, we must ask what cultural relationship users have with medical information. In the context of what I have called a logic of connective incompatibility, we must ask what cultural relationship users in the developing world have with sense making at large. And this ought to concern researchers in international health *communication*.

References

Alexander, Cynthia J., and Stafford, Sue P. 1998. "The cutting edge? Gender, legal, and ethical implications of high-tech health care." In Cynthia J. Alexander and Leslie A. Pal, eds., *Digital Democracy: Policy and Politics in the Wired World*, 195–218. New York: Oxford University Press.

Allen, Anita L. 1996. "Constitutional law and privacy." In Dennis Patterson, ed., *A Companion to Philosophy of Law and Legal Theory*, 139–55. Cambridge, Mass.: Blackwell.

Altman, Dennis. 1994. *Power and Community: Organizational and Cultural Responses to AIDS*. London: Taylor & Francis.

Anderson, Mark. 2000. "Six levels of health care IT: Integrated delivery systems." In David Davidson, ed., *Health Information Systems*, 97–108. New York: Auerbach.

Appadurai, Arjun. 1996. "Disjuncture and difference in the global cultural economy." In *Modernity at Large: Cultural Dimensions of Globalization*, 27–47. Minneapolis: University of Minnesota Press.

Atkin, Charles, and Marshall, Alicia. 1996. "Health communication." In Michael B. Salwen and Don W. Stacks, eds., *An Integrated Approach to Communication Theory and Research*, 479–96. Mahwah, N.J.: Erlbaum.

Bayer, Ronald. 1989. *Private Acts, Social Consequences: AIDS and the Politics of Public Health*. New York: Free Press.

Bin Mansor, Dato' Ismail. 1996. "Application of information technology in health care: The Malaysian context." In Carol Ann Charles, ed., *Proceedings of the GIIC Asia Regional Meeting and International Conference for National Information Infrastructure for Social and Economic Development in Asia*, 37–43. Washington, D.C.: Center for Strategic and International Studies.

Bruntland, Gro Harlem. 1998. In sustainable development, health issues must play role. *Earth Times*. http://earthtimes.org/whodirectory/healthinsustainablefeb17_98.htm.

Edejer, Tessa Tan-Torres. 2000. Disseminating health information in developing countries: The role of the Internet. *British Medical Journal* 321 (7264): 797–800.

Erni, John Nguyet. 1998. "Redressing *Sanuk*: "Asian AIDS" and the Practices of Women's Resistance." In Nancy L. Roth and Linda K. Fuller, eds., *Women and AIDS: Negotiating Safer Practices, Care, and Representation*, 231–56. New York: Harrington Park.

Godlee, Finoa, Horton, Richard, and Smith, Richard. 2000. Global information flow. *British Medical Journal* 321 (7264): 776–77.

India: Annan announces charter of development 2000. *Global News Wire*, April 5.

Keane, Christopher. 1998. Globality and constructions of world health. *Medical Anthropology Quarterly* 122: 226–40.

Krause, Micki. 2000. "Healthcare and the regulatory environment: Information privacy, confidentiality, and security." In David Davidson, ed., *Health Information Systems*, 171–90. New York: Auerbach.

Lerner, D. 1958. *The Passing of Traditional Society: Modernizing the Middle East.* Glencoe, Ill.: Free Press.

Lown, Bernard, Bukachi, Fred, and Xavier, Ramnik. 1998. Health information in the developing world. *Lancet* 175: SII34–SII38.

Maibach, E., and Parrott, R. 1995. *Designing Health Messages: Approaches from Communication Theory, and Public Health Practice.* Newbury, Calif.: Sage.

Ministry against IDs for HIV testing. 2002. *Gleaner,* February 4.

Mullaney, John. 1996. SatelLife: Pioneering the path for electronic communication and health information in the developing world. www.isoc.org/isoc/whatis/conferences/inet/96/proceedings/a3/a3_2.htm.

Patton, Cindy. 1994. *Last Served? Gendering the HIV Pandemic.* London: Taylor & Francis.

———. 1998. "Critical bodies." In Kuan-Hsing Chen, ed., *Trajectories: Inter-Asia Cultural Studies*, 314–29. New York: Routledge.

Ray, E., and Donohew, L. 1989. *Communication and Health: Systems and Applications.* Hillside, N.J.: Erlbaum.

Reiman, Jeffrey. 1997. *Critical Moral Liberalism: Theory and Practice.* Lanham, Md.: Rowman & Littlefield.

Rogers, E. M. 1962. *Diffusions of Innovations.* New York: Free Press.

Schramm, Wilbur. 1964. *Mass Media and National Development: The Rule of Information in Developing Countries.* Stanford: Stanford University Press.

Stevenson, Robert L. 1996. "International communication." In Michael B. Salwen and Don W. Stacks, eds., *An Integrated Approach to Communication Theory and Research*, 181–94. Mahwah, N.J.: Erlbaum.

Sundram, F. 1998. Scientific publication is dominated by First World countries. *Area Academy of Medicine Singapore* 27: 147.

Thajchayapong, Pairash. 1996. "Towards social equity and prosperity: Thailand's IT policy into the 21st century." In Carol Ann Charles, ed., *Proceedings of the GIIC Asia Regional Meeting and International Conference for National Information Infrastructure for Social and Economic Development in Asia*, 21–26. Washington, D.C.: Center for Strategic and International Studies.

Treichler, Paula. 1999. *How to Have Theory in An Epidemic: Cultural Chronicles of AIDS.* Durham, N.C.: Duke University Press.

United Nations Development Program. 2000. Report of the meeting of the high-level panel of experts in information and communication technology, April, New York, 17–20. www.undp.org/info21/new/necosoc.html.

Walker, Robert. 1995. "Smart cards" to cut health costs, Edmonton Journal Online, June 15. www.southam.com/edmontonjournal/archives/0103sma9.htm.

Wellman, Carl. 1997. *An Approach to Rights: Studies in the Philosophy of Law and Morals.* Dordrech: Kluver.

Zielinski, C. 1995. New equities of information in an electronic age. *British Medical Journal* 310: 1480–81.

II

THE GLOBAL VECTORS OF COMMUNICATION

Mehdi Semati

GLOBAL PROCESSES HAVE DRASTICALLY altered many facets of life and compli-cated the analysis of social life by rendering our categories and concepts precarious. The rise of global networks, the material flow of all kinds across borders, and the radical interconnectivity of life in all regions across the globe have rendered the very concept of "society" unstable. Complex mobile economies of signs and people have contributed to a shift from the "social" to the "informational" and "communicational" (see Lash and Urry 1994; Castells 1996). International communication technologies are implicated in many of these processes. This section focuses on global media as important vehicles for both accommodating and resisting the global in its various manifestations.

The chapters in part II, "The Global Vectors of Communication," have two overarching objectives. First, they explore the global media circuit from new perspectives. Second, they offer a new mode of *writing* international communication research. The poststructuralist (and "postmodern") views give students and researchers a new perspective to see our objects of analysis differently. This mode of writing international communication research gives us a different way of comprehending our problematics.

It is generally accepted that we live in the age of the disappearance of distance, whereby spatiality is collapsed into temporal parameters (an always already present). There is an accelerated dematerialization of time and space (e.g., time-space compression). Space is said to be fluid, not limited by boundaries. Global media are among the agents that make this context possible. In this context, global media become the stage on which a global consciousness works out its possibilities, as well as its contradictions and conflicts.

Studies of global media in international communication research tend to be either institutional analyses (e.g., study of media corporations) or product analyses (e.g., study of texts, narratives). Furthermore, they tend to treat production and consumption in isolation from each other. The components of global media are considered in discrete units and in isolation form the larger matrix in which they operate. These studies continue to be relevant and indispensable. We also need, however, a way of apprehending the global media as a circuitry, an apparatus, and an assemblage. This approach emphasizes the fluidity of the global media as a whole. It emphasizes the spatial and temporal characteristics that make global media as a circuitry distinct, where the circuitry has a set of properties that are qualitatively different from the individual components that make up the circuitry. This approach gives us an appropriate vocabulary to comprehend the global media in a unique way.

The term "vector," deployed effectively in various writings by McKenzie Wark to address global communication technologies (e.g., Wark 1994), is borrowed from Paul Virilio's work (e.g., Virilio 1986). Consulting geometry for a definition, a vector is a line of fixed length and direction without a fixed (or necessary) position. Global communication technologies are among the vectors that link positions together at any given time. The worldwide reach of the American Cable News Network (CNN) and the Internet make these obvious examples. Communication scholars have traditionally critiqued global communication technologies as mechanisms of domination and capital expansion (e.g., the political economy critique). That line of critique continues to be vital. This part of the book, however, goes beyond that approach as these chapters explore the contradictions, fissures, and potentials of the global vectors of communication. Global media might act in one context as agents of capture and control in the hands of those whose interest they represent. They might act in another context as agents of escape and liberation. The following chapters explore those tendencies.

François Debrix, an international relations scholar, addresses global communication vectors through a perspective conjoining critical media studies, poststructuralist perspectives on international and social relations, and resistant visual theories. The larger context for Debrix's work in this book and elsewhere (e.g., Debrix 1999) is one in which international communication technologies have become an actor in the conduct of foreign policy and the making of international relations. That the global media circuit (e.g., CNN) has *domestic*-ated *foreign* policy issues and conflicts around the globe through the commodification of news (conflicts as the "content" for "all-news" networks) goes without question. Debrix's point of departure comes in the form of a different question: what happens when the media lose control over the image, when they fail to provide a coherent narrative that can rationalize the terror of the image? If the "mediatrix" facilitates the political rationalization of the new world order led by the United States, it also facilitates the crisis of meaning that terrorizes the dominant narrative of international politics. In short, the mediatrix inadvertently facilitates the contradictions of the global media circuit. Debrix sees in the terror of the image the possibility of a much needed repoliticization of international politics and the return of plural political possibilities repressed by the mediatrix. Debrix's work expands the boundaries of international relations and communication studies in that his "postrealist" approach engages fully with the "rhetorical turn" in international relations (see Beer and Hariman 1996).

McKenzie Wark's chapter continues the interrogation of the global vectors of communication. His notion of the "weird global media event" in the field of vectors addresses issues similar to those addressed by Debrix's use of the terrorizing image in the field of the mediatrix. Both Wark and Debrix are particularly interested in the temporal dimension of the international media because it is on this mode of operation that the global media capitalize (e.g., "real-time" journalism). Moreover, they are interested in the moments when there is a crisis of meaning, when the media fail to provide a narrative for the event. Wark introduces a novel way of conceptualizing the spatio-temporal dimensions of global media as vectors whose agency is caught up in the global political field. He is also interested in the place of the discourse that he and other intellectuals produce in the same field of vectors (or mediatrix). His self-reflexivity is more than an act of acknowledging the contingency of one's own position. It is also a question of exploiting the vector's power against itself. More important, at least for the purposes of the present volume, is the stylistic intervention of this chapter: Wark's concern with writing and its modalities, his style of engaging his objects of analysis (e.g., global media vectors), and his theoretical allegiances all work to produce a form of discourse that has been resisted by scholars of international communication. Wark invites us to respond to the complexities of the globalized condition by exploring alternative forms of comprehending and analyzing its constituent elements.

John Downing also addresses the role of intellectuals and their contribution to the global vectors of communication. He does so vis-à-vis reflections on *Empire*, a provocative and wildly popular book (Hardt and Negri 2000) that has become part and parcel of the global condition it seeks to explain. Downing challenges *Empire* for its difficulties in addressing "the negative" (especially war) and the place of communication media in its conceptual schemas. Downing's interest in a book like *Empire* as an international communication scholar is not surprising, given his ongoing research in radical and alternative media across the globe (e.g., Downing 1988, 2001). Downing provides a useful intellectual and political context in which we can appreciate Hardt and

Negri's Marxist lineage (e.g., the "autonomism" movement). At the heart of autonomist Marxism is a reaffirmation of Marx's original idea that it is labor—creative human energy—and not capital that is constitutive of society. "Cycles of struggle," the processes of working-class recomposition, come about through labor's resistance against capital. Hardt and Negri are not alone in their invocation of the concept of cycles of struggle. Dyer-Witheford (1999), for example, deploys Marx's concept of "the circuit of capital" to show how the sites of social activities, which capital depends on for its continued operation and exploitation, may become sites of struggle, insurgency, and subversion. Such a view of the circuits of capital has not been debated widely in the field of international communication. In this context (alternative) global media play a crucial role, and Downing's chapter provides a valuable assessment of alternative media.

References

Beer, F., and Hariman, R. eds. 1996. *Post-realism: The rhetorical turn in international relations.* East Lansing: Michigan State University Press.

Castells, Manuel. 1996. *The rise of the network society.* Oxford: Blackwell.

Debrix, F. 1999. *Re-Envisioning Peacekeeping: The United Nations and the Mobilization of Ideology.* Minneapolis: University of Minnesota Press.

Downing, J. 1988. Alternative public realm: The organization of the 1980s anti-nuclear press in West Germany and Britain. *Media, Culture, and Society* 10, no. 2: 165–83.

———. 2001. *Radical media: Rebellious communication and social movements.* Thousand Oaks, Calif.: Sage.

Dyer-Witheford, N. 1999. *Cyber-Marx: Cycles and circuits of struggle in high-technology capitalism.* Urbana: University of Illinois Press.

Hardt, M., and Negri, A. 2000. *Empire:* Cambridge, Mass.: Harvard University Press.

Lash, S., and Urry, J. 1994. *Economies of sign and space.* London: Sage.

Virilio, P. 1986. *Speed and politics.* New York: Semiotext(e) Foreign Agent Series.

Wark, M. 1994. *Virtual geography: Living with global media events.* Bloomington: Indiana University Press.

5

The Terror of the Image: International Relations and the Global Image Circuitry

François Debrix

M AIMED AND DISFIGURED Tutsi children patiently waiting for water and food supplies in a UNHCR (U.N. High Commissioner for Refugees) refugee camp in eastern Zaire. A crater in the middle of Sarajevo's main marketplace, with middle-aged women's dismembered bodies thrown about by a sudden mortar attack. A live shot of a train full of Serb and Kosovar passengers blown to pieces by NATO forces as it crosses a bridge. A couple of commercial airliners aiming straight at skyscrapers in downtown New York and leaving behind them nothing but two giant balls of fire that turn a famous cityscape into a postapocalyptic scene. The past ten years of global politics have been replete with graphic scenes of terror, horror, destruction, fear, and often incomprehension. When those scenes come from places far away from Westerners, such as Rwanda or the former Yugoslavia, these ghastly sights almost go unnoticed. They are lost in the global flow of media images of war, ethnic crises, and humanitarian dramas. When the images hit closer to home, however, the terror is less easily cast away. Over the past ten years, Western news media (behind the leadership of CNN Time Warner) have turned the image of terror—a common global televisual reality—into a prized commodity, consumed in real time by more or less mesmerized and/or attentive audiences (from TV viewers to Western politicians). But sometimes, despite the media's desire to control the flow of visual information, the image of destruction goes out of control. The media lose control over the live picture. The global disastrous event strays beyond the media's reach as journalists and media pundits fail to provide a coherent narrative that can rationalize the scene being broadcast.

In this chapter, I want to focus on two scenes that reveal moments when the global news media lose control over the content of the image and are caught unaware by a reality that they did not expect to display. The first scene takes us back to 1993, when Western media were eager to proudly broadcast the exploits of American troops in the sands of Somalia, running after and hopefully capturing a so-called rogue local clan leader (Mohammed Farah Aidid). Instead, they showed to the rest of the world horrific pictures of tortured U.S. soldiers dragged down the streets by a local mob. The second scene is the September 11, 2001, shocking and, for many, incomprehensible picture of an American Airlines jet, hijacked by terrorists, crashing into one of the World Trade Center towers, turning the skyscraper into a surreal scene of urban catastrophe and later causing the collapse of the entire structure. In those two instances, the global production of terror images by news media conglomerates is interrupted. The image, though, continues to display a terrifying reality. But the global media have no prepackaged explanation or rationalization for these unexpected sights.

In this chapter, I call these sights of unbuffered media terror "primal scenes." I borrow this term from Marshall Berman (1988) and his analysis of Charles Baudelaire's vivid prose poems, which denounced the squalid conditions of a modern urban life in the 1870s that many romantic spirits were championing at the time. I do not want to attribute to the primal scenes of post–Cold War video terror the kind of critical romantic and antimodernist message conveyed by Baudelaire. Still, in a form reminiscent of Baudelaire's way of bringing critical thought to bear on contemporary realities, I believe that primal scenes show how "a repressed reality creaks through" (Berman 1988, 152) even when all seems to be going well and when control over the meaning of the image (and its message) appears to have been established. The primal scenes are disturbingly and sometimes brutally ironic. They reveal the excesses of media culture at the moment when the viewer least expects it.[1]

In the following pages, I try to make sense of why it appears that only in these horrific moments the "global swarming" of the media recedes.[2] I wonder whether there is something about the global image, frightening as it may be, that can resist "media packaging" or whether there exist specific social-cultural contexts in which the primal scene is more likely to take its viewers and producers by surprise. By asking these questions, I place my analysis at the juncture of critical media studies, postmodern perspectives on international and social relations, and resistant visual theories. In order for me to ask such questions, I take for granted the postmodern condition of hyperreality observed by scholars like Jean François Lyotard (1984) and Jean Baudrillard (1983b), and I recognize the crucial input of Marshall McLuhan's revolutionary thinking (1994), more than thirty years ago, on the meaning of the image in an age when the medium has become the primary message. I also draw critical insight from more recent media philosophy, particularly the writings of Steven Shaviro (1993) and Mark Taylor and Esa Saarinen (1994). Both Shaviro's and Taylor and Saarinen's philosophies of the image are critical additions to McLuhan's vision of a global village, a closed-circuited, media-driven universe within which interconnectedness between objects and subjects is realized. Unlike McLuhan, Shaviro suggests that the visual is never fully captured since the image has the ability to proliferate traces (residues) that "haunt" the spectator well after the visual production has been deployed. Taylor and Saarinen recognize the closed circuitry of the global image and mobilize the notion of the "mediatrix" to make sense of this phenomenon. But they add that the mediatrix can offer pockets of visual resistance at the same time that it is engaged in operations of visual uniformity and conformity. Shaviro and Taylor and Saarinen provide alternatives to McLuhan's (pre)postmodern conclusion that, in today's media universe, only two subject positions are allowed: either one euphorically believes (and takes part) in the so-called liberating but endless flow of media images (contemporary journalism and those who crave journalistic events) or one passively lets the global swarming of the visual do the acting and provide cognitive experience on one's behalf (the postmodern viewer).

By turning to Shaviro's and Taylor and Saarinen's theories, I do not intend to offer answers (with fixed meanings attached) to the question of why the global circuitry of today's media representations of international events is interrupted by crucial moments of visual terror(ism). Rather, I seek to use these theoretical challenges to interrogate global media productions. In international relations (IR), the recognition of the importance of international communication is a recent discovery. International communication (IC) was officially recognized as a subfield of international relations inquiry a few years ago as the International Studies Association (ISA) granted IC the status of independent section of ISA. Studies in the subfield of IC have so far been fairly traditionalist in the sense that they have expanded classical international relations research frameworks to the domain of international communication.[3] A relatively new subfield of IR, IC is already filled with analyses eager to explain the meaning of global visual phenomena and processes (Strobel 1997; Edwards 2001). Often dominated by institutionalist concerns over the formation of international telecommunication regimes (Cowhey 1990; Zacher and Sutton 1996), the globalization of information as a form of power (Sassen 1996; Golding and Harris 1997), and the challenges that digital technologies present to territorial sovereignty (Simon 1998; Warkentin and Mingst 2000), these mostly IR-influenced analyses of global communications have a tendency to "consume" the global visual event and leave untouched the productive media that unleash the images. Recent studies have tried to remedy these attempts at "capturing" international communication events by offering critical interdisciplinary perspectives on global media governance (Morris and Waisbord 2001; Siochru, Girard, and Mahan 2002). Moving away from institutionalist analyses, these studies have sought to bring together critical scholars from both communication studies and international relations to reflect on the role and place of the state, international organizations, and media networks in newly developing configurations of governance, hegemony, and power. While more promising than institutionalist approaches to IC, these studies still fail to refocus on the image. Instead, they are generally obsessed by processes and procedures of power that make possible the production of the image; they take the image (its meaning or lack thereof) for granted and thus leave it unanalyzed. By bringing the primal scene back into the picture and reflecting on its reign of visual terror, I also intend to suspend the growing certainties of international communication (both within and beyond international relations) before these certainties start to shape the contours and discipline of this emergent field of study.[4]

Primal Scenes

On October 3, 1993, American special forces (Marines, U.S. Rangers) received the order from the U.S. military command to launch a raid on the compound of Somali rebel clan leader Mohammed Farah Aidid in Mogadishu. The anticipated success of the operation (capturing Aidid, dismantling his network) would end the infighting between rival clans in Somalia that had forced the United Nations and later the United States to intervene in the first place. Getting Aidid (dead or alive) became the priority for the U.S. military command in Somalia so that order could be restored and humanitarian organizations and the United Nations could deploy their peacekeeping and nation-rebuilding mission.[5] But the intended final onslaught against Aidid and his men turned out to be a disastrous operation (Debrix 1999a, 97–134) and became one of the most horrid visual spectacles of U.S. post–Cold War interventionism. As Sidney Blumenthal (1993) recalls, "Within hours, horrifying pictures materialized on television screens: the corpses of American soldiers dragged through the streets of Mogadishu and burned by jubilant crowds, and a bloodied and bruised American hostage reciting his name and job in a monotone terror" (50). American audiences, accustomed to foreign policy victories and U.S. triumphalist scenes since the aftermath of the Gulf War, were not prepared to understand these images. American politicians, taken by surprise, were unable to provide an appropriate spin to the events. Even Bill Clinton, who up to this point had supported the operation and backed the strategy of going after Aidid, remained speechless. Blumenthal notes that "the appearance of a hostage turned Clinton into one himself: it was a picture of impotence and defeat, recalling, without any commentary necessary, the fate of the last Democratic president" (1993, 51). Television networks were not sure what they should do with those pictures: show them again and again or hide them (Strobel 1997, 176–77). In the hours that followed the failed military assault, both strategies were chosen. The images were eventually pulled from most networks, but they returned later, albeit in freeze-frame fashion, as front covers and color shots in daily newspapers and weekly magazines (Katz 1993; Sharkey 1993).[6] It was too late then to buffer the public from what had been seen. The image spoke for itself. The U.S.-sponsored brave new world order championed by George Bush Sr. and others after the Gulf War had come to an abrupt halt (Debrix 1999a, 126–34). Images of new American military heroes standing by the side of U.N. peacekeepers and paving the way for a more humane and democratic world suddenly gave way to the vision of tortured American soldiers, caught in a war that may not have been in America's interest to fight. On October 3, 1993, in Mogadishu, and hours later in the rest of the world, unexpectedly bloody images of warfare interrupted the global flow of humanitarian and interventionist images and rendered far less acceptable the political ideologies and military strategies that such a visual flow seemed to legitimize.

Eight years later (give or take a few weeks), another trauma, another image, and another American war. Slightly before 9:00 A.M. on September 11, 2001, an American Airlines jetliner flew into the north tower of the World Trade Center in New York City's Lower Manhattan. Most Americans did not catch what was later known as the "first attack" in real time. But fifteen minutes later, as CNN and other cable networks had already dispatched camera crews into the area, a second airliner slammed into the south tower, impaling the building from one side to the other and almost immediately unleashing a huge ball of fire as the kerosene-filled aircraft exploded inside the tower. Everybody saw that one, even if they had missed the first hit. Viewers who were glued to the television screen that morning (including this writer) after the first plane collided with the north tower could not miss it. People at work or on the street were told about it and rushed to the first TV screen they could find (We Watched and Wept 2001).[7] Although clearly not prepared for the images, all networks (not only CNN) had captured the image of the second plane even though live broadcasters were incapable of finding words to make sense of the scene.[8] In the hours and days that followed, every American who was not (tele)present when the live image jumped onto the screen would be given the chance to see this unfathomable sight over and over, from every possible angle, with still shots if necessary. Video footage of the first collision, which had not been caught live by most TV networks, was hunted down and released to the public. But the subsequent replay of the initial visual shock is less interesting. In a sense, it is expected, not only to guarantee viewership but, in this case, to cope with the unreality of the event too. What is more interesting though, similar to the initial moment of hesitation in the media that followed the images of the tortured U.S. soldiers in Mogadishu, is the virtual silence and absence of meaning on the part of the media networks as the event was shown live (by them) and as the initial event continued to produce unexpected visual consequences (the collapse of both towers hours later; the news of a plane crashing into the Pentagon and another one in a Pennsylvania field; the false information about bombs exploding next to the State Department and the Capitol building in Washington; etc.). The image was allowed to roam free. It was allowed to speak for itself and splash its meanings onto people's screens, at home, at work, in the street. Of course, these meanings were incomprehensible for the public and politicians alike. The media were clueless too. As James Der Derian (2002) remarks, "There was no initial attempt by the media or the government to transform these images of horror into responsible discourses of reflection and action" (para 9, n.p.). These images were replayed over and over and until some intelligibility could be drawn from them (the ultimate message, pronounced by the president and accepted by the population, that America is at war).[9] But even the production and transmission of this message of war against terrorism in the media took a while to be established as the trauma of the image and its cascading flow of related visual terrors created a deep "cognitive gap" (Der Derian's term) between the real and its representation: for several days, "there was much talking but very little meaning" in the media (2002, para. 13, n.p.).

In Mogadishu on October 3, 1993, a war ended because of an image that took everyone by surprise. In Manhattan on September 11, 2001, a war started because of another image that shocked everyone. The role of these images in the logic of war (to launch one or to withdraw from another) is intriguing but lies beyond the scope of this chapter. In both situations, a live image of terror beyond any media control interrupts (sometimes, for several days) regularly programmed and displayed media representations and rationalizations of world events. A reality that does not come from the medium but, rather, from what the medium generally tries to "package" (the so-called real event) comes back to paralyze what Taylor and Saarinen (1994) call the "mediatrix."[10] This reality is the reality of the primal scene. Traumatic as it may be, this reality does *not* look "more real than reality itself" (Baudrillard 1983b) (this is rather the condition of simulated reality in the media) but, in fact, looks more fictive than fiction itself. While all too real for many, the primal scene of media terror looks unreal or surreal. The disastrous attack against a clan leader's compound looks much more like a quagmire film (the *Black Hawk Down* movie as a post–September 11 sequel to the 1980s Vietnam films, but with a narrative of closure), and the terrorist attack on the World Trade Center is first visualized as a technically flawless cinematographic montage made up of scenes from *Towering Inferno* and *Armageddon*.[11] Although too fictive to be real in appearance, primal scenes do not erupt in the normal settings where spectators expect to see fictive representations (movie theaters). More importantly, the primal scenes do not come equipped with the narratives that bring spectators a desirable sense of visual closure. Rather, they mark a moment when narratives of visual closure (generally provided by the media and political leadership) are distinctly absent. Unlike the controlled fear of normalized social relations periodically dispensed by the media and the government, the terror of the image in the primal scene cannot easily be made intelligible and is psychologically destabilizing (Edkins 2001). For the public, the primal scene's primal fear is all the more destabilizing because it completely disables the comforting and buffering narratives of certainty traditionally produced within the closed circuits of the global mediatrix.

Closed Circuitry in the Global Mediatrix

Annabelle Sreberny (2000) notes that "contemporary rhetoric suggests that we live in a unitary world in which space and time have collapsed and the experience of distance has imploded forever" (93). For many, this collapse of time and space is the product of international channels of (tele)communication which, with the advent of cable/satellite TV, cellular phone systems, and the Internet, have granted human relations throughout the world a degree of immediacy and a sense of immanence never experienced before.[12] The realization that world communications are redefining physical demarcations between the global and the local and remediating the linear progression of time is not so novel. Recent media technologies and means of communication, the Internet in particular, have given people the (false) impression that this reconfiguration of time and space is a 1990s phenomenon.

As McLuhan (1994) observed, the collapse of spatiality into new temporal parameters (an always already present) is the fateful, and to some fatal, consequence of the electric age. What McLuhan calls the electric age is a phenomenon that developed throughout the twentieth century and was announced as early as the fifteenth century when Gutenberg discovered the power of printing from moveable types (McLuhan 1995a, 97–148). The electric age is dominated by a form of connectivity that fuses the mechanization of handicraft (the serial production of objects) with technologically enhanced modes of communication between self and other (modern media) to create social communities. Technology is no longer an artifact—the product of the labor of the artificer (man) who constructs tools to guarantee his survival and, in the process, shapes social relations (mostly of mutual exchange) based on the notion of needs/interests realized through manmade instruments.[13] Rather, in the electric age, technology is beyond artifact. It commands and determines human needs and desires, and conditions modernity's forms (and contents) of sociability. No longer an extension of man's physical skills, technology becomes an extension of man's "nervous system." As McLuhan notes, "by putting our physical bodies inside our extended nervous systems, by means of electric media, we set up a dynamic by which all previous technologies . . . will be translated into information systems" (1994, 57). This development of and conditioning by electric technology, what McLuhan calls "the capitulation of Western man to his technology" (69), creates a massive interconnected social body characterized by collective docility (or "social numbness") vis-à-vis information and the media. This docile attitude vis-à-vis information networks is not imposed or forced on the human subject. Rather, it is accepted, desired, and sought after. Reversing Marx's analysis, McLuhan remarks that the passive acceptance of electric media and their technologies is not a matter of alienation of the self to the machine. It is not a question of enslavement or subjugation (hence, Marxist analyses may not be effective tools here). On the contrary, this capitulation to the media and to their networks of communication, information, and object transformation has been utterly "voluntary and enthusiastic" on the part of the mesmerized subjects of the electric age (McLuhan 1994, 69). Again, there is nothing peculiar about late modernity or the last quarter of the twentieth century if one follows McLuhan's analysis. What has happened in the past thirty years is nothing more than a faster growth of the electric network of media that has forced the technologically stimulated "nervous systems" of human subjects to adapt to the transformations at a quicker pace.

Net romancers and cybertopians like Nicholas Negroponte (1995) euphorically proclaim that, over the past ten years, we have moved from the information age to the postinformation age, that human experience has gone from being electric to being digital, and that social life is now governed by bits rather than objects. But they greatly exaggerate the extent of the so-called digital revolution. Negroponte writes that "in the post-information age, we often have an audience the size of one. Everything is made to order, and information is extremely personalized" (1995, 164). Although the personal apparently returns in the age of the Internet, what gives the impression of a unique individualized experience is in fact the dependence of the information system on an ever expanding yet closely connected and at the same time closed-circuited medium. Without the Internet connecting all and one at the same time through a highly depersonalized mediation (where selves and others are always already tele-present and interchangeable), no human sociability is assured (see the ubiquitous power of e-mail), and probably no knowledge is acquired.[14] The fact that information has turned to the Internet as another medium that allows the human nervous system to absorb more electric technology faster would be of no surprise to McLuhan, who in 1969 stated that "the electronically induced technological extensions of our central nervous systems . . . are immersing us in a world-pool of information movement and are thus enabling man to incorporate within himself the whole of mankind" (1995b, 248). McLuhan meant that despite (or rather because of) the social numbness caused by the media, a larger degree of connectivity is achieved through the overdependence of man on what today we call the network. This connectivity is repetitive and, as Jean Baudrillard later said, orbital (Baudrillard 1994). In this "global village" (McLuhan's term) made possible by media technologies, the same social operations are reproduced over and over, and social meaning becomes defined as the ability to get access to the signs and objects displayed by the media and whose worth is determined according to their placement within this media network. While McLuhan was at times tempted to champion the new enlightening and communal (in his language "tribal") potentials of the "global media village," the "psychic reunification" and "global consciousness" of the human family made possible by the human subject's membership to the new interconnected media galaxy (1995b, 233–69), his most useful insight is that the media create a closed circuitry within which subject positions are limited by the type of (nervous) stimulations that are presented.[15] In a social universe where the medium is the message, individual subjects relate to one another, communicate, and exchange on the basis of the form of the information that is being provided. For human subjects, it is no longer a matter of finding and using the proper form of presentation that will best convey the intended message but, rather, of subscribing to and living by globally recognized systems of objects, signs, and media codes within which messages (meanings) circulate everywhere, all the time, and for everyone. Within the closed circuitry of the media (electric, electronic, or digital) a uniformity and conformity of meaning dictated by the adherence to the form is generally found. Whether they are passive participants of a new global psychic experience (McLuhan's electrified subjects), cyber-geekish netizens happily proliferating their decentered personalities throughout the Internet (Negroponte's bit subjects), or terrorized yet avid consumers of an endless flow of television images (post–Cold War world spectators), media subjects answer the calls of the global mediatrix and remain its faithful and docile servants.

A number of studies have shown, in less theoretical terms, how the global media form a closed circuit in which "gaining access" becomes the number one priority for media network participants and consumers. Global media flows, some argue, have developed to the detriment of local cultural forms and meanings, which disappear as human subjects the world over prefer to define their lives in relation to westernized consumer objects and visual cultural signs (Mattelart 1979; Appadurai 1996; Sreberny 2000). Others have demonstrated that live television broadcasts of world events (Prince Charles and Diana's wedding, the fall of the Berlin Wall, the O.J. Simpson trial, etc.) thrill audiences that are not even familiar with the historical and cultural contexts of such events. When these "global media events" are absorbed in nonindigenous societies, they alter local habits and practices (Dayan and Katz 1992; Fiske 1996; Bourdieu 1996). Of course, the use of media, particularly visual media like film or television, has been crucial to the production and reproduction of political beliefs and systems (Iyengar and Kinder 1987). The social numbness created by the media has often been exploited by politicians who use media technology to condition the public to certain discourses (Edelman 1988; Delli Carpini and Williams 1994). Within the media network, political events have been created, social problems have been fabricated, enemies have been produced, defensive strategies have been constructed, and wars have been fought that did not necessarily coincide with real social conditions (Bennett 2001). In the simulacrum of the media, a reality can be generated that does not have to correspond to or find a point of reference in everyday cultural practice (Baudrillard 1988).[16] The more spectacular the political event, the more likely it is to draw audiences and produce acquiescence on the part of the "silent majorities" (Baudrillard 1983a). The closed-circuited world of the global mediatrix is an eminently visual and spectacular world. As Murray Edelman (1995) puts it, "political beliefs and actions spring from assumptions, biases, and news reports. In this critical sense, politics is a drama taking place in an assumed and reported world that evokes threats and hopes, a world people do not directly observe or touch" (1).

It would appear, then, that the conditioning power of the global mediatrix is limitless, that its flow of visual events is destined to keep the numb social masses in awe, and that within the circular logic of media reality there is no possibility to distinguish the original from the copy, the genuine from the fake, the immediate from the mediated. But how is an audience terrorized by an image? Why do some media images take us (media producers and consumers) by surprise? How can primal fear be the outcome of the medium if all the medium does is weave its web of closed circuitry ad infinitum? Are the moments of visual terror mentioned above nothing more than simulacra (too fictive and frightening to be true)?

Mark Taylor and Esa Saarinen's philosophy of the image (1994) provides, if not an answer, at least the ability to make the notion of the terror of the visual somewhat intelligible.[17] Taylor and Saarinen offer an alternative to McLuhan's social numbness without advocating a complicity with the medium. Taylor and Saarinen encourage a participation with the medium that does not just reproduce and expand the signs and codes of the mediatrix but takes the mediatrix at its own game. The mediatrix, "the electro-network that mediatizes the real" (Taylor and Saarinen 1994, "Communicative Practices," p. 5) and appears to provide no escape mechanism, is a symptom of postmodern times. According to Taylor and Saarinen, postmodernism is primordially a visual, information-laden, and media-dominated condition. Postmodernism and its ideological complement, postindustrial capitalism, encourage a decentralization of the human subject throughout the circuits of information. A sense of heterogeneity, singularity, specificity, and difference of identities, behaviors, tasks, and tastes is conveyed by postmodernism. But this is mere appearance, all fictive and superficial. For this appearance to be credible and accepted, the media must "play a central role in the creation and maintenance of the culture of heterogeneity" (Taylor and Saarinen 1994, "Simcult," p. 9). Taylor and Saarinen intimate that "from hypertexts and email to video and virtual reality, economic processes [of late modernity] are regulated by . . . multiple codes for local interests" ("Simcult," p. 9; my inserts). Without the omnipresent message and form of the mediatrix, the articulation of singularity and heterogeneity crucial to both postmodernism and postindustrial capitalism could not be so effortlessly realized.[18]

Extirpating the subject from the numbing condition of postmodernism and freeing man from the tentacles of the global mediatrix can only take place through terror, fear, misunderstanding, and discomfort, Taylor and Saarinen believe. Their philosophy of the image, what they call imagology, may be read as a radical attempt at making visible what in the visual condition of the mediatrix is repressed, hidden, cast away, and disavowed.[19] "Imagology is the return of the repressed," they claim, and "images must be inhabited, not simply interpreted" (1994, "Media Philosophy," pp. 2–3). What I take this to mean is that the subject of the mediatrix must make a conscious effort no longer to accept as given, necessary, and beneficial the flow of images that lulls this postmodern being into a false comfort.[20] Some images offer an opportunity for the postmodern subject to escape the closed circuit of the visual. Representing an excess of the mediatrix, some visual scenes beg not to be understood. Springing from the mediatrix and yet strangely foreign to its rules, these images are not readily interpretable and acceptable. But instead of being brushed away and quickly replaced by reassuring explanations, the initial misunderstanding and terror of these sights should be seized on by the postmodern viewer. Only in these moments of misunderstanding can the tightly knit global media web be pried open and pluralized. This is precisely the challenge of Taylor and Saarinen's imagology. Imagology's dare is to make the subject aware of the importance of these moments when the misunderstanding and terror of the image must be embraced. Taylor and Saarinen intimate that "for those who still believe in the dream of transparent inter-subjectivity [e.g., Negroponte's netizens] or in an ideal speech community of the experts who trade clear and distinct ideas, essences and concepts [the theory of an ideal speech community where pure communication is achieved through beneficent media], misunderstanding constitutes an abiding fear. But misunderstanding can release energy. The law of the media is the law of the dirty hands: you cannot be understood if you are not misunderstood" (1994, "Media Philosophy," p. 5; my inserts).

What is gained through the subject's refusal to capitulate to media technology and the simultaneous acceptance of the terror and misunderstanding of the image is a return to reality. This does not mean that a real subject is being restored once the media panoply has been undone, or that greater and better human subjectivity has been recovered by piercing through the veil of the mediatrix. What this means, rather, is that plural experiences can be accessed precisely because the uniform and often universalizing rationalizations of the mediatrix (and its proponents) have been left behind, even if only temporarily. To use Taylor and Saarinen's words, "the aleatory irruption of difference" has taken over the "eternal return of the same," and a "politics of hope" has displaced "the aesthetics of despair" imposed by the media ("Media Philosophy," p. 20). Through misunderstood or rather nonunderstandable images which often terrify, a plurality of meaning can be discovered if the postmodern subject takes the pain to face the image rather than recline back into the mediatrix.

I am in no way suggesting that the images of terror, like the primal scenes from Somalia or Manhattan mentioned above, should be interpreted as positive, enlightening, liberating, or even pleasing. I am not claiming that the political reality/message they supposedly reveal ought to be supported. What I am arguing, rather, is that the silence, misunderstanding, and moment of trauma experienced in the media and by those who are caught in it need to be taken advantage of since, in a media-saturated universe, it is only in those fleeting moments that the predictable rationalizations and prepackaged justifications of the mediatrix recede.[21] The images of terror must be faced and the short-lived absence of meaning they provoke must be left as is (in suspense) before the global media have a chance to recuperate every possible residue of meaning. It is perhaps only in those suspended moments of terror and incomprehension that the reality of politics can be experienced, often in all its cruelty and visual irrationality. It is also in those moments that postmodern subjects can voice original political strategies (including response strategies to what has just happened) which refuse to reproduce the normal, accepted, and common-sensical ideological responses (often in the form of retaliations) of those who, buffered and supported by the mediatrix, are in charge of policymaking and control the political message. Simply, it is in those passing moments, when questions are asked but clear answers are not found, that the subjects of the mediatrix may become political subjects (again). To quote Taylor and Saarinen, "to construct meaning is an act of repression that closes as much as it opens. To embrace meaninglessness is not to despair but to welcome the incomprehensible plurality that is our destiny" (1994, "Superficiality," p. 3).

The Haunting of the Image

Although Taylor and Saarinen do not explain why some images of terror suddenly appear on people's television screens, they nonetheless make intelligible some of the reasons why such images breed incomprehension and anxiety. Images of terror terrorize, they suggest, because they escape the power of the mediatrix. They are incomprehensible not so much because they do not signify but because postmodern viewers have not been prepared by the mediatrix to reflect upon them. Reflection requires time, analysis, distance, and introspection. When the postmodern subject watches images in the global mediatrix, reflection has already been obliterated and replaced by immediate interpretation/translation (what you see is this). What then appears to be an absence of meaning in the moment of terror and misunderstanding is in fact a plurality of signification released away from the mediatrix but nonetheless terrifying since the mediated subject has not been accustomed to think outside the media's frames. Again, what traumatizes and is sometimes expressed as the irruption of the real into the postmodern subject's imaginary is the silence of the media and their unexpected lack of explanation.[22] The prospect of an aleatory, uncertain, and unstable reality, so unlike the global media's own version of what is visually real, is discomforting yet, as Taylor and Saarinen would have it, necessary for the subject to recover dignity, integrity, and political significance.

It would appear, then, that the terror of the image has very little to do with the content of the image (what it shows, no matter how gruesome), but that it is rather explained by the way the mediatrix has established a formula for linking visual content with form in a given cultural context. If the mediatrix commonly and matter-of-factly displays images of urban terrorism and destruction, scenes of chaos and torture, photos of warfare and death in news reports or on the covers of newspapers, such images are unlikely to shock the post-modern viewer. One could imagine that terrorist attacks caught live or recorded and then replayed on TV would have a different effect for audiences in Lebanon and Israel for instance than they would have for an American audience. In fact, it is quite possible that the terror of the image would not have occurred among the American population if the September 11 attacks had taken place in Jerusalem or Beirut. Middle Eastern and American television viewers are not so different. They all partake of the global mediatrix and receive their daily doses of visual information. But the mediatrix filters to them differential meanings that are apt to rationalize different interpretations of given political situations/events in seemingly different cultural contexts. At least, the mediatrix makes it look like these are different cultural contexts. What then makes an image look different in the global mediascape, when this image is transposed from one cultural context to the next, is less the cultural context and the substance of politics in this context (which becomes a media fabrication) than the meaning the media choose to give to the political event and its image. Thus the same image of terror may create unfathomable angst in one region of the global mediascape and produce completely indifferent attitudes in other parts of it. Once again, as Taylor and Saarinen mentioned, the global mediatrix thrives when it propagates the appearance of heterogeneity (of cultural identities) and singularity (of political meaning). While the meaning of the image may look different in various subdivisions of the mediatrix, all these (simulated) meanings only make sense in relation to one another (not individually), based on their relative place in the closed circuit of the global mediatrix. The images' supposedly unique and differential meanings are in fact dependent on a common media code that globally makes the process of signification and political rationalization uniform, limited, and saturated. To repeat, it is not the content of the image that terrorizes. Rather, it is its ability to bring a crisis of meaning, to proliferate questions about the process of political rationalization in the media (which never dared to associate this image's particular content with this particular form in this particular context), that is found to be troubling and destabilizing.

In the aftermath of September 11, with its images of terror and their interruption of meaning, it is doubly ironic that some media commentators and pundits chose to accuse postmodernism for what took place (both the attacks and the sight of these attacks) (Rothstein 2001; Beinart 2001). The irony of their reaction is that, as active participants of the mediatrix, they showed their complete impotence with regard to the moment of terror and misunderstanding ushered in by the images. Unable to escape the global media's rationalizations, they sought to explain the attacks by blaming the excesses of postmodernism (its decentering of the subject; its calls to political relativism).

By blaming postmodernism for the attacks, these pundits revealed that they cannot think beyond the mediatrix and that, in the face of visual terror, they crave the mediatrix's interpretations even more. In their attacks against postmodernism, these media participants have proven to be exemplary postmodern subjects (in Taylor and Saarinen's sense) who have been totally decentered and disarmed by the mediatrix and yet cannot live without it. At the same time though, the irony of their response to September 11 is doubled by the fact that, in a sense, they are correct. But they do not know why they are correct. It is indeed the postmodern mediatrix that brought terror and incomprehension since, as we have seen, global media networks in the postmodern condition do not allow pluralized meanings and plural political possibilities to be visually presented. When different visual realities jumped onto the screen on September 11 in an otherwise visually controlled media environment, images terrorized many and could not be understood.

To conclude the theoretical investigation of the image of terror and its global effects, I wish to supplement the critical insight offered by Taylor and Saarinen with Steven Shaviro's reflection on the "fear of images." Shaviro's own philosophy of the visual (1993) pushes further the question of why certain images bring terror and, beyond their moment of shock and incomprehension, continue to haunt the visual spectrum. What Shaviro suggests is that, even when the moment of misunderstanding and anxiety caused by the image has passed and the mediatrix has regrouped and reconstituted meaning, traces or residues of visual uncertainty remain that unsettle the closed circuitry of global media networks.

Shaviro believes that all filmed images, not only those that represent a blatant scene of terror, have the capacity to terrorize. What is frightening about images is what Shaviro describes as "their weird fullness" (1993, 17). Images are the registers of the material in the visual. They capture an object, a reality, an event. And despite the repeated attempts of those in the mediatrix who want to "subdue and regulate the visual," images remind the viewer that the material object they show "is never distant or absent enough" (16–17). There is always something about material reality (the real outside the mediatrix) that is caught by the film even as more images roll on. This is what it means for the image to be a trace or residue. Images periodically, and often unexpectedly, bring back a reality that media codes, the political spectacle, and (post)modern systems of rationalization hoped had been buried once and for good. But what is this reality outside the mediatrix that the media fear?

What the media fear in the image is the physical ability of the subject, elicited by the image, to produce something unexpected, personalized, unconnected to the rest of the mediatrix. For Shaviro, this is what the terror of the image is all about. What is commonly perceived as a terror of the image is in fact the mediatrix's own fear, that is to say, the fear that subjects who watch the image will make something spontaneous as a response to what they see, something the media networks may not be able to catch on film or, even if they catch it, will not be capable of interpreting. The haunting of the image takes place when an unexpected reaction (not on the program) gives rise to new actions on the part of the subject. Off the programmatic charts, these actions can be very political too. However, this political (re)action is no longer dictated by the codes of the mediatrix. In a sense, going back to Taylor and Saarinen, these spontaneous reactions to the image can be said to be all the more political since they are not conditioned by the media spectacle and are not justified by media scripts. Sometimes, the haunting of the visual can give rise to its own images as well. The CNN reports out of Mogadishu days and weeks after the military raid on the compound failed also showed the Somali population grabbing TV cameras from the hands of Western stringers to film scenes of Somali life from their own perspective (Debrix 1999a, 256).[23]

The terror of the image is the fear that the image, even before it is interpreted by the media, may seduce human subjects and steer them away from the reality of the mediatrix. This fear haunts the mediatrix, and the global media try to bury it under multiple layers of visual fictions (from news reports and cinema to the Internet and virtual reality). Shaviro explains that this fear of the image is an old problem in Western metaphysics going all the way back to Plato and his (fearful) warning against shadows and reflections on the wall of the cave (1993, 15). The fear of spontaneous seduction by the image reveals the anxiety that man may be carried away by his visceral reactions and physical impulses. Most of Western philosophy's desire to privilege mind over matter, soul over body, finds its origin in this fear of the visual. Shaviro notes that people react to images with their physical senses, often in the most elementary fashion.[24] This is the power of the image: the ability to play with the body and to require of it an unmediated and often immediate response. This power is the reality that remains as traces in most of the contemporary images of the global mediatrix. All images possess this capacity to awaken the body. All objects and events captured on film and broadcast to a mass audience have remnants of this power to establish a "continuity between the physiological and affective responses of my own body and the appearances and disappearances, the mutations and perdurances, of the bodies and images on screen" (Shaviro 1993, 255–56). But the mediatrix seeks to "destroy the power of images, or at least restrain them within the bounds of linguistic discursivity" (16) because the mediatrix's own credibility is precisely dependent on subjects passively receiving the uninterrupted flow of media messages and forms.

In a postmodern age, all the image can do is haunt the global mediatrix, hoping that these ghostly and often ghastly appearances can awaken the body.

The image of terror is the trace of a materiality which refuses to disappear. Contrary to what the mediatrix would like people to believe, the image of terror haunts and destabilizes (again, it haunts the mediatrix mostly), but not because of its visually graphic nature. If it were so, the same image would terrify audiences the world over. But then, how would one explain the fact that American television spectators barely paid attention to the images of death, destruction, war, and terrorism in Rwanda, Bosnia, Somalia, or the Middle East broadcast by their favorite networks more or less at the same time as the images from Mogadishu and New York were being shown? The image of terror terrorizes because it irrupts in a media system that is not prepared for it and strives to eliminate the visceral from the visual.

Conclusion

In an age when global economic productions, global commercial exchanges, and global visual information have taken over what counts as political and determine the place and role of the subject (and its desires) in structures and systems of meaning that endlessly recirculate signs, objects, and images, critical scholars who have been concerned with both international relations and international communication have sometimes adopted a resigned, passive, and almost understanding attitude. Not envisioning any possible way for the postmodern subject to escape the closed circuitry of the mediatrix, these scholars have often been left to reproduce the same fateful and fatalist diagnoses (since no new prognosis seems possible) (Baudrillard 1987, 1990). For Taylor and Saarinen, and Shaviro as well, there is hope and there is a challenge. The challenge is found in the image itself, an image that terrorizes but, precisely because it does not readily make sense, offers radical opportunities. The image, Shaviro suggests, can provide its own means of resistance, its own form of reaction to the global mediatrix. The image is political to the extent that it revitalizes the human body, shakes it, and remobilizes it to break free, even if only temporarily, from the power of global media networks and their codes of visual uniformity and rational conformity. Surprisingly enough, through the use of the image, a neither global nor local politics of the body resurfaces that may offer novel strategies and plural cultural possibilities to think the material and the political.[25]

Against the grain of Western metaphysics (the postmodern mediatrix is the virtual technological enhancement of Western metaphysics), the image remains to show us that bodies matter, that bodies are/make politics, and that political bodies and body politics are quite material. Perhaps the moment of suspense, the misunderstanding, and the sight of terror that prompt the human subject's reflection (through an initial lack of understanding) about the body's place inside and outside the mediatrix will be able to spread to more mundane and less graphic images of the global mediascape once the work of haunting (of and with the image) is recognized as a vital critical enterprise in international relations and international communication circles.[26]

Returning to the primal scenes of visual terror that opened this chapter, what makes these scenes noteworthy for the critical scholar interested in making intelligible the moments of terror and misunderstanding introduced by these images is not the global political condition that they allegedly represent and according to which they are generally interpreted by the media (post–Cold War U.S. interventionism in Somalia and anti-American terrorism in New York). Too many stories have been and will again be told about the supposedly political contents and implications of these images of terror. What is interesting about these primal scenes, and what must be sought after, is a politics of haunting (Derrida 1994; Debrix 1999b). The politics of haunting looks for radical possibilities, ways of challenging the global mediascape before this mediatrix has a chance to impose its predictable answers onto the visually witnessed material events. This politics of haunting tries to maintain the silence and the incomprehension that follow the vision of terror in order to create a necessary gap between the event and the media. In this gap, different political strategies, different strategies voiced by different people (other than journalists, media pundits, and politicians buffered by the media spectacle) can take place to offer more than one way of dealing with the materiality of the event. In this space, the voices of those who do not necessarily subscribe to the political strategy affirmed by the media-political establishment or, instead, the voices of those who may well support the general political objective championed in the media but would like to see politics result from a more open, democratic debate may be heard.

Politics in the age of the global mediatrix supposedly occurs anywhere, anytime, and for anyone. But politics in the world of CNN and many other mega-media networks is not international politics anymore as most people the world over experience a mediated reality supported by the same visual code. In today's global mediatrix, international politics is neither political nor international. It is merely a depoliticized uniformization of media-filtered reality. Primal scenes, despite their terror, or rather *because* of their terror, must be looked at, faced, and embraced because they represent the rare moments in our media-saturated global condition when plural political possibilities become available. In this sense, international politics needs the terror of the image.

Notes

I would like to thank Clair Apodaca, James Der Derian, Larry George, Tim Luke, Mehdi Semati, and Cynthia Weber for their comments and suggestions on this chapter.

1. It has also been argued that contemporary postmodern American novelist Don DeLillo has the ability to mobilize primal scenes as a literary visual genre (Lentricchia 1998).

2. I borrow the phrase "global swarming" from Der Derian 1996.

3. For a more original study that draws on traditions other than international relations theory, see Deibert 1997.

4. For a more sustained study that tries to blur the disciplinary distinctions between international relations, cultural studies, communication studies and sociology, see Debrix and Weber 2003.

5. The objectives of this mission are summarized in Hirsch and Oakley 1995.

6. See also the cover of *Time*, October 18, 1993, displaying the tortured and bloodied face of the helicopter pilot taken hostage by the Somali mob.

7. See, for example, Carol Banks, a travel agent from Los Angeles who recounts: "The phone rang. It was a coworker, crying her eyes out. She told me to turn on the TV. I put on the news and I started sobbing" (Ground Zero 2001, 17). Or Sue Levytsky, a freelance copywriter from Michigan, who explains: "I was watching TV in Michigan and when the towers went down I felt like the core of my being was ripped out" (18).

8. On the incomprehension of the journalists immediately after the attacks, see "Ground Zero: For the Dedicated TV Newspeople Covering a Day of Infamy, There Was Unexpected Danger and Overwhelming Sadness" (2001). Fox News anchor Shepard Smith recalls, "We decided to set up our cameras on the roof of the Fox News building. Fighter jets were buzzing over our heads. We couldn't process it, and everybody was breaking down. People were vomiting. It was impossible to be a dispassionate journalist. . . . I lost it repeatedly during the show" (38).

9. On the replay/return of time as a consequence of the September 11 events, see Campbell 2002.

10. For Taylor and Saarinen, the "mediatrix" is the dominant symptom of postmodern society. In postmodern society, the media and the Internet form a matrix of communication within which exchanges are staged and understanding of the real is disseminated through the power of information (1994, "Communicative Practices," pp. 10–13). The page numbers in Taylor and Saarinen 1994 are not consecutive but are renumbered for each section of the book.

11. The first reaction of Glendale, California, law student Armen Der Abrahamian, on seeing the images of the towers on CNN, was, "It was something out of Armageddon. It didn't look real; the people looked like movie extras, running around with powder all over them" (Ground Zero 2001, 18).

12. This was recently seen in the use of video phone technology by "embedded" journalists in the war in Iraq in April 2003.

13. This is more or less the definition of "artefact" provided by Hobbes in *Leviathan* (1985, introduction, part I).

14. For a somewhat more nuanced approach to digital connectivity, see Hayles 1999.

15. For a critical review of McLuhan's "global village" notion, see Genosko 1999, 100–11.

16. A popular cultural example of this is the film *Wag the Dog*.

17. I take to heart the notion of intelligibility: a narrative providing a satisfactory interpretation of a situation, event, or problem can be advanced while knowing that this narrated interpretation is provisional and aleatory. This interpretation holds no claim to truth whatsoever. It is one possible way (among many) of making sense, for the time being, of an observed situation or of a problem that has presented itself. On the notion of intelligibility, see Shapiro 1992, 37–41.

18. Taylor and Saarinen's mediatrix is at times reminiscent of the now famous "matrix" represented and theorized by the Wachowski brothers in their blockbuster film *The Matrix*. As David Weberman notes, the mediatrix/matrix "gives us just about everything we could want from the shallowest to the deepest of gratifications . . . [It] gives us the opportunity to visit museums and concerts, read Shakespeare and Stephen King, fall in love, make love, raise children, form deep friendships, and so on" (2002, 235–35).

19. Imagology takes advantage of "the disappearance of the signified in the endless field of signifiers" ("Styles," p. 9). Imagology approaches this cultural condition "not with a heavy heart" but rather "affirms it in all its creative richness" ("Styles," p. 9).

20. My reading of Taylor and Saarinen may be somewhat generous to the extent that it sometimes remains unclear, based on their mainly aphoristic and lapidary style of writing/presentation, whether they fully support the radical possibilities of the image that I allege they champion. While I believe I am reading Taylor and Saarinen's philosophy of the image very closely, this reading is also influenced by the argument I make in this chapter regarding the terror of the image.

21. For another perspective on the void of meaning and the silent relief of the image of terror, see Campbell 2001.

22. On the irruption of the real in the imaginary of the subject, see the Lacanian psychoanalytic interpretations of popular culture offered by Žižek 1992, 1993.

23. "Stringers" are freelance cameramen (often journalism students) taken from the local community to broadcast images on behalf of Western media networks (Strobel 1997, 68–69).

24. Shaviro writes: "[When watching a film], I laugh and cry, I shudder and scream, I get tense or pissed off or bored, I restlessly glance at my watch and the person next to me, or I sink into a state of near-catatonic absorption. But in any case, I do not actively interpret or seek to control" (1993, 255).

25. Patricia Zimmermann (2000) has recently offered a series of examples of visual strategies that take the global image at its own game and use this image to recover a politics of the body. For Zimmermann, documentary film in a postmodern era has the ability to take advantage of the images produced by the global mediatrix to reveal plural political realities both locally and internationally. Among the visual strategies Zimmermann suggests (and describes) are visual testimonies by war victims (raped Muslim women in Bosnia in particular) and camcorder technology used by women to

voice their preferences in the debate over reproductive rights and to regain possession of their bodies.

26. I have developed an argument along these lines in *Re-Envisioning Peacekeeping* (1999a, particularly chapter 6). See also Foster 1996 on this topic.

References

Appadurai, A. 1996. *Modernity at Large: Cultural Dimensions of Globalization.* Minneapolis: University of Minnesota Press.

Baudrillard, J. 1983a. *In the Shadow of the Silent Majorities.* New York: Semiotext(e).

———. 1983b. *Simulations.* New York: Semiotext(e).

———. 1987. *The Ecstasy of Communication.* New York: Semiotext(e).

———. 1988. "The Implosion of the Social in the Media." In M. Poster, ed., *Jean Baudrillard: Selected Writings*, 207–19. Stanford: Stanford University Press.

———. 1990. *Fatal Strategies.* New York: Semiotext(e).

———. 1994. *The Illusion of the End.* Stanford: Stanford University Press.

Beinart, P. 2001. Sidelines. *New Republic,* September 24. www.thenewrepublic.com/092401/trb092401.html.

Bennett, W. L. 2001. *News: The Politics of Illusion.* New York: Longman.

Berman, M. 1988. *All That Is Solid Melts into Air: The Experience of Modernity.* New York: Penguin.

Blumenthal, S. 1993. Why Are We in Somalia? *New Yorker,* October 25.

Bourdieu, P. 1996. *Sur la télévision* [About Television]. Paris: Liber.

Campbell, D. 2001. Imaging the Real, Struggling for Meaning. *Info-Tech-War-Peace,* Info Interventions, October 6. www.watsoninstitute.org/infopeace/911/index.cfm?id=4#.

Campbell, D. 2002. Time Is Broken: The Return of the Past in the Response to September 11. *Theory and Event* 4, no. 4. muse.jhu.edu/journals/theory_and_event/v005/5.4campbell.html.

Cowhey, P. 1990. The International Telecommunications Regime: The Political Roots for Regimes of High Technology. *International Organization* 44, no 2: 158–76.

Dayan, D., and Katz, E. 1992. *Media Events: The Live Broadcasting of History.* Cambridge, Mass.: Harvard University Press.

Debrix, F. 1999a. *Re-Envisioning Peacekeeping: The United Nations and the Mobilization of Ideology.* Minneapolis: University of Minnesota Press.

———. 1999b. Specters of Postmodernism: Derrida's Marx, the New International, and the Return of Situationism. *Philosophy and Social Criticism* 25, no. 1: 1–21.

Debrix, F., and Weber, C. 2003. *Rituals of Mediations: International Politics and Social Meanings.* Minneapolis: University of Minnesota Press.

Deibert, R. 1997. *Parchment, Printing, and Hypermedia: Communication in World Order Transformation.* New York: Columbia University Press.

Delli Carpini, M., and Williams, B. 1994. Methods, Metaphors, and Media Research: The Use of Television in Political Conversations. *Communication Research* 21: 782–812.

Der Derian, J. 1996. Global Swarming, Virtual Security, and Bosnia. *Washington Quarterly* 19, 3: 45–56.

———. 2002. The War of Networks. *Theory and Event* 4, no. 4. muse.jhu.edu/journals/theory_and_event/v005/5.4derderian.html.

Derrida, J. 1994. *Specters of Marx: The State of the Debt, the Work of Mourning, and the New International.* New York: Routledge.

Edelman, M. 1988. *Constructing the Political Spectacle.* Chicago: University of Chicago Press.

———. 1995. *From Art to Politics.* Chicago: University of Chicago Press.

Edkins, J. 2001. The Absence of Meaning: Trauma and the Events of September 11. *Info-Tech-War-Peace,* Info Interventions, October 5. www.watsoninstitute.org/info-peace/911/index.cfm?id=4#.

Edwards, L. 2001. *Mediapolitik: How the Mass Media Have Transformed World Politics.* Washington, D.C.: Catholic University Press.

Fiske, J. 1996. *Media Matters: Race and Gender in U.S. Politics.* Minneapolis: University of Minnesota Press.

Foster, H. 1996. *The Return of the Real: The Avant-Garde at the End of the Century.* Cambridge: MIT Press.

Genosko, G. 1999. *McLuhan and Baudrillard: The Masters of Implosion.* New York: Routledge.

Golding, P., and Harris, P. eds. 1997. *Beyond Cultural Imperialism: Globalization, Communication, and the New International Order.* London: Sage.

Ground Zero: For the Dedicated TV Newspeople Covering a Day of Infamy, There Was Unexpected Danger and Overwhelming Sadness. 2001. *TV Guide.* Terror Hits Home special ed. 49, no. 39: 12–16, 38–42.

Hayles, N. K. 1999. *How We Became Post-Human: Virtual Bodies in Cybernetics, Literature, and Informatics.* Chicago: University of Chicago Press.

Hirsch, J., and Oakley, R. 1995. *Somalia and Operation Restore Hope: Reflections on Peacemaking and Peacekeeping.* Washington, D.C.: U.S. Institute of Peace Press.

Hobbes, T. [1651] 1985. *Leviathan.* London: Penguin.

Iyengar, S., and Kinder, D. 1987. *News That Matters: Television and American Opinion.* Chicago: University of Chicago Press.

Katz, L. M. 1993. Graphic Photos from Somalia Gave "Urgency." *USA Today,* October 13, 8A.

Lentricchia, F. 1998. "Don DeLillo's Primal Scenes." In D. DeLillo and M. Osteen, eds., *White Noise: Text and Criticism,* 412–16. New York: Penguin Classics.

Lyotard, J. F. 1984. *The Postmodern Condition: A Report on Knowledge.* Minneapolis: University of Minnesota Press.

Mattelart, A. 1979. *Multinational Corporations and the Control of Culture.*: Atlantic Highlands, N.J.: Humanities.

McLuhan, M. [1964] 1994. *Understanding Media: The Extensions of Man.* Cambridge: MIT Press.

———. 1995a. "The Gutenberg Galaxy." In E. McLuhan and F. Zingrone, eds., *Essential McLuhan,* 97–148. New York: Basic.

———. 1995b. "The Playboy Interview." In E. McLuhan and F. Zingrone, eds., *Essential McLuhan,* 233–69. New York: Basic.

Morris, N., and Waisbord, S., eds. 2001. *Media and Globalization: Why the State Matters.* Lanham, Md.: Rowman & Littlefield.

Negroponte, N. 1995. *Being Digital.* New York: Vintage.

Rothstein, E. 2001. Attacks on U.S. Challenge the Perspective of Postmodern True Believers. *New York Times,* September 22. www.nytimes.com/2001/09/22/arts/22conn.html.

Sassen, S. 1996. *Losing Control? Sovereignty in an Age of Globalization.* New York: Columbia University Press.

Shapiro, M. 1992. *Reading the Postmodern Polity: Political Theory as Textual Practice.* Minneapolis: University of Minnesota Press.

Sharkey, J. 1993. When Is a Picture Too Graphic to Run? *American Journalism Review,* December, 188.

Shaviro, S. 1993. *The Cinematic Body.* Minneapolis: University of Minnesota Press.

Simon, C. 1998. "Internet Governance Goes Global." In V. Kubalkova, N. Onuf, and P. Kowert, eds., *International Relations in a Constructed World,* 147–69. Armonk, N.J.: M. E. Sharpe.

Siochru, S., Girard, B., and Mahan, A. 2002. *Global Media Governance: A Beginner's Guide.* Lanham, Md.: Rowman & Littlefield.

Sreberny, A. 2000. "The Global and the Local in International Communications." In J. Curran and M. Gurevitch, eds., *Mass Media and Society,* 93–119. London: Arnold.

Strobel, W. 1997. *Late-Breaking Foreign Policy: The News Media's Influence on Peace Operations.* Washington, D.C.: U.S. Institute of Peace Press.

Taylor, M., and Saarinen, E. 1994. *Imagologies: Media Philosophy.* New York: Routledge.

Warkentin, C., and Mingst, K. 2000. International Institutions, the State, and Global Civil Society in the Age of the World Wide Web. *Global Governance* 6, no. 2: 237–57.

We Watched and Wept: Americans Express Shock, Anger, and Sorrow over the Events They Witnessed on Television. 2001. *TV Guide.* Terror Hits Home special ed. 49, no. 39: 17–19, 43.

Weberman, D. 2002. "The *Matrix* Simulation and the Postmodern Age." In W. Irwin, ed., *The Matrix and Philosophy,* 225–39. Chicago: Open Court.

Zacher, M., and Sutton, B. 1996. *Governing Global Networks: International Regimes for Transportation and Communications.* Cambridge: Cambridge University Press.

Zimmermann, P. 2000. *States of Emergency: Documentaries, Wars, Democracies.* Minneapolis: University of Minnesota Press.

Žižek, S. 1992. *Looking Awry: An Introduction to Jacques Lacan through Popular Culture.* Cambridge: MIT Press.

———. 1993. *Tarrying with the Negative: Kant, Hegel, and the Critique of Ideology.* Durham, N.C.: Duke University Press.

6

The Weird Global Media Event and the Tactical Intellectual

McKenzie Wark

Media Times

THE ALMOST INSOLUBLE TASK IS to let neither the power of others, nor our own powerlessness, stupefy us."[1] Theodor Adorno was writing of the intellectual's challenge in comprehending Hitler, but the same injunction may apply to more recent events. As with Hitler, so with Osama bin Laden: to a psychologist both might be pathological cases, but "people thinking in the form of free, detached, disinterested appraisal" are "unable to accommodate within those forms the experience of violence which in reality annuls such thinking."

Traditional scholarship characteristically assumes a certain kind of time within which the scholarly enterprise can unfold. Scholarship is knowledge occupying an abstract, homogeneous, formal time. Indeed scholarship may be defined as the production of precisely this kind of time. A scholar's primary duty is to patiently work through what her predecessors and colleagues deposited for her in the archive.

As a consequence, scholarship has difficulties with images that, as Walter Benjamin said, "flash up in a moment of danger."[2] Such images interrupt the time of scholarship, breaking the thread of its apparent continuity. There are always parallel times—the news media ticks over at a faster rate than scholarship. The time of everyday life takes its distance and insists on its own rhythms. These times may occasionally synchronize, but mostly they follow their own beat.

Every now and then an event interrupts all such discrete and parallel times, cutting across them and marking them all with the image of a moment of danger. September 11 interrupted the time of news media. The evidence is there in videotapes of CNN and other live news feeds. The news story suddenly confronted its opposite, which I would call the event. A routine news story has a narrative structure that preexists any given circumstances. Facts, when they emerge, can be fitted into a story. An event is as an irruption of raw facticity into the news, for which a story is not ready at hand.

The event, when it occurs in news media, opens up a certain abyss. One stares at the evidence of an event for which the story is lacking or, rather, lagging. News media respond with a range of coping strategies to paper over the evident fact that events have violated the narrative control and management of the news media, at least for the moment.

One coping strategy is repetition. News feeds reiterate a cluster of images and sounds over and over, as if the facticity of the event could only be acknowledged through repetition. Exploratory attempts are made using file footage to construct a beginning to the event. Events always irrupt into news as if in the middle. News responds by speculating on the beginning point for the story. As the narrative arc of the event is unknown or unstable, wise white-haired gentlemen are recruited to provide a speculative trajectory, a template, that reduces the event to some familiar variant on the common stock of stories.

The event now has the capacity to synchronize many diverse local times, spilling over into the living rooms, bars, bazaars, and places of worship of many different kinds of people. Local and communal rhythms suddenly appear to be connected to global forces and relations. Yet for all that, it proves remarkably difficult to think back from one's experience to the causes of the event itself. The *New Yorker* put some of the most distinguished writers in town on the job of recording their experiences of September 11. The results were remarkably banal. Star writers from Jonathan Franzen to Adam Gopnik could all provide richly detailed versions of their whereabouts on the day, connected to nothing but trivial remarks about the more abstract forces at work.

As Fredric Jameson notes, this is an era in which the forces that determine one's life chances are abstract and global, yet the means by which one would usually communicate about one's life chances with others, one's immediate experience, appears as merely an effect of unseen forces. "There comes into being, then, a situation in which we can say that if individual experience is authentic, then it cannot be true; and that if a scientific or cognitive model of the same content is true, then it escapes individual experience."[3] This is a problem, as Jameson notes, for art; it is also a problem, as he doesn't note, for critical theory.

While I agree with Jameson on the disconnect between appearances and relations, which in art is the disconnect between naturalism and realism, I think there is a solution. One needs to displace the terms a little. The disconnect can be expressed as a difference between kinds of time. The time of everyday life not only differs from the time of news media and the time of scholarship, it differs from the time of capital flows and global power. The latter appear in everyday life as images that flash up, not just in moments of danger but as moments of danger. The moment when they flash up is the moment of the event. The event opens a critical window onto the disjuncture between different kinds of time precisely because it is the moment when times suddenly connect, even if, in connecting, the usual means of making sense of time within the horizon of a specific temporal narrative is obliterated.

So if one is not to be stupefied by the power of others, or one's own powerlessness, one needs to know something of the time in which power operates. But this is a temporality to which one usually does not have access, either in everyday life, scholarship, or art—it is even doubtful if the news media is all that proximate to the most effective times of power and powers of time. But there are moments, interruptions in the polyrhythmic flow, in which a kind of knowledge is possible.

These moments are events. Or to give them the full specification I have given them elsewhere, "weird global media events."[4] They are events because they interrupt routine time. They are media events because they happen within a space and time saturated in media. They are global media events because they traverse borders and call a world into being. They are weird global media events because each is singular and none conform to any predetermined narrative. They introduce a new quality of time.

The event not only breaches the separation among what we might call after Marx superstructural times, but between them and what we might call infrastructural times of political and economic power. As Jameson notes, Marx borrowed this terminology from the railways. Superstructure and infrastructure are the rolling stock and the rails. In these terms, the event might be the juncture at which both the track and the train change paths.

Media Spaces

Where do events come from? Do they fall from the sky? Yes they do. From the comsat angels in orbit overhead or thrown from a truck onto the ground in front of your local newsstand. Robert McChesney points out that these vectors from whence we get the information to form an ongoing map of the world and its histories becomes increasingly concentrated in fewer and fewer corporate hands. These corporate owners are increasingly integrating diverse media holdings to more profitably coordinate print and audiovisual flows.[5] No matter how many channels we can get, our main news feed comes from few hands indeed.

Herbert Schiller once argued that the growth of transnational corporations, who seek rich offshore markets and cheap offshore labor forces, necessitates an internationalization of media vectors. The deregulation of economic flows during the Reagan years went hand in hand with a deregulation of information flows and attacks on public control and access to information.[6] The media that feed us are not only more and more concentrated, but increasingly global in both ownership and extent. Since business consumes a vast amount of media information, and business is increasingly global, so too are the information providers. Three developments come together: the globalization of business communication, the communication of global business, and the business of global communication.

The global media vector does not connect us with just anywhere. It connects us most frequently, rapidly, and economically with those parts of the world which are well integrated into the major hubs of the vector. It comes as no surprise that New York is a major media hub, as it is a major business hub, but so too is the Middle East. Hamid Mowlana points out that the Middle East has a long history of integration into the international media vector. At the turn of the century, Lord Curzon described British interests in the Persian Gulf as "commercial, political, strategical and telegraphic."[7] Some of the world's first international telegraph lines passed through there. British communications with India flowed along this route. With the recognition of the strategic value of oil for propelling the mechanized vectors of war from 1914 on, the region became important in its own right.

An event that connects an expatriate Saudi to New York so spectacularly is, not surprisingly, an event that punctures the time of everyday life with a major impact. One should, however, add Tariq Ali's caveat: "To accept that the appalling deaths of over 3,000 people in the USA are more morally abhorrent than the 20,000 lives destroyed by Putin when he razed Grosny or the daily casualties in Palestine and Iraq is obscene" (Ali 2002, 290). In proposing that September 11 is a weird global media event, I am not assuming that the violence of that moment somehow trumps these other instances of violence. The point is rather that the globalization of media flows is subject to very uneven development. One of the characteristics of the event is precisely to reveal the uneven topography of the vectoral landscape along which media messages speed.

One of the striking things about September 11 is that the event happened in a major node in the media network, and hence was rapidly and thoroughly reported, thus provoking remarkably different responses around the world. Ali records some of the range of responses: "In the Nicaraguan capital, Managua, people hugged each other in silence. . . . There were celebrations in the streets of Bolivia. . . . In Greece the government suppressed the publication of opinion polls that showed a large majority actually in favor of the hits. . . . In Beijing the news came too late in the night for anything more than a few celebratory fireworks" (Ali 2002, 2). The centralization and concentration of media has some effect on what events may spark across the vector field of time and space, but does not necessarily determine how they may be interpreted, which still depends on the tempos of everyday life and of local media envelopes. The people make meaning, but not with the media of their own choosing.

The "global village" is a fractious and contentious place, particularly when the lightning strike of an event gives way to the thunder of a thousand pundits explaining it away. Local interpretive strategies and authorities invariably script the event in terms that make it appear as if it were meant to make sense within the dominant local framework. John Hartley suggests that "news includes stories on a daily basis which enable everyone to recognize a larger unity or community than their own immediate contacts, and to identify with the news outlet as 'our' storyteller" (Hartley 1992, 207). The protocols of everyday life appear here as the imagined categories of a far more vast and unevenly global terrain of what I call telesthesia, of perception at a distance. This world of telesthesia is organized temporally in terms of "visible, distant visions of order," but where these are highlighted negatively by "the fundamental test of newsworthiness," namely, "disorder—deviation from any supposed steady state" (Hartley 1992, 140). Telesthesia is organized spatially by what Hartley calls Theydom. "Individuals in Theydom are treated as being all the same; their identity consists in being 'unlike us,' so they are 'like each other.'"

Slavoj Žižek and Edward Said offer a general and a specific theory respectively that may help us reconstruct, after the event, our own narrative about how the narrative of Theydom works. To start with the specific theory: Said proposes the category of Orientalism to account for the doubling of a Wedom with a Theydom, in which the defining characteristics of Wedom come into focus against the background of a Theydom. The opening up of the Middle East to European trade, conquest, and most importantly communication opens up a vector field in which information may flow across boundaries for the purpose of commerce or colonization, but where that flow produces an anxious desire for a sense of border or boundary. That boundary is defined by Orientalism, a discourse by, for, and secretly about Wedom, sustained by the image of a Theydom, in which it is axiomatic that the "attributes of being Oriental overrode any countervailing instance."[8]

For Žižek, the Orientalist image of Theydom might count as a local and specific variant on a general structure: "We always impute to the 'other' an excessive enjoyment; s/he wants to steal our enjoyment by ruining our way of life and/or has access to some secret, perverse enjoyment."[9] As if to illustrate such a theory, one of the more popular images to circulate via e-mail shortly after September 11 was a Photoshop collage of Osama bin Laden sodomizing President George

W. Bush. For Žižek, the other is dangerous because Theydom either pursue enjoyment too much or too little. In the construction of a Theydom in the wake of September 11, the focus is usually on terrorist as denier of pleasure, as a fanatic, a militant. But curiously, this image keeps flipping over into its other. The terrorist is also the one panting after the seventy virgins promised in paradise or putting liquor and lap dances on the al Qaeda credit card.

So far we have two things defining the space of September 11. One is the presence of a vector from where the World Trade Center is to wherever you are. The other is a set of everyday conventions operating to make the fate of its victims, who belong to Wedom, the subject of sympathy or mourning, and an evil Theydom. There is a connection and a convention, in time and space, making those fatal flights fall from the sky into our lives.

Whatever the virtues of the work of Said and Žižek, neither really offers a narrative of the dialectic of Wedom and Theydom that takes full account of the role of the time of the event in creating and recreating the boundaries, nor do they highlight the role of telesthesia in the formation of Wedom and Theydom on a global scale. The weird global media event is more than an anomaly in the "normal" functioning of culture; it is the moment that disrupts its normal functioning, and in the wake of which a new norm will be created.

How then can such a weird global media event be conceptualized? The event as I define it is something that unfolds within the movement of telesthesia along media vectors. These media vectors connect the site at which a crisis appears with the sites of image management and interpretation. Vectors then disseminate the flows of images processed at those managerial sites to the terminal sites of the process, so they fall from the sky into our lives. In this instance the vector connects a bewildering array of places: New York, Managua, Beijing. Into the vision mix went images hauled off the global satellite feed, showing us file footage of Osama bin Laden one second and live footage of Mayor Giuliani the next, as if the mayor were responding to that absent figure. The vector creates the space of telesthesia where one can appear quite "naturally" to respond to the other, in the blink of an edit. We witnessed the montaging of familiar and surprising sites into the seamless space and staccato time of the media vector. The terminal site of the vector is the radio, television, or Internet terminal within reach—directly or indirectly—of almost everyone almost everywhere.

Vectors and Antipodes

A word on this word "vector." I've adapted it from the writings of Paul Virilio. It describes the aspect of the development of technology that interests him most and the style of writing he employs to capture that aspect. It is a term from geometry meaning a line of fixed length and direction but having no fixed position. Virilio employs it to mean any trajectory along which bodies, information, or warheads can potentially pass. The satellite technology used to beam images from Afghanistan to America can be thought of as a vector. This technology could link almost any two such sites, and relay video and audio information of a certain quality along those points at a given speed and at a certain cost. It could just as easily have linked Copenhagen to Chiapas, or quite a few other combinations of points. Yet in each case the speed of transmission and its quality could be essentially the same. That it often is not points to the politics and economics that shape the infrastructure of the vector field, but which it in turn also shapes.

This is the sense in which any particular media technology can be thought of as a vector. Media vectors have fixed properties, like the length of a line in the geometric concept of vector. Yet that vector has no necessary position: it can link almost any points together. This is the paradox of the media vector. The technical properties are hard and fast and fixed, but it can connect enormously vast and vaguely defined spaces together and move images, and sounds, words, and furies between them.

In every weird global media event, new dimensions to the vector field are "discovered" and new technical properties of the vector implemented. After September 11, the Western world discovered—as if for the first time—the significance of al-Jazeera satellite television.[10] During the Gulf War, most of the Middle East was more or less effectively contained within state-controlled national media envelopes, at least as far as television was concerned. Al-Jazeera changed all that. Or to take a more poignant instance: it seems that while people all over the world knew that one of the WTC towers had collapsed, the firefighters in the other tower did not, as the vectors along which information might pass to them were disrupted by the collapse of the tower itself. Telesthesia failed at the point where it was most pressingly required.

In the analysis of the weird global media event, a theoretical approach that highlights the technical, such as the concept of the vector, is crucial but must be handled as a critical tool. Everyone marvels at what the latest media technologies make possible in the moment of the event. It is one of the most immediate ways of constructing a narrative for it. But then the material means by which the space in which the event happens is constructed tends to be pushed to the background. The knowledge of the vector that the event highlights passes imperceptibly into an unacknowledged part of the information landscape we take for granted. Victor Shklovsky once said that the real reveals itself in culture in much the same way as gravity reveals itself to the inhabitants of a structure when its ceiling caves in on them.[11] That might stand as a good emblem for the event.

It is not only media technologies that have this vectoral aspect. The hijacked 767s were also a vector. So too are the bombs and missiles rained down on Afghanistan in what Ali calls the "lightly disguised war of revenge" (Ali 2002, 3). All of these vectors had certain fixed technical properties: payload, range, and accuracy. Yet they could be launched at any point within a given radius. On the other hand, one could think of the entire U.S. invasion force that mobilized for what President Bush initially called Operation Infinite Justice as a vector too. The fixed properties here have to do with the length of time it takes to deploy a force of a given size. Yet that force could be deployed almost anywhere. Indeed, in an age of proliferating media vectors, perhaps the public spectacle of a threat to the interests of imperial powers will provoke the deployment of this other kind of vector. The alternative, something we also saw on TV during the war in Afghanistan, is the vector of diplomacy: diplomats can shuttle between any series of points negotiating an apparently limitless range of demands with seemingly limited results. The time pressures introduced by the military and media vectors pose a serious problem for the tactful tempo of diplomacy.

The beauty of Virilio's concept of vector is that it grasps the dynamic, historical tendency of weird global media events, but it is not a concept limited to media technologies alone. It also provides a way of thinking about the other aspects of such events. Virilio homes in on the apparent tendencies that seem to result from the relentless, competitive development of vectors. For instance, the tendency toward a homogenization of the space of the globe. Its tendency to become an abstract, geometric space across which powerful vectors can play freely, producing new differentials of Wedom and Theydom.

Virilio grasps the novel kinds of crisis this seems to engender: "An imperceptible movement on a computer keyboard, or one made by a 'skyjacker' brandishing a cookie box covered with masking tape, can lead to catastrophic chains of events that until recently were inconceivable. We are too willing to ignore the threat of proliferation resulting from the acquisition of nuclear explosives by irresponsible parties. We are even more willing to ignore the proliferating threat resulting from the vectors that cause those who own or borrow them to become just as irresponsible."[12]

There is a limit to the way Virilio conceptualizes the vector, in that he doesn't distinguish the vectors of telesthesia, which move information, from those that move bodies and things, labor and commodities, subjects and objects. Thus he loses focus on the way telesthesia creates a space for the logistical tracking of objects and subjects in movement, and for ordering that movement. The second nature of labor and commodities, of work and leisure, of private and public worlds, is traversed by an emergent space composed of vectors capable of moving information more quickly than people or things can move. Just as second nature is built out of the historical transformation of the raw materials of nature, so too a third nature arises, built out of the historical transformation of second nature by the vectors of telesthesia.

Perhaps it is worth hitting the video pause button at this point in the replay, just as the image of the 767 hitting the WTC comes into view. Here we have a vector of second nature, the ubiquitous passage of the 767 through the skies, which is only made possible by the existence of a third nature, of radio and radar and global positioning technology. And here we have the rerouting of the aircraft, using that same technology of telesthesia, to new coordinates, bringing about an event in the most built up part of second nature, New York City, which in turn disrupts the third nature of the news media.

What bears critical attention is the way telesthesia is part and parcel of what killed people in both New York and subsequently in Afghanistan. The event takes place at the level of the physical vector and the media vector conjointly. In terms of vectoral power in general, the media are part of the problem of power, not merely a separate space of reportage or critique of emergent forms of power that exist elsewhere. Needless to say, this chapter too is a part of that problematic and does not exist outside, in a neutral space. It is in the worst of all possible worlds: within the regime of power created by the media vector, but relatively powerless there, within. What is indeed stupefying is that the ability to think critically about the event depends on the same vectoral power that produces its violence.

Reading the critical coverage of September 11 and the subsequent war in Afghanistan in journals such as the *Nation*, I am struck first by the double bind its correspondents found themselves in, and second by the curious way that the critical response to imperial power nevertheless participated in the same way of seeing the world. As Michel Feher notes, the leftist response to such events is caught between two desires. One desire is to oppose American imperial power, in which case it can appear to lend support to dictatorial anti-Western regimes. The other desire is to overturn tyranny in dictatorial anti-Western regimes, in which case it ends up lending support to American imperial power.[13] Either way, the rhetorical structure of Wedom versus Theydom is reproduced, without really addressing the vectoral power that underlies the production of their relation in the first place.

The massive presence in the media flow of American stories, images, faces, voices, is sometimes all that stabilizes the flow of meaning in third nature. Take away America's imaginary domination and the domination of the imaginary of America, and meaning would drift and eddy, caught in impossible turbulence and glide.[14] Not only the instant media coverage, but also the critical coverage relies on this stabilization of the referents, either positively or negatively. The frightening paradox of September 11 is how this attack on actual human lives in New York and Afghanistan is at the same time merely an attack on abstract signifiers of Wedom and Theydom. The trick, if this is not to stupefy us, is to look for a way of displacing the terms within which the event is understood.

Nightly Chimeras

By starting with the appearance of the vector in everyday life, we can trace it back to a general problematic of the velocity of power. The "departure lounge" for this is not some abstract concept of everyday life in general, not the life of others, under the microscope, but *this* life, *these* events. A vectoral writing strategy considers the production of events within the media as the primary process that nevertheless gives the appearance of merely *reflecting* "naturally occurring" moments outside all such apparatus.

This may sound counterintuitive, since we all tend to take it for granted that regardless of how much the media constructs a particular view of an event the media still *reports* something outside of itself. While not disputing the fact that violent and momentous conjunctures arise whether the media report them or not, once the media takes up such conjunctures they assume a quite different character. A vectoral approach looks at movements of information transgressing the boundaries between what were once historically distinct sites. It looks at the effect of this movement on the outcomes of conjunctures. It looks at the event as a peculiar and historically emergent form of communication—or rather of noncommunication.

Writing about September 11 as an event happening in a network of global vectors, which made it that much more instant, that much more deadly, struggles to recall that we are not just spectators. The whole thing about the media vector is that its tendency is toward *implicating* the entire globe. Its historic tendency is toward making any and every point a possible connection—everyone and everything is a potential object and/or subject of a mediated relation, realized instantly. In September 11, to see it was to be implicated in it. There is no safe haven from which to observe, unaffected. Nor is there a synoptic vantage point, above and beyond the whole process for looking on in a detached and studious manner. We are all, always, already—there, in third nature.

As the possibility of an extensive war of revenge increased, the media's role changed, ever so imperceptibly. No longer did it exist in a relation to an audience assumed to be a mass of consumers or a public to be educated.[15] The event turns the media into part of a feedback loop connecting the spectator to the action via the vagaries of "opinion" and the pressures of the popular on political elites. The media user becomes a vague and quixotic, unpredictable yet manipulatory "delay" in the circuit of power.[16]

This is the curious thing about telesthesia. It can make events that connect the most disparate sites of public action appear simultaneously as a private drama filled with familiar characters and moving stories. The vector blurs the thin line between political crisis and media sensation; it eclipses the geographical barriers separating distinct cultural and political entities; and it transgresses the borders between public and private spheres both on the home front and the front line. There is no longer a clear distinction between public and private spaces, now that the vector transgresses the boundaries of the private sphere.

As Donna Haraway suggests, "we are all chimeras, theorized and fabricated hybrid of machine and organism."[17] Our chimerical confusion may result from the dissolution of the spaces that kept aspects of the social order separate. Indeed, one of the defining characteristics of the event is that it exposes the ironic ability of the vector to disrupt all seemingly stable distributions of space and the more or less water-tight vessels that used to contain meaning in space and time. As September 11 unfolded, the hallowed ground bled into the profane domain—of media. One keeps the sense of what it means to be in public life as opposed to private life by keeping them spatially separate. The horror of bodies jumping from the towers—a rare image, quickly edited out—has a layer to it that draws on the horror of the separate and excluded part reappearing in the everyday sphere of "normality."

The reasons why these interpretations should spring to mind stem from another sense of separation, the separation of such things off from Wedom and their projection into an other. Yet here they are, returned to haunt us, in an uncontrollable way. Here they are in everyday life, intersected by the rays of the screen. To adapt a line from William Burroughs, in an incongruous yet strikingly apt context: "These things were revealed to me in the Interzone, where East meets West coming around the other way."[18] The interzone is this space where chimerical and monstrous images become a part of everyday life. The interzone is the experience, in everyday life, of the ironizing impact of the event.

The media weave a Wedom and a vast map of Theydoms together as the light and dark strands of a narrative distinction within the event as it of threads its way across these other kinds of border. In breaking down solid old boundaries, the vector creates new distinctions. Flexible distinctions airily flow through the story-time realm of information. They selectively replace the heavy walls and barriers that compartmentalized information in days when vectors were less rapid and less effective. This cruder narrative structure can be applied to more sudden and diverse events to produce the same effect of apparent narrative seamlessness. The application by the media of simple temporal structures, in a flexible fashion, produces more rigid and uniform stories about events.

There are many analyses of these wartime bedtime stories that expose the interests of capital and empire that lie behind them.[19] What matters is telling convincing stories, which show others ways to account for the facts—and for the way facts are produced. Or persuasive stories, which help as many people as possible to credit this version of the event over other ones. The democratic forces that want to rewrite this event as a chapter in the story of, say, American imperialism or Orientalist racism, must learn the tools and the tricks of the story trade—and prevail.

As the technology of persuasion grows more complex, the art of telling stories in the wake of events grows both more complex and more instantaneous. If this chapter is less concerned with telling these alternative stories it is not because such things are not important. It is because it is also important to understand the nature of weird global media events and the power field of the vector. This is the field of becoming within which a certain kind of power is immanent. A field in which democratic forces need to speak, and attempt at least to make good sense, for and with, the many against the few. But the tools for doing so may have less to do with the hypocritical earnestness of Wedom and more to do with pushing the ironic spatial and temporal displacements of vectors to the limit.

Tactical Media and Tactical Knowledge

As Montaigne remarked, there are certain viewpoints that expose us to our own fundamental state of ignorance. Confronting an event in the media is such a viewpoint. This is not to celebrate stupidity, merely to recognize that there are no authorities one can evoke when genuine, full-blown, out-of-control events occur. And this is precisely why outlets like CNN wheel out the white-haired authorities at the first whiff of a weird global media event. There is, however, always a store of useful information and sets of conceptual tools that might help. Access to these is a form of power that can be very unevenly distributed. The vector is a form of power. Rapid and effective access to useful information is a vector. Not all vectors are extensive ones, seeking to cover the span of the globe. Some are intensive. They seek microscopic paths through the labyrinthine mazes of data stored in the cores of the information-rich archives of the West.

Some of the really useful information is "classified." It will be released very slowly and to few people. On the other hand, conceptual tools for extracting the most out of the information that is freely available about any actual or potential event are available to a much wider pool of people. I believe this "tactical response" to the media vector to be a worthwhile skill to learn, to teach, to practice and communicate. But there is a caveat. When responding in a timely fashion to events that stupefy, it is important not to respond stupidly, reactively, with a reflexive negation that merely reproduces the dialectical terms of Wedom and Theydom. Rather, one has to deploy tactics that display a certain ironic knowledge about how the vector works and attempts to reach that everyday interzone where, in the wake of the event, boundaries seem to dissolve and irony finds its intemperate time.

Geert Lovink and David Garcia speak of a tactical media that might free itself from the dialectic of being an alternative or opposition that merely reproduces the sterile sense of a Wedom versus a Theydom in the media sphere.[20] They claim that the "identity politics, media critiques and theories of representation" that were the foundation of oppositional media practices "are themselves in crisis." They propose instead an "existential aesthetic" based on the temporary "creation of spaces, channels and platforms." Lovink and Garcia's seminal text on tactical media doesn't entirely succeed in extracting itself from the oppositional language of Wedom versus Theydom, but it points toward an alternative strategy to the negation that paradoxically unites Osama bin Laden, George W. Bush, and the writers of the *Nation* as purveyors, not of the same worldview but of worldviews constructed the same way. It is a question of combining tactical media with a tactical knowledge, of using the extensive vector of the media in combination with the intensive vector of the scholarly archive.

In a nominally democratic country, one acts as part of a public sphere in the sense Alexander Kluge gives to the term.[21] A public sphere—a matrix of accessible vectors—acts as a point of exchange between private experience and public life; between intimate, incommunicable experience and collective perception. Public networks are arenas where the struggle to communicate takes place. Two aspects of this concept are relevant here. For Kluge, writing in postwar Germany, the problem revolves around the historic failure in 1933 of the public sphere to prevent the rise of fascism. "Since 1933 we have been waging a war that has not stopped. It is always the same theme—the noncorrelation of intimacy and public life—and the same question: how can I communicate strong emotions to build a common life?"[22] For Kluge, the public sphere is a fundamentally problematic domain, caught between the complexities of the social and the increasing separation of private life.

For whom does Kluge imagine he speaks? Perhaps there are other experiences of the relation between the time of intimate experience and the time of the public sphere, buried out there in popular culture. Perhaps it is only intellectuals who feel so estranged from the time of information in the era of telesthesia. After all, the mode of address adopted by most popular media doesn't speak to a highly cultured intellectual like Kluge—or even a provincial one like me. We were trained in slower ways of handling information and have a repertoire of quite different stories with which to filter present events. How could we claim to know what goes on out there in the other interzones, in quite other spaces where different flows from different vectors meet quite other memories and experiences of everyday life? After all, we intellectuals keep finding more than enough differences among ourselves.

A tactical knowledge of media may have among its merits the fact that it takes these other interzones seriously. It tries to theorize the frictions between Kluge's intimate experience and the network of vectors, or it actually tries to collect and interpret accounts of such experiences.[23] It is necessary to at least attempt to maintain a self-critical relation to the codes and practices of the interzone specific to intellectual media experiences. After all, "our" training, "our" prejudices in relation to the vector might be part of the problem. Nothing exempts "our" institutions and interests from the war of the vector, the struggle to control the trajectories of information.

With the spread of the vector into the private realm, a window opens that might be used to create a line along which the communication of intimate experience and collective feeling might take place, in those eventful moments when their separation collapses. The protocols of tactical media are not given in advance. As Gilles Deleuze says, "Experiment, never interpret."[24] What is at stake is not the recreation of the public grounds for a universal reason, but finding the tactical resources for a far more differentiated and diverse struggle to communicate, that simple thing so hard to achieve.[25]

The maintenance of democracy requires a practice within the public networks for responding to events that it was never quite designed to handle. Virilio asks whether democracy is still possible in this era of what he calls "chronopolitics." Perhaps democracy succumbs to "dromocracy"—the power of the people plowed under by the power to technological speed.[26] The only way to forestall such pessimism is to experiment with tactics for knowing and acting in the face of events. One has to experiment with relatively freely available conceptual tools and practices and base a democratic knowledge on them. This may involve moving beyond the techniques and procedures of the academy. In Antonio Gramsci's terms, the academic intellectual risks becoming merely a traditional intellectual, one of many layers of cultural sediment, deposited and passed over by the engine capital and the trajectory of the vector, caught up in a temporality that is not even dialectically resistant but is merely residual. One has to make organic connections with the leading media and cultural practices of the day.[27]

Nevertheless, the historic memory and living tissue of scholarship store resources that are useful and vital. In studying an event like September 11, a tactical knowledge can build on the best of two existing critical approaches. To the schools that concentrate on the structural power of transnational capital flows and military coercion it adds a close attention to the power of transgressive media vectors and the specific features of the events they generate. To the schools that study the space of the media text in the context of periodic struggles for influence with the national-popular discourse it adds an international dimension and a closer attention to the changing technical means that produce information flows. The event is a phenomenon a little too slippery for either of these approaches. Hence the need to examine it in a new light, as the chance encounter of the local conjuncture with the global vector—on the operating table.

The chance encounter of Osama bin Laden with CNN, like the meeting of the umbrella with the sewing machine, has a surreal, "surgical" logic specific to it. It is not entirely reducible to the long-term temporalities of capital or military power and lies in the spaces between national-popular discourses. Writing the vector is not really something that can be practiced with the tools of the Herbert Schiller school of political economy or the Stuart Hall school of cultural studies alone, although a tactical knowledge might owe something to both.[28] A tactical intellectual practice that uses the moment of the event to cross the divide between infrastructural and superstructural time.

The event is not reducible to the methods of the "areas specialists." When studying events from the point of view of the site at which they originate, they always remain the province of specialists who deal with that particular turf. Events often generate valuable responses from area specialists, but these usually focus on the economic, political, or cultural factors at work in the area the specialists know firsthand. They do not often analyze the vectoral trajectories via which the rest of the world views the event. A tactical knowledge borrows from area studies without being caught within its territorial prerogatives.

In an age when transnational media flows are running across all those academic specialties, perhaps it is time to construct a discourse that follows the flow of information and power across both the geographic and conceptual borders of discourse. Perhaps it is time to start experimenting, as Kluge has done, with modes of disseminating critical information in the vector field. Perhaps it is time to examine intellectual practices of storing, retrieving, and circulating knowledge. Without wishing to return to the practice of the "general intellectual," it may be worth considering whether the development of the vector calls for new ways for playing the role of the tactical intellectual.[29] The tactical intellectual would combine the practices of tactical media and tactical scholarship, while being careful not to fall into the temporality of either journalism or the academy, but rather remain alert to the moments in which such distinct times are brought into crisis by the time of the event.

Afghan eXplorer

The Afghan eXplorer is described on its Web site as "a tele-operated, robotic war reporting system, able to provide images, sound, and interviews in real time."[30] It bears an uncanny resemblance to the Mars Explorer. As the Web site notes, "One central advantage of Afghanistan over Mars is that Afghanistan features tens of thousands of miles of functioning roadways." Its makers state that "the system may be retrofitted, with only minor software modifications, to work in other potential hotspots, such as Palestine, Israel, Iraq, Syria, Sudan, Lebanon, Indonesia, Pakistan and Qatar." These might all qualify, in the eXplorer's subtle and ironic displacement, as alien landscapes to Western journalism and its audience.

Chris Csikszentmihályi, who led the team that designed it at MIT's Media Lab, reports that when journalists started to hear about the eXplorer, interest rapidly snowballed.[31] Journalists love to write about themselves, and journalists tend to write about what other journalists are writing about. So Csikszentmihályi found himself fielding calls from journalists in a wide range of media, all interested in the eXplorer. The eXplorer touches on the interzone of journalistic experience.

Csikszentmihályi says he studied Noam Chomsky's approach to responding to interviews, and learned from Chomsky the practice of ignoring the journalist's questions and hammering away at one's own agenda. The agenda as far as he was concerned was to emphasize the military's closing the field of conflict to fair and unbiased reporting, and the use of what he calls "robotic killing machines" in Operation Infinite Justice. The eXplorer calls attention to the effect of the vector in a double sense: the robotic war vector appears in a displaced form as the robotic journalism vector, which in turn refers to the absence of journalists from infrastructural deployment of military vectoral power.

While Csikszentmihályi would not necessarily embrace the term, I want to use the Afghan eXplorer as a striking instance of tactical intellectual work. Csikszentmihályi was able to exploit mainstream media's fascination with its own practices of reporting, and also a fascination with technological solutions to political problems to his advantage, inserting a point of view into the media feed that is not oppositional but cuts across Wedom and Theydom at an ironic tangent, displacing the terms within which one may think about the event. The eXplorer manages to reconnect the naturalism of the experience with its quirky form and function, with the realism of the abstract relations of vectoral power for which it is so ironic, and iconic, an interzone.

Csikszentmihályi was able to insert at least some mention of this other perspective into interviews with journalists not only in the United States but also in Pakistan and at the BBC World Service. He notes that live radio and television interviews were particularly good tactical opportunities. Print media journalists usually plug the facts of the Afghan eXplorer story into preexisting scripts. The eXplorer provides the tactical leverage for a fact-gathering mission into what for many artists or scholars is the alien world of news media time.

One way of disentangling this practice of the tactical intellectual from oppositional or alternative media strategies is to see it as being a kind of microevent in itself. The media tactician presents an image that endangers the conventions of journalistic narrative time yet is capable of inserting itself into it. This kind of tactical media ironically displaces the boundaries drawn by the machine of the news story. The moment when such a tactic is most likely to be successful is when news media time has itself already been disrupted by an event of a much larger scale—a weird global media event, for instance. In that moment of instability, the ironic displacement of a tactical media microevent may find its purchase on media time.

Notes

1. Theodor Adorno, *Minima Moralia* (London: New Left Books, 1974), 57.

2. Walter Benjamin, "Theses on the Philosophy of History." In *Illuminations* (London: Fontana, 1973).

3. Fredric Jameson, "Cognitive Mapping," in Cary Nelson and Lawrence Grossberg, eds., *Marxism and the Interpretation of Culture* (Urbana: University of Illinois Press, 1988), 349.

4. McKenzie Wark, *Virtual Geography: Living with Global Media Events* (Bloomington: Indiana University Press, 1994), 21–24.

5. Robert McChesney, *Rich Media, Poor Democracy* (New York: New Press, 2000).

6. Herbert Schiller, *Culture Inc: The Corporate Takeover of Public Expression* (New York: Oxford University Press, 1989).

7. Quoted in Hamid Mowlana, "Roots of War: The Long Road to Intervention," in Hamid Mowlana et al., eds., *Triumph of the Image: The Media's War in the Persian Gulf—A Global Perspective* (Boulder, Colo.: Westview, 1992), 30–50, at 36.

8. Edward Said, *Orientalism* (Harmondsworth, U.K.: Penguin, 1978), 231.

9. Slavoj Žižek, "Eastern Europe's Republics of Gilead," *New Left Review*, September 1990, 53–54.

10. Mohammed El-Nawawy et al., *Al Jazeera: How the Free Arab News Network Scooped the World and Changed the Middle East* (Boulder, Colo.: Westview, 2002).

11. Victor Shklovsky, *Mayakovsky and His Circle* (London: Pluto, 1978).

12. Paul Virilio, *Speed and Politics* (New York: Semiotext(e), 1986), 143–44. See also McKenzie Wark, "On Technological Time," *Arena* 83 (1988).

13. Michel Feher, *Powerless by Design: The Age of the International Community* (Durham, N.C.: Duke University Press, 2000).

14. See McKenzie Wark, "From Fordism to Sonyism: Perverse Readings of the New World Order," *New Formations* 15: 1991.

15. Ien Ang, *Desperately Seeking the Audience* (London: Routledge, 1991).

16. Gilles Deleuze, *Bergsonism* (New York: Zone, 1988). Deleuze's thinking takes the form of a reading of the first chapter of Henri Bergson, *Matter and Memory* (New York: Zone, 1991).

17. Donna J. Haraway, "A Cyborg Manifesto," in *Simians, Cyborgs, and Women: The Reinvention of Nature* (New York: Routledge, 1991), 150.

18. William Burroughs, "Word," in *Interzone* (London: Picador, 1989), 137.

19. See, for instance, Noam Chomsky, *9-11* (New York: Seven Stories. 2002); Michael Parenti, *The Terrorism Trap* (San Francisco: City Lights Books, 2002).

20. Geert Lovink and David Garcia, "The ABC of Tactical Media," www.ljudmila .org/nettime/zkp4/74.htm.

21. On the public sphere, see Alexander Kluge and Oskar Negt, "The Public Sphere and Experience: Selections," *October*, no. 46, Fall 1988; and Stuart Liebman, "On New German Cinema, Art, Enlightenment, and the Public Sphere: An Interview with Alexander Kluge," *October*, Fall 1988.

22. Liebman, "New German Cinema," 45.

23. See, for example, John Fiske, *Television Culture* (London: Methuen, 1989); Ien Ang, *Watching Dallas* (London: Methuen, 1985).

24. Gilles Deleuze and Claire Parnet, *Dialogues* (New York: Columbia University Press, 1987), 48.

25. Writings by Kluge and Oskar Negt on the public sphere, such as "The Public Sphere and Experience: Selections," *October*, Fall 1988, are a critical response to Jürgen Habermas, *The Transformation of the Public Sphere* (Cambridge: Polity, 1989).

26. Paul Virilio, *Pure War*, Foreign Agents Series (New York: Semiotext(e), 1983), 58.

27. Antonio Gramsci, "The Intellectuals," in *Selections from the Prison Notebooks* (New York: International, 1980).

28. Schiller, *Culture Inc;* Stuart Hall, *The Hard Road to Renewal* (London: Verso, 1988).

29. Russell Jacoby laments the decline of the public intellectual in *The Last Intellectuals* (New York: Farrar, Straus & Giroux, 1989). He argues that while radical academics have inserted new content into academic discourses, they have not changed the form. While I agree with this assessment, I am less inclined toward nostalgia for the public intellectuals of the past.

30. http://www.afghanexplorer.net.

31. Presentation by Chris Csikszentmihályi at the Blur conference, Parsons School of Design, April 12, 2002; www.nsu.newschool.edu/blur.

References

Adorno, T. 1974. *Minima Moralia.* London: New Left Books.
Ali, T. 2002. *The Clash of Fundamentalisms.* London: Verso.
Ang, I. 1985. *Watching Dallas.* London: Methuen.

————. 1991. *Desperately Seeking the Audience.* London: Routledge.

Benjamin, W. "Theses on the Philosophy of History." In *Illuminations* (London: Fontana, 1973).

Burroughs, W. 1989. "Word." In *Interzone.* London: Picador.

Chomsky, N. 2002. *9-11.* New York: Seven Stories.

Deleuze, G. 1988. *Bergsonism.* New York: Zone.

El-Nawawy, M., et al. 2000. *Al Jazeera: How the Free Arab News Network Scooped the World and Changed the Middle East.* Boulder, Colo.: Westview.

Feher, M. 2000. *Powerless by Design: The Age of the International Community.* Durham, N.C.: Duke University Press.

Fiske, J. 1989. *Television Culture.* London: Methuen.

Gramsci, A. 1980. *Selections from the Prison Notebooks.* New York: International.

Habermas, J. 1989. *The Transformation of the Public Sphere.* Cambridge: Polity.

Hall, S. 1988. *The Hard Road to Renewal.* London: Verso.

Haraway, D. 1991. *Simians, Cyborgs, and Women: The Reinvention of Nature.* New York: Routledge.

Hartley, J. 1992. *The Politics of Pictures: The Creation of the Public in the Age of Popular Media.* London: Routledge.

Jameson, F. 1988. "Cognitive Mapping." In Cary Nelson and Lawrence Grossberg, eds., *Marxism and the Interpretation of Culture.* Urbana: University of Illinois Press.

Liebman, S. 1988. "On New German Cinema, Art, Enlightenment, and the Public Sphere: An Interview with Alexander Kluge." *October* 46.

Lovink, G., and Garcia, D. n.d. "The ABC of Tactical Media." www.ljudmila.org/nettime/zkp4/74.htm.

McChesney, R. 2000. *Rich Media, Poor Democracy.* New York: New Press.

Mowlana, H. 1992. "Roots of War: The Long Road to Intervention." In H. Mowlana et al., eds., *Triumph of the Image: The Media's War in the Persian Gulf—A Global Perspective,* 30–50, at 36. Boulder, Colo.: Westview, 1992.

Parenti, M. 2002. *The Terrorism Trap.* San Francisco: City Lights.

Said, E. 1978. *Orientalism.* Harmondsworth, U.K.: Penguin.

Schiller, H. 1989. *Culture Inc: The Corporate Takeover of Public Expression.* New York: Oxford University Press.

Shklovsky, V. 1978. *Mayakovsky and His Circle.* London: Pluto.

Virilio, P. 1983. *Pure War.* Foreign Agents Series. New York: Semiotext(e).

————. 1986. *Speed and Politics.* New York: Semiotext(e).

Wark, M. 1988. "On Technological Time." *Arena* 83.

————. 1991. "From Fordism to Sonyism: Perverse Readings of the New World Order." *New Formations* 15.

————. 1994. *Virtual Geography: Living with Global Media Events.* Bloomington: Indiana University Press.

Žižek S. 1990. "Eastern Europe's Republics of Gilead." *New Left Review* September: 53–54.

7

Empire, War, and Antiwar Media

John D. H. Downing

IN THIS CHAPTER I ADDRESS the question of war—a well-established mode of international and intranational communication—and antiwar alternative media through a critical evaluation of *Empire*, by Michael Hardt and Antonio Negri (2000), a widely circulated treatise on the contemporary global conjuncture. The twin problems in the text that I address are (1) its failure to engage with the negative on any profound level, with war in particular and (2) the authors' sloppily conceived analysis of communication. The text has strengths as well (and still further weaknesses), but in view of its widespread reception in many circles as both authoritative and penetrating, a kind of *Lonely Planet* guide to the dynamics of our era, its putative contribution to debates about international communication requires some tough-minded evaluation.

Two historically influential explanations for people's readiness to communicate by fighting wars are unconvincing. This issue is central, for effective antiwar media must be based on a thorough understanding of what may spur people to fight wars in the first place. I undertake a critical discussion of *Empire* along the lines indicated and then discuss antiwar alternative media, focusing on the currently emerging contribution of independent media centers. Although it is tiny and potentially evanescent at the present time, it merits careful examination as a serious attempt to enable horizontal linkages and to amplify the voices of those whose vision transcends the savagely armed kindergarten politics of war.

Two Views of War

Two explanations are often offered for why people agree en masse to wage war in the modern era, the one conservative and the other radical. Conservatives have pointed to the history of modern war with the aim of pouring scorn on any attempt to insist that war defeats the general public's true concerns, or— more cynically—they have argued that manipulative appeals to xenophobic militarism will always outbid any sense for international solidarity. Their standard example for nearly a century has been the alacrity with which in the "Great" War proletarians appeared to leap into deadly combat with each other rather than casting off the common chains of their capitalist exploitation. Freud (1974, 179), for example, argued for the existence of what he termed the thanatos instinct, or death drive, in human beings:

> consider the Great War which is still laying Europe waste. Think of the vast amount of brutality, cruelty and lies. . . . Do you really believe that a handful of ambitious and deluding men without conscience could have succeeded in unleashing all these evil spirits if their millions of followers did not share their guilt?

Thirteen years later he wrote:

> As a rule this cruel aggressiveness waits for some provocation or puts itself at the service of some other purpose, whose goal might also have been reached by milder measures. In circumstances that are favorable to it, when the mental counter-forces which ordinarily inhibit it are out of action, it also manifests itself spontaneously and reveals man as a savage beast to whom consideration towards his own kind is something alien. (Freud 1973, 48–49)

Some feminist writers, even before Freud but continuing into the present, have produced similarly absolute but more targeted explanations, zeroing in on masculinist aggression rather than the human death drive as the source of war (cf. Israels Perry 1994).

Against this view I cite the empirical realities of the World War I military draft, which often fell well short of supercharged patriotic fervor.[1] Among many other sources, Pat Barker's *Regeneration Trilogy* (1996), Sebastian Faulks's novel *Birdsong* (1993), and Joseph Losey's 1964 feature film *King and Country* draw on World War I oral histories that evince a complex variety of motivations for joining up and for staying in. These included not least the social and legal sanctions for refusing to serve—conscientious objectors were officially stigmatized as cowards bordering on traitors and were harshly treated in jail—and the commitment to sticking with one's comrades caught up in the mayhem. Not to mention execution for desertion. The contemptuous rumor popular in northern Europe in the twentieth century that Italian soldiers lacked the required guts for combat contentedly neglected to acknowledge that many Italians remained sensibly unimpressed by the rationale of fighting in World War I (or later for Mussolini).[2] Later, in World War II against the Axis powers, the rationale for fighting was a great deal plainer, but that too, as Studs Terkel underscored in his oral history *The Good War* (1984), was a conflict whose daily purpose was a lot less plain or heroic than the antifascist crusade. I might add the youthful experience of an eminent German cultural critic of my acquaintance, whose Catholic farmer parents were totally uninterested in any form of politics whatsoever until the Allies saturation-bombed Cologne near where they lived, as well as Hamburg and Dresden. Overnight they became fanatical Nazis, convinced Hitler was their only defense against inhuman savagery, and enrolled their ten-year-old in the Nazi Youth. The psychological "hard-wired aggressiveness" explanation of people's readiness to fight war is too tidy, even though it may help explain some facets of war's barbarism.

Lenin's radical explanation for World War I in his enormously influential *Imperialism: The Highest Stage of Capitalism* (1916) began from the position that rivalry between imperialist powers was its fundamental cause. Pivotal within this process, however, in leading masses of people actually to fight, was the action of union and socialist leaders in many European nations who rallied for war bonds in 1914 to finance the fighting. Lenin argued they were largely representing "labor aristocrats," skilled and relatively well-paid industrial workers whose concerns were simply with bread-and-butter issues that would enhance their affluence and economic security. Military budgets would stabilize the economy and improve their members' financial situation. Voting for war spending would also demonstrate beyond doubt the socialist parties' patriotism (and disloyalty to international solidarity). Hence Lenin's accusation that these superficially socialist organizations had effectively been "bribed" into agreeing to war budgets and policies.

With his pen this was a barb, an impotent cheap shot meant to sting into shame and try however feebly to encourage opposition to the established socialist leadership. But it became gospel to subsequent generations of self-defined communists, an authoritative and in a way comforting "explanation" of why proletarians had spent four long years blowing each other to bits with the aid of weapons considerably supplied by patriotic arms manufacturers. Everyone can understand the bottom line.

Both Freudian and Leninist perspectives fail the test of credibility as macroexplanations, whether the "natural" bellicosity of humans or the blinkered venality of socialist leaders manipulating the masses. While the true range of causes of war lies far beyond the scope of this chapter, to grasp the hinge of *mass* motivations for participating in war it seems much more productive to focus on a very common phenomenon, namely, *a collective sense of extreme vulnerability*, from which it appears to follow all too persuasively that attack will be the only imaginable scenario to guarantee physical security over the long term. Russian, Japanese, Israeli, Palestinian, German, Afrikaner, and nuclear weapons history all demonstrate with particular clarity the tragic appeal and manipulative mediatic potential of this lethal non sequitur.

Understanding the sources of war, and the related question of antiwar media, also both connect to our conventional, half-buried mnemonic images of wars past—so often shoved to the back of our minds, uninspected because of their terrors—and their mainstream media sources. Yet we must not siphon off these matters to the recesses of our imaginations. We live in an era in which wars have become and are becoming more and more commonplace—the 1980–1988 Iraq–Iran war, the 1990–1991 Gulf War, long drawn-out civil wars in Sri Lanka, Colombia, Congo, Bosnia, Chechnya, and elsewhere, the endless Israeli–Palestinian conflict, not to mention Indo-Pakistani nuclear saber rattling, other emergent nuclear powers, ongoing U.S. "police" actions (sometimes, like the Korean War, under U.N. auspices), and neokamikaze attacks. These should spur thinking and action, not ostrichism. Wars will continue to be part of our future until we deploy our collective intelligence with far more energy than so far to peaceful conflict resolution. This is why *Empire*'s failure to engage successfully with war or communication matters.

My discussion is designed ultimately to contribute to answers to the following questions, though it is too brief to engage with them in real depth. How may we develop media that effectively communicate a vivid concern for our fellow humans in other nations *as well as* the suicidal face of war for those whose leaders safely initiate it? And through those media, render steps to war significantly harder to take? How do we do so in an era in which making warfare (for those who wage it) safe has been the objective of so much technological innovation?[3]

Empire: Intellectual and Political Context

My complaints against the Hardt and Negri book are several, and I will briefly put them, or more particularly Antonio Negri, in intellectual and political context. That context was post–World War II Italy (Negri was born in 1931), where many contradictory political tendencies were in play, most of which cannot be listed here. The conservative pro-Vatican Christian Democratic party governed the country from 1948 to the mid-1980s without a break. It was faced with the largest communist party in western Europe, regularly pulling around 30 percent of the national vote, but a party that, depending on your viewpoint, was the most reasonable, the most deceptive, or the most co-opted of major communist parties. During the 1970s there emerged an effective working rapprochement between it and the Christian Democrats, the so-called Historic Compromise. Yet as the Communist party drew closer to power, so almost inevitably it began to lose connection to significant elements of its normal base, especially the most militant and active.

Thus from 1969 onward large elements of the radical younger generation in particular began to pull away and to commit themselves to more assertive politics. As the tensions grew between their increasingly activist ranks and the forces of the state, especially during the 1970s but noticeably too in the preceding decade, there developed a wave of terrorist attacks. Interpretations differ sharply as to their sources, some ascribing them to ultra-leftist extremists, others to elements within the state, posing as urban guerrillas in order to create a public mood receptive to tough law-and-order policies that would, in turn, enable endemic labor unrest to be harshly disciplined.

Within this context, one of the political strands on the left was termed "workerism" (*operaismo*) in the 1960s, and then "autonomism" in the 1970s and 1980s. Negri was one of those most closely identified with the autonomist school of thought, so much so that when the leading guerrilla group, the Red Brigades—very plausibly sponsored by state security services—kidnapped and killed a liberal conservative premier, Aldo Moro, Negri found himself quickly tagged by the Italian state as the brain of the organization and jailed. His checkered career thereafter included being elected as a deputy (with parliamentary immunity from prosecution) to the Italian legislature, political exile in France (where he was closely associated with Deleuze and Guattari), and eventually a 1997 return to Italy in the knowledge that he would be returned to jail.

To summarize Marxist autonomist thought, albeit in its barest outline, we need to move away from the typical nostrums of communist, Trotskyist, or anarchist thinking. It represented an attempt at an independent evaluation of Marxism, relying much more on Marx than on his epigones, including Lenin, and took Marx's *Grundrisse* (rather than *Kapital*) as the central text of his work. At autonomism's core was the notion that wage earners represent a collective creative force increasingly responsible for running the mechanisms of capitalist economy for and by themselves, and that they have represented the *initiating* force in successive reorganizations of capitalist production, from Fordism to Toyotism as they put it, namely from the planned assembly line to the interacting and coordinating labor force.[4]

Tidy traditional notions of the proletariat, based in factories in a given nation, as the heart of the working class, gave way to a much more inclusive definition—the *societal* factory[5]—of active, reflective wage laborers at all levels of technical skill functioning across nations, not merely within them. In turn, these people—"the multitude" as Hardt and Negri call them, rather than "the people"—were increasingly demanding a societal wage from the wealth created under advanced capitalism—a support for all members of society, for housework and child rearing, during illness, for the young and the elderly. The multitude increasingly was refusing to labor under capitalist conditions, not necessarily based on some advanced political theory as such, but simply expressing their basic human desires to live meaningful lives (here there are strong echoes of the fundamental themes of Marx's *Economic and Philosophic Manuscripts of 1844* (Marx 1973).

On this level, as an attempt to utilize Marx's work creatively, as a dismissal of literalist readings of it, as a rejection long before 1989–1991 of Soviet and Chinese communist "solutions," and at the same time as a refusal of passive fatalism about the possibilities of challenging capitalist priorities, Italian autonomist Marxism undoubtedly has its appeal. So where are the flaws?

Empire: Some Acute Flaws

Principally, aside from the quite unnecessary opacity of Hardt and Negri's writing at times, my objection is to their version of a secular eschatology. We are, they claim, on the threshold of a dynamic and positive shift in world affairs:

> The capacity to construct places, temporalities, migrations and new bodies already affirms its hegemony through the actions of the multitude against Empire. Imperial corruption is already undermined by the productivity of bodies, by cooperation, and by the multitude's designs of productivity. The only event that we are still awaiting is the construction, or rather the insurgence, of a powerful organization. The genetic chain is formed and established in ontology, the scaffolding is continuously constructed and renewed by the new cooperative productivity, and thus we await only the maturation of the political development of the posse. (Hardt and Negri 2000, 411)[6]

Much in the tradition of Italian autonomist Marxism as it developed in the 1970s, their analysis sweeps with self-confident magisterialism over the political, economic, cultural, and historical landscape, constantly flattening its asymmetries by reducing them to a series of politico-arithmetic averagings. There is a considerable amount that is analytically provocative and intellectually exciting in this tradition, but its proponents often seem a cross between rock-hopper penguins and entrail diviners. As rock hoppers, they leap nimbly from crag to crag, but with scant interest in the specifics of what lies in between; as diviners they claim a finely trained nose for dynamic movements deep within history's bowels. The almost papal assertion that they have a hotline to the inner reading of reality, that it just *is* so, with a scattering of polymathic, sometimes quirky Deleuze and Guattari–style allusions (cf. Deleuze and Guattari 1987) to mostly European philosophers stretching back beyond Machiavelli to St. Augustine and Polybius, or to contemporary analysts of digital technology and corporate trends, all to underpin the "it *is* so," is a hallmark of their style. One which, despite their shafts of genuine insight, can be alternately ludicrous and irritating. "The genetic chain is formed and established in ontology," is just one case in point.

In a key discussion in the book, the authors discuss what they define as a transition from an earlier phase of an "international cycle of struggle." This term was very popular in autonomist writing of the 1970s and denoted a period of almost simultaneous explosions of labor unrest around the world.[7] In the current period they argue these to have ceded to political upsurges that are still fundamentally connected on a deep-structure level, but extremely specific, so much so that

> struggles not only fail to communicate to other contexts but also even lack a local communication and thus often have a very brief duration where they are born, burning out in a flash. This is certainly one of the central and most urgent political paradoxes of our time: in our much celebrated age of communication, *struggles have become all but incommunicable.* (Hardt and Negri 2000, 54; their emphasis)

This passage is a good example of the rhetorical überspin of their analysis, not least in relation to communication issues (to which I will return below). The instances they offer to support the claim above are remarkably specific but also global in impact: Tiananmen Square, the first Intifada, the Los Angeles "Rodney King verdict" explosion, the Zapatista uprising in Mexico, and the strike waves in France (1995) and South Korea (1996). So far so good, on one level. Yet on another, there is a depressingly formulaic quality to their association of these moments, which fairly or unfairly gives the feeling of focused newspaper readers—of the *Financial Times, New York Times, El País* perhaps, *Asian Wall Street Journal* perhaps—sifting through the news media they simultaneously despise and love, in order to discover a progressive essence of hope in capitalist chaos while staying safely away from the messy realities of the individual events.

To take one example out of the six: the Rodney King explosion, totally justifiable on one plane as a response to the cynical, immoral refusal of justice by a jury specifically selected for its obsession with crimes by people of color, was also a moment in which innocent citizens were brutalized and even lost their lives. It was a moment in which some people took the opportunity simply to steal—not to demonstrate, organize, or solidarize. Unless we subscribe to Proudhon's claim that all property is theft, it is hard to see how their actions disturbed rather than cemented the status quo. Armchair academics, so long as their own laptops are not imminently threatened with seizure, can comfortably revel in the expropriation and burning down of other people's livelihoods—Korean, Latino, and black shopkeepers being the obvious case in this particular instance. The Los Angeles police were too busy putting a defensive shield around Beverly Hills to protect the people actually under threat.

My complaint is *not* that the "Rodney King verdict" explosion was really an act of self-destruction and nothing more, only that Hardt and Negri comfortably corral its meaning into being a sign of the movement of the times and nothing more. It is an index of their consistent difficulty, as I see it, in handling the negative, especially war. Of course they acknowledge fascism, Stalinist dictatorship, colonialist wars, labor repression. They are not idiots. But in their diagnosis of the present it is quite extraordinary how hard it is to find a treatment of the enduring and increasing menace of warfare, whether enabled by the American, French, Russian, Brazilian, British, Israeli, and other weapons industries, or directly sponsored by the United States or other nations (Ramonet 2002; De La Gorce 2002; Parsons 2002; Coryell 2002).

Instead, they present the immanent movement of society as headed toward a different and fully cooperative future, even if it has to deal with unspecified traumas along the way. They argue, for example, that these "horizontally . . . incommunicable . . . struggles . . . leap vertically and touch immediately on the global level . . . and attack the imperial constitution in its generality" (Hardt and Negri 2000, 55–56).[8] As an article of faith this assertion may give comfort to the godly, but its spatialized theology is almost comic.[9] The metaphors get richer—or in this case come back to earth—a little further on, where they assert that "today's struggles slither silently across these superficial, imperial landscapes. . . . Simply by focusing their own powers, concentrating their energies in a tense and compact coil, these serpentine struggles strike directly at the highest articulations of imperial order" (Hardt and Negri 2000, 57–58).

Hardt and Negri come late, like Bourdieu (1996), to the study of media communication, which in any given instance may offer the strong advantage of a fresh perspective (this is not a professional jealousy issue), but in this case leads to some very clumsy and inadequate conceptualizations. We have already seen their assertion both that certain conflicts are incommunicable and yet that they mystically unite at the global level, both leaping and slithering. Things get worse when they directly engage in discussing the communication process (Hardt and Negri 2000, 321–24, 346–48). In the former passage they rely heavily on Guy Debord's (1994) notion of the society of the spectacle, which they take as unvarnished fact and proceed on that basis to claim that "traditional forms of struggle . . . become inconceivable" (Hardt and Negri 2000, 322). They also say that the society of the spectacle operates principally by creating "forms of desire and pleasure that are intimately wedded to fear. . . . It seems as if there is no place left to stand, no weight to any possible resistance, but only an implacable machine of power" (Hardt and Negri 2000, 323). They nonetheless assert that "new and more powerful" forms of struggle are emerging.

Despite its welcome attack on the political fatalism visible in some countries in the face of triumphant neoliberalism in the 1990s and 2000s, this Debordian analysis hardly constitutes a coherent account of the global roles of media in the contemporary world, and one is left wondering where to begin in order to make their schema viable in this regard. Yet given their uncompromising insistence on the crushing power of the spectacle, this remains a huge gap, which they gesture at filling by citing Herman and Chomsky's *Manufacturing Consent*, and Said's *Covering Islam*, in a footnote (Hardt and Negri 2000, 464 n. 7). Both are important and influential texts but hardly serve to summarize the insights or debates in contemporary media research.

In the second of the two passages noted above, communication is defined as one of "three global and absolute means" of control by empire (Hardt and Negri 2000, 345), the first two being nuclear weapons and money.[10] For reasons having more to do with rhetorical balance than hermeneutical efficacy, they actually deploy the term "ether" rather than communication: "Ether is the third and final fundamental medium of imperial control" (Hardt and Negri 2000, 346). Passing smoothly over the tiresome distraction that a great deal of communication today does not avail itself of ether, they proceed to hypostatize "communication" as an active force in its own right: "communication is not satisfied . . . it attacks . . . it imposes" (346–47). And then they haul Debord back in to produce a one-way, overwhelming impact of the society of the spectacle:

> Education and culture too cannot help submitting to the circulating society of the spectacle. . . . The space of communication is completely deterritorialized. . . . Communication is the form of capitalist production in which capital has succeeded in submitting society entirely and globally to its regime, suppressing all alternative paths. (347)

However, with no link specified to the assertion that all alternative paths have been suppressed, they fleetingly propose on the very next page (348) that this means "empire" has to confront "the power of all those who contribute to the interactive production of communication." For them it is a basic statement of autonomist principle: precisely those who staff the system of production are those who contain within their expertise the potential to transcend it, who are in fact the source of all significant changes within it even though to date those changes (Fordism, Toyotism, etc.) have been under the managerial control of capital.

I propose to take this passing hint and inflate it in directions that I think more productive of understanding the contemporary conjuncture, namely, the ways in which radical alternative media uses have challenged and continue to challenge transnational corporate priorities and the wars they sponsor, spark, or connive at. These media operate in both territorialized and deterritorialized modes: the divorce Hardt and Negri propose between the two is spurious (Downing forthcoming). I will refer especially to the new independent media center movement, but without constraints on space, it would easily be possible to address other instances. Autonomist Marxism has its virtues—the germ of the idea is sound that we contain within ourselves the possibility of another world—but very urgently, if it is ever to escape the stratosphere in which it is mostly confined in *Empire*, this approach needs to be complicated with the real. As opposed to humans trying dimly to divine what the gods are up to, Hardt and Negri seem often to be sitting on Olympus peering through cloud cover and trying to divine what is going on down here. But more than simply dissecting the mechanisms of oppression, they have faith in us, and that's refreshing.

Antiwar Media

Given the intimate relation between military objectives and the emergence of communication technologies (Mattelart 1994), the ever blurrier line between civilian and military technology (De Landa 1991), and the ways television has been intensively used to represent what war means (Cumings 1992; Kellner 1992), it is indeed a pity that Hardt and Negri did not explore the crucial interconnections between war and communication (as well as war as a means of communication). Here however our focus will be on antiwar media as examples of autonomous media.

Such media have a long story, partly but not exclusively associated with the pacifist movement, but one that largely remains to be written. Peck (1985) has provided an account of alternative media during the U.S. war in Southeast Asia in the 1960s and 1970s, and Aronson (1972, 198–226) of the antiwar newspapers produced inside the U.S. armed forces in that period. McCrea and Markle (1989) have focused on protest against nuclear weapons, especially the *Bulletin of Concerned Atomic Scientists*. I (Downing 1988) explored the 1980s antinuclear media of the German Federal Republic and Britain, a period of tremendous European protest against nuclear war. This handful of studies is hardly comprehensive: in the United States alone in the 1980s there was a flood of documentary films, books, fliers, and magazine articles either against nuclear war or in solidarity with Guatemala, El Salvador, and Nicaragua, all three nations experiencing a very severe military repression enthusiastically supported by the Reagan presidency.

For those who are prepared to swallow the dismissive *public* attitudes of corporate and government officials to such protest and solidarity micromedia as if they were their *actual* attitudes, then of course there is hardly anything worth analyzing here. Fleabites, no more. Yet reading the memoirs of such officials we repeatedly find after the event how acutely conscious they were of a major battle to be fought for public opinion, a public opinion fed and aroused in significant measure by these micromedia. This, the trajectory of the Star Wars program (Strategic Defense Initiative) to 2000 shows rather well (Fitzgerald 2000). To take just one example, Reagan's original crackpot notion in the mid-1980s of a defensive antinuclear shield around the United States almost certainly sought to steal the clothes of the nuclear freeze movement, which had mounted a million-strong march in New York City and had won significant resolutions in Congress. Why trouble to steal the clothes if they were irrelevant?

I have discussed at length this basic proposition about the importance of micromedia elsewhere (Downing 2001). Here I simply draw attention in conclusion to the rapidly expanding "indymedia" phenomenon, the independent media center movement that was born in the Seattle WTO confrontation of 1999, as a potentially very effective expression of autonomous politics within a war-prone epoch.[11] Let me briefly trace out why.

There were at the time of writing around eighty independent media centers (Downing 2002), the great majority concentrated in the United States and Canada, but with around twenty in Europe, Australia, and New Zealand, and ten or so outside nations typically defined as Western (e.g., India, Russia, Palestine, Brazil). In less than three years since the Seattle IMC had been started, this represented a phenomenal rate of growth. Levels of activity varied considerably between IMCs, but nonetheless with links available easily between the servers of each one, this represented an extraordinary opportunity for up-to-the-minute connectivity across over thirty nations and thus for mutual information and coordination inside, for the most part, the affluent OECD countries whose corporate and government elites typically called the shots on which wars to support. Still photographs, cartoons, audio and video files were all available. Local trends in global political economy, challenges to it, and civil or military conflicts part and parcel of all these, were easily accessible on an ongoing basis. They offered the prospect of cutting down the typical isolation among the progressive movements in different nations.

These were enabling centers, not directing centers. They were in no sense some kind of new Communist International, marching to a single beat. They simply used options possible within digital technology to store, archive, update, hyperlink, put into contact and facilitate debate, and overwhelmingly to do so on a nonsectarian basis. Thus in terms of war issues, the potential here became considerably greater than before for mobilizing international resistance against bombing Iraq and starving Iraqis, for example, policies which constituted such an obsession within the 2001–2005 Bush administration and the Clinton administration before it.

This is an example of the potential in the indymedia movement only. Writing in the middle of 2002, this was not meant to predict either a huge imminent upsurge of the movement to oppose the bombing or the instant demise of U.S. punishments of ordinary Iraqis for the actions of their unelected regime, only to indicate that information nodes to feed a new global groundswell of opposition to U.S. military were much more readily and cheaply available than ever before. Despite the carefully constructed blanket over information about the war in Afghanistan that began in 2001, the possibilities for opening up its real conduct and horrors were also far greater with the advent of the IMC network and its multiple additional hyperlinks. Not to be dismissed either, was the availability of these materials in a number of major world languages on the Seattle site and a number of others.

At the same time, the utility of these sources and options was inexorably bound up, interactively, with the vigor of local political activities of all kinds. Merely having the information available would not of itself change anything.

Furthermore, though, the realities of war needed more than simply horror stories or exposés. As military strategy and technology grow increasingly dominant, widespread public understanding of both is simply necessitated. To take the simplest of examples, the notion of a purely defensive, "inoffensive" missile shield is attractive to many U.S. citizens because they have not thought through that (1) the more effectively defended any nation, the less it has to fear attacking other countries because it need not worry so much about retaliation, (2) any defensive weapon can also be used offensively, and (3) investing in a crackpot vision can still produce extremely dangerous offensive weapons, for there is no requirement that the original vision must be held to in the face of new technical developments.

To take a slightly more technical example, the ability to intercept a rather primitive Iraqi Scud missile—though the U.S. military wildly exaggerated its success in doing so at the time of the second Gulf War—is a very long way from being equivalent to intercepting an intercontinental ballistic missile coming in from outer space. To take a primarily software/organizational example, the roles of intelligence gathering in warfare—the U.S. intelligence failures at the time of Pearl Harbor and in relation to 9/11 are just two very salient instances of a more general phenomenon—are also a critical component of the picture.

These are just three examples of the depressing but essential requirement today for alternative education in the fundamentals of war and defense. These are a priority, over and above attempts to get at what is happening on the ground in Afghanistan, Kosovo, and other military theaters. And they are a priority for pacifist and nonpacifist media alike.

A second priority is to find imaginative means to convey the full dimensions of war. "Facts," horrors, analyses, all have their necessary place. But the range of possibilities of cheap digital communication, via IMCs and similar bodies, that engage with the whole human being is considerable. Two brief examples will have to suffice. One, on the Israeli IMC Web site in 2002, is the constantly updated blinking number of the number of refuseniks, Israeli soldiers publicly refusing to serve in the occupied Palestinian territories. Another is the "Boomerang Politics" cartoon by Brazilian cartoonist Latuff, available via the Brazil IMC Web site, which shows two boomerangs labeled "US Interventionist Policies" slamming into the two World Trade Center buildings. The simple fact that people in many different parts of the world can sit and absorb these graphic visual images for as long as they choose is a contribution to international mobilization against wars and their causes.

Conclusion

This brief reflection was intended to raise a series of international communication issues about wars and opposition to them, and the potential and actual roles of micromedia within that matrix. It has both critiqued and drawn on Hardt and Negri's *Empire*, chosen because of its widespread circulation at the present time. Major gaps in their analysis concern war and communication, these gaps being putatively the results of a rather Panglossian rhetoric that from time to time afflicts their analysis, and of their lack of systematic reflection upon communication issues. On the other hand, their sense for the ongoing subversive potential of the "multitude" draws our attention to initiatives such as the indymedia movement and the international applications of digital technology in the service of peace and justice that it so dynamically illustrates.

Notes

1. George Washington was compelled to institute the draft for the American Revolutionary War, supposedly an outpouring of nearly homogeneous sentiment in favor of liberty.

2. The same was true of Americans. Both the Italian Socialist Party and the American Socialist Party opposed involvement; Italy did not join in until 1915, the United States, 1917.

3. This is often dated to the so-called smart bombs of the second Gulf War of 1990–1991 (the first having been the Iran–Iraq war of 1980–1988), but effectively goes back to the saturation and nuclear bombing strategy of World War II. A former Vietnam War pilot with whom I spoke, by that time deeply ashamed of his role, observed that dropping bombs from four miles up easily numbed moral disquiet since the human targets were less visible than ants and totally unknown to the bomber pilots.

4. This perspective is clearly articulated on pages 268–76 of *Empire*.

5. Usually translated the "social" factory, but this adjective doesn't give the sense so well.

6. The term "posse" is one to which they give a particular meaning (Hardt and Negri 2000, 407–11), as is the term "multitude" in this excerpt (60–66, 209–18, 357–63).

7. It has found its way into the social movement literature via the work of Sidney Tarrow, who rephrases the term as "cycle of protest" (cf. Tarrow 1989).

8. For the authors, "imperial" is not the same as "imperialist," which refers to colonialism and neocolonialism by specific nations, whereas "empire" and "imperial" denote for them the current global order that has no identifiable center, despite the leading role of the United States.

9. It is hard for this reader not to be reminded of the French knight in Monty Python and the Holy Grail standing at the castle battlements and proclaiming to John Cleese, "I fart in your general direction."

10. Since I complained above that the authors pay no attention to war, let me just note that at this juncture in the book they do provide a single long paragraph claiming that nuclear weapons have destroyed national sovereignty except for nations that possess them, and that nuclear war between possessing states is unthinkable. Every war is now "a limited conflict, a civil war, a dirty war" (Hardt and Negri 2000, 345). They conclude with an infantile syllogism, that as a result of nuclear weapons "Empire is the ultimate form of biopower insofar as it is the absolute inversion of the power of life" (Hardt and Negri 2000, 346). In other words we can blow the planet up if we want to. Their compulsion to produce papal *obiter dicta* that glide effortlessly over awkward specifics—the Israeli nuclear arsenal, the Indo-Pakistani-Chinese nuclear triangle—is never more evident than here.

11. IMCs, in the most rudimentary terms, are activist groups utilizing one or more servers.

References

Aronson, James. 1972. *Deadline for the Media*. New York: Bobbs-Merrill.
Bourdieu, Pierre. 1996. *Sur la Télévision*. Paris: Liber Éditions.
Coryell, Schofield. 2002. Au Vietnam, le napalm tue encore. *Le Monde Diplomatique* (March): 12.
Cumings, Bruce. 1992. *War and Television*. New York: Verso.
Debord, Guy. 1994. *The Society of the Spectacle*. New York: Zone.

De La Gorce, Paul-Marie. 2002. Bombarder pour mieux contrôler, Washington a défini sa stratégie. *Le Monde Diplomatique* (March): 10–11.

De Landa, Miguel. 1991. *War in the Age of Intelligent Machines.* New York: Zone.

Deleuze, Gilles, and Félix Guattari. 1987. *A Thousand Plateaus: Capitalism and Schizophrenia.* Minneapolis: University of Minnesota Press.

Downing, John. 1988. Alternative Public Realm: The Organization of the 1980s Antinuclear Press in West Germany and Britain. *Media, Culture, and Society* 10, no. 2: 165–83.

———. 2001. *Radical Media: Rebellious Communication and Social Movements.* Thousand Oaks, Calif.: Sage.

———. 2002. "Independent Media Centers: A Multi-Local, Multi-Mediatic Challenge to Global Neo-Liberalism." In Marc Raboy, ed., *Global Media Policy.* Luton, U.K.: Luton University Press.

———. Forthcoming. *The Indymedia Phenomenon: Space-Place, Democracy, and the New Independent Media Centers.*

Faulks, Sebastian. 1993. *Birdsong.* New York: Random House.

Fitzgerald, Frances. 2000. *Way Out There in the Blue: Reagan, Star Wars, and the End of the Cold War.* New York: Simon & Schuster.

Freud, Sigmund. [1930] 1973. *Civilization and Its Discontents.* London: Hogarth.

———. [1917] 1974. *Introductory Lectures on Psychoanalysis.* Harmondsworth, U.K.: Penguin.

Hardt, Michael, and Antonio Negri. 2000. *Empire.* Cambridge, Mass.: Harvard University Press.

Israels Perry, Elizabeth. 1994. "Image, rhetoric, and the historical memory of women," in Alice Sheppard, ed., *Cartooning for Suffrage,* 3-19. Albuquerque, NM: University of New Mexico Press.

Kellner, Douglas. 1992. *The Persian Gulf TV War.* Boulder, Colo.: Westview.

Lenin, Vladimir. [1916] 1975. "Imperialism: The Highest Stage of Capitalism." In *Collected Works.* Vol. 22. Moscow: Progress.

Marx, Karl. [1844] 1973. *Economic and Philosophic Manuscripts of 1844.* London: Lawrence & Wishart.

Mattelart, Armand. 1994. *Mapping World Communication: War, Progress, Culture.* Minneapolis: University of Minnesota Press.

McCrea, Frances, and Gerald Markle. 1989. *Minutes to Midnight: Nuclear Weapons Protest in America,* 43–60. Thousand Oaks, Calif.: Sage.

Parsons, Robert James. 2002. De la réalité des armes à l'uranium appauvri. *Le Monde Diplomatique* (March): 12–13.

Peck, Abe. 1985. *Uncovering the Sixties: The Life and Times of the Underground Press.* New York: Pantheon.

Ramonet, Ignacio. 2002. *Les Guerres du XXI Siècle.* Paris: Galilée.

Tarrow, Sidney. 1989. *Democracy and Disorder: Social Movements in Italy, 1965–1975.* Oxford: Clarendon.

Terkel, Studs. 1984. *The Good War: An Oral History of World War II.* New York: Pantheon.

III

MODELS AND TOOLS FOR INQUIRY IN INTERNATIONAL COMMUNICATION

Mehdi Semati

PART III, "MODELS AND TOOLS FOR Inquiry in International Communication," reexamines some established tools of research and explores new models for inquiry in international communication. The areas covered include regulation in media as a mechanism to achieve cultural protection, democratization process and the media, and ethnography as a research tool in international communication. Two sets of issues persist in most international communication classrooms of all levels: first is the question of regulation and legal maneuvers for cultural protectionism, which often accompany issues of national and regional identities, language, cultural traditions, and heritage; second is the question of media in relations to political culture, civil society, and democratization, which often accompany issues of government control. In chapter 8, Clifford Jones addresses the first set of issues in the context of regulation in the European Union and its attempts at regional integration and protection against the perceived threat of American cultural domination. In chapter 9, Rick Rockwell examines the second set of issues as he considers democratization in Central America. By providing continent-wide analyses, both of these chapters provide valuable tools for comparative analysis in international communication.

In chapter 10, Michael Evans reconsiders ethnography as a research tool in international communication. His chapter is devoted to a set of philosophical, epistemological, and theoretical questions that arise in many international communication teaching and research settings.

Clifford Jones, a legal scholar, addresses a set of recurrent issues in international communication from a regulatory perspective, including many of the

cultural and political themes discussed under the auspices of cultural imperialism. Attempts to create a "United States of Europe" have been motivated by
various factors. Chief among these are the desire to create a common market
capable of massive growth, the aspiration to be competitive against the United
States, and the need to create favorable conditions for regional integration of
various kinds. In this context, the attempts to create regional cultural integration have been made against the threat of American cultural domination. The
cultural and communicative issues that are caught up in the struggles within
and among regional identities constituting the European formation have
rarely been addressed in a regulatory and legal framework. Jones's discussion
of the legal maneuvers and underpinnings of cultural integration and protectionism, with all the contradictions and complexities that such projects entail,
highlights the legal-political-cultural implications of communication (media)
that cross cultural-political frontiers. One implication of the study of transfrontier media law is that other regional cultural-political configurations
might benefit from the European experience, such as the Middle East, Africa,
Latin America, and Asia. In this sense, Jones's chapter provides additional
tools for comparative studies of international media.

Rick Rockwell, an academic and a practicing journalist who has worked in
Central America, focuses his chapter on corruption as a major factor in his
consideration of democratization and the media. Corruption, Rockwell argues, has not received sufficient scholarly attention as a theoretical and empirical object of analysis. In the aftermath of the tumultuous 1980s in Central
America, many media systems, as part of larger structural changes, began to
move away from dictatorial control and underwent a process of transformation. Rockwell advocates developing theoretical explanations of the relationships among media systems, political institutions, and structures of civil society as frameworks for studying corruption. He proposes a new method for the
evaluation of media systems in their transition from authoritarianism. His
analysis of corruption as a limiting factor in the advancement of professional
standards for media practices gives his chapter a unique empirical edge. Given
the ongoing movement across the globe toward privatization and liberalization of media systems, his study is relevant to analyses of media systems beyond Central America. Rockwell's chapter addresses a long-standing need in
the field of international communication to develop analytic tools for comparative international media studies.

In the last chapter of part III, Michael Evans addresses ethnography as a
tool for research in international communication. His chapter is inspired by
the debates over ethnographic audience research in cultural studies and communication media research and the critiques of "active audience theory" that
have emerged during recent years. For example, opponents of cultural studies

have decried ethnographic cultural studies as mere revisionism (e.g., Curran 1990) while proponents have expressed concerns over new "theoretical orthodoxies" (e.g., Morley 1997). These debates prompt Evans to appraise ethnography in its anthropological and communication applications in a way that is cognizant of both humanistic and social scientific sensibilities. His reflections on ethnography entail both theoretical and methodological questions and identify diverging perspectives as well as persistently vexing issues. Most critical among these questions and issues for international communication research are the self-other problem, the question of context, and the relationship between representation and the lived experience. Evans does a thorough job of cataloging the opportunities and challenges international communication researchers face in considering ethnography.

References

Curran, J. 1990. The new revisionism in mass communication research: A reappraisal. *European Journal of Communication* 5, no. 2–3: 135–64.

Morley, D. 1997. "Theoretical orthodoxies: Textualism, constructivism, and the 'new ethnography' in cultural studies." In M. Ferguson and P. Golding, eds., *Cultural studies in question*, 121–37. Thousand Oaks, Calif.: Sage.

8

Transfrontier Media, Law, and Cultural Policy in the European Union

Clifford A. Jones

Who would accede to the Russian plea that no broadcast should criticise the Leninist interpretation of Marx? What answer would be given to the primitive savage who wished to protect his family against the American Way of Life? Let us acknowledge here and now that there is no prospect of international agreement on the intellectual or cultural quality of this, or any other mass medium. Everyone will receive what anyone transmits. . . . The time will come when peoples must be plunged into the cold seas of world opinion, and can no longer swim in the warm baths that their Governments would prefer them to enjoy. (Lord Kilbrandon 1968, 104)

European Integration, Culture, and the Broadcast Media

THE END OF WORLD WAR II brought measures designed to replace centuries of European history featuring warring nation-states with some form of pan-European integration that would prevent future and potentially even more devastating conflicts. Winston Churchill (1946) once called for a "kind of United States of Europe," a goal that is not yet achieved.

In 1950, France and Germany called for the creation of a common European organization to assume international control over the coal and steel resources of the participating countries and, through this control of essential war materiel, make further conflicts impossible (Schuman 1950). The result was the European Coal and Steel Community, the precursor to the European Community,[1] the "Common Market" now often referred to as the European Union.[2]

The European Economic Community, now renamed the European Community, followed in 1958 and extended the sectoral arrangements making up the Coal and Steel Community by the creation of a general Common Market in which goods of all kinds, capital, services, and people were gradually freed to circulate among the member countries for the most part without heed to national borders. One of the objectives of the European Community was the creation of a "single market" for all types of services, including broadcasting. In addition to the obvious economic-oriented provisions of the various treaties and secondary Community legislation, there was a strong desire to develop a European identity and perhaps a European culture distinct from yet alongside the national identities and cultures of Europe.

Television (and radio) broadcasting systems in Europe during the early years of the EC were governed by national law of the member states who strictly regulated broadcasting with the objective of ensuring public service goals (Ungerer 1996). The European public broadcasting tradition contrasted sharply with the lightly regulated commercial system that developed in the United States. However, as technical advances have occurred, there has been an increase in the amount of spectrum available to broadcasters, as first cable systems, then satellite systems, and now digital television technology have arrived. The scarcity of spectrum rationale that initially justified the public broadcasting monopolies of Europe has gradually lost its force. Since the early 1980s, private commercial broadcasting has become increasingly important and public broadcasting in Europe is less dominant.

In the European Community, a number of initiatives combined with the Community's general objective of creating a common market in broadcasting led to a recognition of television broadcasting's importance as a tool in encouraging the economic and cultural integration of Europe. One of the most important initiatives stemmed from the Hahn Report, which emphasized the role of broadcasting in the integration of Europe:

> Information is a decisive, perhaps the most decisive factor in European unification. . . . European unification will only be achieved if Europeans want it. Europeans will only want it if there is such a thing as a European identity. A European identity will only develop if Europeans are adequately informed. (1982, 8–10)

A variety of proposals were considered and an experimental "European" television channel, Eurikon, actually operated for five weeks with programs provided by five member state public broadcasters (Machet 1999). The European Commission (1983, 22) supported the idea of European television service and suggested that "the development of a truly European spirit will therefore become possible in national audiences, who will, of course, retain their full cultural identity."

A series of EP resolutions followed, resulting in the Commission's famous green paper best known as Television Without Frontiers (European Commission 1984). This document embodied discussions of the social and cultural aspects of broadcasting as well as the economic and legal dimensions. One of its declared purposes was to demonstrate the importance of broadcasting for European integration and for the free democratic structure of the European Communities (European Commission 1984). Following protracted and contentious negotiations, the so-called Television Without Frontiers directive (TWF)[3] was adopted in 1989. It was amended in 1997 (TWF 2) and reviewed in 2002 for possible further amendments.

The Council of Europe, which is not an EU institution, prepared the European Convention on Transfrontier Television (ECTT) in parallel with the first TWF directive and its language is in most respects similar, if not identical to the first directive. The ECTT convention was opened for signature in 1989 and was intended to allow participation in its drafting by European nations that were not EC members. It has been suggested that the convention was "substantially inspired by cultural and human rights arguments," while the "mainspring" for TWF was the view that "broadcasting is an economic service" (Barendt 1995, 236).

There has been a continuing debate in Europe over threats, real and imagined, to European culture in the form of cheap imports of American television sitcoms, soap operas, and movies. *Dallas* and *Dynasty*, much to the chagrin of European elites, proved that inferior American culture can be popular in Europe. Ironically, an unlikely comedy set in a World War II German POW camp, *Hogan's Heroes*, has proven astoundingly popular in Germany. Some in Europe advocated increased transfrontier broadcasting regulation on a pan-European basis in order to rescue Europe and its television and film production industries from Hollywood's economic power. Some supported it because they perceived that lowbrow American cultural imperialism would degrade and ruin a higher European culture unless legal measures limited the amount of American shows on European television. Others supported it to ensure that television broadcasts circulated throughout the EC, to create a single market in broadcasting, promote economic development, and break down national control of the media in favor of building a European identity. Whatever the disparate motives, the result has been a cultural and economic communications transformation that is still under way.

Transfrontier Broadcasting in the EU: The Early Years

The influence of Community law on broadcasting did not begin with the TWF directives, although some thought that the commercial and economic nature of Community law meant it had no application in the field of broadcasting. However, because broadcasting is a service normally provided for remuneration, it falls within the scope of Community law (Schwartz 1986; Barendt 1995), in particular, articles 49–55 of the EC Treaty (1957) as amended. Article 49 EC provides that "restrictions on freedom to provide services within the Community shall be progressively abolished . . . in respect of nationals of Member States who are established in a State of the Community other than that of the person for whom the services are intended." National laws that prevented reception of television signals from other member states thus infringed Community law.

As cable television began to appear, the public broadcasting monopolies in Europe saw their exclusivity threatened. In *Sacchi* (1974), Giuseppe Sacchi created a business consisting of placing television sets connected to the cable network in public places such as train stations where people could watch programs and he could receive income from advertisements delivered over the cable. The Italian public broadcasting monopoly at the time, RAI, took a dim view of this entrepreneurial effort and prosecuted Sacchi for not having paid his license fees to receive television broadcasts.[4] The ECJ declared that Sacchi's ad hoc cable network fell under the Treaty because it was a service: "In the absence of express provision to the contrary in the Treaty, a television signal must, by reason of its nature, be regarded as a provision of services. It follows that the transmission of television signals, including those in the nature of advertisements, comes, as such, within the rules of the Treaty relating to services" (*Sacchi* 1974, 426).

In two later cases, *Debauve* (1980) and *Coditel* (1980), the position that broadcasting constituted a service was reaffirmed. *Debauve* involved criminal prosecution of cable television company executives in Belgium who allowed German television programs that included advertisements to be retransmitted over the Belgium cable network in violation of Belgian law prohibiting advertising on television. The defense argued, inter alia, that the prohibition on advertising was incompatible with the EC Treaty provisions on freedom to provide services across borders. However, the Belgian regulatory scheme at issue prohibited commercial advertising on television broadcasts originating within Belgium as well as those originating in other member states. *Debauve* made it clear that the Treaty applied only to *transfrontier* broadcasting, and in the absence of harmonization of national laws, a member state could restrict domestic broadcasting as it chose so long as it did not discriminate against nationals of another member state or create artificial barriers to trade between member states. Therefore, Belgium was allowed to ban commercial advertising from abroad so long as the ban applied equally to domestic advertising.

After *Debauve*, it was clear that restrictive national laws could still represent serious obstacles to broadcasts from other EC members. This prevented the existence of a common market in broadcasting and made the emergence of pan-European broadcasting channels that might help construct a European identity unlikely. This situation led to the Hahn Report and the TWF directives.

However, the ECJ handed down a number of other decisions prior to the passage of the TWF directive. Between 1988 and 1994, the compatibility of the public broadcasting rules in The Netherlands with the EC Treaty came before the ECJ five times. In the course of these rulings, the Court greatly refined the application of the Treaty to public broadcasting and substantially narrowed the role national concepts of culture would be allowed to play in the Common Market for broadcasting. These cases demonstrate the substantial impact on the public broadcasting systems of Europe of economic principles of EC law even without provisions aimed specifically at constructing a European culture.

The Dutch system (at the time) was generally in the European tradition of state-owned or controlled public broadcasting but with the added element of "pillarization," in which there is no single state broadcaster but a selection of secular and religious societal segments ("pillars"), each of which is authorized to broadcast its own programming (Price 1994; Altes 1993). Groups competed for and received broadcasting time according to membership, with the largest groups receiving the largest proportion of time (Price 1994). The aim of this form of noncommercial broadcasting organization is affirmative support of various cultural and pluralistic components of Dutch society, structurally defined by factors such as religion, language, and political affiliation.

By 1984, limited commercial advertising was permitted through an independent foundation, the STER, which administered the advertising, and a broadcasting fund, which financed the production of programs for the groups permitted to broadcast (Altes 1993). The groups were obligated to use the NOPB studios for production of all radio programs and 75 percent of television productions.

In the *Dutch Advertisers* case, the ECJ struck down Dutch cable regulations prohibiting retransmission of radio and television programs originating in other member states and containing advertising intended for the public in The Netherlands. The purpose of the prohibition was to protect the Dutch national broadcasting services from competition for advertising revenues. The ECJ said these constituted restrictions on the rights of broadcasters in other member states to advertise across borders in violation of article 49 EC.

The ECJ further battered the Dutch system in two cases decided together, *Gouda* (1991) and *Kingdom of the Netherlands* (1991). In *Gouda*, the revised

Dutch law restricted commercial advertising to broadcasters that were structured identically to the Dutch STER. Naturally, the Dutch broadcasters through use of the STER met these criteria, but foreign broadcasting organizations did not. The revised Dutch broadcasting law was a not-too-subtle attempt to devise a scheme that ostensibly would be applied equally to domestic and foreign broadcasters and avoid ECJ scrutiny while preventing the latter from competing with the Dutch STER.

The Netherlands argued that its requirements for broadcasters allowed to transmit advertisements were nondiscriminatory and necessary to support Dutch cultural policy in the audiovisual sector. The aim of the policy was said to be to safeguard the freedom of expression of the various social, cultural, religious, and philosophical components of The Netherlands by allowing that freedom to be exercised on radio and television, an objective that could be jeopardized by the excessive influence of advertisers on program content. The ECJ accepted in principle that "a cultural policy understood in that sense may indeed constitute an overriding requirement relating to the general interest which justifies a restriction on the freedom to provide services" (*Gouda* 1991, at 23).

Nonetheless, in practice the Court found no causal connection between this policy and the structure of broadcasting organizations in other member states. The Netherlands could maintain its cultural policy by governing its own broadcasting organizations without attempting to dictate organizational structures in other member states. The ECJ concluded that the purpose of the restrictions was still economic—to protect STER revenues—and the restrictions therefore infringed article 49 of the EC Treaty.

In *The Netherlands* (1991), the ECJ held that requiring use of the NOPB studio to produce advertisements violated the EC Treaty because it limited the opportunity of production companies in other member states to sell their services in The Netherlands. In *Veronica* (1993) and *TV10* (1994) Dutch regulators blocked signals from broadcasters who set up in other countries in order to evade Dutch regulation. The ECJ found this treatment did not infringe the EC Treaty.

The Belgian rules governing retransmission of broadcasts originating abroad came under attack in *Flemish Cable* (1992). The Commission alleged that four aspects of the Belgian system were incompatible with the Treaty, including rules forbidding broadcasters from relaying on their systems programs originating in another member state that were not in the language of the member state of origin. Belgium conceded three rules were invalid but argued that its language rules were justified by three cultural policy objectives: (1) maintenance of pluralism in the printed press, which benefited directly from advertising revenues of Belgian national television broadcasting stations,

(2) the preservation and development of artistic heritage, and (3) the economic viability of the Belgian national broadcasting stations.

The ECJ rejected all three objectives, noting that the first and third ones established that the purpose of the restrictions was economic and their effects were discriminatory. Because economic restrictions could not be justified as "public policy," they were insufficient. The second justification, to preserve artistic and cultural heritage, was rejected because the rule had the effect of reducing the number of television productions in the Dutch language and was therefore counterproductive to the claimed justification.

By the time the TWF directive (1989) was enacted, it was already clear that many if not most of the national rules that threatened the free circulation of television broadcasts throughout the EC related to programming from commercial broadcasters, particularly broadcasts that carried advertisements. By this time, many state public broadcasters were deriving some revenue from advertising in addition to their licensing fees. An important motivation for the TWF directive was the harmonization of national rules on television advertising to prevent disparate and discriminatory national laws from stifling transnational broadcasting in the Community. Blockage of transfrontier advertising had the effect of blocking transfrontier broadcasting as a whole because broadcasts were produced with the advertising already embedded in the program.

The Television Without Frontiers Directives and the Common Market in Broadcasting

The fundamental principle underlying the TWF directive is that a television program legitimately broadcast in one member state may be rebroadcast in another member state without restriction (Wallace and Goldberg 1989). The TWF directive (1989) laid down minimum standards for broadcasts in certain fields and charged member states with ensuring that broadcasters in a member state comply with broadcasting law in that member state. This means that in general national broadcasting regulators are no longer permitted to exclude programs initiated in other Member States. The TWF (1989) requires in article 2(2) that "Member States shall ensure freedom of reception and shall not restrict retransmission on their territory of television broadcasts from other Member States for reasons which fall within the fields coordinated by this Directive."[5] The directive contains chapters devoted to promotion of television program production and distribution (TWF 1989, chapter 3, arts. 4–9), protection of minors (TWF 1989, chapter 5, art. 22), television advertising and sponsorship (TWF 1989, chapter 4, arts. 10–21), and a right of reply (TWF 1989, chapter 6, art. 23).

The TWF directive (1989) also laid down two controversial policies that have a quota-like effect on broadcasting in the EU. First, the directive requires member states to ensure "where practicable and by appropriate means" that broadcasters reserve for "European works" a majority of their transmission time, exclusive of news, sports events, games, advertising, and teletext services (TWF directive, art. 4). This effectively protects 50 percent or more of transmission time so defined from foreign (non-European) competition. The second quota, designed to stimulate the production of European drama work, requires broadcasters to reserve 10 percent or more of their transmission time or, alternatively, 10 percent of their programming budget, for European works created by producers who are "independent of broadcasters" (TWF directive, art. 5).

A key feature of the TWF directive (1989) is its focus on harmonizing or coordinating the television advertising rules in the member states. The rules contained in the TWF directive displace any preexisting national rules the member states might seek to apply to transfrontier broadcasts. The directive sets content and placement standards for television advertising and requires it to be readily recognizable as such and separated from other parts of the program. Advertising is allowed to be scheduled within programs (as opposed to in blocs between programs) only if done without prejudice to the "integrity and value of programs" or their natural continuity. If the program is structured to have breaks or intervals (such as sports or performances) the ads must come during the intervals. Films can be interrupted only every forty-five minutes, and in general spot advertising may consume no more than 15 percent of daily broadcast time and no more than 20 percent of a given one-hour period.

The directive permits member states to lay down stricter requirements concerning advertising for broadcasters *under their own jurisdiction* in order to "reconcile demand for televised advertising with the public interest," having particular regard for "the role of television in providing information, education, culture and entertainment" and "the protection of pluralism of information and of the media" (TWF 1989, art. 19). This means that the Dutch or Belgian regulatory authorities, for example, may continue to restrict their own broadcasters as much as they wish, but restrictions addressed in the TWF directive cannot be applied to broadcasters in other member states. In fact, very first judgment of the ECJ on the TWF directive (1989) confirmed that France could ban entirely television advertising in the retail distribution sector (gasoline sales at supermarkets) for its own broadcasters even though it could not apply that rule to foreign broadcasters (*LeClerc-Siplec* 1995). In *De Agostini* (1997), Sweden was allowed to ban ads promoting dinosaur-related magazines and toys aimed at children from being aired on a Swedish station but was required to permit the same advertising to be aired in Sweden when broadcast by a channel originating in the United Kingdom. Similar rulings occurred in *RTI* (1996) and *Pro Sieben* (1999).

Transnational Media Systems: Culture and Protectionism

The TWF directive had its origins in the concept of stimulating European identity and European culture, at least for some proponents. In practice, this ideal led to quotas for European works. To some Europeans, the quotas were legitimate means of preserving national and regional identities. To other Europeans, the increasing numbers of Hollywood movies, dramas, and sitcoms being aired on European television were both a cultural disaster and an economic one. The cultural one is obvious. The economic disaster was that Hollywood programming, having already had its costs fully amortized in the U.S. market, was available cheaply to European stations. The result was that for some years, European producers could not create new programs at anywhere near the low prices available from the U.S. market (European Commission 1998b). The increasingly profit-oriented commercial channels (and even public broadcasters) bought foreign, primarily American, programming. European audiovisual producers lost much business and in some cases the economic viability of the European industry was much in doubt. The solution ultimately incorporated into the TWF directives was the quota requirements for European works and independent producers.

Article 4 of the TWF, the main quota provision, drew sharp criticism on the basis that the alleged grounds of cultural protection were a subterfuge for economic protectionism (Salvatore 1992). The thrust of article 4(1) is the requirement that broadcasters reserve "a majority proportion" (more than 50 percent) of "their transmission time" (exclusive of news, sports events, games, advertising, and teletext services) for "European works" as defined in article 6 of the TWF. Even one of the most fervent proponents of the quotas, the Italian Communist MEP Barzanti, noted in his report to the European Parliament that the quota measures "smacked of old-fashioned protectionism, relies on artificial barriers and aims at building up protection against competition" (Barzanti 1987, 52). While some supporters of the directive undoubtedly had protectionist as opposed to purely cultural motives, several member states, including Germany, Belgium, Denmark, Luxembourg, and the United Kingdom, opposed the quota provisions (Machet 1999). The resulting directive contained extremely weak quota language that is probably impossible to enforce. Moreover, a protocol (no. 15 1989) to articles 4–5 of the directive recited that the EC Council and Commission agreed that the quota provisions were a "political" obligation (not a legal one).

There are a number of problems with the text of the quota that make enforcement efforts problematic. Article 4(1) of the directive refers to reserving the majority proportion of transmission time to European works "where practicable and by appropriate means." Salvatore (1992, 978–79) has called this "an almost unique example of language vagueness" that leaves him "without a doubt that we face a loophole, which enables member states to escape any mandatory requirement." To this day, the Commission has not attempted to enforce compliance with quota provisions against any member state. In the (amended) second directive adopted in 1997, no change to this text was made despite the efforts of France and other proponents to strengthen the language (Machet 1999).

The Commission has monitored the European works content being broadcast based on data supplied by the national television authorities. The Commission's reports on articles 4–5 of the directive indicate that in the 1991–1992 period 70 of 105 channels (66.7 percent) met the 51 percent quota (European Commission 1994), in 1993–1994, 91 of 148 channels (61.5 percent) met the quota (European Commission 1996a), and in 1995–1996, 62.7 percent of 214 channels were considered to meet the quota (European Commission 1998a). In the 1996–1998 period, 53.3 percent to 81.7 percent of 367 channels, depending on the country, of broadcast time featured European works (European Commission 2000). The Commission has stated that "many of those channels not reaching the majority proportion were recently launched channels and/or satellite channels with limited audience share, often providing specialist programming on a pay-TV basis" (European Commission 1996b, 1). The Commission considers that the quota provisions of the directive have achieved their objectives.

The directive's quotas have not prevented American programming exports from hitting the airwaves in Europe for several reasons. First, the meaning of "European works" in article 6 is sufficiently broad that coproductions involving U.S. firms that are properly structured can readily cause a film or program episode to be a "European work" (Schwartz 1986). Second, growth in the European broadcasting market has expanded the demand in Europe. Projections at the time of the adoption of the directive expected increases in European television stations from 61 in 1987 to 86 by 1992. In fact, by 1992 there were 105 stations in the European Union, by 1994, there were 148, and by 1996, 214. By 1998, Europe had 367 television channels (European Commission 2000). As the growth of digital television increasingly enlarges broadcasting capacity, the continuing increase in demand for content makes it unlikely that European works alone will fill the need for programming in Europe.

The European Court of Justice has considered one case concerning article 4, Belgium's attempt to ban the reception of Turner Broadcasting's TNT/

Cartoon channel, which was broadcast via satellite from the United Kingdom. This is a theme channel, consisting of fourteen hours of cartoons and ten hours of classic movies each day, subtitled in the native languages of most of the nations receiving the broadcast (Shelden 1994). Although the TNT/Cartoon channel's programming is 100 percent U.S. origin, TNT's position was that compliance with the directive was "impracticable" within the meaning of article 4. The grounds asserted were that (1) the "theme" of the channel was U.S. cartoons and movies, so that it should be exempt for cultural reasons (!), and (2) the start-up costs of the new network made it economically impracticable to purchase European-made programming.

The U.K. Department of National Heritage (now the Ministry for Culture, Media, and Sport), which is charged with implementing the directive, notified TNT that it will need to comply with the quotas but set no specific deadline (Shelden 1994).[6] France objected to TNT broadcasts as a violation of the quota and threatened to sanction French cable operators who retransmitted the channel. Belgium's media authorities initially banned the channel, but the ban was overturned by the Belgian Commercial Court, which referred questions of law to the ECJ.

In *Denuit* (1997), the Belgian authorities for the French Community of Belgium refused the cable operator Coditel Brabant permission to distribute the TNT/Cartoon channel for failure of the channel (which originated in the United Kingdom) to satisfy the European works quota in the TWF directive. In *Denuit*, the Belgian authorities argued that TNT/Cartoon was not "under the jurisdiction" of the United Kingdom because it had not forced TNT/Cartoon to meet the broadcasting quotas. Belgium also argued that since TNT/Cartoon's programming originated from a nonmember state, the United States, it could be banned. The ECJ rejected both arguments, stating that the origin of the programs and the broadcaster's compliance with the quotas were "irrelevant" to a determination of which member state had jurisdiction (*Denuit* 1997, at 959). The judgment in *Denuit* thus confirms that Belgium could not exercise secondary control over a television broadcast from a broadcaster established in the United Kingdom even if Belgium believed that the United Kingdom was not enforcing the quota. Accordingly, the Belgian authorities could not maintain their ban on the TNT/Cartoon channel.

The Second Directive: Sports and Shopping

Even if the amendments in the second TWF directive (1997) did not strengthen the "cultural" quota provisions, two other changes stand out amid a larger number of technical amendments. First, and most importantly, rules were put in place allowing the member states to designate "events of major importance to society"—sporting events—which in effect had to be broadcast on free TV (TWF 2 directive 1997, art. 3a). Second, the rules governing "teleshopping" were altered to allow channels to greatly expand this boon to commerce, if not culture (TWF 2 directive 1997, art. 19).

The term events "of major importance for society" is not defined in TWF 2, but the history of the measure makes it clear that the motivation for this amendment is grounded in the perceived risk that pay-per-view TV or other "premium" subscription channels would obtain exclusive rights to sporting events that had been available on free television in the past (European Commission 1997). The TWF 2 does not literally restrict such events to *sporting* events, but no example of an event of major importance to society of any other kind was cited as a justification for these provisions. Recital 18 to the TWF 2 directive (1997) refers to the need to "protect the right to information and to ensure wide access by the public to television coverage of national or non-national events of major importance for society, *such as the Olympic games, the football World Cup and European football Championship*" (emphasis supplied).

The goal of new article 3a is to ensure that a broadcaster in one member state does not obtain exclusive rights to events of "major importance" and thereby prevent the event from being televised on "free" television in that or another member state. By restricting the conditions under which a broadcaster may obtain or exercise exclusive rights to sporting events, this provision virtually may compel a broadcaster to engage in transfrontier broadcasting of its coverage of important cultural (sporting) events.

A significant part of the motivation for article 3a must have been the fear that public service broadcasters might be unable to secure coverage of major sporting events if exclusive rights were obtained by private commercial broadcasters. Public service broadcasters depend less on advertising revenues than some private stations, but the prospect of losing an audience whose demographics are beloved by advertisers was of grave commercial concern even to the public stations. The economic disadvantage was described by the Commission:

> In-the-clear broadcasters, be they publicly or privately funded, are increasingly having to compete with pay TV providers. The latter are prepared to accept a large increase in costs in order to acquire exclusive sports rights. The most remarkable "quantum leap" (1,000 percent) was in 1996 with the deal on acquiring the world football championship for the years 2002 and 2006. In a study dated August 1996, "London Economics" expressed the view that 'the financial strength of pay TV providers, who are in a better position to extract the consumers' valuation for a specific content, implies that they are the likely winners in this competition.' While fewer viewers may watch an event on pay TV than on

in-the-clear TV, the revenues can be significantly higher. It has been calculated that the transmission of the 1996 European Football Championship final on a pay-TV basis to 25 million paying viewers would have resulted in a total cost to those viewers three times higher than the amount paid for in-the-clear transmission of all 33 matches, including the final. In fact, the event was broadcast on in-the-clear TV and each match was watched by an average of 150 million viewers, with 250 million watching the final. (European Commission 1997, 2)

Another motivation may have been the fear that exclusive rights obtained by pay TV channels would make televised events unavailable to many. The Commission noted that pay TV covers approximately 20 percent of TV households in France and the United Kingdom, but less than 5 percent in other member states. While pay TV growth continues, the concern was that close to 95 percent of TV households would be unable to view major sporting events on television (European Commission 1997, 7).

New article 3a is implemented by each member state that chooses to do so (it is not mandatory) by drawing up a list of designated events, national or non-national, that it considers "of major importance for society." Broadcasters are then prevented from exercising their exclusive rights for those listed events unless they contract with free TV broadcasters with sufficient national reach to also air the event.

The TWF 2 directive (1997) does not specify how disputes over the price to be agreed with free TV broadcasters will be resolved. The Danish implementation, for example, provides that the Danish Competition Council may set the price according to prevailing competitive market conditions if agreement cannot be reached by the broadcasters (Ministerial Order 1999, sec. 7). The Exclusive Television Rights Act of Austria (2002) contains similar provisions. The rules also vary widely as to what audience share member states consider sufficiently widely available on free TV. For example, Denmark requires 90 percent, Austria 70 percent, and Germany 66 percent.

The right to watch football and other sporting events is not usually thought of as a major component of European culture, yet the TWF 2 directive goes further in this area to ensure that transfrontier broadcasting takes place in any other field. As the transnational media system develops in the EC, it comes more and more to contain compromises between those who see its objective as cultural and those who perceive its greatest importance as economic. In the case of the exclusive broadcasting rights rules found in the second directive, the EC seems to have given more weight to protecting the economic interests of public broadcasters than to the promotion of European culture (except the culture of sport) or the free market.

Shopping, particularly on TV, is also an area that is not usually considered a major cultural activity. Rather, provisions in the new directive relating to teleshopping seem obviously aimed at expanding the commercial aspects of the Common Market. In recital 36 of the preamble to TWF 2 (1997), teleshopping is described as "an economically important activity for operators as a whole and a genuine outlet for goods and services within the Community."

In the second directive, teleshopping is defined and a legal framework established for teleshopping programs and channels, partially aligned with many of the rules on advertising. "Teleshopping" means "direct offers broadcast to the public with a view to the supply of goods or services, including immovable property, rights and obligations, in return for payment" (TWF 2, directive 1997, art. 1[f.]).

The second directive frees teleshopping channels from many of the restrictions on advertising in the original directive. The European works quota contained in article 4(1) does not apply to teleshopping. The previous one hour per day limit on teleshopping contained in former article 18(3) was deleted from the second directive, and the percentage limitations of transmission time allowed for advertising [art. 18(2)] are not applicable to teleshopping channels (TWF 2, art. 19). This effectively removes the general advertising rules as barriers to full-time shopping channels. In addition, shopping channels themselves may carry advertising, and channels that are not teleshopping channels may carry "teleshopping windows" with a minimum duration of fifteen minutes up to a maximum of three hours per day of such "windows." Under the amended TWF directive, a hypothetical general channel with an eighteen-hour broadcasting day could devote 6.6 hours of it to teleshopping spots and windows under the new provisions. This is culture indeed!

Conclusion: Transnational Media and Culture in an Era of Convergence and Expansion

Nearly fifteen years have elapsed from the formal initiation of the European Community's transnational broadcasting policy in the form of the adoption of the first TWF directive (1989). After a decade of Television Without Frontiers, Machet (1999, 48) observed that "we are far from the ideal of a common European television programme aimed at fostering a European identity which was at the core of the first initiatives of the European institutions in the field of media policy." Indeed, the experimental pan-European broadcasts have fallen by the wayside, and there is today no "Eurochannel" in the sense envisaged during the European media policy debates of the 1980s. The citizens of all member states do not turn on the same broadcast every night to receive "European identity" socialization as may have occurred on a national basis in the first three decades following World War II. If that were the sole benchmark of success, then efforts at a transnational media system have failed.

A more generous view of the success of European-level (transnational) media policy may be taken when one considers that national identities did not develop only with the onset of national public broadcasters and certainly did not arise in a decade's time. It could not realistically have been expected and surely was not expected that a European "national" identity would spring full-blown into being as the consequence of a few short years of watching a common European channel.

While it is too early to attempt a comprehensive assessment of the role of transnational broadcasting in supporting the creation of a European identity, certain trends and challenges can be identified. First, the TWF directives were never merely concerned with European culture and identity as such. The European Community itself was envisaged as an economic arrangement that would lead in a practical fashion through concrete steps to a Common European Market and the process of building it would lead to a common European identity and perhaps a "United States of Europe." The TWF directives were concerned with building a common market in broadcasting and that process would be a concrete achievement that would ultimately contribute to the formation of a collective European identity. Therefore, while Machet is correct that we are far from a common European television program (in the sense of pan-European channels) in the present iteration of European media policy, this is not to say that a process is not under way that will contribute to the formation of a European identity.

Second, the dominant purpose of the TWF directives as adopted was always the development of a European common market in broadcasting, especially commercial broadcasting. Free circulation of programs (including advertising) originating in any member state among the others could only have been conceived of as an aid to a common market and never as building "one" European identity. Many have said there is no such thing as one "European" culture, and there are numerous cultures in Europe. There is much truth in this. Henry Kissinger once allegedly commented that "Europe doesn't have a phone number." Europe also doesn't have a channel. Europe has many channels.

What TWF has accomplished is the increasingly free circulation of all national channels distributed throughout the member states via cable and satellite systems. Viewers, whether in France, Germany, the United Kingdom, Austria, or wherever can watch multiple channels originating in multiple European nations. If this does not constitute exposure to European culture, it is difficult to say what does. European culture is not unity in culture but diversity in culture, and the free circulation of television systematically has begun to break down national frontiers of broadcasting through the power of the economic marketplace. Not all proponents of the TWF directives may have realized that it would be economic forces that would break down national control of the broadcast media, but that is the process identifiably under way.

Third, what TWF does is admit the programs of other countries and other cultures into the broadcasting system for viewers to make of what they will. The primary aspects of TWF seriously thought to be justified on the basis of protection of European culture are the quota provisions for European works and productions. However, these provisions have such overly broad definitions of European works that there is little possibility of their having this effect. This is because, as in *Fediciné* (1993), the quota rules favor films or programs based on origin, not content or quality. Films or TV shows may qualify as European works if they are made or produced by European firms or "coproductions" with European firms. They need not be about any aspect of European culture or have any European content. The most that can be said is that they might (or might not) be in a European language, of which English is one.

For example, the Brazilian actress Xuxa is to star in remakes of the U.S. TV comedy *I Love Lucy* to be filmed in Spain based on the original *Lucy* scripts (McNeill 1998). One is hard put to think how remaking shows from original American scripts would help build European culture. A Spanish remake of *Lucy* would certainly create profitable work in Spain, but it would not necessarily reflect European culture.

One only has to consider the famous series of films (including *Per qualche Dollari in più* and *Per un Pugno di Dollari*) known as "Spaghetti westerns" starring Clint Eastwood, directed by Italian director Sergio Leone, and produced in Italy to grasp the point.[7] Italian culture would not measurably be enhanced by production of films ostensibly depicting the American Old West. European-produced films are protected by the quotas without having any necessary connection to European content or culture. It would not be wrong to say the European works quotas could not be justified as cultural in nature because they protect the "good, the bad, and the ugly" (*Il Buono, Il Brutto, Il Cavitta*)—and the American—in European films.

As well, Turner Network Television formed a French division so that its productions would count as European works. Its first project: a joint venture with the French channel Canal+ to produce a show titled *The Native Americans* (Shelden 1994). Such programs are European works within the meaning of the directives, but their principal contribution to European culture is economic.

Fourth, what this indicates is that the quota provisions were intended to have their effects by providing work and income for European audiovisual or cinematic firms, not by changing the cultural content of the shows being aired. They represent "industrial policy," not cultural (de Witte 1995, 112). Some studies have shown that the European works quotas actually may be counterproductive to the economic well-being of European producers, artists, and technicians (Machet 1999). Nonetheless, some view the economic support of the industry as cultural preservation:

> The culture industry will tomorrow be one of the biggest industries, a creator of wealth and jobs. Under the terms of the Treaty, we do not have the resources to implement a cultural policy; but we are going to try to tackle it along economic lines. It is not simply a question of television programmes. We have to build a powerful European culture industry that will enable us to be in control of both the medium and its content, maintaining our standards of civilization, and encouraging the creative people amongst us. (DeLors 1985, 98)

Fifth, there are numerous challenges ahead for European media policy in general and Television Without Frontiers in particular. The second directive (1997) provided for a complete review of the directive in 2002, and that review is now under way. Efforts will likely be made by some groups to abolish the European works quotas entirely and others will argue to strengthen them and make them enforceable. The result may be, like in 1997, that no change will result because of sharp differences of opinions within the member states.

New broadcasting technologies such as split screens and virtual advertising (e.g., electronically placing an advertiser's logo on the picture of a football field which in reality is green) blur the distinctions between programs and ads, especially when the two run simultaneously. Digital "multiplexing" enables the provision of multiple program streams in a single spectrum allocation, and blurs even the question of what is a channel? How the TWF directives' rules on advertising and European content apply to such techniques is yet to be determined, and there may be amendments in store. Advertising and teleshopping restrictions were lessened in 1997, and there may be more of that as commercial channels continue to increase in numbers and public channels increasingly rely on advertising for revenue.

The greatest challenge facing European transnational media policy is not the details or interpretations of the rules, but rather new geographic frontiers. The new frontier is the impending expansion of the fifteen-member Community by ten new member states in 2004 and up to three more within the next three to six years. When these countries join the EU, its frontiers expand to embrace new European cultures in the common market for broadcasting. The transition from Communist state-controlled broadcasting to a dual system of commercial and public service broadcasting for these countries involves significant challenges, including:

> How to overcome political resistance to relinquishing control over the state broadcaster; how to develop the commercial sector without sacrificing the public one; how to ensure economic viability and autonomy of public service broadcasters by

giving them ample access to advertising, and at the same time prevent their commercialisation; whether or not to promote local entrepreneurs (who may need a considerable development period before being able to provide a service of full range and quality); and how to ensure high professional standards in journalism (independence, objectivity, effective training, etc.). (European Commission 1998b)

By the time the 2002 review of the TWF directive is completed and legislation is proposed, some of these incoming member states will have influence on the changes to be implemented. How and in what direction that influence will be exercised remains to be seen. If the steps toward a transnational media system taken thus far are to facilitate the development of a European identity in the long run, ways must be found to integrate the economies and cultures of current member states with nearly as many new member states that are still struggling in the transition from command to market economy and from totalitarian states to democracy.

Broadcasting technology, law, politics, and economics have combined to at least begin the process of breaking down the national control of broadcasting that once existed in Europe. While this process began with the objective of European unification and helping to build a European "national identity," the implementation of transfrontier European broadcasting has also contributed to the transfrontier broadcasting of non-European (e.g., American) programming in substantial amounts. These factors have, as Price (1994, 696) has said, increasingly limited "one of the most important aspects of state power: the effectiveness of intervention by governments to protect an internal cartel from the destabilizing cacophony of the world." Lord Kilbrandon's (1968, 104) prophetic remarks, which opened this chapter, bid fair to have come to pass: "peoples must be plunged into the cold seas of world opinion, and can no longer swim in the warm baths that their Governments would prefer them to enjoy." In the European Union, national broadcasting systems have been forced to open their electronic frontiers to outside forces and messages that will bring cultural changes whose end cannot be clearly foreseen. The influx of outside messages pouring in from the "cold seas of world opinion" includes not just European cultures but global culture as well. This is no bad thing.

Notes

1. As of January 1, 1995, there are fifteen member states. In order of accession, they are France, Germany, Italy, Belgium, The Netherlands, Luxembourg (the original "Six"), the United Kingdom, Ireland, Denmark, Greece, Spain, Portugal, Austria, Sweden, and Finland. Thirteen additional countries have applied for membership, and ten will join in 2004. Those are Slovenia, Hungary, Estonia, Malta, Cyprus, Czech Republic, Poland, Slovakia, Latvia, and Lithuania. Longer-term candidates include Bulgaria, Romania, and Turkey.

2. The terms "Community" and "European Community" ("EC") are used interchangeably, all denoting the organization formerly known as the European Economic Community (EEC). Since the Maastricht Treaty, the Treaty on European Union, was ratified in 1993, it has become acceptable usage to refer to the European Union (EU) instead. This chapter generally uses the terms interchangeably.

3. A "directive" is a form of Community legislation that requires the member states to revise and harmonize or "coordinate" their laws to conform to the rules laid down in the directive. These are binding on the member states.

4. Owners of television sets in European countries pay a license fee to own or use a television set. Historically such fees exclusively financed the public television networks of Europe and advertising was not allowed on television. This has now changed.

5. Suspension of retransmission of broadcasts on a provisional basis is allowed under TWF only in the case pornographic or violent material that might impair development of minors.

6. Or, as some have called it, the "Ministry of Fun."

7. Known in the United States as *A Fistful of Dollars* and *For a Few Dollars More*. The series also includes *The Good, the Bad, and the Ugly*. For the culturally disadvantaged, these films depicted countless bloody gun battles featuring mercenaries, bounty hunters, bandits, and others in the American Old West engaged in diverse economic and cultural pursuits involving firearms.

References

Books and Journals

Altes, W. F. K. 1993. "European Law: A Case Study of Changes in National Broadcasting." *Cardozo Arts & Ent. L.J.* 11: 313.

Barendt, E. 1995. *Broadcasting Law: A Comparative Study.* Oxford: Oxford University Press.

Barzanti, R. 1987. "Barzanti Report." European Parliament Doc. A2-246/87, PE 113.272/def.

Churchill, W. 1946. "The United States of Europe." In R. James, ed., *Winston S. Churchill: His Complete Speeches, 1897-1963.* Vol. 7. London: Chelsea House 1974.

Collins, R. 1994. "Unity in Diversity? The European Single Market in Broadcasting and the Audiovisual 1982–92." *J. Common Mkt. Stud.* 32: 89.

Delors, J. 1985. "Address to the opening of the European Parliament on March 12 1985." In R. Collins, "Unity in Diversity? The European Single Market in Broadcasting and the Audiovisual 1982–92." *J. Common Mkt. Stud.* 32, 1994: 89.

European Commission. 1983. *Realities and Tendencies in European Television: Perspectives and Options, An Interim Report.* COM (83) 229 final.

———. 1984. *Television Without Frontiers: Green Paper on the Establishment of the Common Market for Broadcasting, Especially by Satellite and Cable,* COM (84) 300 final.

———. 1994. *Television Without Frontiers: Report on the Implementation of the Directive for 1991 and 1992.* COM (94) 57 final.

————. 1996a. *Television Without Frontiers: Report on the Implementation of the Directive For 1993 and 1994.* COM (96) 302 final.

————. 1996b. *Press Release IP/96/645.* Brussels: Commission.

————. 1997. *Exclusive Rights for TV Broadcasting of Major (Sports) Events.* Brussels: Commission.

————. 1998a. *Third Communication from the Commission to the Council and the European Parliament on the Application of Articles 4 and 5 of Directive 89/552/EEC "Television Without Frontiers" for the Period 1995-96 Including an Overall Assessment of Application over the Period 1991-96.* COM (98) 199 final.

————. 1998b. *The Digital Age, European Audiovisual Policy: Report from the High Level Group on Audiovisual Policy.* http://europa.eu.int/comm/avpolicy/legis/key_doc/hlg_en.htm#top.

————. 2000. *Fourth Communication from the Commission to the Council and the European Parliament on the application of Articles 4 and 5 of Directive 89/552/EEC "Television Without Frontiers" for the period 1997-8.* COM (2000) 442 final. Brussels: Commission.

Hahn Report. 1982. *European Parliament Report on Radio and Television Broadcasting in the European Community.* O.J. C-87 of 5 April 1982.

Kilbrandon, L. 1968. In Consultative Assembly of the Council of Europe's *Symposium on Human Rights and Mass Communication.* Strasbourg: Council of Europe.

Machet, E. 1999. *A Decade of EU Broadcasting Regulation: The Directive "Television Without Frontiers."* Dusseldorf: European Institute for the Media.

McNeill, H. 1998. "Ball Spin." *Dallas Morning News*, January 2, 1998, 2A.

Price, M. 1994. "The Market for Loyalties: Electronic Media and the Global Competition for Allegiances." *Yale L. J.* 104: 667.

Salvatore, V. 1992. "Quotas on TV Programs and EEC Law." *Common Mkt. L. Rev.* 29: 967.

Schuman, R. 1950. "'The Declaration of May 9 1950,' in Commission." 1988. *European Documentation Series.* 5/1988.

Schwartz, I. 1986. "Broadcasting and the EEC Treaty." *Eur. L. Rev.* 11: 7

Shelden, J. 1994. "Televison without Frontiers: A Case Study of Turner Broadcasting's New Channel in the Community: Does It Violate the Directive?" *Transnat'l Law* 7: 523.

Ungerer, H. 1996. "EC Competition Law in the Telecommunications, Media, and Information Technology Sectors." *Fordham Int'l Law J.* 99: 1111–77.

Wallace, R., and Goldberg, D. 1989. "Television Broadcasting: The Community's Response." *Common Mkt. L. Rev.* 26: 717.

de Witte, B. 1995. "The European Content Requirement in the EC Television Directive: Five Years After." *Y.B. Media & Ent. Law.*, 101. Edited by E. Barendt.

Laws

EC Treaty. 1957. *Treaty Establishing the European Economic Community (Treaty of Rome).* 298 U.N.T.S. 3. Referred to as the EC Treaty or Article 49 EC.

Exclusive Television Rights Act of Austria. 2002. O.J. C 16/06 19.1.2002.

Ministerial Order of the Kingdom of Denmark. 1999. O.J. C 14/ 05 19.1.1999.

TWF. 1989. *Council Directive 89/552 of 17 October 1989 on the Coordination of Certain Provisions Laid Down by Law, Regulation, or Administrative Action in Member States Concerning the Pursuit of Television Broadcasting Activities* 1989 O.J. (L 298) 23. Herein referred to as TWF or the First Directive.

TWF 2. 1997. *Council Directive 97/36 of 30 July 1997 Amending Council Directive 89/552 on the Coordination of Certain Provisions Laid Down by Law, Regulation or Administrative Action in Member States Concerning the Pursuit of Television Broadcasting Activities* 1997 O.J. (L 202) 60. Herein referred to as TWF2 or the Second Directive.

Court Cases

De Agostini. 1997. Joined Cases C-34/95, C-35/95 and C-36/95, *Konsumentombudsmannen v. De Agostini (Svenska) Förlag AB* [1997] ECR I- 3843, [1998] 1 CMLR 32.

Coditel. 1980. Case 62/79, *Coditel v. Cine Vog Films* [1980] ECR 881.

Commission v. Belgium. 1996. Case C-11/95 [1996] E.C.R. I-4115, 2 C.M.L.R. 289 (1997).

Debauve. 1980. Case 52/79, *Procureur du Roi v. Debauve* [1980] ECR 833.

Denuit. 1997. Case C-14/96, *Paul Denuit* [1997] E.C.R. I-2785 , 3 C.M.L.R. 943 (1997).

Dutch Advertisers. 1988. Case 352/85, *Advertisers' Association v. Netherlands* [1988] ECR 2085 [1989] 3 CMLR 113.

Fediciné. 1993. Case C-17/92, *Federacion de Distribuidores Cinematograficos v. Estado Espanol* [1993] E.C.R. I-2239.

Flemish Cable. 1992. Case C-211/91, *Commission v. Belgium* [1992] E.C.R. i-6757.

Gouda. 1991. Case C-288/89, *Gouda v. Media Commission* [1991] E.C.R. 4007.

Kingdom of the Netherlands. 1991. Case C-353/89, *Kingdom of the Netherlands v. Commission* [1991] E.C.R. 4069

Leclerc-Siplec. 1995. Case C-412/93, *Societe d´Importation Edouard Leclerc-Siplec v. TF 1 Publicite sa* [1995] E.C.R. I-179, 3 C.M.L.R. 422.

Pro Sieben. 1999. Case C-6/98, *Arbeitsgemeinschaft Deutscher Rundfunkanstalten (ARD) v. PRO Sieben Media AG* [1999] E.C.R. I-7599.

RTI. 1996. Joined Cases C-320, 328-9 & 337-339/94, *RTI v. Ministero Delle Poste E Telecomunicazioni* [1996] E.C.R. I-6471, 1 C.M.L.R. 346 (1997).

Sacchi. 1974. Case 155/73, *Italy v. Sacchi* [1974] E.C.R. 409 1974 (2) C.M.L.R. 177.

TV10. 1994. Case C-23/93, *TV10 s.a. v. Media Commission* [1994] E.C.R. i-4795.

Veronica. 1993. Case C-48/91, *Veronica v. Media Commission* [1993] E.C.R. 487.

9

Democratization and the Media: Reflections on the Central American Experience

Rick Rockwell

THE FIGHT AGAINST CORRUPTION in the Central American media began in 1993 with an editor staring down the barrel of a gun. The gun was pointed at Vilma Gloria Rosales, the editor of *El Tiempo*, a popular and respected newspaper in Honduras. Rosales had discovered a ring of corrupt reporters who were on the illicit payroll of the Honduran electoral tribunal. The person pointing the gun at Rosales was one of her own reporters, a ringleader of the corrupt pack. Rosales was told to forget what she had uncovered or else. Instead, she called the reporter's bluff. She printed the names of the corrupt reporters and most lost their jobs, a watershed event that swept most overt corruption out of Honduran newsrooms (Rockwell 1998).

But media corruption was far from dead in Honduras.

Six years later, another Honduran journalist who had faced death threats for her work, Sandra Maribel Sanchez, stood up at an international forum on journalism and denounced the widespread underground corruption in her country. She called many of her colleagues "insatiable gangsters." She also said the trail of media corruption started with reporters covering the country's president and soliciting payoffs. The trail of corruption eventually led to various levels of the media (Fliess 1999).

Examples abound throughout Central America of the media's battles against corrupt influences in their ranks along with the stories of those who have succumbed to corruption's siren call.

In Nicaragua in 2000, popular television news anchor Danilo Lacayo was swept up in a corruption scandal. Lacayo had struck a deal with the Nicaraguan comptroller, General Agustin Jarquin Anaya, to share investigative information with Jarquin's office. Jarquin, a prominent Sandinista, was involved in an intense effort to reveal the corrupt practices of Nicaragua's former president, Arnoldo Alemán. Jarquin would also pay a monthly bribe to ensure placement of news items on Lacayo's program, *Buenas Dias Nicaragua*, one of the most popular television programs in the country. Although meant to combat state corruption, Lacayo's arrangement with Jarquin was built on an unethical foundation. When news of the arrangement finally leaked out, Jarquin faced the full wrath of the state: he lost his job and went to jail briefly (Dye, Spence, and Vickers 2000). Lacayo lost his position as the top anchor at Canal 2, Nicaragua's most popular network. He eventually became the news anchor for a UHF station in Managua regularly seen by only 1 percent of the city's viewing audience (UCA 2001).

In Panama in 2001, investigative editor Gustavo Gorriti was forced to return to his native Peru after confronting state corruption through his work for six years at *La Prensa*. A corporate coup had allowed allies of Gorriti's investigative targets to gain control of the newspaper. After Gorriti led an exodus of some of the paper's best talent out of the publication and out of the country, he wrote on October 12, 2001, that "any serious attempt to conduct investigative journalism in thoroughly corrupt societies will be a very difficult and precarious endeavor" (Gorriti 2001).

The Analytical Framework

These examples show the ongoing struggle with corruption in Central America as the media attempt to find new standards amid a period of democratization. The story of Rosales at *El Tiempo* is indicative of that struggle. Central American journalists are moving past a period of authoritarianism where direct violence was often used to curb free expression and control the media. However, instead of facing threats at gunpoint as Rosales did at *El Tiempo*, as the 1990s came to a close, the threat to the free flow of ideas in Central American society came mostly from corrupt influences. As the millennium began, monitors of violence and threats against the media noted that the possibility of states using violence or prison against the media had diminished, although journalists in Guatemala and Panama remained at some risk (Canton 1999).

During the 1990s, most of the isthmus of Spanish-speaking countries strung between Mexico and Colombia went through a period of profound change. The United States invaded Panama in 1989 to depose dictator General Manuel Noriega and restore a democratic form of government. After losing an election, Nicaragua's Sandinistas left control of that country to others in 1990 and thus ended the U.S.-backed military counterrevolution against their socialist cause. In 1992, the civil war in El Salvador also ended. Guatemala's long-running guerrilla war finally finished officially as 1996 came to a close. With the end of these conflicts, the United States dismantled most of its military presence in Honduras and that country's military finally came under civilian control in 1999. Only Costa Rica seemed to make it through this period without much turmoil, although Nicaragua's counterrevolutionary war spilled across Costa Rica's northern border. As a result, the entire region was caught up in transformation using the tools of democracy, something that had not been attempted since the region's independence from Spain in the nineteenth century.

After this tumult, it is important to assess the progress the media have made in contributing to this transformation. This chapter proposes a new method for evaluating media systems undergoing the transition from authoritarianism.

One of the critical issues in this context, and one that has been neglected in scholarly studies of the media, is the importance of corruption as a limiting factor in the advancement of professional standards for media practices. This chapter will argue that corruption should be considered in theoretical explanations of media systems and how those systems relate to political institutions and structures for civil society.

In their work on corruption in Latin America, Joseph Tulchin and Ralph Espach note that "corruption has an overall negative effect on economic growth and stability and on democratic consolidation" (Tulchin and Espach 2000, 5). Further, Tulchin and Espach feel there is a consensus that state bureaucracy has failed at combating corruption, and free market means toward transparency, including civil society groups and the media, should be the main tools in the fight. Tulchin and Espach represent a group of Latin American specialists who point to strong, independent media as a cornerstone in the construction of new societal standards as a means of limiting state and corporate corruption and advancing democratic forms of governance.

Of course, the media are not separate from these structures. The political and corporate agendas of media owners, leaders in the journalistic field, and other media figures also affect how the media deal with corruption (Lins da Silva 2000; Hallin 2000). As with Lacayo in Nicaragua, the motives and methods of the media are not always pure. Sometimes there is collusion between elements of the state and the media, with political gain for all parties.

One of the difficulties with the examination of corruption, as economist Alberto Ades and scholar Rafael Di Tella point out (2000), is that its definition shifts, depending on the cultural context. Luis Moreno Ocampo of Transparency International, a nongovernmental organization (NGO) focused on promoting anticorruption programs, suggests a multistandard approach in assessing corrupt systems (2000). Under Moreno's system, formalized rules of behavior for groups should be studied along with operational norms of groups to determine what can be defined as corruption. Tulchin and Espach suggest a narrow definition of corruption: "the application of public property or license for private gain." However, this definition proves too narrow when applied to the media. This definition proves useful for the media to apply when assessing state corruption but seems inadequate in any self-reflective gaze. In addition, Tulchin and Espach point to a compounding problem documented by various Latin American specialists: corruption is not just endemic in the working systems of the region and culture; it often is the system. So how to define it using the suggestions of Moreno?

Citizens in the proto-democracies of Latin America perceive that corruption in general has actually increased in the transition away from authoritarian government (Tulchin and Espach 2000). Although corruption certainly exists in authoritarian and totalitarian systems, the onset of democracy often causes a public reaction calling for institutions to reveal past and current abuses. This call for transparency has historically left many with the impression that in periods of democratization in Europe and Latin America corruption actually increases (Little and Posada-Carbó 1996). As Tulchin and Espach theorize (2000), "It is in the periods between the delegitimizing of old sets of rules or systems and the formulation of new ones that corruption is most likely to expand." This also increases the burden on the media to provide a balanced focus on corruption as part of the process of providing a more representative form of government and as a way to bolster civil society.

Various media analysts have called for a rejection of generalized standard theories when considering the Latin American experience, including the rejection of neoliberalism, Marxism, the political economy approach, or dependency theory (Fox 1997; Hallin 2000; Waisbord 2000a). In going beyond those boundaries, some experts have invoked the need to understand how the media, civil society, and the state work while negotiating power. Defining corruption starts by examining those power bases.

Although completely answering Moreno's question in Central America is beyond the scope of this chapter, it is important to note that journalism educators, media owners, and international journalism organizations have attempted at various times to set standards of media behavior for Latin America (Heise and Green 1996). In the past, most have agreed that imposing an ethical framework imported to the region from the United States would be folly. This view rejects cultural imperialism and acknowledges the shortcomings of the U.S. media system (Bennett 2000; McChesney 1997). Some of those shortcomings, like the weakness of the public sector in the media system, are also part of the Central American experience. There are similarities between the United States and Central America because of U.S influence in the region during the Cold War era, when broadcasting was established in these countries (Fox 1997). So a shared definition for corruption may be appropriate. The definition provided by Tulchin and Espach can be broadened to encompass the media: corruption is the application of power for personal gain and enrichment beyond that allowed by law or ethical construct.

Some of the analysis of the region, this chapter included, is made from a cultural standpoint that is not native to Central America. Nevertheless, it provides a further understanding of corruption to shed light on the structural impediments for the development of attempts at a democratic political system.

This chapter proposes a framework for assessment of media systems in nations undergoing postauthoritarian transition as a way to gauge the influence of corruption. Five factors seem to be influential in assessing the level of media standards to determine the democratic potential of a given media system for a particular nation: (1) the distance in time from watershed political-military events (e.g., civil wars, guerrilla wars, major military invasions), (2) general economic conditions for journalists, (3) demonstrable generational shifts in ideology and ethics, (4) genuine state policies aimed at curtailing corrupt practices, and (5) the political and cultural influence of the United States in a particular country (e.g., U.S. support for educational programs for journalists, cultural exchange, or other international assistance programs). In this context, media corruption becomes theorized as part of the dynamic nexus where these formative factors struggle, the end result being the power and legitimacy of various media actors.

This examination of media systems also allows an assessment of the growing so-called media-ocracy that has arisen in many of these countries under transition, if not the developed world too (Heywood 1996; Bennett 2000). Such systems are characterized by a decline in party loyalty and importance while television advertising and media campaigns influence the electorate. In such systems, revelations of high-level corruption can spell doom for the powerful. The end of power for Fernando Collor de Mello in Brazil, Alberto Fujimori in Peru, and Carlos Andrés Pérez of Venezuela partially due to corruption exposed by the media speaks to this growing media power throughout Latin America.

The analysis of these factors surrounding corruption also could have future applications to media systems outside Latin America. Studies of the media systems in Indonesia, the Balkans, the Middle East, and the nations making up the Commonwealth of Independent States (the former Soviet states) could adapt this analytical framework. This chapter takes for granted that in today's globalized society with its various cultural and political conflicts the need for democratic media systems is greater than ever. Ultimately, this analytical framework has value in allowing a deeper assessment of Western/northern theoretical models for the development of democratic media systems.

The factors that make up this analytical framework are drawn from a variety of sources. Ades and Di Tella have identified different prisms for studying the effects and approaches to creating anticorruption standards. They propose a three-pronged view: legalistic, corporate, and economic. Those views are reflected in several of the core factors of the framework. Likewise, John Nerone (1994) in his work on the transition away from violence as a controlling factor of the media in the United States has identified various factors that cue journalists to higher ethical and professional standards. Later, Nerone (1996) distilled his views on these historic factors of media evolution to show the transition from violent controls of the media to more sophisticated means coincides with the process of media professionalization. The analysis of that process in the United States to attain higher media standards and a less corrupt and violent system also informs this analytical framework.

The Corruption Perception Index

Transparency International's annual rating (2001) of corruption in various nations is an important assessment guide to the development of professional standards for media systems in the region (see table 9.1). The perception index is assembled through polling and interviews to construct a rating of the influence of corruption in government, politics, and business, the perceived connections of institutions to criminal elements, and the acceptance of corrupt practices in the course of daily social activity. Although this rating ranks corruption in general for various societies, it gives observers clues about the level of corruption the media must face. As various experts have noted (Lins da Silva 2000; Tulchin and Espach 2000), the media play the role of both monitor and

TABLE 9.1
Transparency International's Corruption Perception Index

	2000	1999	1998	1997	1996	1995	Avg.
Chile	7.5	6.9	6.8	6.1	6.8	7.9	7
Costa Rica	4.5	5.1	5.6	6.5	—	—	5.4
Panama	3.7	—	—	—	—	—	3.7
El Salvador	3.6	3.9	3.6	—	—	—	3.7
Guatemala	2.9	3.2	3.1	—	—	—	3.1
Nicaragua	2.4	3.1	3.0	—	—	—	2.8
Honduras	2.7	1.8	1.7	—	—	—	2.1
Argentina	3.5	3.0	3.0	2.8	3.4	3.2	3.2

Note: The index is a survey rating on a 10-point scale, with 10 being the rating for the least corrupt. Not all countries are rated each year. Chile and Argentina are included here with the Central American countries for comparative purposes.

participant in such systems. This rating does not give a pure assessment of media corruption and therefore a reading on the scale of media professionalism in these countries, but it provides a starting point for analysis.

As benchmarks for assessment, the two leading countries in the Transparency International rankings in Latin America are Chile and Costa Rica. Despite their different paths toward governance in the latter half of the twentieth century—Chile charting the neoliberal course and Costa Rica a social interventionist route—both countries have historically fought the casual bribery many stereotypically pin on Latin America. Both countries have records stretching back to colonial times for anticorruption campaigns (Whitehead 2000; Knight 1996).

By comparison, the remainder of Central America seems to rank closer to Argentina. The corruption of the administration of Carlos Menem in Argentina partially fueled a resurgence of investigative reporting in that nation during its postauthoritarian, neoliberal transition (Waisbord 2000b).

Costa Rica and Honduras

Despite *El Tiempo*'s open fight against journalistic corruption, the high level of Honduran media corruption was one of the central topics at a regional conference on journalism in Panama in 1999 (Fliess 1999). This correlates to the Transparency International scale, which ranks Honduras as the most corrupt country in Central America during the past few years.

Conversely, Costa Rican journalism is often hailed as a cornerstone bolstering the longest-running democracy in Latin America (Whitehead 2000). The differences and gaps between these nations can partially be explained through the analytical framework proposed here.

Nerone, in his various works on the transition from turbulence in a media system controlled by violence and corrupt practices to one with solid professional standards, has noted the need for elite members of society and government to agree to accept social cleavages and partisanship as part of one holistic system, and to accept how those differences are debated in the media. Although Nerone based his analysis on the U.S. media system, Central American, Latin American, or other cultural systems do not need to adopt U.S. standards and practices. Although various analysts have pointed to how Latin America has borrowed from both U.S. and European models, local culture and politics have played strong roles in creating interesting new blends for media systems (Straubhaar 2001; Waisbord 2000a). Nevertheless the various Central American blends, like the U.S. system, are characterized by a system that is easily manipulated by elite forces (Bennett 2000). Some media systems have adapted a less partisan approach at balancing political news, which in many ways is predicted by Nerone's research.

What Nerone's work illustrates is a process of media evolution. Because Nerone traces the beginning of those changes to the resolution of the U.S. Civil War, looking at how nations resolve internal conflicts over partisanship and social cleavages becomes an important tenet in this analysis. Honduras and Costa Rica exhibit wide differences when viewed through that prism.

Some might question whether Honduras has resolved the issue of accepting differing viewpoints in the media or society in general. Unlike its neighbors, Honduras did not endure a civil war in the twentieth century. In 1999, the military finally relinquished control to civilian authorities after forty-five years of either directly running the country or being an unchecked and independent force that could nullify civilian government (Skidmore and Smith 2001; Cuevas 1999). When Honduran journalists decided to expose how the state had shackled them economically through bribery in 1993, they also grew bold enough to confront the military. *El Tiempo* was in the forefront of a short investigative crusade that linked the Honduran military to extrajudicial death squads, connections to narcotics rings, and journalism repression. When the home of the newspaper's publisher, Yani Rosenthal, was firebombed, the crusade to monitor the military ended (Quintanilla 1994; Schulz and Sundloff Schulz 1994). Former President Carlos Flores, who owns *La Tribuna,* was noted for pressuring various media outlets to stifle criticism during his time in office (Rockwell and Janus 2001). Although his methods were more subtle than those of the military, they did not encourage the debate necessary to foster democracy. By Nerone's standards, there is a question of whether Honduran elites have resolved ideological differences enough to accept that differing viewpoints can coexist in the same system.

By contrast, Costa Rica fought a forty-day civil war in 1948. Although communist groups were repressed after the civil war, the country abolished its military and adopted a social welfare approach to democracy (Paige 1997). Even the communists became part of the country's political scene by the 1970s.

At the same time, Costa Rica's media system was renowned in Latin America for its support of democracy. Costa Rica had a press law guaranteeing freedom from government interference as early as 1835. For decades, the Costa Rican media system has been marked by its debate of policy issues in search of compromise and consensus building (Vanden Heuvel and Dennis 1995).

Other points along the analytical scale also underscore the differences between Costa Rica and Honduras. Although average pay rates are difficult to determine, in general, Costa Rican journalists earn more than Honduran journalists. In the mid-1990s the Latin American Association of Journalists estimated that most of its journalists earned between $200 and $800 monthly (Waisbord 2000b). Maribel Sanchez of Honduran Radio America, who made the charges of corruption at the 1999 conference in Panama, noted in her statements that corrupt journalists often earned $300 to $400 per month at their media jobs (Fliess 1999). This pegs Honduran journalists in the lower half of the pay range. Costa Rican journalists are comfortably part of the middle class and receive higher rates of pay. These differences also can be seen in the wider economy. In 1999, per capita income in Honduras was $2,200 while in Costa Rica it was $5,500 (Goodwin 2000).

In terms of the third and fourth areas of the analytical framework, in response to poor pay conditions, journalists in Honduras traditionally have turned to the government for bribes, in effect government subsidies for their complicity. In the 1980s in Honduras, many journalists held jobs with both the government and media outlets, compromising their independence (Rockwell 1998). Although that practice waned somewhat in the 1990s, Sanchez's criticisms show that journalists continue to turn to the state in both open and illicit ways to supplement their meager pay. The state has not curtailed its practice of open subsidies or clandestine bribes in the Honduran system, at least not during the Flores years through 2001. This is similar to bribery systems in other Latin American countries such as Mexico (Fromson 1996; Hallin 2000; Rockwell 1999).

In Costa Rica, a push for higher journalism standards began to make headway after the civil war, which parallels the evolution Nerone has tracked in the United States. In the 1940s, most Costa Rican newspapers were aligned officially with a political party. For instance, the now defunct *Diario de Costa Rica* was the political base of publisher Otilio Ulate Blanco. Ulate won the 1948 elections, but the National Republican Party refused to transfer power to him and the civil war began. At the time, *La Tribuna* backed the Republicans. *La Nación*, although not aligned with a formal political group, represented the interests of Costa Rica's coffee elite and was founded by the rich, conservative Jimenez de la Guardia family.

Today, both *Diario de Costa Rica* and *La Tribuna* have disappeared. *La Nación* changed its approach to journalism and became an outlet for a less openly partisan, U.S.-style journalism. Media outlets in Costa Rica are currently known for their lack of partisan displays and have no direct connections to political parties (Vanden Heuvel and Dennis 1995).

The Costa Rican government is one of the largest advertisers in the country, but unlike most other governments on the isthmus, it has not exerted political leverage against media outlets to gain favorable coverage. As Tulchin and Espach note, a country that tends to follow the rule of law and has strong democratic institutions, especially an independent judiciary and a probing media to check executive power, usually has lower levels of corruption. As demonstrated in Costa Rica, the firewalls remain intact between the media, political, and judicial actors to keep them working at the democratic ideal.

What this analysis shows is that after the civil war period Costa Rican journalism and the media took less partisan stands. Partisan media outlets disappeared. This generational shift in approach, coupled with Costa Rica's long history at fighting public sector graft and corruption, are two major differences compared to the Honduran system.

The final area to consider is U.S. influence in each country. Although El Salvador was the greatest beneficiary of U.S. aid to the region from 1989 through 1999 (see table 9. 2), Honduras received a significant amount, about $808.2 million. The Honduran figure was more than double the aid sent to Costa Rica. However, these figures measure total U.S. aid to the region, not aid aimed directly at media development in the form of ethics programs or anticorruption programs. The influence of U.S.-inspired ethics programs for the media may be less quantifiable.

One way to track this influence is to review the performance of the journalism training program sponsored by the U.S. Agency for International Development (USAID) in the region. Known as the Latin American Journalism Program (LAJP), for a decade the program focused most of its efforts on Central America to raise the standards of reporting, improve the skills of reporters and editors, and infuse ethics into journalism (Heise and Green 1996). The program, administered by Florida International University, held seminars in the region and ran training sessions in the United States. For the program's first phase, the recipients from each country were tracked (LAJP 1994). Because of poor U.S. relations with Panama and Nicaragua in the first phase of the program, participation from those countries skewed lower. During this first phase, 25.7 percent of all participants were from El Salvador, 24.2 percent from Honduras, and 19.5 percent from Costa Rica (LAJP 1994).

In the latter half of the program, participation by country was not tracked (Heise and Green 1998). As political conditions changed in Panama and Nicaragua, more training sessions were held there. The LAJP regional training center in Costa Rica was relocated to Panama and eventually became the headquarters of the independent Center for Latin American Journalism. Although training sessions held in the various countries of the region were not exclusive to journalists from those nations, often journalists from the host country of a particular seminar dominated attendance. Examining the number of participants of journalism training seminars sponsored by USAID in each country (see table 9.3) produces a clearer picture about where training was focused. In the decade the LAJP existed, Honduras received the lowest amount of training. During all phases of the program, journalists in Costa Rica were well represented with the third highest total of training slots. Also, having a training center in Costa Rica for the region was bound to have some symbolic impact on raising standards.

TABLE 9.2

U.S. Assistance to Central America, 1989–1999 (U.S.$ millions)

	1989	1990	1991	1992	1993	1994	1995	1996	1997	1998	1999	Total
Costa Rica	121.9	95.3	44.9	26.7	27.6	12.1	6.2	2.1	0.1	0.7	1.1	338.7
Panama	0.9	397.1	40.1	21.1	8.9	6.7	4.9	7.4	4.8	5.5	6.9	504.3
El Salvador	307.0	246.7	227.7	268.8	214.3	56.8	63.2	78.4	31.2	40.2	48.9	1583.2
Guatemala	147.2	114.8	92.3	61.8	68.2	67.9	39.2	37.3	61.4	82.5	101.4	874.0
Nicaragua	3.9	223.2	218.7	74.9	149.8	93.1	31.4	27.3	26.8	54.3	65.5	968.9
Honduras	88.1	192.6	123.8	89.3	59.6	47.2	29.7	25.8	28.5	21.1	102.5	808.2

Note: All figures provided by the U.S. Agency for International Development (USAID). Totals include all economic assistance loans and grants.

TABLE 9.3
USAID-Sponsored Training
Sessions in Central America, 1988–1997

Country	Number of Participants
Costa Rica	692
Panama	938
El Salvador	680
Guatemala	587
Nicaragua	853
Honduras	398

Note: Totals exclude training sessions conducted in the United States and other countries outside of Central America. Totals also exclude registrants for annual conferences or meetings sponsored by the training groups supported by USAID. Totals are meant to reflect the number of persons trained in each country during the decade of the journalism training program. The Latin American Journalism Program sponsored by USAID was a $13.9 million project with its main training focus on Central America, although Andean nations were added in the final phase of the program. The program concluded in 1998.

Central American Comparisons

If Costa Rica and Honduras represent the separate poles of this assessment framework, it is now possible to sketch in the remainder of the region.

Panama has the second-highest ranking in the region on Transparency International's corruption index, a ranking similar to Mexico and the Slovak Republic. Although Panama has not had a civil war since its independence from Colombia in 1903, Operation Just Cause, the U.S. invasion of 1989 that deposed General Noriega, proved to be a political watershed. The invasion restored democracy to the country, and both pro-Noriega and anti-Noriega politicians have held the presidency since the invasion. The country eliminated its military after the invasion. Since the invasion, Panama's media remain partisan (Gorriti 2001). However, Panama's *La Prensa* and *El Universal* both made important attempts at lessening partisanship in their news columns in the 1990s.

Pay rates for journalists were generally between $300 and $600 monthly in Panama (Freedom Forum 1999), making salaries a bit higher than in Honduras. Government policies vis-à-vis journalistic corruption have a mixed track record in Panama. Although government bribes for journalists were readily available in the 1990s, Panamanian journalists tried to expose media corruption (Guerrero 1995). Panama's new president, Mireya Moscoso, promised sweeping changes in media policy when she was inaugurated (Freedom Forum 1999), but the promised changes have been slow in coming. Panama had extensive contact with U.S. efforts to raise media standards in the 1990s. The ethics training of the Center for Latin American Journalists in Panama has resulted in a sustained effort to create higher standards for a new generation of journalists. But again, the record is mixed. Gorriti's ouster at *La Prensa* and his complaints about the corrupt nature of Panamanian society point to the deep-seated nature of corruption in the country.

On the Transparency International scale, El Salvador rates just behind Panama, with perceptions of corruption in general comparable to Egypt and Turkey. El Salvador's civil war ended in 1992, but the media remain polarized (Rockwell, Janus, and Neubauer 2001). In the latter part of the 1990s, salaries for journalists were listed as some of the lowest in the region, as little as $100 monthly for radio journalists (Janus 1998a). At Salvadoran daily *El Diario de Hoy*, management brought in a new generation of reporters with higher ethical standards in the postwar era (Smeets 2000). To combat corruption, *El Diario de Hoy* also raised salaries. The paper launched an anticorruption campaign against the government and the conservative ARENA party (Fliess 1999), although the publication has generally tilted toward the conservative government and ARENA in the past. Another factor hemming in some of the systemic media corruption in El Salvador is the influence of ethical standards from outside the country. U.S. and other foreign journalists maintained a higher presence in El Salvador than any other Central American country during the war years of the 1970s and 1980s. Today, many Salvadoran journalists credit these foreign correspondents with changing local attitudes to create higher standards (Smeets 2000). Although El Salvador had the fourth highest amount of USAID journalism training in the 1990s, the country was also the top recipient of total U.S. aid in the region. All this leaves El Salvador with an improving record but in the middle of the Central American pack.

Guatemala ranks lower on the Transparency International index than El Salvador and is comparable to the Philippines or Zimbabwe in regards to overall corruption. Since the end of the guerrilla war in 1996, Guatemala's media have worked to become less partisan. At least one of the country's newspapers, *Siglo Veintiuno*, has been recognized as one of the best in Latin America (Mower 1999). However, the country's broadcasters have not made similar strides (Smeets 2000). Although violence against journalists has subsided, it has not been eliminated completely, unlike the situation in most other countries in Central America (Smeets 2001). The quality split among newspapers and broadcast operations was also reflected in pay. Television journalists in the late 1990s were making as little as $50 per month (Barrios Reina 1998), while at newspapers, salaries were more in line with the Latin American average.

One factor that curbed media corruption was a move by Guatemala's former president Alvaro Arzú in 1996. Arzú stopped all official media subsidies and published a list of corrupt journalists. However, Arzú's policy was part of a scheme to use state advertising as a fulcrum to get the media to bend to the president's wishes (Chasan 1999). The president's moves coincided with a trend among media outlets to write new ethics policies and enforce them (Berganza 1998). Although Guatemala had the second lowest level of interactions with the USAID journalism programs, many journalists cited these outside contacts for improving Guatemalan standards (Smeets 2000; Berganza 1998; Barrios Reina 1998).

In Nicaragua, the trend for more ethical practices has begun to reverse. In Transparency International's latest rankings, Nicaragua had the worst general corruption in the region, comparable with Côte d'Ivoire. This relates to the revelations of state corruption at the end of the term of President Alemán (Dye, Spence, and Vickers 2000). Some researchers cite Nicaragua as a worst-case example for the "sultanistic" style of the Somoza dictatorships, showing how the state can become a vehicle for looting and personal enrichment (Whitehead 2000). Although the Sandinista and Chormorro eras saw less corruption, the restoration of Somoza's Liberal Party to power also returned corrupt state policies. The Lacayo scandal also showed that younger journalists, who supposedly eschewed the dishonest practices of the past, could fall back into the old ways.

Nicaragua's movement away from corruption and violence has been uncertain. Since the Contra War ended in 1990, violence, threats, and censorship against the media have stopped. Although many partisan divisions remain in the media, *La Prensa*, the country's oldest newspaper, has become more balanced in its presentation (Kodrich 2001). Canal 2, the most powerful network, has also moved away from its partisan roots. Both *La Prensa* and Canal 2 have instituted ethics codes and improved salaries. Although salaries remain relatively low, they range from $300 to $700 monthly for journalists, putting them near the top end of the scale for Central America (Janus 1998b). Nicaragua also had the second-highest level of USAID journalism training in the region. The question in Nicaragua is whether the media can maintain momentum in the push toward professionalism or will they backslide.

The Comparative Matrix

Several factors that are often part of evaluating media systems are missing from this framework. First, the structure of media ownership is not a consideration. Broad similarities do exist among the structures of media ownership in the region. In general, the media of the region are characterized by concentrated ownership with strong ties to conservative political elites (Rockwell and Janus 2001). The determination of owners and managers to fight corruption, as demonstrated at *El Tiempo* in Honduras and *El Diario de Hoy* in El Salvador, is crucial. Equally crucial is maintaining those standards over time. Sanchez's complaints in Honduras six years after *El Tiempo's* anticorruption fight show that the extraordinary efforts of one media organization are not enough to change the entire system permanently. The Lacayo scandal in Nicaragua juxtaposed against the reform efforts of *La Prensa* and Canal 2 show the push and tug of the fight against media corruption and the battle to set new standards. Lacayo, who worked at Canal 2, shows that the efforts of owners and media leaders are not enough to change the system.

This comparative framework is useful across media systems with different ownership structures. The media in Central America provide a wealth of different examples while working within generally free market republics. For instance, Guatemala's system is characterized by a foreign-owned monopoly television structure, while print media are divided among conservative and moderate owners from inside the country. Honduras, Costa Rica, El Salvador, and Nicaragua have mixed broadcast systems with external and internal ownership structures. El Salvador, Nicaragua, and Panama all have quasi-monopoly television systems where one ownership group dominates. Although the print and broadcast media are dominated by conservative messages in most of these countries, important exceptions exist in El Salvador and Nicaragua.

When considering Mexico, media analyst Daniel Hallin (2000) suggests that any framework of analysis should consider ownership structures—a factor that undercuts the political economy approach and the liberal framework for media analysis. Arguably, media owners could change the atmosphere for media corruption in the region if they would uniformly pay workers a higher wage. In effect, the system of corruption has created a black market for information that subsidizes reporters and others in the media to the real market price of their services. Higher pay and a stronger hand dealing with those who are caught—even harsher market penalties for transgressors like Lacayo in Nicaragua—would reduce the level of corruption in the system. Although to outsiders media owners seem to operate as a cartel, often ego, political ambition, and other factors keep them apart. For now, the likelihood of media owners banding together to combat corruption in the region seems remote.

Parallels exist between the Mexican system in Hallin's analysis and Central America. For instance, the weakness of the rule of law when applied to broadcasters and the strength of broadcasters versus state attempts at regulation are similar in Central America to the Mexican experience. As usual, Costa Rica stands out as an exception. However, that too may be changing with the forceful movement of one Mexican broadcaster into Costa Rica's network structure (Rojas 2000).

Although Hallin's analysis skims past corruption as an important controlling factor, on the surface there are parallels in this area between the Mexican experience and Central America. Before Vicente Fox became Mexico's president, many major media outlets were controlled through state subsidies or graft. Arzú's use of state advertising in Guatemala is just one example of attempts to create similar structures of control in Central America. However, most of the broadcast operations in Central America are strong enough to ignore such state pressures. By building diversified structures to acquire revenue, publications like the leftist *El Nuevo Diario* in Nicaragua and the moderate *Prensa Libre* in Guatemala have successfully fought state efforts at control. The popularity of these papers and strong circulation buffered them against such pressure. Arguably *La Nación*, perhaps the most profitable paper in the region, would also be immune to such pressures although they are unlikely to arise given the political development of Costa Rica. Again, the unique features of the media systems in these various countries work against using some of the broader factors for analysis outlined by Hallin and other media analysts. Considering the political change in Mexico with Fox's election, Central America may become more of a barometer to show Mexico's future evolution rather than the other way around.

Political structures also differ in the various countries of the isthmus. The strong contrast between the oldest democracy in Latin America in Costa Rica and the renewal of democratic forms in Honduras, where civilian government finally reasserted itself after forty-five years, illustrates the differences. The Honduran system retains the classic conservative–liberal split that is rooted in the politics of the mid-nineteenth century, while Costa Rica's political structures were remade after its civil war in 1948. In Guatemala, political party structures are so unstable that the dominant parties of the 1990s did not even exist in the 1980s: no party has been able to win back-to-back presidential elections since the U.S.-backed coup in 1954 that destroyed the country's political evolution. In Nicaragua, the shadow of the Cold War conflict between the Sandinistas and the Somozas still hovers over the political system. Likewise the politics of El Salvador and Panama seem to be shaped by the partisanship surrounding recent wars or invasions. To simply lump these nations together as part of the neoliberal wave affecting other nations in the region like Mexico and Argentina would be to oversimplify.

Although the force and influence of the United States undeniably looms over Central America, and the influence of the superpower to the north is a part of the analytical framework proposed here, this influence is the least important part of that framework. As Latin American specialist Silvio Waisbord

(2000b) has argued, the embrace of U.S.-style journalism in Latin America has only been "halfhearted." Although U.S. journalism and media standards remain important cultural referents, the different structure of the state vis-à-vis the media in Central America has called for a different response to corruption. Even the USAID-sponsored journalism training in Central America did not take the paternalistic view that the U.S. model was the only one to emulate (Heise and Green 1996).

Conclusion

Media analyst W. Lance Bennett (2000) argues that attempts at political balance have actually weakened debate and undercut democratic forms in the United States and for countries following the U.S. model. In Bennett's view, balance has constrained political coverage to a narrow alley instead of considering the wide plain that makes up the real spectrum of opinion.

In the Central American context, a partisan media opens itself to more manipulation and corruption from party structures, political advertising, and state subsidies that may be offered above or below the table. Bennett maintains that a media system which filters partisanship is open to manipulation by organized elites. The Central American experience shows organized elites are often more powerful in partisan systems, especially when they can use the state structure for further manipulation.

In fighting corrupt practices of the state and corporate interests, some media outlets in Latin America have shown they can set the agenda even when parts of the elite structure are fighting to restrain them (Waisbord 2000b). Powerful media outlets in Latin America can also amplify the call of civil society to bring about major political change (Lins da Silva 2000). When the media in Guatemala propelled the protests that stopped the abrogation of the country's constitution in 1993, the Central American media showed similar strength. In recent years, the anticorruption investigations across party lines by Guatemala's *Prensa Libre* and *elPeriodico*—two papers working toward more balanced coverage—show the continuation of that tradition. The investigations into former president Alemán by the revamped *La Prensa* in Nicaragua and the anticorruption campaign of *El Diario de Hoy* in El Salvador show that trend is slowly emerging across the region.

Media outlets must also turn inward to combat media corruption, as Panama's *La Prensa* and Honduras's *El Tiempo* have done in the past. The consideration of corruption's influence on the media systems of Central America is important. The media's role as a counterbalance to power is compromised if the media are infected by the same disease that inflicts the societies and governments of the region. For the media to rise above the political fray, they must not be encumbered by conflicts of interest, monetary and otherwise. This also speaks to why partisanship should be reduced. If the media are to serve as a conduit for progress and a means to strengthen the advance of democracy, then these ideals must truly dominate their work, rather than the pursuit of illicit gains. If the media of Central America hope to contribute to a democratic transition in the region, and strengthen the rule of law while turning government institutions toward working for the populace, then dealing honestly with the amount of corruption in their own ranks is paramount. For this reason, a system of analysis to evaluate various media systems is essential.

References

Ades, Alberto, and Rafael Di Tella. 2000. "The New Economics of Corruption: A Survey and Some Results." In *Combating Corruption in Latin America*. Edited by Joseph S. Tulchin and Ralph H. Espach. Washington, D.C.: Woodrow Wilson Center Press.

Barrios Reina, Marco Tulio. 1998. Interview by author. Guatemala City, Guatemala. Managing editor, Noti7, Canal 7 Guatemalan television network.

Bennett, W. Lance. 2000. "Media Power in the United States." In *De-Westernizing Media Studies*. Edited by James Curran and Myung-Jin Park. London: Routledge.

Berganza, Gustavo. 1998. Interview by author. Guatemala City, Guatemala. Berganza is managing editor of *Siglo Veintiuno*.

Canton, Santiago A. 1999. *Report of the Office of the Special Rappaorteur for the Freedom of Expression*. Washington, D.C.: Organization of American States.

Chasan, Alice, ed. 1999. *Attacks on the Press in 1998*. New York: Committee to Protect Journalists.

Cuevas, Freddy. 1999. "Honduran President Fires Military Officials, Denies Coup Attempt." Associated Press, July 31.

Dye, David R., Jack Spence, and George Vickers. 2000. *Patchwork Democracy: Nicaraguan Politics Ten Years after the Fall*. Cambridge, Mass.: Hemisphere Initiatives.

Fliess, Maurice. 1999. "Honduran Press Called Tarnished by Corruption." *free!* [Online journal of the Freedom Forum]. September 13. www.freedomforum.org/international/1999/9/13mediaatmill.asp.

Fox, Elizabeth. 1997. *Latin American Broadcasting: From Tango to Telenovela*. Luton, U.K.: University of Luton Press.

Freedom Forum. 1999. "Salaries are 'Sore Spot' for Journalists." In *Media at the Millennium: Latin America*. Arlington, Va.: Freedom Forum.

Fromson, Murray. 1996. "Mexico's Struggle for a Free Press." In *Communication in Latin America: Journalism, Mass Media, and Society*. Edited by Richard R. Cole. Wilmington, Del.: Scholarly Resources.

Goodwin, Paul B. 2000. *Global Studies: Latin America.* Guilford, Conn.: Dushkin/McGraw-Hill.

Gorriti, Gustavo. 2001. E-mail message to author, October 24. Gorriti is the former editor of *La Prensa* Panama.

Guerrero, Alina. 1995. "Las Relaciones Peligrosas" [Dangerous Relations]. *Pulso,* April-July.

Hallin, Daniel. 2000. "Media, Political Power, and Democratization in Mexico." In *De-Westernizing Media Studies.* Edited by James Curran and Myung-Jin Par. London: Routledge.

Heise, J. Arthur, and Charles H. Green. 1996. "An Unusual Approach in the United States to Latin American Journalism Education." In *Communication in Latin America: Journalism, Mass Media, and Society.* Edited by Richard R. Cole. Wilmington, Del.: Scholarly Resources.

———. 1998. *Latin American Journalism Program: A Final Review.* North Miami: International Media Center, Florida International University.

Heywood, Paul. 1996. "Continuity and Change: Analysing Political Corruption in Modern Spain." In *Political Corruption in Europe and Latin America.* Edited by Walter Little and Eduardo Posada-Carbó. London: Macmillan/Institute of Latin American Studies, University of London.

Janus, Noreene. 1998a. *Latin American Journalism Program: El Salvador.* Washington, D.C.: U.S. Agency for International Development.

———. 1998b. *The Nicaraguan Program of the Latin American Journalism Project.* Washington, D.C.: U.S. Agency for International Development.

Knight, Alan. 1996. "Corruption in Twentieth-Century Mexico." In *Political Corruption in Europe and Latin America.* Edited by Walter Little and Eduardo Posada-Carbó. London: Macmillan/Institute of Latin American Studies, University of London.

Kodrich, Kris. 2001. "Professionalism vs. Partisanship in Nicaraguan Newsrooms; Journalists Apply New Professional Standards." *Pulso* [Online journal of the International Media Center at Florida International University], September 6. www.pulso.org/English/Current/Ing-Professionalism-Nica010906.htm.

Latin American Journalism Program [LAJP]. 1994. "Statistical Highlights on Academic and Technical Training." North Miami: International Media Center, Florida International University.

Lins da Silva, Carlos Eduardo. 2000. "Journalism and Corruption in Brazil." In *Combating Corruption in Latin America.* Edited by Joseph S. Tulchin and Ralph H. Espach. Washington, D.C.: Woodrow Wilson Center Press.

Little, Walter, and Eduardo Posada-Carbó. 1996. Introduction to *Political Corruption in Europe and Latin America.* Edited by Walter Little and Eduardo Posada-Carbó. London: Macmillan/Institute of Latin American Studies, University of London.

McChesney, Robert W. 1997. *Corporate Media and the Threat to Democracy.* New York: Seven Stories.

Moreno Ocampo, Luis. 2000. "Structural Corruption and Normative Systems: The Role of Integrity Pacts." In *Combating Corruption in Latin America.* Edited by Joseph S. Tulchin and Ralph H. Espach. Washington, D.C.: Woodrow Wilson Center Press.

Mower, Joan. 1999. "Newspapers Called Vital in Advancing Democracy in Latin Amer-ica." *free!* [Online journal of the Freedom Forum], July 15. www.freedomforum.org/international/1999/7/15pagina.asp.

Nerone, John. 1994. *Violence against the Press: Policing the Public Sphere in U.S. History.* New York: Oxford University Press.

———. 1996. "Lessons from American History." *Media Studies Journal* 10, no. 4.

Paige, Jeffery M. 1997. *Coffee and Power: Revolution and the Rise of Democracy in Central America.* Cambridge, Mass.: Harvard University Press.

Quintanilla, Germán. 1994. "La Policia y Los Medios de Comunicacion: El Caso de Honduras: The Police and the Communication Media: The Case of Honduras." *Periodismo, Derechos Humanos y Control de Poder Politico en Centroamerica* [Journal-ism, Human Rights and the Control of Political Power in Central America]. Edited by Jaime Ordûòez. San Josè, Costa Rica: InterAmerican Institute of Human Rights.

Rockwell, Rick. 1998. *Honduran Journalism: Searching for New Boundaries, Confronting Systemic Problems.* Washington, D.C.: U.S. Agency for International Development.

———. 1999. "Killing the Messenger: Methods of Media Repression in Mexico." In *Mexico: Facing the Challenges of Human Rights and Crime.* Edited by William Cartwright. Ardsley, N.Y.: Transnational.

Rockwell, Rick, and Noreene Janus. 2001. "Integracion de Monopolios y la Oligarquia de los Medios en Centroamerica" [Vertical Integration and Media Oligarchy in Cen-tral America]. *Realidad* 82: 481–99.

Rockwell, Rick, Noreene Janus, and Kristin Neubauer. 2001. "Expose Could Signal End of El Salvador TV News Magazine." Pacific News Service, May 24.

Rojas, Ana Cristina. 2000. "Television Sin Arbitraje" [Television without Arbitration]. *Actualidad Economica,* May.

Schulz, Donald E., and Deborah Sundloff Schulz. 1994. *The United States, Honduras, and the Crisis in Central America.* Boulder, Colo.: Westview.

Skidmore, Thomas E., and Peter H. Smith. 2001. *Modern Latin America.* New York: Oxford University Press.

Smeets, Marylene. 2000. "Speaking Out: Postwar Journalism in Guatemala and El Sal-vador." In *Attacks on the Press in 1999.* Edited by Richard Murphy. New York: Com-mittee to Protect Journalists.

———. 2001. "Guatemala." In *Attacks on the Press in 2000.* Edited by Richard Murphy. New York: Committee to Protect Journalists.

Straubhaar, Joseph. 2001. "Brazil: The Role of the State in World Television." In *Media and Globalization: Why the State Matters.* Edited by Nancy Morris and Silvio Wais-bord. Lanham, Md.: Rowman & Littlefield.

Transparency International. 2001. Corruption Perceptions Index 2001. [Internet data-base.] www.transparency.org/documents/cpi/2001/cpi2001.html#cpi.

Tulchin, Joseph S., and Ralph H. Espach. 2000. Introduction to *Combating Corruption in Latin America.* Edited by Joseph S. Tulchin and Ralph H. Espach. Washington, D.C.: Woodrow Wilson Center Press.

Universidad CentroAmericana (UCA). 2001. *Resultados de Encuesta: Preferencia de Medios* [Results of the Poll: Media Preferences]. Managua, Nicaragua: Universidad CentroAmericana.

Vanden Heuvel, Jon, and Everette E. Dennis. 1995. *Changing Patterns: Latin America's Vital Media.* New York: Freedom Forum Media Studies Center.

Waisbord, Silvio. 2000a. "Media in South America: Between the Rock of the State and Hard Place of the Market." In *De-Westernizing Media Studies.* Edited by James Curran and Myung-Jin Park. London: Routledge.

———. 2000b. *Watchdog Journalism in South America: News, Accountability, and Democracy.* New York: Columbia University Press.

Whitehead, Laurence. 2000. "High-Level Political Corruption in Latin America: A 'Transitional' Phenomenon?" In *Combating Corruption in Latin America.* Edited by Joseph S. Tulchin and Ralph H. Espach. Washington, D.C.: Woodrow Wilson Center Press.

10

The Promises and Pitfalls of Ethnographic Research in International Communication Studies

Michael Robert Evans

IN YUENDUMU, 150 MILES up the treacherous Tanami Highway from Alice Springs in the heart of the Australian outback, Randall Wilson grabs a video camera. Reports of a murder near Ti Tree had made their way to Yuendumu, along with descriptions of the suspected culprit and speculations about his next destination. The man supposedly stopped a British couple who were backpacking around the Red Centre; he killed the boyfriend and chased the woman for hours through the brush. Now Wilson's neighbors insist they saw the murderer drive through Yuendumu.

Wilson, a member of the Warlpiri Aboriginal group, is part of the Warlpiri Media Association, a professional video, radio, and music-recording organization located in Yuendumu. He and some others from the WMA decide to find the local police and follow them as they pursue this new lead. Four videographers leap into the media association's battered, dusty truck and bounce down the corrugated road in search of a story.

On the Akwesasne Mohawk Reservation in upstate New York and Ontario, Joyce Mitchell sits at a desk in a tidy two-story office building near the clinic, overlooking part of the Saint Lawrence Seaway system. Mitchell, one of the leaders at the *Indian Time* newspaper, is trying to decide how to play a story about the tribal government. *Indian Time* is among the few tribal newspapers in the United States that are not owned by the tribal governments themselves, so the paper has quite a bit more freedom than do most of its counterparts on other reservations.

Although keeping the tribal government on its toes is a serious priority at *Indian Time*, the weekly paper also has a nice photo-and-text package about a local man who is considered a hero among the Akwesasne Mohawks. He almost single-handedly brought the group back from dispersal, assimilation, and ruin, and Mitchell wants to give the article and photos about him prominence on the front page. She heads down the hall to the layout room to get a better sense of how the other page-one stories look.

✦

Zacharias Kunuk brings the snowmobile to a quick stop. Paulossie Qulitalik, an elder and the chairman of the local school board, is finishing the construction of an igloo outside the entrance tunnel to a large, half-underground hut called a *qarmaq*. Kunuk, chief producer of the Igloolik Isuma videography company, is directing the production of a feature-length movie based on an Inuit legend; this place will serve as the set for several of the scenes. On this snowy plain outside the tiny Arctic village of Igloolik, in Canada's new territory of Nunavut, Kunuk offers direction to the people who have successfully auditioned for parts in the movie.

The cast members—not one of whom is a professional actor—read their lines and discuss the scenes. Shooting will begin in just a few days.

✦

In these situations and hundreds like them around the world, groups work to produce and disseminate information about themselves for the benefit of their own people and others. A great deal remains to be learned about such groups and their impact, intercultural and international. Some studies have been done, of course, using a wide range of methodologies. Following the call of Gans (1999), Denzin (1997, 1999), Wolcott (1999), and others, this chapter seeks to demonstrate the value that can be brought to international communication studies by an ethnographic approach that gathers and systematizes large amounts of information about cultures, societies, and communication across boundaries.

Taking into account classic and innovative approaches to ethnography, this chapter begins with a consideration of ethnography itself, as both a methodology and a theoretical framework. The focus then shifts to major questions that surround ethnography, including Self and Other, presentation and representation, active audience theory, and the importance of context. It ends with an exploration of the performance of communication and the ways in which ethnography can help us understand that performance.

Ethnography

Ethnography is the close, long-term study of human activity and insight, conducted in service of greater understanding of culture. As Frow and Morris put it, ethnography helps us "get at the particularity of responses to and uses of" a site, "to understand it as lived experience (or lived textuality, to use a more precise phrase)" (1993, xvii). Connections between facts, relationships among people, and underlying reasons and rationales for certain activities can be discerned through ethnographic research.

Taking ethnography as an approach to the study of culture, we must grapple, at least briefly, with the idea of culture. Frow and Morris offer a useful perspective:

> Culture is thought of as directly bound up with work and its organization; with relations of power and gender in the workplace and the home; with the pleasures and the pressures of consumption; with the complex relations of class and kith and kin through which a sense of self is formed; and with the fantasies and desires through which social relations are carried and actively shaped. In short, "culture" is a term that can designate, in Raymond Williams' phrase, the "whole way of life of a social group as it is structured by representation and by power." . . . It is a network of representations—texts, images, talk, codes of behaviour, and the narrative structures organizing these—which shapes every aspect of social life. (1993, viii)[1]

Following Herder's concept of cultures (*plural*)—differing but concurrent and equally valid systems of interaction held by nations and by groups within nations—ethnography seems particularly well suited to the exploration of the second and third of Raymond Williams's three categories of the term's usage. The second—"a particular way of life, whether of a people, a period, a group, or humanity in general" (1983, 90)—presents opportunities for ethnographers to study social structures in depth, cutting across particular forms of activity. The third—"culture is music, literature, painting and sculpture, theatre and film" (1983, 90)—guides ethnographers in the examination of specific endeavors, including international communication. As I have already indicated, it is in this manner that I conducted my own ethnographic studies; I focused first on art (especially Inuit sculpture), and since then I have focused on such indigenous media as Inuit videography and Aboriginal radio, exploring not just these products but also the processes by which they were created and the role of those processes in the larger sociocultural fabric. It is not necessary, however, to be too rigid with Williams's categories. As he notes, "It is the range and overlap of meanings that is significant" (1983, 91).

An ethnographic framework can shed light on often hidden aspects of human experience. In the realm of international communication, it can offer insights into issues of audience, cultural context, and the performance of communication production, among others. In each of these facets, people work within social parameters to affect the world around them, with teleological ends in mind. As Morris notes, citing Mica Nava (1987), "consumers are not 'cultural dopes,' but active, critical users of mass culture; consumption practices cannot be derived from or reduced to a mirror of production; consumer practice is 'far more than just economic activity: it is also about dreams and consolation, communication and confrontation, image and identity'" (1990, 21–22).[2]

Ethnography can be seen as both a set of research methodologies and as a theoretical framework—a "way of looking" and a "way of seeing," in Wolcott's terms (1999). Methodologically, ethnography is relatively straightforward. The central method is participant observation, in which the researcher participates in the activities of the community being studied. When I conducted ethnographic fieldwork among the Inuit of Igloolik, I went out on whale hunts and caribou hunts with families, I helped build igloos and set up tents, and I took part in community-wide games. (I almost won a hammer once, but it was in my best interest to concede defeat to the elder woman who opposed me in the finals.) Because I was there to learn about Inuit videographers, I participated in videographic activities undertaken by the three video groups in the settlement. I also have worked with Aboriginal video, music, and radio professionals in Alice Springs and Yuendumu, and I spent time with the staff of *Indian Time* on the Akwesasne Reservation. In similar ways, Wolcott participated in the community life of the Kwakiutl (1999), Michaels worked with the Warlpiri (1984, 1986, 1994), Glassie lived with the citizens of Ballymenone (1983, 1995a), and so on. Michaels describes his ethnographic immersion this way:

> Most of what I know and present in this report came from working alongside Aboriginal people for three years and sharing in activity with them. This included especially the video work. But it also meant hunting trips, attending ceremonies, running errands, going to community dances, and participating in meetings. With the senior men, most of my relationships were based around the activity of painting and the sociability that developed around the Yuendumu Doors project and the subsequent Warlukarlangu Artists' Association. (1986, xviii)

Through this long-term working contact, the researcher can observe activities over time, at close range, and—through trust gained by mutual effort—in settings and situations that would be off-limits to casual visitors.

Participant observation is the central method in ethnography, but it is not the only one; as Wolcott notes, "one of the unsung features of ethnographic research is its embrace of multiple techniques" (1999, 43–44). Along with participant observation comes a host of other methods, all gathered under the "ethnography" umbrella. Wolcott offers a trilogy:

- *Experiencing.* This is his term for participant observation.
- *Enquiring.* This term refers to active interviewing, the solicitation of information. Interviews can range from quick chats at the street corner to full-blown, formal, taped question-and-answer sessions. Wolcott offers this typology for the range of interview types included in ethnographic research: casual conversation; life history, life cycle interview; key informant interviewing; semistructured interview; structured interview; survey, household census, ethnogenealogy; questionnaire (written and/or oral); projective techniques; other measurement techniques (1999, 52). Other scholars would carve that list differently, of course. Some, for example, would balk at the inclusion of surveys and questionnaires, insisting that ethnography necessarily involves face-to-face, informant-driven communication.
- *Examining.* Here Wolcott refers to gleaning information from the works of others—archival research, in short (1999, 46–48).

To this list Wolcott adds observation without participation (1999, 48–51). At times, the researcher wants to watch what is going on without actually getting involved in it. This can be an especially prudent approach when getting involved would radically change the very activity being studied.

Nightingale offers her own inventory of ethnographic tools:

- Participant observation
- Group interviews
- Letters solicited by the researchers
- Letters written without solicitation to newspapers or television channels
- Informal discussions (1993, 152)

Merging the lists offered by Wolcott and Nightingale, I would add the reciprocal ethnographic techniques advocated by Lawless, in which the subjects read and respond to the developing ethnography, and the research includes those reactions in the final product (1993).

Methodologically, ethnography and its approaches have been criticized at times. Even the concept of participant observation has been challenged by scholars who find conflicts inherent in the bringing together of those two words. Cruikshank argues that although she learned in college that participant

observation is the cornerstone of anthropological research, she found it difficult to maintain that position.

> Like every other anthropology student, I was jolted by the contradictions in that
> definition when I had my first opportunity to do fieldwork, in the Yukon Terri-
> tory in 1968. Returning to graduate school in 1969 at the height of the debate
> about ethical dilemmas of anthropological research only increased my sense that
> the methodological goals of observation and participation seemed incompatible,
> at least in the climate of that discussion. (Cruikshank 1990)

Despite such concerns, which trouble everyone who experiences the clash
between the theory of participant observation and the realities of fieldwork,
participant observation remains the eminent component of ethnographic research. Nevertheless, I must reveal my bias and side with Gans when he declares that participant observation, the cornerstone of ethnographic pursuits,
"is still my preferred method" (1999, 540). He finds participant observation
"particularly useful for elaborating, explaining, and even debunking the findings of the quick-and-dirty legwork on which journalists must base their feature stories about American society. Perhaps even more important, PO could
supply empirical findings about little known or stereotyped populations, particularly those outside the mainstream" (1999, 540).

Another logistical area of contention in ethnography centers on the necessary scope of the fieldwork. In an effort to demand an appropriate degree of
heft from ethnographic research, many scholars hold the "if it isn't a year or
longer, it isn't ethnography" stance; Werner, for example, calls for a general
agreement among scholars that longer stays in the field are preferable to
shorter ones (1998). But others, including Berg, hold out hope for "mi-
croethnographies" that narrow their compass and shorten their duration
(1998). Gans maintains that such shorter-duration ethnographies are fine, noting that investigative journalists have been doing short-term participant observation for years (1999, 546). He urges those who employ these approaches,
however, not to fall into the trap of shallowness, pursuing inquiries that are
"dominated by small studies of exotic sites such as dance halls and strip joints,
for which the fieldwork is sometimes mainly an excuse for the researcher to ru-
minate on how the site felt to him or her" (1999, 541–42). Wolcott agrees:

> Ethnography has slowly become dislodged from the conceptual framework once
> so closely associated with it. As a consequence, for some researchers, an ethno-
> graphic question may simply be a question that is amenable to study through
> *techniques* (or *methods*, if you prefer) comparable to those employed by the early
> ethnographers. The orienting question need not call for interpretation at all,
> only description, with finely *detailed* description substituted for, and perhaps
> even misconstrued for, carefully *contextualized* description. (Wolcott 1999, 67)

Morris takes a similar stance. She defines ethnography as "finding out what the people say and think about their culture," but she laments "voxpop techniques common to journalism and empirical sociology—interviewing, collecting background, analyzing statements made spontaneously by, or solicited from, informants" (1990, 22). Morley, too, harkens back to a "purer" form of ethnography that resists some of the more recent variations and instead embraces "sociological materialism, epistemological realism and methodological pragmatism" (1997, 122). Denzin, on the other hand, calls for a more literary "interpretive" ethnography that "is simultaneously minimal, autoethnographic, vulnerable, performative, and critical" (1999, 510). He prefers ethnography rich and deep in personal description, as can be seen in this excerpt from his work, "Performing Montana, Part 2":

> Nelson . . . reminds us that "A person moving through nature . . . is never truly alone." It is midday. I am knee-deep in the Soda Butte River, chasing a huge brown trout. Having crossed the line into Yellowstone National Park, I am more than a little nervous. I do not have a park-fishing permit. I turn back at the sound of a noise behind me. There, on a sandy spit of land reaching out into the river, stand four deer, a young buck, two smaller does, and a fawn. They are staring wide-eyed at me, as if I had invaded their home, walked into their back yard so to speak. Of course I had. And I left as quickly as possible. Later, like Senior . . . I struggled to put words to the images of how to describe the "velvet-textured scent of the wild moss flowers" I brushed against as I looked back at the doe as she "spanked her fawn with a forehoof." (Denzin 1999)

Strategies and Theories

Getting at the disparate structures of a complex site "is never simply a descriptive activity," notes Frow and Morris (1993, xvi). One way to break out of the "circular" and "narcissistic" enterprise that shallow ethnography can promote, Morris herself maintains, lies in the development and application of theory (1990, 22).

Wolcott concurs: "ethnography comes to mean more than method" (1999, 68). Ethnography assembles a useful and rich methodology for researchers, but many scholars condemn studies that limit their "ethnographic work" to research and description only. Lamenting such studies, Nightingale (1993, 152–54) calls for an ethnography that embraces not only a methodology but also a research strategy that adheres to the definition that Marcus and Fischer give us:

> [Ethnography is] a research process in which the anthropologist closely observes, records, and engages in the daily life of another culture—an experience labeled as the fieldwork method—and then writes accounts of this culture, emphasizing

descriptive detail. These accounts are the primary form in which fieldwork procedures, the other culture, and the ethnographer's personal and theoretical reflections
are accessible to professionals and other readerships. (Marcus and Fischer 1986, 18)

Marcus and Fischer note that the main innovation of ethnography lies in
bringing together into an integrated professional practice the previously separate processes of (1) collecting data on the scene and (2) armchair theorizing
and analysis done by the academic anthropologist (1986, 18). The marriage of
method and theory has resulted in some potent cultural explorations, including work done by Agee and Evans (1939), Abrahams (1963), Glassie (1995a),
Foley (1995), Wachowich (1999), Hinson (2000), and others.

Ethnography presents a unique set of opportunities and challenges. Ethnography is not, however, a clean, clear, uniform system that researchers can employ, like chemists dipping litmus paper into still ponds and reading the results.
At its heart, it is scuffed by conflict, and any student—or practitioner—of
ethnography would be well advised to understand the points of contention
going in. For example, definitions offered for the term are as varied as scholars
themselves. Neither Morley's nor Denzin's previously stated description of
ethnography fully meshes with Nightingale's set of concepts: "The term
'ethnographic' possesses connotations which include *cultural, community-
based, empirical,* and *phenomenal*" (1993, 154). The distinctions among these
lists of characteristics is subtle but deliberate; each list is intended to fore-
ground certain elements of ethnography and relegate others to the background—or eliminate them altogether.

Debates over the definition of ethnography and over the relative merits of
one approach or another can be useful, but behind these debates lies an essential question: What value do ethnographic approaches offer? In the framework of this chapter, the question can be sharpened even further: What value
do these approaches offer the study of international communication? This
chapter explores major issues, concerns, and opportunities that ethnography
brings to scholars of international communication.

The value to international communication is clear. Because international
communication necessarily involves communication across cultural divides,
studies of this communication must grasp the meaning and consequences of
this intercultural linkage. Ethnography's ability to collect and analyze cultural
data make it a vital tool for this research.

Another of ethnography's strengths is that participant observation "is the
only [approach] that gets close to people. In addition, it allows researchers to
observe what people do, while all the other empirical methods are limited to
reporting what people say about what they do" (Gans 1999, 540). Because of
this trait, Gans considers ethnography the most "scientific" of the research
methods (1999, 540).

Frow and Morris adhere to a similar position. "Structures are always structures-in-use, and . . . uses cannot be contained in advance" (1993, xvi). For the same reason, uses cannot be anticipated, imagined, or deduced fully from afar. Ethnography, properly done, helps the scholar avoid the errors that spatial and temporal distance can introduce to the study of culture.

Ethnography also brings the researcher into close contact with numerous informants from a society, often in a marathon of individual and small-group encounters. Among ethnography's advantages, then, is that it acknowledges the significance of the individual actor. Audiences can function as groups, and we often study them as indivisible masses, but they are made up of individuals, each of whom carries a unique perspective, history, and set of expectations. Producers of mediated messages operate in similar fashion. By working with individuals among audiences or producers, ethnographers can create a mosaic that strives to represent social realities accurately. "Macro structures can only be reproduced through micro-processes," Morley notes, urging us to address the "interplay of biography and history in the 'sociological imagination'" (1997, 126). Ethnography allows researchers to explore the broad compass of society while at the same time achieving the depth that sustained contact with informed individuals can provide. It also allows scholars to appreciate the interplay between the individual and the collective, embracing simultaneously the broad sweep of sociological approaches and the penetrating gaze of psychological and literary methods.

MacDougall rightly cautions us against a gaze too tightly focused on the individual, however, pointing out that the experiences of individuals offer a suggestive but ultimately unreliable indicator of collective experience (1995, 218). "Although the raw unit of . . . study remains the individual, the individual must be left by the wayside on the road to general principle," he observes (1995, 220). Morley agrees, arguing that the situated strength of ethnography should not be taken so far as to embrace the ideology of individualism (1997, 127).

Balancing the tension between the individual and the collective, ethnography gives researchers the ability to understand a culture more fully than does any other method; as Wolcott puts it, "ethnography has always been associated with and intended for studying culture" (1999, 67). Like Gans, Morley notes that ethnography is valuable because it helps us reshape theories to better represent the complexity of local situations (1997, 127; citing Marcus and Fischer 1986, 88). To adapt Glassie's explication of folklore, ethnography is at home with the personal, the social, and the teleological in ways that other forms of research cannot match (1992). Denzin puts it this way:

> Interpretive ethnography seeks to ground the self in a sense of the sacred, to dialogically connect the ethical, respectful self to nature and the worldly environment. In so doing, it recognizes the ethical unity of mind and nature. . . . It seeks

to embed the self in storied histories of sacred spaces. This epistemology presumes a feminist moral ethic, stressing the sacredness of human life, dignity,
truthtelling and nonviolence. (Denzin 1999, 510)

Embraced as theory, ethnography offers the international communication
scholar a set of philosophical perspectives with which to inform his or her inquiry. Morley puts forth this argument:

> Some of the theoretical debates which have surrounded the practice of ethnog-
> raphy in recent years . . . are of considerable importance, not just to anthropol-
> ogy, but also for scholars in the field of media research. In the first place, these
> debates (initially concerning the relations of power, as well as of knowledge, be-
> tween representor and represented) concern not only the dilemmas of the white
> anthropologist who produces forms of knowledge of "exotic" or "tribal" peoples.
> They also concern media researchers, in so far as they too are in the business of
> investigating and representing others, whether or not those others wear exotic
> tribal dress: working-class audiences, youth audiences, gendered audiences, eth-
> nic audiences. (Morley 1997, 128)[3]

Self and Other

One of the fundamental dichotomies in ethnographic work lies in the relationship between the researcher and the researched: the Self and the Other.
The concern over this relationship stems from an increasing interest in the
impact that ethnographic study has on the people involved. Some ethnographers have been criticized for conducting studies or handling research in ways
that engendered feelings of alienation, confusion, and even betrayal among
the people being studied. In some extreme cases, researchers have been ac-
cused of actually causing serious physical harm to the people they were learning about; in perhaps the most famous case, Napoleon Chagnon has been ac-
cused of disrupting the Yanomamo society and exacerbating disease and other
problems there (Albert 1990; Mann 2000; Tierney 2000; Turner 2001).

The Self-and-Other divide brings with it complicated repercussions. To
view a person or a group of people as an "Other" suggests that I (as "Self") am
aware of a barrier between us—but cultural research strives to reduce that
barrier in an effort to enhance understanding. The dichotomy also raises
problems of power relations, ethics, and even possession: *They* are *my* "Other."
Morris points to another concern in this area. Any theory grounded on the
category of otherness tends to result in a unification of "others" into an
"Other" that derives its value only from its negation of the writing subject
(1990, 36–37). So, she notes, alienation from everyday life becomes a constitutive feature of the scholar's enunciative place.

As Clifford and Marcus (1986) point out, one postmodern reaction to these legitimate concerns lies with reflexivity, making the researcher openly aware of the role he or she is playing in the study, in the lives of the people being studied, and so on. I would extend to ethnography the point that Frow and Morris offer that "cultural studies tends to incorporate in its object of study a critical account of its own motivating questions—and thus of the institutional frameworks and disciplinary rules by which its research imperatives are formed" (1993, xviii). The very nature of pursuing the "open-ended social life of texts" requires cultural studies to "question the authority or finality of its own readings" (1993, xix). Wolcott put it this way: "Today, we no longer have to pretend to a level of objectivity that was once fashionable; it is sufficient to recognize and reveal our subjectivity as best we can, thus to maximize the potential of fieldwork as personal experience rather than to deny it" (1999, 46). With increased attention to reflexivity—to thinking through what we are doing, why we are doing it, and what impact our actions may have—ethnographers hope to develop research processes and products that offer greater sensitivity, awareness, and sophistication. But it would be overstating the case to argue that this focus on reflexivity is a uniquely postmodern phenomenon; Gans reminds us that participant observation "has always required reflexivity, or else researchers would lose the rapport without which the research cannot proceed" (1999, 541). Worth and Adair raised reflexive concerns back in 1972, during their project with Navajo filmmaking: "Research is designed to formulate and solve problems, to ask and to answer questions. All of us doing research, and our students working with us and being trained to become researchers on their own, are concerned about the kinds of questions and answers we provide. . . . What will [the people we are studying] think about what we did? How will they benefit from our research and findings?" (1997, 5). With these concerns in mind, Worth and Adair included in their project a detailed description of what the researchers did and felt.

The question of Self and Other also raises issues of "ethnographic distance." For decades, jokes and cartoons have poked fun at researchers who have "gone native," emerging from the bush or the jungle or the tundra bedecked in native garb, pierced in interesting places with bones or blunt wooden pegs, and sporting elaborate and frightening tattoos. Such researchers—or, more properly, any real-world counterparts who drift too close to the subjects of their work—find themselves facing a difficult dilemma. Ethnographers are supposed to get close to their informants, to develop rapport, enhance trust, and gain access to information that is typically withheld from superficial passersby. But getting too close can lead to trouble when a critical book emerges from the research—or when the closeness prevents the book from emerging at all. Gans staunchly defends the need for professional distance: "Once researchers fail to distance themselves from the people they are studying . . . or fail to allow them the same distancing, the rules of qualitative reliability and validity are sidestepped, reducing the likelihood that sociologists and their work will be trusted by their readers" (1999, 542–43). But too much distance might prevent the researcher from learning about certain aspects of the culture, aspects that might have been revealed to someone who allowed himself or herself to be more fully integrated into the society. This tension can be difficult for the researcher to handle. As MacDougall put it, "If I am to understand this sociocultural system properly, I must not adopt the indigenous view; but if I do not adopt the indigenous view I cannot understand it properly" (1995, 217–18). Titon framed the tension this way: "How can an ethnographer make the strange familiar, yet keep it strange?" (1992, 89). With Malinowski urging us to "go inside" the culture and Levi-Strauss urging us to "stay outside," MacDougall notes, ethnographers are left with interdependent but not mutually compatible directives (1995, 217).

The reflexive corrective to insensitive research brings with it another point of debate: how fully the researcher should appear in the book or article being created. Some scholars, such as Gans, look with disdain at the increasing trend toward autoethnography as an approach that "represents not only the climax of the preoccupation with self that is at the heart of too much contemporary ethnography but also the product of a postmodern but asocial theory of knowledge that argues the impossibility of knowing anything beyond the self" (1999, 542). Countering that position are such scholars as Denzin, who is a strong fan of autoethnography (1999). To Denzin, an ethnographic project "asks that I make myself visible in my text. I am the universal singular, universalizing in my singularity the crises and experiences of my historical epoch" (1999, 511). The challenge, it would seem, lies in acknowledging, in the text, one's own presence, role, relationships, and impact—to the best that these can be discerned—without shifting the spotlight too far away from the people being studied and toward our own personal angst.

Underlying all the attention paid to the ethnographer's role is a concern over the power relations between the researcher and the researched. This power relationship, as has been noted already, can be destructive—either insidiously or explosively. Such power relationships always influence the process, Nightingale argues, and so should be studied and revealed, and she aims specific advice at scholars studying communication:

> The relationship between the researcher and the researched is foregounded as problematic once the term "ethnography" is used to describe it. In this sense, the very use of the term acts as a reminder of the differences (of class, education, religion, gender, age, etc.) between them, differences which are often unacknowledged, especially when the researcher is of equal or lower status than the researched, as where television executives or production personnel are concerned. (Nightingale 1993, 153)

One term that cuts through the myriad sides of this debate holds some promise for resolution. Werner, in his call for ethnographic standards, cites Roscoe (1995, 492–504) to support his claims regarding the privileged, authoritative position held by many ethnographers in the field, and then he urges researchers to increase the "vulnerability" of their statements by reducing that position (Werner 1998, 1). By exposing our statements to scrutiny, backed by our field notes and tape recordings, reinforced with fieldwork journals and other reflexive tools, we can enhance the degree to which our positions in the communities we study can be assessed.

Understanding that position is essential not only because ethnographers can do damage in the field, but also because any ethnographic writing represents a filtered reality, a situation colored by the ethnographer's own subjectivity. Researchers cannot help but extrude the world they see through the world they know. MacDougall offers us an interesting challenge: "How can any representation approximate the self that every self knows itself to be?" (1995, 220). Titon also puts it well:

> Ethnographers write as if they represent other people "as they are," but in truth they represent them as they appear to the ethnographer, whose gender, class, appearance, wealth, skills, knowledge, relation to the nearby power structure, and culture of origin, among other things, affect what the other people say and do in the ethnographer's presence, and whose ethnographic analysis is based on his or her own personal as well as cultural and academic history. So long as ethnographers assume the authority to represent other people, they control how others will appear in their texts, even if the ethnographer allows others to speak their own (though translated) words. Attempts at observational neutrality, inductive reasoning, cross-checking with multiple informants (and ethnographers), and other methods meant to transcend individual bias, have not prevented some ethnographers from writing colonialist, racist, sexist, and elitist ethnographies. And when these reify stereotypes they have the power to harm. (1992, 89–90)

As always, however, some scholars wisely caution against going too far. Wolcott, for example, decries the "postmodern critique and its 'crisis of representation' that has sought to upbraid ethnographic authority and make literary form a central preoccupation in ethnographic discourse" (1999, 14). MacDougall adds his voice—and a twist—to such concerns when he asks "is the attempt to reveal the subjective an act of communion or merely of invasion?" (1995, 248).

This power of translation, of representation, of subjective filtering compels ethnographers toward precision, caution, skepticism, and circumspection. But it need not cripple the ethnographer who wishes to offer a valid and useful account of communication. Morley argues that "the fact that the analyst finally produces an account of his subjects' activities which is not expressed in their own terms, and which may in fact be different from the account they would offer of their own activities, hardly invalidates it, but is perhaps precisely the necessary responsibility of the analyst" (1997, 130–31). Worth and Adair put it this way:

> We have accepted the obvious: that pretending we are not part of our culture, that we have no preconceived ways of viewing the world or of viewing a film, is impossible. Dismissing culture is no answer to the problem of cultural relativity. What we have tried to do is describe what we saw as honestly as possible, putting as much light upon ourselves as we could and hoping that the reader can make judgments within his framework, sometimes recognizing that we organize the world the way he does and sometimes recognizing differences. We hope that whatever issues develop will aid rather than hinder clarity and understanding. (1997, 9–10)

In other words, emic (internally derived) terminologies, genre categories, and worldviews are often unable to transcend the society in which they are current; etic (externally derived) structures and approaches are necessary to carry communication to another group.

Perhaps awareness offers the surest path through this thicket. Ethnographers could benefit by embracing Denzin's insistence that ethnography (in his case, existential ethnography in particular) "understands that there can be no value-free, objective, dispassionate, value-neutral account of a culture and its ways. . . . The ethnographic, the aesthetic, and the political can never be neatly separated" (1999, 512). MacDougall's solution carries similar echoes, calling for "a way of looking at the world that is intersubjective and, finally, communal" (1995, 250).

Audience Research

When defined and executed well, ethnography can be a powerful tool for the study of audiences (Nightingale 1996, 113–17). Before such work can begin, however, a conceptual understanding of audience is necessary. Some scholars position the audience as a fiction, a kind of imagined recipient of the material being created by communicators. Morley dismisses such claims, arguing that "audiences do in fact exist outside the terms of . . . discourses" (1997, 135). That audiences do maintain this existential reality is difficult to dispute, but audiences also exist as ideas in the communicator's mind. It is through the communicator's interaction with the idea—or the expectation, or the anticipation—of an as-yet-unformed audience that societies are able to constrain the otherwise myriad and chaotic galaxies of possibilities that each communicator faces.

That audiences can exist in the realm of the mind and the realm of physical reality seems reasonable; as audiences form and disperse, no two are ever the same—but the imagined constitution of a future audience, based on experiences with past audiences, can exert a potent influence on a communicator.

When audiences do gather, how can ethnography help us understand them? A key component to the answer lies in an understanding of where meaning resides. As Spitulnik notes, "central to this theoretical reformulation of media power is the crucial problem of where to locate the production of meaning and ideology in the mass communication process, and how to characterize processes of agency and interpretation" (1993, 295).[4] At the heart of the matter is the question of the locus of meaning: Is it in the communication itself, or is it created as the audience interprets the communication?

To address this issue, Morley notes two common assumptions about audiences. The first is that the audience is always active, meaning that the audience invariably plays a significant role in the development of meaning (1997, 123). The meaning does not lie entirely embedded within the text—in this discussion, within the video or film, the article or book—but rather is the product of a negotiation between the audience and the text. Each person in the audience brings to the activity a history, a set of expectations, a particular aesthetic, and a worldview. When the content of the communication is put forth, it interacts with the peculiarities within the audience to produce a situated meaning.

That meaning, then, is subject to changes with shifts in audience composition or in the circumstances of the communication; even with the same people in the audience, a later showing or reading will produce a different result because the audience has had additional experiences and conversations, because the audience is undoubtedly in a somewhat different mood, and because, of course, everyone in the audience has experienced this communication before.

The second assumption regarding audiences is that media content is always polysemic and hence open to interpretation (Morley 1997, 123). It is this assumption that allows us to consider the negotiated meaning produced by the interaction between audience and text. If media content were self-limiting to only one possible interpretation, then the "activity" of the audience would be moot.

Despite these assumptions, however, Morley and Hall maintain faith in a degree of textual determinacy, arguing that we must give some weight to the notion to avoid an excessive eroding of the idea of media power (Hall 1986; Morley 1997, 124). This position, however, raises interesting questions about the *degree* to which the interpretation of a communication can be negotiated. Hall offers the notion of a preferred reading, maintaining that while several interpretations might be possible, only one is intended and hence desirable from the communicator's standpoint (Morley 1997, 124). This position has been eroded in recent years by the "active audience" theory, which was "considered radical" in its early days (Nightingale 1996, 7). Nightingale criticizes Morley for positioning meaning too fully in the text alone, without sufficient recourse to readers (1993, 151).

To the extent that the active audience theory is valid, however, ethnography offers a vitally important tool for the research of communication. It is difficult to grasp the nature of the audience—and all that the audience brings with it—without deep, close, and extensive research conducted in person at the time. The value of ethnography becomes even more apparent when the realm of study involves international or cross-cultural communication. When a researcher is working with an audience that holds cultural, political, or social values that differ to any significant degree from his or her own, ethnography offers a unique ability to reveal those values and make them clear, within the bounds of research competency, to the researcher. By observing the audience engaged in the communication, by listening to the comments and other reactions offered by the audience at the time, by talking with various members of the audience individually and in groups, by learning all that can be gleaned about the society and culture embraced by these people—only then can we begin to appreciate the nature of the negotiation taking place during the communication.

The debate over the active audience stems largely, it seems, from a clash over competing models. One model positions the text at one end of a straight line and the audience at the other, with meaning flowing from text to audience. Dismissed as overly simplistic and determinant, this model has been modified to accept some degree of interpretation by the audience, even if the idea of a preferred meaning remains intact. Now the text, which is polysemic, offers the potential for multiple interpretations—although one interpretation remains the intended or preferred version.

Moving even further along this spectrum, the next model shows the text offering multiple meanings without granting a privileged position to any of them. The audience members choose from among the possible meanings based on their own backgrounds and outlooks.

And taken to its extreme, the final model shows the text simply existing in the world, without directing or limiting any interpretations whatsoever. In this view, the audience members are entirely responsible for the generation of meaning, as they would be if discussing the shapes of clouds.

The most likely reality grants the communicator and the audience the power to negotiate not only the meanings themselves but also where along the above spectrum the negotiation should function. In this mode, ethnography is an essential means by which these negotiations can be revealed and explored. The ethnographer, then, breaks out of any linear model whatsover, positioning himself or herself in relation to both the text and the audience.

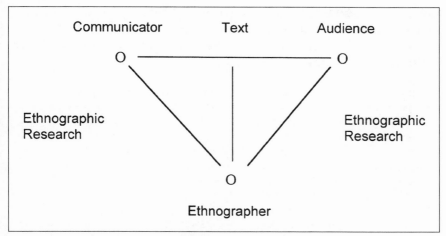

FIGURE 10.1
The Ethnographer's Perspective on the Structure of Communication

In this way, the communicator, through the text, negotiates with the audience for meaning and the locus of meaning. In addition, the researcher, apprehending and interpreting the text directly, negotiates with both the communicator and the audience in an effort to discover and explore the meanings of the communicative act itself.

With cultural negotiations comes the influence of power. On this level, the power in question involves the relationship between the communicator and the audience. Issues of hegemony, resistance, colonialism, and other power dynamics come to sharp focus in the arena of communication (cf. Condit 1989, 1994; Mumby 1997; Gramsci 1971, 1978). The locus of power in communicator/ audience negotiations is rarely open to an equal interplay of influences. "The power of viewers to reinterpret meanings is hardly equivalent to the discursive power of centralized media institutions to construct the texts which the viewer interprets" (Morley 1997, 125). To further understand these issues, ethnography ventures beyond the immediate communicative situation to explore the cultural, social, and political context in which such a communication occurs.

The Fabric of Context

Communication, of course, never happens in a vacuum. Anytime one person communicates with another—or with many—that enterprise takes place within a rich and complex context, the confluence of history, culture, and personality. It is the ethnographer's duty to reflect this context as fully as possible. "This science will work by establishing a second center of experience distinct from our own.

Around it facts will be built into a true portrait of another way of life so rich and complete it can stand on its own" (Glassie 1995a, 12).

Frow and Morris frame cultural studies in a manner that can be applied specifically to ethnography as well:

> Cultural studies often operates in what looks like an eccentric way, starting with the particular, the detail, the scrap of ordinary or banal existence, and then working to unpack the density of relations and of intersecting social domains that inform it. Rather than being interested in television or architecture or pinball machines in themselves—as industrial or aesthetic structures—it tends to be interested in the way such apparatuses work as points of concentration of social meaning, as "media" (literally), the carriers of all the complex and conflictual practices of sociality. (1993, xviii)

Communication studies that attempt to answer narrow questions without regard to context run the risk of producing results that are overly simple, misdirected, or just plain wrong. Ethnography, with its ability to press outward from the communication event to the *circumstances* of the communication event, offers a path of inquiry that can bring context to bear on text. As Wolcott states, "Context has always seemed to be the ethnographic long suit. Context is something one can expect (and insist on) from ethnography that is most apt to be stripped away in any more narrowly focused approach. . . . To be commended for well-contextualized reporting should bring satisfaction to any ethnographer for having successfully resolved the tension between providing irrelevant or excessive detail and providing too little" (1999, 79).

In the realm of international communication, the contextualizing power of ethnography becomes all the more significant. In reaching across national, cultural, and political boundaries, studies run even greater risks of misunderstanding and misrepresentation than do purely intracultural inquiries. The more remote the researched is from the researcher, both geographically and culturally, the greater the chance for breakdowns in the process of understanding. Ethnography—by compelling researchers to go to the society being studied, spend large amounts of time there, and test theories and ideas in multiple ways—can offer a potent (but ever imperfect) corrective to the kinds of errors that can creep into long-distance or impersonal studies. In considering the role of ethnographic contextualization with regard to indigenous video and film, Weiner put it this way:

> Is there something I need to know about the tenor and shape of Inuit or Aboriginal or Native American social engagement that would allow me to see this portrayed interaction differently or perhaps from my point of view more effectively? . . . That explanatory passage I refer to is no more or less than the critical ethnographic background to the film, and in such a case we would desire that the

anthropologist perform the same role that we expect of the successful film critic: We want him/her to tell us something about the film that we cannot see for ourselves. (1997, 197)

Gans notes that participant observation, his favorite ethnographic tool, can "supply empirical findings about little known or stereotyped populations, particularly those outside the mainstream" (1999, 540). As Werner put it, "perhaps the greatest strength of ethnographies is the contextualization of native knowledge" (1998, 3).

Examples of this approach to communication studies are plentiful. They begin, in one sense, with Worth and Adair, who gave film cameras to the Navajo and watched closely to see how they would create films and what these films would show (1997). Worth and Adair were aware of the limitations of verbal language to describe complex cultural outlooks, and they applauded efforts to capture such outlooks in other ways (1997, 12–14). "We reasoned that if a member of the culture being studied could be trained to use the medium so that with his hand on the camera and editing equipment he could choose what interested him, we would come closer to capturing his vision of his world" (1997, 14).

Similarly, Ginsburg has done important work with the Inuit and the Aborigines (1991, 1993, 1994, 1995). Citing Michaels (1984), Ginsburg offers comments about the text of Aboriginal videos but then observes that "of equal if not more importance is the social organization of media production; the ways in which tapes are made, shown, and used reflect Warlpiri understandings of kinship and group responsibilities for ceremonial production and the control of traditional knowledge" (1993, 566). While much of Ginsburg's work functions in the theoretical, academic realm, she also turns to her own ethnographic fieldwork to make points about Aboriginal society and culture:

The recent development of the Tanami Network offers a telling contrast to Imparja [the large, Aboriginally owned television station in Alice Springs]. In this case, western video technology is being used in the service of Aboriginal communication needs, creating a completely innovative use of televisual media. In 1992, when I worked in Central Australia for the second time, criticisms of Imparja by more remote Aboriginal media associations had escalated. Regarding Imparja as deaf to their complaints, WMA members and others at Yuendumu became engaged in an effort to harness new communications technologies in ways more suited to their concerns and activities. Along with other Aboriginal communities in the Tanami area of Central Australia (Lajamanu, Willowra, and Kintore), they formed the Tanami Network, a video-conferencing system that uses satellite signals to link these settlements to each other and to the cities of Alice Springs, Darwin, and Sydney. (1993, 571)

Turner's work with the Kayapo also falls into this contextualizing realm, in which the world around the communicators and their audiences is allowed to carry weight within the research project and its results (1990, 1991, 1992a,b). And my own work in the Arctic and the Outback tends toward this approach, offering contextual details not as superficial color but rather as significant pieces of information that give shape to communication and to our thinking about it.

In advocating existential or interpretive ethnography, Denzin urges us to use ethnography to better understand the context of oppression and commodification within a culture: "The moral ethnographer searches for those moments when humans resist these structures of oppression and representation, and attempt, in the process, to take control over their lives and the stories about them" (1999, 512). This and related approaches might be seen as an alternative to the more heavily textualist focus that has become eminent since Clifford and Marcus published *Writing Culture* (1986). "An existential ethnography offers a blueprint for cultural criticism, a criticism grounded in the specific worlds made visible in the ethnography," Denzin notes (1999, 512). He argues that ethnography provides a way to achieve the essential contextualization that helps us make sense of communication and its role in the world. "A vulnerable, performative ethnography . . . asks the ethnographer to always connect good and bad stories to the circumstances of the media, to history, to culture and political economy. . . . In connecting the personal to the historical, the political and the representational, the writer contextualizes the story being told" (1999, 514).

Ethnography of Communication Performance

One interesting direction in which ethnography can shed light on international communication lies in the area of performance. Following the work of Hymes (1975, 1981), Glassie (1983, 1989, 1992, 1995a,b), Bauman (1975, 1986), and other scholars of performance—and responding to Hall's call for greater research into textual production (1980)—I find enormous potential for ethnographic studies of communication that focus their gaze on the side of communicator and creation. In the realm of performance studies, and with particular relevance to the performative study of international communication, ethnographic approaches are vital tools in the effort to understand just what goes on when a communicator creates a communication, whether intended for an intimate audience or an enormous one. Spitulnik notes:

> Mass media—defined in the conventional sense as the electronic media of radio, television, film, and recorded music, and the print media of newspapers, magazines, and popular literature—are at once artifacts, experiences, practices, and processes. They are economically and politically driven, linked to developments

in science and technology, and like most domains of human life, their existence is inextricably bound up with the use of language. Given these various modalities and spheres of operations, there are numerous angles for approaching mass media anthropologically: as institutions, as workplaces, as communicative practices, as cultural products, as social activities, as aesthetic forms, and as historical developments. (Spitulnik 1993, 293)

Here, she points to the possibility of studying the mass media from the point of view of communicative art. As Hymes notes, "performance is not to be considered simply an outward manifestation of an individual and inner competence. It may take on properties that are intrinsically interactive, and social, in the sense of transcending individual contribution" (1975, 353). Frow and Morris make a similar, but not identical, observation; culture, they note, has to do with "the *practice* (rather than the implementation) of structures of meaning—genres or codes, for example—and with the construction of social space out of the weaving together, the crisscrossing of such practices" (1993, xix). In other words, the performance of communication can and should focus on the social interaction between communicator and audience. How *does* the communicator get his ideas across to an audience, especially when separated from that audience spatially and temporally, as in the case of mass media?

Morley calls on us to integrate Hall's vertical dimension—involving questions of ideology, power, and politics—with his horizontal dimension, involving consumption, uses, and functions of media (1997, 127–28). But this integration, while sound, continues to overlook the creation/performance/art of communication, in which a person, inspired by a vision of something to be communicated and constrained by the limits placed upon her, implicitly or explicitly, by her culture, creates a work intended to transcend personal boundaries and convey the idea from her mind to the minds of others. This performative aspect of communication, especially on the larger scale of mass communication, has been largely overlooked, and ethnography is especially well suited to explore it.

An important consideration in the performance of communication—mass as well as personal—is that the audience gives shape to the communication through active response. In personal, face-to-face communication, the communicator can adjust his performance "on the fly" in reaction to the audience's response in service of the desired end (Bauman 1986; Lord 2000). In mass communication—video, for example—the social filter enters through the *anticipation* of the audience response. When Zak Kunuk makes a video about Inuit hunting practices, for instance, he determines the response he wants to engender in the audience and then creates a video that will, to the best of his competence, bring about that result. History enters the picture as well; Kunuk recalls the reactions he has received in the past and, with the benefit of competence enhanced by that experience, creates a new work that will, he hopes, more fully bring about the reactions he seeks. Communicators, functioning on the mass or the personal level, craft their communication in an effort to achieve the laughter, tears, gasps, or sighs that they hope to elicit from their audiences. Continued ethnographic research among communicators will result in further refinement of our understanding of the ways in which they go about this process.

Conclusion

Ethnography has been framed as a way of researching, a way of organizing thought, a way of thinking, writing, and seeing. Despite Gans's correct observation that "empirical ethnography is now a synonym for virtually all qualitative research except surveys and polls" (1999, 541), I agree with Nightingale's call for another look at ethnography as anthropology defines it, as both "a heritage and as future direction" (1993, 159). By "ethnography," she means the kind of study that embraces entire cultures and focuses broadly on people, rather than the narrow, attenuated textual studies that have too often come to pass for ethnography. As Gans put it in his corrective for the superficial ethnographies that he has seen, "in the long run, the only ethnography that will be useful to students and researchers is that enabling people to learn more about their society" (1999, 543–44).

In the realm of international communication, thick with opportunities for missteps and unintentional harm, ethnography offers a means by which the cultural significance and cultural ramifications of an act of communication can be discerned. Other forms of inquiry, both theory and method, offer strengths of their own, but ethnography gives the international-communication scholar an opportunity to understand the underlying, situated nature of communication more thoroughly.

This chapter has touched on several of the current, major questions surrounding ethnography today, but it has by no means exhausted the list. Dialogue abounds around the issue of the ethnographic artifact, for example— the degree to which the written ethnography should be seen as a window to another culture or as a subjective literary work in its own right.

Amid the definitions and disagreements, the clashes and the camps, one fact should be held dear: the goal of international, intercultural understanding, aided well by the use of ethnography, may be impossible to fully realize but *is* worth the effort. As Scholte put it, "While we may never know the whole truth, and may not have the literary means to tell all that we think we know of truth . . . shouldn't we nevertheless keep trying to tell it?" (1987, 39).

Notes

1. The passage quotes Williams 1961.
2. The term "cultural dopes" comes from Hall 1981.
3. Nightingale dismisses this last point, however, arguing that "the senses in which the mass audience, or parts of it, can be seen as an 'other culture' are . . . tenuous" (1993, 153).
4. "Since the early 1980s, one intriguing component of this move toward the 'interpretive' audience has been the embracing of anthropology and the ethnographic method as empirical antidotes to the prevailing theoretical overload" (Spitulnik 1993, 298). Spitulnik adds that few audience studies have been truly ethnographic, although I would point out that several indigenous media studies have used ethnography as their primary approach. (For examples, see Michaels 1984, 1994.)

References

Abrahams, R. D. 1963. *Deep Down in the Jungle: Negro Narrative Folklore from the Streets of Philadelphia*. New York: Aldine de Gruyter.

Agee, J., and Evans, W. 1939. *Let Us Now Praise Famous Men*. Boston: Houghton Mifflin.

Albert, B. 1990. On Yanomami Warfare: Rejoinder. *Current Anthropology* 31, no. 15: 558–63.

Bauman, R. 1975. Verbal Art as Performance. *American Anthropologist* 77: 290–311.

———. 1986. *Story, Performance, and Event: Contextual Studies of Oral Narrative*. Cambridge: Cambridge University Press.

Berg, B. L. 1998. *Qualitative Research Methods for the Social Sciences*. Boston: Allyn & Bacon.

Clifford, J., and Marcus, G. E. 1986. *Writing Culture: The Poetics and Politics of Ethnography*. Berkeley: University of California Press.

Condit, C. M. 1989. The Rhetorical Limits of Polysemy. *Critical Studies in Mass Communication* 6: 103–22.

———. 1994. Hegemony in a Mass-Mediated Society: Concordance about Reproductive Technologies. *Critical Studies in Mass Communication* 11, no. 3: 205–30.

Cruikshank, J. 1990. *Life Lived Like a Story: Life Stories of Three Yukon Native Elders*. Lincoln: University of Nebraska Press.

Denzin, N. K. 1997. *Interpretive Ethnography: Ethnographic Practices for the 21st Century*. Thousand Oaks, Calif.: Sage.

———. 1999. Interpretive Ethnography for the Next Century. *Journal of Contemporary Ethnography* 28, no. 5: 510–19.

Foley, D. E. 1995. *The Heartland Chronicles*. Philadelphia: University of Pennsylvania Press.

Frow, J., and Morris, M., eds. 1993. *Australian Cultural Studies: A Reader*. Urbana: University of Illinois Press.

Gans, H. 1999. Participant Observation in the Era of "Ethnography." *Journal of Contemporary Ethnography* 28, no. 5: 540–48.

Ginsburg, F. 1991. Indigenous Media: Faustian Contract or Global Village? *Cultural Anthropology* 6, no. 1: 95–114.

———. 1993. Aboriginal Media and the Australian Imaginary. *Public Culture* 5, no. 3: 557–78.

———. 1994. Embedded Aesthetics: Creating a Discursive Space for Indigenous Media. *Cultural Anthropology* 9, no. 3: 365–82.

———. 1995. "Mediating Culture: Indigenous Media, Ethnographic Film, and the Production of Identity." In L. Devereaux and R. Hillman, eds., *Fields of Vision: Essays in Film Studies, Visual Anthropology, and Photography,* 256–91. Berkeley: University of California Press.

Glassie, H. 1983. *All Silver and No Brass: An Irish Christmas Mumming.* Philadelphia: University of Pennsylvania Press.

———. 1989. *The Spirit of Folk Art.* New York: Harry N. Abrams.

———. 1992. "The Idea of Folk Art." In J. M. Vlach and S. J. Bronner, eds., *Folk Art and Art Worlds,* 269–74. Logan: Utah State University Press.

———. 1995a. *Passing the Time in Ballymenone.* Bloomington: Indiana University Press.

———. 1995b. Tradition. *Journal of American Folklore* 108, no. 430: 395–412.

Gramsci, A. 1971. *Selections from the Prison Notebooks.* New York: International.

———. 1978. *Selections from Cultural Writings.* Cambridge, Mass.: Harvard University Press.

Hall, S. 1980. "Encoding/decoding." In S. Hall et al., eds., *Culture, Media, Language.* London: Hutchinson.

———. 1981. "Notes on Deconstructing 'the Popular.'" In R. Samuel, ed., *People's History and Socialist Theory,* 227–39. London: Routledge & Kegan Paul.

———. 1986. Introduction to *Family Television: Cultural Power and Domestic Leisure,* 7–10. London: Comedia.

Hinson, G. 2000. *Fire in My Bones.* Philadelphia: University of Pennsylvania Press.

Hymes, D. 1975. Folklore's Nature and the Sun's Myth. *Journal of American Folklore* 88: 345–69.

———. 1981. *"In Vain I Tried to Tell You": Essays in Native American Ethnopoetics.* Philadelphia: University of Pennsylvania Press.

Lawless, E. 1993. *Holy Women, Wholly Women: Sharing Ministries of Wholeness through Life Stories and Reciprocal Ethnography.* Philadelphia: University of Pennsylvania Press.

Lord, A. B. [1960] 2000. *The Singer of Tales.* Cambridge, Mass.: Harvard University Press.

MacDougall, D. 1995. "The Subjective Voice in Ethnographic Film." In L. Devereaux and R. Hillman, eds., *Fields of Vision: Essays in Film Studies, Visual Anthropology, and Photography,* 217–55. Berkeley: University of California Press.

Mann, C. 2000. Anthropology: Misconduct Alleged in Yanomamo Studies. *Science* (September 29, 2000): 2251.

Marcus, G., and Fischer, M. 1986. *Anthropology as Cultural Critique: An Experimental Moment in the Human Sciences.* Chicago: University of Chicago Press.

Michaels, E. 1984. The Social Organisation of an Aboriginal Video Workplace. *Australian Aboriginal Studies* 1: 26–34.

———. 1986. *The Aboriginal Invention of Television in Central Australia: 1982–1986.* Canberra: Australian Institute of Aboriginal Studies.

———. 1994. *Bad Aboriginal Art: Tradition, Media, and Technological Horizons.* Minneapolis: University of Minnesota Press.

Morley, D. 1997. "Theoretical Orthodoxies: Textualism, Constructivism, and the 'New Ethnography' in Cultural Studies." In M. Ferguson and P. Golding, eds., *Cultural Studies in Question*, 121–37. Thousand Oaks, Calif.: Sage.

Morris, M. 1990. "Banality in Cultural Studies." In P. Mellencamp, ed., *Logics of Television: Essays in Cultural Criticism*, 14–43. Bloomington: Indiana University Press.

Mumby, D. K. 1997. The Problem of Hegemony: Rereading Gramsci for Organizational Communication Studies. *Western Journal of Communication* 61, no. 4: 343–75.

Nava, M. 1987. Consumerism and Its Contradictions. *Cultural Studies* 1, no. 2: 204–10.

Nelson, R. 1983. *Make Prayers to the Raven.* Chicago: University of Chicago Press.

Nightingale, V. 1993. "What's 'Ethnographic' about Ethnographic Audience Research?" In J. Frow and M. Morris, eds., *Australian Cultural Studies: A Reader*, 149–61. Champaign: University of Illinois Press.

———. 1996. *Studying Audiences: The Shock of the Real.* London: Routledge.

Roscoe, P. 1995. The Perils of "Positivism" in Cultural Anthropology. *American Anthropologist* 97: 492–504.

Scholte, B. 1987. The Literary Turn in Contemporary Anthropology. *Critique of Anthropology* 7, no. 1: 33–47.

Senior, D. 1997. "Never Alone." In L. Hasselstrom, G. Collier, and N. Curtis, eds., *Leaning into the Wind: Women Write from the Heart of the West*, 335–36. New York: Houghton Mifflin.

Spitulnik, D. 1993. Anthropology and Mass Media. *Annual Review of Anthropology* 22: 293–316.

Tierney, P. 2000. *Darkness in El Dorado: How Scientists and Journalists Devastated the Amazon.* New York: Norton.

Titon, J. T. 1992. Representation and Authority in Ethnographic Film/Video: Production. *Ethnomusicology* 36, no. 1: 89–94.

Turner, T. 1990. The Kayapo Video Project: A Progress Report. *Commission on Visual Anthropology Newsletter*, 7–10.

———. 1991. The Social Dynamics and Personal Politics of Video Making in an Indigenous Community. *Visual Anthropology Review* 7, no. 2.

———. 1992a. Defiant Images: The Kayapo Appropriation of Video. *Anthropology Today* 8, no. 6: 5–16.

———. 1992b. The Kayapo on Television. *Visual Anthropology Review* 8, no. 1: 107–12.

———. 2001. *The Yanomami and the Ethics of Anthropological Practice.* Ithaca, N.Y.: Cornell University, Latin American Studies Program.

Wachowich, N. 1999. *Saqiyuq.* Montreal: McGill-Queen's University Press.

Weiner, J. F. 1997. Televisualist Anthropology: Representation, Aesthetics, Politics. *Current Anthropology* 38, no. 2: 197–235.

Werner, O. 1998. Short Take 24: Do We Need Standards for Ethnography? *Cultural Anthropology Methods* 10, no. 1: 1–3.

Williams, R. 1961. *The Long Revolution.* London: Chatto & Windus.

———. [1976] 1983. *Keywords: A Vocabulary of Culture and Society.* New York: Oxford University Press.

Wolcott, H. F. 1999. *Ethnography: A Way of Seeing.* Walnut Creek, Calif.: AltaMira.

Worth, S., and Adair, J. 1997. *Through Navajo Eyes: An Exploration in Film Communication and Anthropology.* Albuquerque: University of New Mexico Press.

IV

ON THE POLITICAL-THEORETICAL HORIZONS OF INTERNATIONAL COMMUNICATION

Mehdi Semati

PART IV, "ON THE POLITICAL-THEORETICAL Horizons of International Communication," consists of chapters that anticipate new problematics and trajectories for the field of international communication. In different ways, all of these chapters explore borders and the politics of crossing frontiers: transnational cross-border insurgencies escaping governance and posing security threats; articulating hybridity, multiplicity; cultural and political frontiers demarcating inside from outside, "the West" from "the rest"; clash of civilizations.

In chapter 11, Heidi Brush explores electronic communication technologies and their entanglement in the discourses of the security state. She clearly demonstrates the difficulties of regulation, governance, and control of an entity such as the Internet. A decentralized network with abundant redundancy as a Cold War defense strategy made sense in a bipolar world. The very same structure as a mechanism that permits porosity and resists containment, however, becomes a powerful tool in the hands of those who wish to escape hierarchies, borders, and control (be it national or transnational). Brush counterposes "counter-Net," as an heterarchical entity, to the Internet, and casts "netwar," or nonstate and nonmilitary actors taking up specific causes, in contrast to "cyberwar," a hierarchical military application of information technologies. These distinctions make explicit the ideological and administrative contradictions inherent to the regulation of an entity characterized by complexity in connectivity. I find the implications of Brush's analysis intriguing, especially as they connect with the arguments by Debrix, Downing, and Wark, if we take the Internet as emblematic (and as a component) of the global vectors of communication that resist capture. Here I would use the theoretical language of Deleuze and Guatarri (1987) to conceptualize an alternative approach to international communication. Communication technologies (e.g., counter-Net) supply rhizomatic structures that in turn provide "smooth space," which is counterposed to the "striated space" of the state. The counter-Net makes possible the "line of flight" that resists the state as the "apparatus of capture." To revisit the contradictory and ambivalent power of the vector, a line of flight might enable freedom (e.g., utilizing it for a politically progressive cause) or it might bring death and destruction (e.g., terrorists exploiting open systems). Brush's analysis introduces a set of heuristic distinctions that cannot be ignored by those interested in international communication technologies and governance. Her argument highlights the degree to which communication media might be rooted in technologies and discourses of security, military, and governmentality.

Marwan Kraidy explores some of the past conceptual trajectories within the field of international communication in chapter 12. His exploration of "the cultural" in international communication literature underlines certain unease in regard to the category of culture in international communication literature. Consideration of the cultural in the present globalized condition is bound to encounter the notion of hybridity with all its putative fecundity. As Kraidy shows, the much touted notion of hybridity could be articulated either progressively or hegemonically. Since many of the debates on globalization end up addressing the cultural, the concept of hybridity becomes a convenient tool. In that context, his discussion demonstrates the centrality of communication and culture in many of the arguments on globalization, arguments that purport to address the political, social, and economic forces that make up globalization. I maintain, however, that addressing communication and culture in those arguments creates a certain tension within them. By contending that international communication provides the space of articulation for the economic and the cultural, Kraidy raises the complexities of and contestations over the theoretical moves that can be made. Take, as an example of such moves and contestations, an interview on their work in *Empire*, in which Hardt and Negri (2002) dismiss the distinction between cultural, political, and economic as "no longer very satisfying" (181). For them, the concept of "empire," the "nonimperialist" current global order without a fixed center, is a more useful concept than "globalization" for addressing "the new biopolitical order." Yet as Downing's chapter in this volume demonstrates, this view is challenged by other theoretical moves that can be understood to articulate the cultural, political, and the economic differently. These difficulties indicate that the frontiers of international communication are dynamic and contestable.

Marouf Hasian addresses the discourse of eugenics at the dawn of the twenty-first century in chapter 13. Biopolitics and global governance is the backdrop against which attention to this discourse becomes pressing. "Eugenics" became a dirty word in the latter half of the twentieth century. However, the discourse of eugenics in Anglo-American thought, a topic Hasian (1996) has addressed in a book on the subject, has a complex history. He questions the purported disappearance of the discourse of eugenics in his analysis of the Chinese "eugenics" laws of 1995, and the reactions to these laws as reflected in the press. One of the benefits of such an analysis is that we gain insights into the symbolic "markers" used to demarcate the frontiers between "east" and "west," "north" and "south," "developed" and "underdeveloped," and so on. More important, I would argue, is a larger context in which such an analysis becomes indispensable: the expanding globalization with its population movement (e.g., emigration and diaspora), interventions in world population growth (e.g., the discourses of the U.N.), concerns with world health and the movement of medicalized bodies across national frontiers (e.g., global AIDS crisis), and the politicization of bodies in geopolitical conflicts across borders (e.g., the birthrate among Palestinians in the occupied territories). These are among the instances where the discourse of eugenics might return under the guises of liberal policies and seemingly objective political rhetoric. In all of these cases, "biopower," in the sense Michel Foucault understood it, is the organizing principle across international boundaries. In sum, Hasian's chapter demonstrates that international communication scholars are in a position to contribute critically to the political analysis of eugenics across its various manifestations.

In the final argument of the book, presented in chapter 14, S. Sayyid reflects on the topic of Islamism. Although it should be self-evident in some ways why the topic of Islamism should be included in a book exploring new frontiers in international communication, I would like to provide a larger context for its inclusion. There is a growing awareness that international communication needs to include non-Western perspectives in its conceptual and philosophical worldviews. Attempts to formulate an "Islamic perspective" in international communication (e.g., Mowlana 1996) are part of this context. So are the international (political and cultural) frameworks in which discussions of globalization and/or the new world order incorporate assumptions and views about Islam. The so-called clash of civilizations as a new global condition is an example of such a framework (e.g., Huntington 1993). A set of perspectives on globalization in which the "modern" (i.e., Western) world is positioned against the "traditional" (i.e., "Islamic") world is another such framework (e.g., Barber 1994).

Against this background, S. Sayyid, a political theorist, examines Islamism and its relationship to Eurocentrism. Sayyid's writings on political Islam incorporate poststructuralist theoretical tools (e.g., Sayyid 1997, 2003). One of his main lines of argument is that Islamism in its various forms is not reducible to a convenient label such as "Islamic fundamentalism." Various sociological and political explanations have been offered, particularly in the aftermath of September 11, to explain the emergence of Islamism in various societies across the world. However, there has been a general failure to demonstrate why Islamism and not a competing ideology (e.g., classic liberalism, socialism) should emerge as the final vocabulary for such political formations. In his chapter, Sayyid argues that Islamism is not only a direct challenge to a conception of the West as the universal narrative of emancipation and political destiny, but also an attempt to articulate an alternative subjectivity (i.e., a Muslim subjectivity). In the current rush to "explain" Islam and its followers, and in the context of growing international cultural conflicts associated with globalization, a scholarly treatment of Islamism is a critical addition to the list of our problematics in international communication. In sum, it is the contention of this book that international communication needs to be at the forefront of the research that tackles the question of cultural and civilizational conflicts.

References

Barber, B. 1994. *Jihad vs. McWorld*. New York: Ballantine.

Deleuze, G., and Guatarri, F. 1987. *A Thousand plateaus: Capitalism and schizophrenia*. Translated by B. Massumi. Minneapolis: University of Minnesota Press.

Hardt, M., and Negri, A. 2002. The global coliseum: On empire. *Cultural Studies* 16, no. 2: 177–92.

Hasian, M., Jr. 1996. *The rhetoric of eugenics in the Anglo-American thought*. Athens: University of Georgia Press.

Huntington, S. 1993. The clash of civilizations? *Foreign Affairs* 73, no. 3: 22–49.

Mowlana, H. 1996. *Global communication in transition: The end of diversity?* Thousand Oaks, Calif.: Sage.

Sayyid, S. 2003. *A Fundamental fear: Eurocentrism and the emergence of Islamism*. 2d ed. London: Zed.

11

Cells, Nets, and the Security State: Transnational Political Organizations and the Governing of the Internet

Heidi Marie Brush

TALES OF TRANSNATIONAL TERRORISTS finding refuge in dark alcoves of the Internet appear regularly in newspaper headlines and governmental security reports (Schwartau 2000; Ludlow 2001). The discourse of cyberspace security positions the Internet as a vulnerable national infrastructure, alongside other boundary panic sites such as airline systems and the immune systems of its citizens. Warding against the transnational flows of information and the attendant threats of rogue state electronic espionage, terrorist chat rooms and online activists (or hacktivists) has become the preoccupation of governmental agencies such as the National Security Agency (NSA), the Federal Bureau of Investigation (FBI), the RAND Corporation, and the National Infrastructure Protection Center (NIPC), to name a few. After September 11, 2001, calls for increased cyberspace security have discursively positioned the Internet as a vulnerable and porous system, emblematic of the "networked society" we inhabit (Castells 1996; Urry 2000).

In this chapter, I argue that various security discourses position the Internet as a bounded, circumscribable entity that may operate *architecturally.* Through techniques of security and law enforcement, the Internet can be (at least rhetorically) rendered into a structure of containment and control, as opposed to the chaotic, lawless, transnational, and ungovernable system frequently described (Ludlow 2001; Schwartau 2000; Campbell 2002). The goal of cellular operations, be they criminal networks, transnational insurgent groups, or counterglobalization hacktivists, is to reconstruct the existing architecture. They operate by means of *anarchitecture* beneath and through detectable nodes on the network.

The construction of cyberspace and the Internet as a *frontier* situates the Internet as nationally bounded territory in need of defense. After September 11, Internet and cyberspace security has taken center stage as a doomsday threat. As distinctions between military and civilian blur, cyberspace has become a new battleground as state forces attempt to control ever expanding territory (Virilio 1998). As Kathy Rae Huffman (1996) suggests in "Video, Networks, and Architecture," the new electronic territory is media information: "this is an invisible architecture without the interface of technology, and it faces new challenges in the public domain" (206). Cellular groups using network techniques present a crisis of national security, threatening law enforcement and even tax collection.

Crises over the governability of the Internet are not new (Ludlow 2001; Stocker and Schopf 1998). However, in light of the September 11 attacks on the World Trade Center and the Pentagon, cellular organizations are now viewed as smooth, slippery, unlocatable, and uncontainable as the Net. Cellular operators have become synonymous with terror, and the Net provides camouflage for hatching terror plans in the counter-Net, along with other ungovernables such as data pirates, music file swappers, corporate spies, and global black market profiteers. On March 22, 2001, National Security Adviser Condoleezza Rice and Richard Clark issued a warning about the vulnerabilities of the Internet. Rice remarked, "It is a paradox of our times that the very technology that makes our economy so dynamic and our military forces so dominating also makes us more vulnerable" (Benner 2001). Furthermore, the national security discourse has elided the distinctions between crime and terror, a tension that was brought into sharp focus in debates surrounding Internet security.

In this chapter, I examine the relationship between an "official" nationally circumscribed Internet conceived topographically as a frontier or highway in need of defense counterposed with the ungovernable transnational and heterarchical smooth spaces of what I call the *counter-Net*. Injected with and indebted to concepts from Deleuze and Guattari's treatise on nomadology in *A Thousand Plateaus* (1987), I interrogate the materiality and spatiality of Internet governance and insurrection. Using *netwar* as one example, I will show the national security crisis surrounding Internet governance to be an attempt to capture and reterritorialize transnational flows into a regulatable grid for defense, while the counter-Net deterritorializes, eludes, and outstrips the state apparatus of capture.

Internet Architectures

In *Postmodern War*, Chris Hables Gray writes that the "continual outbreaks of war are almost contained by the spread of worldwide high-speed communications, the integration of the world economy, and the proliferation of peace initiatives" (1997, 20). The global network has produced what Paul Virilio calls *pure war*—acts of war without war. New forms of war and conflict arise alongside significant societal shifts that have led writers to locate the present in an information age of a network society. The interests of a transnational network society have moved the field of operations to the realm of cyberspace. As capital, people, and information mobilize in transnational flows or scapes (Appadurai 1996), governmental and legalistic calls for regulation and containment hearken back to an earlier form of war architecture—the decentralized national information infrastructure known as Arpanet.

Originally designed as a decentralized network of nodes between key governmental and academic sites, the Internet was implemented in order to electronically connect the critical *information infrastructure*. Nationally circumscribed, the Internet was not designed to protect against the threat of international or transnational flows. Instead, in the binary Cold War logic, decentralization assured maximum redundancy in case of physical or nuclear attack (Abbate 2000; Edwards 1997).

What was once a defensive strategy against a Cold War enemy has now become a liability through porosity and transnationality. With satellite and massive nodal connections, the decentralized Internet became transnational, relying on unregulated flows and new mobilities of people, money, and information. As a regime of governance and control, national security agencies discursively construct the "official" Internet, counterpoised against what I call the counter-Net—the zone of encrypted documents, Web sites offering pirated software and music files, and the techniques of encryption and steganography that offer private communications and mobilities, escaping the capture of surveillance. Crypto-anarchist cypherpunks and cyberlibertarians imagine a counter-Net that outstrips the ability of the surveillance and control of the security state. For example, cyber anarchists have called for an alternate global banking system that would evade taxation by nations (Ludlow 2001; Agre 2001). Escaping detection, the counter-Net has become aligned purely with crime and terror in security discourse. The connection of al Qaeda with the counter-Net has resituated security discourse of the Internet from threats of crime to the lurking possibility of cyber terror.

Attempting to regulate and govern the massive connectivity of the Internet can be compared to controlling the weather or predicting the stock market. As De Landa (1991) writes in *War in the Age of Intelligent Machines*, "When networks reach a certain level of connectivity, they begin to form 'ecologies' resembling insect colonies or even idealized market economies" (107). Complexity is the bane of the state production of space. The Internet itself provides a good example of complexity in connectivity. In such complexity lies the crisis of governability as unbounded computer connections render the network itself "capable of spontaneously generating computational processes not planned by its designers" (9). Faced with a network so complex that it is an active and productive system, one starts to glimpse the dynamism of the Internet and may draw the analogy of policing national borders of network activities as akin to circumscribing boundaries on weather patterns. However, a self-organizing system can also be brought to states of turbulence, a threat the security state strives to ward off.

Against complexity, state space and the architecture of control segment and homogenize, or *striate*. Against the "smooth space" of boundless connectivity, porous systems, and rhizomatic structures afforded by the Internet network, the state attempts to maintain a "striated space" of control and capture. In *Nomadology: The War Machine*, Deleuze and Guattari (1987) describe state space: "[The] state constructs spaces which have a kind of gravitational effect, thereby making it the central organizational organism which attempts to regulate (not always successfully) the movements of persons and goods within and through its borders" (298). The state attempts to capture and reterritorialize various flows. Most importantly for my argument, state architecture forms *interiors* and seeks to centrally control and regulate its bounded interiors. The state is a machine of capture that attempts to create measurable striated spaces and a milieu of interiority (Patton 2000, 112). State initiatives to regulate and govern the Internet unambiguously employ the rhetoric of interiors versus exteriors, nation versus others—an outlook confounded by the logics of transnational capital and the smooth spaces of war and cyberspace.

Against interiority lie the tactics of the counter-Net, the tactics of creating smooth spaces. As Deleuze and Guattari write, "And each time there is an operation against the State—insubordination, rioting, guerilla warfare, or revolution as act—it can be said that a war machine has revived, that a new nomadic potential has appeared, accompanied by the reconstitution of a smooth space or a manner of being in space as though it were smooth" (1987, 386). The irruptive, insurgent events of the counter-Net such as data piracy, hacking, and information-hiding techniques such as steganography threaten the ability of security forces to contain and capture these flows.

The topography of the smooth and the striated on the Internet has been mapped out by Nunes in "Virtual Topographies: Smooth and Striated Cyberspace" (1999). Arguing that topography effectively creates a territory, Nunes calls attention to the two dominant conceptualizations of the Internet: the information superhighway and the surfable Net. The information superhighway exemplifies a striated space of "lines and trajectories subordinated to points" (Deleuze and Guattari 1987, 478). When cyberspace is conceived of in land-based terms such as the information superhighway or a frontier position, the Internet is territory in need of regulation and defense. A terrestrial network such as the highway system embodies a rationalized system of control that labels all nodes on the networks and follows centralized state governance and control. A highway system extends the mobility of the state in order to regulate, as well as facilitating sanctioned flows of capital. Flows move according to prescribed and legally coded directions and speeds. Little debate exists surrounding new uses or appropriations of highway systems—even hitchhiking is prohibited. The superhighway metaphor typifies the urge for a striated and enclosed network—an architecture of control.

Against the grid system of the "official" Internet, the information superhighway, is the complex, sealike surfable Net. Instead of the striation of territory, the surfable Net operates through deterritorialization in which "points are strictly subordinated to the paths they determine . . . every point is a relay and exists only as a relay" (Deleuze and Guattari 1987, 380). Sadie Plant describes smooth space in *Zeros + Ones* (1997): "webs of footnotes without central points, organizing principles, hierarchies" (10). Smooth cyberspace typifies the decentralized Net and the unlocatable practices of the counter-Net that use elusive techniques to avoid capture.

In "Anarchy, State, and the Internet: An Essay on Lawmaking in Cyberspace," David G. Post notes that the Internet allows escape from detection, as well as from jurisdictional control (2001). Sovereigns can circumscribe no borders around a territory in cyberspace. Security on the Internet revolves around the utter impossibility of tracking and capturing smooth flows in order to capture and govern.

As a locus of national security, the Internet resists regulation and policing because of its robust, decentralized design. Governmental agencies are bureaucracies that excel in controlling through vertical command and control, or hierarchy. As RAND strategists Arquilla, Ronfeldt, and Zanini write, "Nation-state ideals of sovereignty and authority are traditionally linked to a bureaucratic rationality in which issues and problems can be neatly divided, and specific offices can be assigned certain tasks" (2000, 182). Governmental agencies now approach the regulation of cyberspace with the same bureaucratic compartmentalization and striation in the insistence on establishing borders to cyberspace.

One month after the 9/11 attacks on the Pentagon and WTC, the National Infrastructure Protection Center (NIPC) released the following statement that places in tension the boundedness of an infrastructure with the porosity of a network: "Proactive network defense and security management are imperative to the prevention of more serious damage to infrastructure assets" (2001). The uncontrollability of transnational smooth flows proves so threatening that smooth flows have been discursively positioned as *attacks*.

The national infrastructure is state architecture: hierarchical and nonredundant. Cyberspace security guru Richard Clark recently insisted on creation of a new governmental communications network that would be distinct and not connected to the Internet. In the wake of 9/11, Clark proposed "GovNet" to President Bush in October 2001 as yet another classified and secure network not connected to the Internet (Intelink has existed since 1994 and is used by the FBI, CIA, DEA, and NSA). State Internet architecture with clear interiors and exteriors calls into question the threat that terrorists or other attackers could launch against the critical infrastructure. Spatially, while cyberspace is conceptualized as a whole body, individual sites or nodes are established—as Michael Menser calls it, the "organ-izing" function of the state (1996). With more than one protected, isolated, and heavily encrypted governmental intranet intact and open only to insiders, the panic surrounding the potential for threat on the Internet lies not in the ability to attack the critical data infrastructure (as is frequently cited), but rather, a crisis over controlling and governing the Internet. The organs have left the body.

The discourse of the vulnerability of a national infrastructure compromised by the Internet intensified in the late 1990s. In 1998, the Center for Strategic and International Studies (CSIS) released a report, *Cybercrime, Cyberterrorism, Cyberwarfare,* that underscored the potential for global criminal or terror networks to use the Internet, not only to coordinate their organizations but also to gain access to the state architecture of the infrastructure (1998). As early as 1998, the discourse of defending national borders against transnational terror organizations crackled with urgency as the CSIS task force warned, "America's most wanted transnational terrorist Osama bin Laden uses laptops with satellite uplinks and heavily encrypted messages to liaise across national borders with his global underground network" (10). The decentralized Internet threatens hierarchical chain of command state architecture of control simply by unmonitored flows gaining access to the infrastructure.

The task of security forces is to track, confine, and control the counter-Net, which harbors not only crime but also terror. The counter-Net is inevitably constructed as populated by networks and cellular organizations. Warding against the suspect activities of the counter-Net has spawned a voluminous literature of security documents produced by governmental agencies such as the NIPC, the RAND Corporation, and the CSIS task force. Let us now turn our attention to the production of criminal cells and terror networks in one such product of security state discourse, netwar.

Netwar and Counter-Nets

The war in the Persian Gulf inaugurated the precedence of digital technologies on the battlefield, and the move to eliminate (U.S.) soldiers from the battlefield. Norman Schwarzkopf has called Desert Storm a *technology war.* After

Desert Storm, the Internet rose in prominence for individual users, governments, military, corporations, and political organizations (from the far right to the far left). From the perspective of military strategy, conflicts and wars would now occur in the virtual realm of cyberspace. In 1995, RAND prognosticators Arquilla and Ronfeldt announced, "Cyberwar is coming!" Arquilla and Ronfeldt write of the symbiotic relationship between multiorganizational networks and information technologies that make it possible for "diverse, dispersed actors to communicate, consult, coordinate, and operate together across greater distances, and on the basis of more and better information than ever before" (Arquilla and Ronfeldt, 1998, 27).

Cyberwar and netwar provide another example illuminating striated and smooth topographies of the Internet. Cyberwar is defined as a hierarchical military application of computer and information technologies to the problems of high- and middle-intensity warfare, an aspect of the military technology revolution (Schopf 1998, 26). Whereas cyberwar is conducted at the military level, "netwar" is described as "societal-level conflicts waged in part through internetted modes of communication" (Stocker and Schopf 1998, 28). Netwars target information and communications, largely nonmilitary. Whereas cyberwar occurs at a purely military level, netwar includes nonstate actors from the Legion of Doom to the Zapatistas. Cyberwar performs the inevitable outcome of military developments in cybernetics and the computerization of warfare. Cyberwar is a hierarchical, rationalized and state-sanctioned, state-sponsored "defensive" military endeavor. Cyberwars may be waged over the official channels of the information superhighway. Netwar, on the other hand, bears more resemblance to the deterritorialized and decentralized smooth spaces of the surfable oceanic counter-Net.

Both cyberwar and netwar are frequently cited as a national security concern (guarding against netwar, and arming and preparing for waging a cyberwar) throughout the late 1990s and even more urgently in the twenty-first century. Imagining the threat of a netwar has fueled much speculation, and it predicts the current suspicion of transnational flows as potential terrorist threats. In an essay called "On the History of the Theory of Information Warfare" (1998), Friedrich Kittler vividly describes a RAND simulation of a potential netwar:

> In the year 2002, the USA withdraws its military support for a collapsing Saudi-Arabian ruling house because Airbuses full of American tourists are dropping like flies from the sky over Chicago. The Airbus was the first civil plane that needed an on-board computer to remain in the air, just like its military predecessors. In the RAND corporation's war game, Iranian mullahs, who have always thrown oily looks towards Saudi Arabia, have managed to bribe the Indian programmer of the Airbus software to hack his own program. A single artist engineer of that unincidental half-continent, which once created the basis of all things digital with the invention of all things zero, suffices to strategically paralyze the last remaining super power with the transmission belt of the American media democracy. (270–71)

Kittler's recounting of the RAND simulation neatly encapsulates the transnational nature of netwar, while underscoring economic and political motivations for a netwar aimed against U.S. targets. Implicit in this account is that small nations, political organizations, or corporations can gain an advantage over a military superpower simply by using easily accessible, inexpensive digital technologies. The fact that RAND used Islamic fundamentalists as a main enemy has inevitably gained legitimacy in security agencies after the 9/11 events.

The formidable capabilities of a group poised against the United States has caused shockwaves throughout the military throughout the 1990s, and prompted numerous reports from national security experts. While the information superhighway promised a utopian future of electronic commerce for Vice President Al Gore, in 1998, President Clinton delivered the following talk in a commencement address for the U.S. Naval Academy:

> Our security is challenged increasingly by nontraditional threats from adversaries, both old and new, not only hostile regimes, but also international criminals and terrorists who cannot defeat us in traditional theatres of battle, but search instead for new ways to attack by exploiting new technologies and the world's increasing openness. (CSIS, 1998, xii)

The CSIS task force report, *Cybercrime, Cyberterrorism, Cyberwarfare: Averting an Electronic Waterloo,* is peppered with hyperbole and littered with sensationalism, frequently invoking the names Osama bin Laden and Saddam Hussein as possible netwar enemies, or at least models for potential "cyberterrorist" groups. The report released information that coincides with many contemporary theorists who emphasize the erosion of the nation-state into transnational flows of capital and media images: "The nineteenth-century model of an independent state has become one of trappings rather than substance. Information technology is also eroding hierarchies that have long served as information filters for the people they rule or govern, thus constraining the actions of officials within government structures" (CSIS 1998, xvi). These transnational flows of people and information clearly challenge a military and governmental structure dependent on hierarchy and bureaucratic organization.

Transnational flows have become a new form of mobility in the information age, and new digital technologies, especially wireless digital communications devices, accelerate the movement of information and capital. Regulating these transnational flows has become the preoccupation of the United States and other G8 countries in an attempt to protect the relic of their nations while simultaneously protecting trade and information routes. Transnational flows and digitized information and technologies have become synonymous with today's most dreaded forces: "rogue states" and "transnational terrorists."

Political organizations, guerrilla operators, and online activists have found resistant strategies possible in a globalized, corporatized network world. Alternative political strategies frequently include reconceptualizing spaces and practices—for example, subverting a U.S. cyberwar into nonhierarchical arrangements that can disable a network. These nonhierarchical webs and cells also rely on bytes before bombs—their preferred weapons of choice are communications and information technologies (especially the Internet). To paraphrase the EZLN Zapatista spokesperson, Subcommandante Marcos, what governments should really fear is a communications expert. The Zapatistas are credited with being one of the first widely publicized political organizations to use the Web to promote their cause and provoke online protests in the spirit of electronic civil disobedience, cited by Arquilla and Ronfeldt as acts of netwar.

A network war, or netwar, refers not only to the use of new communications technologies and networks, such as the Internet and wireless communications; it also refers to the networked or cellular organization of the actors. Netwar is asymmetrical warfare in which nonhierarchical nonstate actors can use information and communications technologies to disable a hierarchical organization, such as a national infrastructure. Using the Internet for netwar purposes, a cellular operator may employ several different modes of attack, including data attacks, software attacks, hacking, physical attack, exploitation, deception, denial of service (DOS) attacks, and physical destruction of networks. Arquilla and Ronfeldt cite the Chiapas, Mexico, EZLN (the Zapatistas) as a major example of transnational social netwar. "The Zapatistas are insurgents—in some eyes, the first post-communist, postmodern insurgents" (73). Groups that use cellular organization and networked communications are placed on Arquilla and Ronfeldt's list of Netwar participants: "transnational terrorist groups, black-market proliferators of weapons of mass destruction, transnational crime syndicates, fundamentalist and ethnonationalist movements, intellectual property and high-sea pirates, and smugglers of migrants or black-market goods" (2000, 180). Which one of these categories better describes the decidedly nonviolent, noncriminal Zapatistas? Perhaps protesting NAFTA and eradication of indigenous culture may count as netwar if the members carry laptops and evade detection and capture, or if New York activists stage nonviolent online protests in support of the Zapatista cause.

In the security agencies' models of netwar, networked organizations use internetted communications channels to attack, disrupt, or destroy the infrastructure. Again, it is important to note the distinctions between terror and crime that become elided in the netwar literature produced by security agencies such as the NIPC and RAND. Netwar or cyberterror proponents apply the label "war" or "terror" to groups such as global organized crime networks or nonviolent political groups more interested in evading detection on a network than in creating a disruption. War and crime have become elided as the distinctions between the military and the civilian have blurred.

Activities such as pirating software or clandestinely moving funds become attached to the label of netwar as an all-purpose term to describe any nonstate networked organization that uses the Internet or networked communications in order to perpetuate their network of relations. So, netwar refers to the very existence of an organizational structure that defies hierarchical command and control. I argue that netwar suggests, instead, a crisis over accelerated flows, contested borders, and ungovernable cellular operators. Netwar is identification of a counter-Net with warfare and attack, thereby urging a security state toward greater vigilance in drawing lines around its infrastructure and network. I suggest that the netwar literature creates an enemy of cellular operators who do not attack or defend—they simply elude.

Elusiveness and undetectablity are the weapons of netwar, strengths through network design. Although constructed as threats that may attack a national infrastructure, cellular "heterarchical" organizations pose the greatest threat through their redundancy, resilience, and lack of identifiable or predictable nodal coordinates.

An architecture of camouflage, of elusiveness, exists just as the counter-Net operates in tension with the Net. Architect Lebbeus Woods suggests anarchitecture as an escape from the rationality of an architecture of control. Against hierarchical architecture, Woods employs a network organizational structure, a heterarchy. Woods defines heterarchy as a "self-organizing system of order comprised of self-sustaining individuals, the structure of which changes continually according to changing needs and conditions" (1994, 287). The morphing and virtual invisibility of heterarchical organizations have created a ream of security documents devoted to describing the vulnerability of the infrastructure and the difficulty of locating and disabling these acephalous (headless) organizations, morphing through the Net and counter-Net.

The historical precedents for netwar may be located in the networked and cellular organization of assassins, Mafia, tongs, yakuza, and nineteenth-century pirates—nonstate groups that operate outside the reach of national laws or even the laws of capital. Not surprisingly, the security discourse renders the very act of cellular organization as intrinsically linked with criminality, terror, and acts of war.

In a cover story article written for *Wired* magazine, Arquilla and Ronfeldt create an analogy between al Qaeda and music-swapping Napster fans: "In some ways, al Qaeda is to terrorism as Napster is to file sharing. True, declawing Napster did little to put an end to the swapping of MP3 files; smaller, even more decentralized P2P networks have popped up in its place" (2001, 151). Arquilla and Ronfeldt provide an example of a governmental bust of music-trading cellular operators but neglect to remind the reader that the Napster events were resolved through legalistic procedures that criminalized a centralized source for music swapping. By linking Napster with al Qaeda, and thus crime with terror, Arquilla and Ronfeldt create a correspondence/homology between cellular organizations and terror networks.

One recent digital technique, steganography, brings into sharp focus the tensions between architecture and anarchitecture, the Net and the counter-Net, prompting calls for security, regulation, surveillance, and control.

Steganography and Anarchitecture

Steganography, literally "covered writing," is a technique of concealment dating back to the fifth century B.C.E. as a way of hiding messages in plain sight. A common stego technique included tattooing a message on the head of a messenger. By the time the messenger reached the intended audience, the messenger would simply state "shave my head." Other famous techniques of steganography include the use of invisible ink. The allure of steganography lies in the ability to hide messages in the open. It is a guerrilla technique that employs camouflage and uses ordinary surfaces as ripe repositories for embedding messages where they are least suspected.

Recently, steganography has gone digital, allowing users to hide digital messages on the Internet on ordinary surfaces such as a Web site. Stego is hiding data within data, a kind of high-tech invisible ink. Popular uses of steganography range from hiding and protecting corporate secrets to watermarking copyrighted data. Unlike encryption, which scrambles messages, rendering them acutely detectable albeit theoretically untranslatable—steganography relies on the inherent lack of scrutiny given to unencrypted, mundane surfaces. Governmental and law enforcement agencies locate the threat of steganography in the ability of criminal and terrorist networks to coordinate their plans by using steganography. A cell organization posting messages on those most American of pursuits, sports and pornography, has rendered the most innocent or vacuous documents suddenly suspect. Media corporations fear the use of steganography, since CDs, DVDs, or software programs can be made available for free to all those who know where to look.

Steganography allows cellular and networked organizations to camouflage and evade detection by state-sponsored surveillance systems such as Carnivore or Echelon. User-friendly packages such as White Noise Storm, Steghide,

MP3Stego, and Snow are readily available tools for embedding messages within still pictures, audio, and text files.

In February 2001, seven months before the attacks that positioned bin Laden and al Qaeda as capable of any vile action, *USA Today* reported, "Terror Groups Hide Behind Web Encryption; Officials Say Sites Disguise Activities." The story opens by suggesting that terrorist blueprints can be hidden on pornographic Web sites and in sports chat rooms. Erroneously describing the technique as encryption, the article quoted FBI Director Louis Freeh as saying, "Uncrackable encryption is allowing terrorists to communicate without fear of outside intrusion." Of course, steganography is very easy to "crack"— the trouble is only in knowing where a stego message exists.

After September 11—just one day after the attacks—security experts overwhelmingly pointed to the vulnerability and labyrinthine nature of the Internet as a tool for terror and Web sites as beckoning harbors for terrorists. The news media quickly added sensationalism and intensified the panic over the ungovernability of the Internet.

Bolstering the security discourse, the news media perpetuate the construction of steganography and encryption as synonymous with terrorism, and sensationalize the presence of cellular operators in sites as innocuous as sports chat rooms. Stego outstrips the ability to govern smooth cyberspace because of its undetectability. It is the digital purloined letter. The London *Times* frets over the implications for a governable cyberspace in a September 26, 2001, article by Mark Henderson entitled "Secrets Concealed by Software":

> And here's the catch: It's dead simple to retrieve the message, if you know it's there. But if you don't—if you're a government agent trying to intercept terrorist plans—how do you know where to look? There are probably billions of images and sound files online. There's no way any spy hunter could inspect them all. The exploding size of our multimedia Internet provides fantastic cover for such communications. What's more, the recent terrorists' messages are likely in foreign languages that many spy hunters don't speak. (Henderson 2001)

Less than one month after the 9/11 attacks, Congress passed strong laws that made it easy for security and law enforcement agencies to tap into e-mail and Internet communication. With the threat of terrorists lurking on Web sites, operating in chat rooms, and exchanging e-mail, the call for more governance of the Internet received wide approval and enthusiasm—except from cyber libertarians and crypto anarchists who claim that terror is used as an excuse for more attempts at governmental regulation of the Internet. The cyber libertarians and crypto anarchists' case is presently supported, as no evidence suggests that bin Laden or al Qaeda used steganography or any other Internet tool or practice to coordinate the 9/11 attacks. Bin Laden's associations with cells and camouflage have marked the counter-Net as yet more extensive and labyrinthine enemy territory to scrutinize and attack.

Media panics fed by a will to national security have constructed the Internet as a threat precisely because of the pockets of lawlessness suggested by practices such as steganography. Steganography threatens the ability of security agencies to detect these vacuoles of nonlocatability.

Alongside free encryption programs, piracy, and hacking, steganography has been popularly coded as tools for terrorists, technologies of waging a netwar or a covert, camouflaged attack against the U.S. infrastructure. Julian Dibbell writes that many advocates of encryption, cypherpunks, did not believe the bin Laden steganography-porn story, labeling it as "yet another attempt by the Three-Letter Agencies to soften up the populace for restrictions on crypto, and they may well have been right" (Dibbell, nettime-l-request@bbs.thing.net 2001).

Steganography opens what Bruce Sterling and Hakim Bey have called "Islands in the Net" (Ludlow 2001). Heterarchitecture produces free spaces for "free action" as an architectural assemblage, a self-organizing system (Menser 1996). Against state architecture, for anarchitecture, the "arche and its organ functions are ripped up or thrown outside, placed along an exterior" (300). Anarchitecture refuses hierarchy and self-organizes in tissues, networks, matrices, and heterarchies (Woods 1994, 6).

Radical architect Lebbeus Woods designs and theorizes heterarchitecture as escape from urban and war architecture:

> In freespace, what is lost is the familiarity of architectural and societal norms, the reassurance of control by stable authority, and of predictability, certainty, and the routinization of behavior. What is gained is not an answer to the perpetual question of space, but simply a clear articulation of its potential. From this everything else flows. (Woods 1994, 290)

Woods's anarchitecture or heterarchitecture is an architecture of *possibility*, of what Hakim Bey calls "temporary autonomous zones." In *War and Architecture*, Woods reconceptualizes the war-ravaged urban architecture of Sarajevo, building "scars" and "injections" on the ravaged buildings. Against modernist, positivist state architecture, Woods's self-organizing, emergent spaces offer a "dense matrix of new conditions, as an armature for living as fully as possible in the present, for living experimentally" (Woods 1994, 21).

Like anarchitecture, cellular organizations may use steganography as a way to communicate and form new alliances. Just like tentacles that self-organize, the cellular organization can rely on the seemingly infinite surfaces onto which they may inscribe meanings and connections. In "The Haptic Morphology of Tentacles," Tom Wiscombe writes that tentacles resituate themselves tactically based on other bodies in their grasp (1998, 27). Steganography provides digital camouflage and free zones for online self-organizing cellular operations. These pockets of lawlessness escape capture, control, and regulation by the state security forces. Steganography provides a repository for the anxieties about the ungovernability of the Internet, and the undetectability and uncontainability of transnational cellular operators.

Conclusion

Reconceptualizing cyberspace as a smooth, self-organizing *heterarchitecture* or *anarchitecture* defies state attempts to govern and control by imposing an architecture of hierarchy, compartmentalization, and striation. Instead of cyberspace as a "no place" or utopia, cyberspace and the Internet threaten national boundaries through an elusive yet tangled web of connections where information, identities, and capital flow and resist capture. Cyberspace security forces construct a crisis surrounding the impossibilities of regulating transnational flows.

Online cellular operators through their network design threaten through undetectability, flexibility, and ability to camouflage. When cellular organizations use the smooth spaces of the Net, security forces attempt to impose and architecture of control. The security literature produced by such governmental agencies as the NIPC, the RAND Corporation, and the CSIS task force position the very act of eluding the architecture of control as attacks, or netwar.

Rhetorically linking bin Laden's cellular organization with online practices such as encryption and steganography positions the practices of the counter-Net with terror, and terror with cellular organizations. Techniques of the counter-Net, such as organizing through cells and using steganography to trade information and maintain cohesion and communication through self-organization, have been coded as inherently suspect by security forces. Architectures of control and regulation will continue to attempt capture of the ever morphing technologies and tactics of the counter-Net.

References

Abbate, J. 2000. *Inventing the Internet.* Cambridge: MIT Press.

Agre, P. 2001. Imagining the Next War: Infrastructural Warfare and the Conditions of Democracy, September 14. http://commons.somewhere.com/rre/2001/RRE .Imagining.the.Next.W.html.

Appadurai, A. 1996. *Modernity at Large.* Minneapolis: University of Minnesota Press.

Arquilla, J., and Ronfeldt, D. 1996. *The Advent of Netwar.* Santa Monica: RAND.

———. 1998. "Cyberwar Is Coming!" In G. Stocker and C. Schopf, eds., *Infowar*. New York: Wien.

———. 2001. Fighting the Network War. *Wired*, 9. 12 (December), 148–55.

Arquilla, J., Ronfeldt, D., and Zanini, M. 2000. Information-Age Terrorism. *Current History*, April, 179–85.

Benner, C. 2001. The Phantom Cyber-Threat: We Should Stop Worrying about Computer Terrorism and Learn Who Our Real Enemies Are, April 4. Salon.com .http://dir.salon.com/tech/feature/2001/04/04/cyberterrorism/index.html.

Campbell, R. 2002. Technical Solutions to Cyber Security. Paper presented at the Arms Control, Disarmament, and International Security Millennium Series, Urbana, Ill.

Castells, Manuel. 1996. *The Rise of the Network Society*. Oxford: Blackwell.

CSIS (Center for Strategic and International Studies). 1998. *Cybercrime, Cyberterrorism, Cyberwarfare*. Washington, D.C.: CSIS Press.

De Landa, M. 1991. *War in the Age of Intelligent Machines*. New York: Swerve.

Deleuze, G., and Guattari, F. 1987. *Nomadology*. New York: Semiotext(e).

Dibbell, J. 2001. E-mail from nettime-l-request@bbs.thing.net. February 20.

Edwards, Paul N. 1997. *The Closed World*. Cambridge: MIT Press.

Gray, C. G. 1997. *Postmodern War*. New York: Guilford.

Henderson, Mark. Secrets Concealed by Software. The London *Times*. September 26, 2001.

Huffman, K. 1996. "Video, Networks, and Architecture." In T. Druckery, ed., *Electronic Culture*. New York: Aperture.

Kittler, F. 1998. "On the History of the Theory of Information Warfare." In *Infowar*. New York: Wien.

Levy, S. 2001. *Crypto*. New York: Viking.

Ludlow, P., ed. 2001. *Crypto Anarchy, Cyberstates, and Pirate Utopias*. Cambridge: MIT Press.

May, T. 2001. "Crypto Anarchy and Virtual Communities." In P. Ludlow, ed., *Crypto Anarchy, Cyberstates, and Pirate Utopias*. Cambridge: MIT Press.

Menser, M. 1996. "Becoming Heterarch." In S. Aronowitz, B. Martinsons, and M. Menser, eds., *Technoscience and Cyberculture*. New York: Routledge.

National Infrastructure Protection Center (NIPC). 2001. www.nipc.gov.

Nunes, Mark. 1999. "Virtual Topographies." In M. Ryan, ed., *Cyberspace Textuality*. Bloomington: Indiana University Press.

Patton, Paul. 2000. *Deleuze and the Political*. London: Routledge.

Plant, Sadie. 1997. *Zeros + Ones*. New York: Doubleday.

Post, D. 2001. "Anarchy, State, and the Internet." In P. Ludlow, ed., *Crypto Anarchy, Cyberstates, and Pirate Utopias*. Cambridge: MIT Press.

Schwartau, W. 2000. *Tangled Web*. Indianapolis: Que Foundation.

Stocker, G., and Schopf, C. 1998. *Infowar*. New York: Wien.

Urry, J. 2000. *Sociology beyond Societies*. New York: Routledge.

Virilio, P. 1998. *The Virilio Reader*. London: Blackwell.

Wiscombe, T. 1998. "The Haptic Morphology of Tentacles." In L. Woods and E. Rehfeld, eds., *Borderline*. New York: Springer.

Woods, L. 1994. *War and Architecture*. New York: Princeton Architectural Press.

12

From Culture to Hybridity in International Communication

Marwan M. Kraidy

T HIS CHAPTER EXAMINES THE TROPE of hybridity in international communication. Hybridity emerged in the post–cultural imperialism malaise of the 1990s as a marker of a new pluralism ostensibly critical of the dominance perspective. It is evident that cultural hybridity, the fusion of formerly disparate elements in recombinant forms, is pervasive in the dynamics of contact and exchange of today's globalizing world. However, it would be a mistake to understand hybridity as a symptom of the withering of dominance. The cultural imperialism thesis tended to focus on cultural homogeneity as a dimension of hegemony. In contrast, proponents of hybridity purport to focus on cultural fusion as a manifestation of pluralism. After addressing the use of culture in international communication and the interdisciplinary rise of hybridity, this chapter revisits the correspondence between the homogeneity-fusion and dominance-pluralism. It concludes that an understanding of culture as synthetic, and not holistic, is a heuristic development, but that hybridity is not necessarily posthegemonic.

International communication theory has been marked by a proliferation of approaches, which has hindered the cumulative theory construction that establishes a distinct field of inquiry. Boyd-Barrett (1998) rightly bemoaned the trajectory of international communication as a theoretical enterprise, writing that "previous models of international communication may be abandoned in a process of linear intellectual development" (157). Boyd-Barrett argues that this process "has moved through theories of international communication as propaganda, through to modernization and free flow, to dependency and cultural or media imperialism, supplanted in turn by theories of the 'autonomous reader' and culminating in discourses of globalization that play upon an infinite variety of 'global' and 'local.'" Boyd-Barrett concludes that "intellectual development in the field of international communication appears not to proceed on the basis of exhaustive testing but lurches from one theory, preoccupation, dimension to another with inadequate attention to accumulative construction" (157).

The institutional bases and historical development of international communication have contributed to this fragmentation. Hardt (1988) has argued that international communication research evolved in response to the political and policy needs of the U.S. government, whose leaders regarded the mass media as a global strategic asset (Curtin 1993).[1] Consequently, international communication as a research enterprise was susceptible to government's influence and dependent on its funding, and did not develop as an intellectual endeavor concerned with theory construction and methodological growth. It was in this environment, where communication served as a strategic weapon in the U.S. superpower rivalry with the Soviet Union, that Lerner (1958), Rogers (1962), and Schramm (1964) developed the modernization paradigm. Whereas modernization theory did not explicitly focus on "culture," its researchers and practitioners conceptualized and implemented communication campaigns whose objectives were to alter traditional sociocultural values in the Third World deemed to be obstacles to development.

A radical critique of modernization crystallized in dependency theory, which emphasized the growing international power imbalance and the connections between First World wealth and Third World poverty. The media/cultural imperialism[2] thesis was the embodiment of the dependency paradigm in international communication research. Boyd-Barrett (1977), Mattelart (1979, 1983), Schiller (1971, 1976), and Tunstall (1977) were among its leading founding figures. They analyzed how Western multinational corporations, with the support of political regimes of wealthy countries and national elite groups in the developing world, dominated international cultural and media flows. This paradigm continued to be influential, especially in the context of the new world information and communication order (NWICO) debate. This discussion, which centered on ways to redress the structural framework of global inequality (see Boyd-Barret 2002; Gerbner, Mowlana, and Nordenstreng 1994 for a detailed discussion of this issue), has bifurcated into related concerns such as human rights and transnational civil society. Interest in issues of culture, however, has grown substantially, including emerging frameworks such as cultural rights but remaining focused on the more established concern about cultural influence.

Culture in International Communication

Since the 1980s, international communication scholarship has taken a cultural turn that has enshrined culture, in contrast to "society" or "national development," as the locus of analysis. Instead of social psychology and positivist political science, international communication scholars increasingly borrowed from cultural anthropology and sociology, literary criticism, and even Continental philosophy, in addition to a continuing tradition in critical political economy. In that environment, the prevailing notion of "culture" has become more complex and no longer sees culture as a by-product or a mere signifier for the political economy of global communication. Rather, this cultural turn has provided the space for interparadigmatic fertilization where international communication has borrowed from a range of disciplines and interdisciplinary areas.[3]

One of the most striking aspects of the cultural imperialism thesis is that some of its leading works did not focus on culture *strictu sensu*, if by culture we mean, following Williams, "structures of feeling." In contrast, cultural imperialism research was inclined to subsume culture to its industries, influenced by the "cultural industries" perspective developed by the Frankfurt School. Herbert Schiller, the doyen of cultural imperialism scholarship, underscored this association of culture with its modes of production in his famous definition in *Communication and Cultural Domination* (1976). "The concept of cultural imperialism," Schiller writes, "best describes the sum of the processes by which a society is brought into the modern world system" (9). In his definition, he also included "how [that society's] dominating stratum is attracted, pressured, forced and sometimes bribed into shaping social institutions to correspond to, or even promote, the value and structures of the dominating center of the system (Schiller 1976, 9). This broad analysis of the large-scale, systemic forces that shape the media industries is valid, but confusion arises in the working out of the details of his vision. The language in Schiller's definition of cultural imperialism, terms such as "world-system," "center," "structure," reflected a political economic approach in which culture tends to be more assumed (as in the "values" of "the dominant center of the system") than engaged.

Other leading proponents of the cultural imperialism thesis offered more culture-centered definitions, but their conception of culture is ripe for reassessment. Tunstall (1977) included culture more explicitly in his definition: "authentic, traditional and local culture . . . is being battered out of existence by the indiscriminate dumping of large quantities of slick commercial and media products, mainly from the United States" (57). Soon after, Beltran (1978) wrote that cultural imperialism is "a verifiable process of social influence by which a nation imposes on other countries its set of beliefs, values, knowledge, and behavioral norms as well as its overall style of life" (184).

While more inclusive of culture than Schiller's notion of cultural imperialism, Tunstall's and Beltran's definitions underscored another prevailing, often unarticulated assumption that guided much of early cultural imperialism work: culture conceived as a holistic, organic entity, usually identified with the nation-state. Animating much of the cultural imperialism thesis and the new world information and communication order is an understanding of culture as *national* culture, assumed to be relatively homogeneous. Based on this notion, which implicitly rejected, or at least neglected, the existence of cultural hybridity, foreign cultural influence is an unwelcome interference. The central challenge, as reflected in a 1980 United Nations Educational, Scientific, and Cultural Organization (UNESCO) report, was "the problem of fostering endogenous cultures in the wake of intrusions from without" (International Commission for the Study of Communication Problems 1980, 162, cited in Morris 1995, 7). While a necessary tactic at specific historical junctures, the rhetoric of cultural homogeneity glosses over the differences and fusions that exist in the overwhelming majority of nation-states.

Revisiting Culture in International Communication

The identification of culture with its structures and technologies, then, and the assumption that cultures are unitary wholes, are compelling reasons to revisit the notion of culture as used in international communication scholarship. The growing concentration of worldwide media in the hands of transnational conglomerates gives these behemoths unprecedented control over the information and electronic culture of the majority of the world's population. Whether this domination of production, content, and distribution leads to hegemony over everyday culture, with its values, beliefs, practices, and traditions remains one of the darkest areas of indeterminacy in research on cross-cultural media influence. Also, the notion that the practices of global media conglomerates, aided by the states that protect their interests, are contaminating and transforming once authentic cultures is untenable because ideas of cultural authenticity and purity are ontologically and politically dubious. This does not mean that foreign media have no influence over local cultures, but that there is a spectrum of cultural diversity ranging from the ideal types of complete homogeneity to total hybridity, and that most cultures gravitate to the middle range of that spectrum. Consequently, a new understanding of global media power ought to be grounded in the disentanglement of the issues of domination from that of homogeneity.

Obviously, other critiques have been leveled at the cultural imperialism thesis. Positivist mass communication researchers have criticized the cultural imperialism thesis on empirical grounds, conservative researchers on political bases; cultural studies scholars have pointed out that it denies social agency. Other scholars have also argued that cultural imperialism was a monolithic concept without clearly defined referents. These critiques range from the serious to the spurious, and the reader interested in their elaboration will find an abundant literature.[4] This chapter will focus instead on highlighting an alternative definition of culture that would in turn lead to a renewed understanding of power in international media dynamics and consequences.

Calls for a more elaborate notion of culture began in the early 1980s and emanated mostly from the critical tradition itself. In his assessment of media imperialism research, critical media studies scholar Fred Fejes (1981) advocated, among other things, a more thorough and complex understanding of culture (287): "While a great deal of the concern over media imperialism is motivated by a fear of the cultural consequences of the transnational media . . . All too often the institutional aspects of transnational media receive the major attention while the cultural impact, which one assumes to occur, goes unaddressed in any detailed manner" (287).

The putative object of media effects is "Third World societies" whose ability to foster national cultures is presumably undercut by foreign cultural influence. Fejes (1981) concludes that cultural imperialism research perceives the mass media a "primarily manipulative agents capable of having direct, unmediated effects on the audience's behavior and worldview" (287).

At the time Fejes (1981) called for a renewed understanding of culture by critics of cultural imperialism, pointing to literary analysis as a possible inspiration, the emerging British cultural studies was formulating theoretical bases and methodological approaches to understand culture and communication as everyday life processes infused with power differentials and negotiated meanings. Its sources of inspiration included Michel de Certeau's notion of everyday life, Antonio Gramsci's seminal development of the concept of hegemony, and Michel Foucault's writings on the micropolitics of power. Cultural studies promptly developed its own founding texts. Stuart Hall's 1980 article "Encoding/Decoding" and David Morley's book *The "Nationwide" Audience* (1997) set the stage for two decades of research into the relationship between texts and audiences. This approach became known as the "active audience formation." Its migration to North America is evident in the *Critical Studies in Mass Communication* 1988 audience symposium and in the special issue on "Ethnography and Cultural Studies" of the *Journal of Communication Inquiry*.[5]

Theories of meaning negotiation, viewer creativity, and quasi-ethnographic methods proved highly popular. New concepts and approaches injected fresh ideas in international communication scholarship, which hitherto had been dominated by world-system and dependency approaches that neglected audiences and cultural processes. The British cultural studies active audience group, the Scandinavian school of reception studies, Latin American cultural theories, and a variety of related media research in Asia, Africa, and Australia have coalesced in what is now commonly referred to as "global media studies" (see Murphy and Kraidy 2003a and 2003b for a systematic treatment).

Leading international communication scholars have questioned active audience research in particular and cultural studies in general. Acknowledging the "considerable influence" of this cultural studies approach, Boyd-Barrett (1997) nonetheless argued that "its discovery of polysemic texts . . . fitted well with a politically conservative era and the re-invigoration of liberal capitalism" (19). Similarly, Curran (1990) criticized active audience research as a "new revisionism" of radical perspectives on the media, espousing the old pluralist perspective and claiming it as a new research agenda. While accusations of this nature were vehemently rejected by some cultural studies scholars (see Ang 1996 for a response to Curran 1990), mainstream appropriation of concepts from critical and cultural theory warrants more scrutiny than it has received, and is visible in the appropriation of the discourse of hybridity by the neo-liberal narrative of democratic capitalism (Kraidy 2002a). There has also been considerable renewal within the community of adherents to the dominance perspective, including Boyd-Barrett (1998), Mattelart (1994), Miller et al. (2001), and Mosco and Schiller (2001). In varying degrees, these scholars focused on the systemic inequities in the global media system but recognized that these imbalances did not necessarily lead to cultural homogeneity; they rather acknowledged the existence of cultural hybridity, albeit one subordinated to the imperatives of power and profit (Kraidy 2002b).

The Advent of Hybridity and International Communication

This recognition of composite cultures mirrors a growing interdisciplinary debate about cross-cultural fusion. The 1990s witnessed the rise of hybridity as a multidisciplinary concern over the fragmentation and fusion of cultural forms.[6] Behind the frenzy surrounding hybridity, akin to the rush to postmodernism's gold mine in the 1980s, lies an ancient preoccupation with the consequences of cross-cultural encounters. This concern is more widespread than the English colonization of America and India, which have inspired the bulk of Anglophone scholarship on postcolonial cultural spaces and the coinage of such seminal concepts as Bhabha's "Third Space" (1994) and Gilroy's "Black Atlantic" (1993). Critics like Gruzinski (1999) in France, Toumson (1998) in the Caribbean, García-Canclini (1989) in Mexico, Martín-Barbero (1993 a, b) in Colombia, and others have used hybridity or its equivalents in their cultural analyses.

These scholars have recognized, like historian Jerry H. Bentley (1993), that "cross-cultural encounters have been a regular feature of world history since the earliest days on the human species' existence" (vii). While Bentley's work focuses on cross-cultural encounters in premodern times, his analysis illustrates that the relationship between hybridity and power is of the utmost importance. Far from being a benign mixture of equal cultural differences, the formation of hybridity is pervaded by political, economic and cultural inequalities. What roles do dominance and resistance play in shaping hybrid cultures? What approach would allow us the best possible grasp of cross-cultural dynamics in their historical and contextual specificities?

From Determination to Articulation in International Communication

The theory of articulation may do the trick. In fact, it may be productive to reformulate transnational media power from a model of determination to a framework of articulation. Many thinkers, including Etienne Balibar, Louis Althusser, Ernesto Laclau, Terry Eagleton, and Stuart Hall, have used articulation. Hall defined articulation as "a connection or link which is not necessarily given in all cases, as a law or a fact of life, but which requires particular conditions of existence to appear at all" (1985, 113). The heuristic potential of such an angle in international communication is considerable, because a model of articulation displaces both monolithic condemnation of domination and populist celebration of resistance. Beyond this initial but far-reaching implication, a model of articulation is productive in unpacking the polyvalent push-and-pull relationships between dominance, homogeneity, diversity, and hybridity.

As I have argued elsewhere (Kraidy 2002a), the deployment of the concept of hybridity can be articulated to a variety of economic, political, and cultural interests. In each case, hybridity has a different meaning and its use a different goal. In postcolonial theory, it is seen as a symptom of subaltern resistance. In international marketing jargon, hybridity is seen as a new strategic weapon in building niche markets. In all these cases, however, hybridity is mediated, that is translated via a communicative process in order to be articulated to particular agendas. If, following Jameson (1999), Hardt and Negri (2000) and others, we agree on the centrality of communication—broadly understood to include all flows of information—in the myriad entangled processes that constitute globalization,[7] then communication should be understood primarily as an articulator—the contingent and selective link between different

(political, economic, cultural, ideological, etc.) spheres. Consider the following
examples of various articulations of hybridity:

1. The prestige press uses hybridity as a meta-construction of global culture. For example, the *Washington Post* published in October 1998 a series of articles on "American culture abroad" that deploy hybridity as the
   primary characteristic of American cultural influence in developing
   countries. As I have argued elsewhere (Kraidy 2002a), this is a politically
   unproductive articulation of hybridity to globalization. It puts forth
   Western technology and non-Western desire for Western freedom and
   culture as the twin engines of cultural hybridity, as Third World audiences use U.S. popular culture to subvert their own authoritarian political and sociocultural systems. The series also uses economic arguments
   to explicate discriminatory practices by Hollywood studios, basically arguing that minority U.S. actors are not cast because foreign audiences
   are not drawn to them, a claim adopted from the studios themselves.
   This rhetorical ploy goes unchallenged in the articles, and so the crucial
   nexus of American multiculturalism and cultural globalization goes unexplored. More importantly, the rhetoric of hybridity used in these stories elides the issue of power altogether, leaving the reader with the impression that the world's cultures are engaged in a shiny, happy process
   of cultural exchange that transforms and renews them. The latent logic,
   however, is one that places U.S. culture at the center of the world and understands cultural hybridity as a result of the relationship between the
   United States and Third World countries, at the detriment of exchanges
   between these countries themselves (Kraidy 2002a).
2. Communities throughout the world have experienced hybridity as a
   positive force that allows them to make sense of their identity, one that
   relates uncomfortably to established categories. This is manifest among
   immigrant communities, whose culture is a mix of their native and host
   cultures, in addition to influences from other immigrant communities
   with whom they share neighborhoods and destinies. The work of Hamid
   Naficy (1993), Marie Gillespie (1995), and others is instructive in that
   regard. Naficy's superb study of the Iranian community in Los Angeles,
   or Tehrangeles, underscores the importance of hybridity as a space
   where immigrants suspended between the United States and Iran feel
   they belong. The "discursive strategies of mimicry and identity" (178)
   Naficy (1993) analyzed are not the fruit of his cosmopolitan imagination
   or poststructuralist license, charges that scholars of hybridity have had
   to contend with; rather, they are "defensive hybrid strategies" (188) that
   sustain the cultural ethos of a community living thousands of miles

away from home since the trauma of the 1979 Islamic revolution. The Punjabi community in the London area of Southall, whose media and cultural life Gillespie (1995) explores, also resorts to hybridity as a way to bring some sense of stability to the tumult of exile. For instance, Punjabi Londoners use Christmas, when British families get together for extended periods of time and watch a lot of television, as an opportunity for their children to meet extended families, eat mother-culture foods, and live some aspects of their ancestral traditions, activities including watching television. Their Christmas is therefore "not the Turkey type" (Gillespie 1995, 101) but rather a subversion of a Christian holiday to perpetuate a hybrid identity between host and mother culture. Moreover, hybridity is crucial not only to diasporic communities, but as a central aspect of the life of local, historically grounded communities such as the Maronites of Lebanon. Young Maronites use global, regional, and local television programs and popular music to fashion a hybrid cultural identity straddling what they articulate as "Western" and "Arab" worldviews, both of which they deem unacceptable as bases of their identities (Kraidy 1999). There is evidence that hybrid cultural identities can influence audience preferences in a way that truncates the political economic structures of media ownership and affiliation (Kraidy 2003). These examples demonstrate that hybridity can be articulated as positive and even progressive force by those straddling different cultural formations.

3. There is a trend of hybrid media texts cross-breeding cultural signs, values, and styles to reach transnational audiences. These include movies whose story lines unfold in several countries, such as *The Red Violin*, reality television programs that include participants from different countries, such as *Survivor Africa*, and programs whose format is adapted or even stolen from elsewhere, such as the *Teletubbies* copycat *TeleChobis* produced by TV Azteca in Mexico. The rise of post-Fordist practices in the global media industries underscores that the hybridity of media texts takes on merely the appearance of growing diversity. Practices of surveillance such as audience research (Maxwell 1996), of targeting such as ethnic marketing (Castañeda Paredes 2001), of decentering such as coproductions (Miller et al. 2001), and of borrowing such as format adaptation (Moran 1998) are shaped by the profit drive of the global media conglomerates. The hybridity they project is a symptom of carefully carved-up niche audiences in the case of ethnic marketing, and of spreading risk, pooling resources, and broadening their transcultural appeal in the case of coproductions and format adaptation. Cross-cultural exchange and cultural fusion are in this case fully integrated in the global

commercial media machine, itself solidly anchored in the liberalized global economy. In the words of Mosco and Schiller (2001), "uneven economic development—and cultural variation—are being reconstituted, rather than eradicated" (4).

These cases indicate that hybridity can be variously articulated, hegemonically or progressively, depending on the forces shaping the local spaces where different forms of hybridity emerge. The outcomes of cultural dynamics can therefore not be preordained, and comprehending their complexity requires a heightened sensitivity to history, context, and specificity. Consequently, hybridity ought not to be used as a metaconstruction of global media culture, lest it become another totalistic paradigm destined to crumble under the weight of its internal contradictions.

Toward a Synthetic Notion of Culture in International Communication

Critical international communication scholarship has often equated cultural homogenization with domination in a model privileging the political economic determination of culture. This chapter has proposed that it may be helpful to consider that domination can also be achieved through cultural hybridization. Conversely, this entails that cultural hybridity is not predicated on the end of domination and on more equal intercultural relations. In its myriad historical, rhetorical, empirical, and textual dimensions and manifestations, hybridity can be articulated with discourses ranging from the progressive to the reactionary. The theory of articulation is helpful in understanding the interactions between local and global, hegemonic and subaltern, economy and culture, power and signification, and other binary equations that have befuddled media and communication scholars.

It could be argued that the peripatetic trajectory of international communication research derives from its taken-for-granted separation of the poles in these equations. Culture and economy are analytically separated, the local and global considered distinct, the hegemonic and subaltern considered opposites, and modernity and tradition are treated as if their chronological distinctiveness was natural. The separation of these spheres is enshrined in both the development and imperialism paradigms, and international communication has yet to fully engage the momentum questioning the value of these separations. This engagement should occur in the space created by the interdisciplinary debate on globalization in the social sciences and humanities, a literature that, as mentioned earlier, considers communication as one of its central dimensions.

Engaging the debate on globalization should not be confused with *embracing* current globalization theories, especially those dealing with culture. A real engagement should in fact be committed to questioning approaches to globalization in their empirical, conceptual, ideological, and rhetorical dimensions. There is broad agreement that globalization has accelerated a double movement of standardization and hybridization, of control and fragmentation. So taking globalization theory to task does not mean sliding into the all too familiar clichés about worldwide monocultural convergence. Rather, it entails examining the conditions in which hybridities are constituted and exploring the forces that bear on their formation. After all, cultural hybridity *is* a pervasive existential condition. It also is a heuristic trope, which it will remain as long as the holistic view of culture is entrenched. Significantly, while hybridity can in some cases be a positive cultural and political force for some communities, "in many cases, the harshness of conditions reduces hybridization to mundane adaptations to increasingly oppressive market conditions" (Escobar 1995, 218).

Notes

1. Research on the international dimensions of communication began as a result of growing interest in the United States in the psychological warfare potential of the mass media. In the 1920s, Lasswell's work on World War I propaganda (1927) and Lippmann's writing on public opinion (1922) were influential in establishing communication as an area of research of interest to U.S. political and military leaders. However, McDowell (2002) remarks that the early cohort of international communication researchers believed that "communication was war continued by other means" (297). After World War II and the onset of the Cold War, the focus shifted to communication as a tool for modernization in the developing world.

2. "Media imperialism" and "cultural imperialism" have been used interchangeably. I prefer cultural imperialism because media imperialism reflects a degree of media-centrism. The term "cultural imperialism" is preferable because it addresses the media in their larger sociocultural environment.

3. The dominant contemporary scholarly form is the interparadigmatic hybrid, examples of which are abundant. Entertainment-education studies (Singhal and Rogers 1999) is an amalgamation of development and popular culture studies, while critical and feminist inroads into developmental thought have asserted the role of power and gender in communication processes (Wilkins 1999; Servaes and Lie 2001). These hybrids are vastly different in theoretical orientation, methodological preferences, and ideological biases, but they are blends whose components are identifiable as research areas. Postcolonial approaches to media are beginning to supplement more canonical forms of media criticism, as evidenced in the special issue on postcolonial approaches to communication of the journal *Communication Theory*

(2002a). In addition to rejuvenating the field, these interparadigmatic hybrids expose the fragility, if not futility, of the notion of paradigm—a unified, overarching worldview with identifiable central assumptions, a core ideology, leading scholars, and methodological arsenal.

4. Many of the criticisms addressed to the cultural imperialism thesis are only valid when applied to some of the cruder studies conducted under the imperialism rubric. There is a tendency to treat cultural imperialism like a monolithic formulation determined by theoretical rigidity and ideological entrenchment. In fact, the cultural imperialism thesis itself has attracted scholars with diverse backgrounds, various methodologies, and different degrees of ideological engagement.

5. Isolated articles appeared before, and many more since, but these two issues of *Critical Studies in Mass* (now Media) *Communication* and *Journal of Communication Inquiry* played a major role in institutionalizing this approach in the United States.

6. This is a long list of fields: anthropology (Thomas 1996), critical race studies (Werbner and Modood 1997), cultural studies (Gilroy 1993), popular music and ethnomusicology (Boggs 1991; Hutnyk 1997), sociology (Nederveen Pieterse 1994, 2001), film studies (Marchetti 1998), literary criticism (Moreiras 1999; Young 1995), migration studies (Papastergiadis 2000), postcolonial theory (Ahmad 1995; Bhabha 1994; Said 1994), performance studies (Joseph and Fink 1999), tourism (Hollinshead 1998), folklore (Kapchan and Strong 1999), sports (Archetti 1999), and economics (Cowen 2003).

7. Literary and philosophical treatments of globalization focusing on the role of communication as hinge between the economic and cultural are instructive in that regard. Fredric Jameson has argued that "globalization is a communicational concept, which alternately masks and transmits cultural or economic meanings" (Jameson 1999, 55). Jameson nonetheless warns: "But the communicational focus of the concept of globalization is essentially incomplete." He concludes with a challenge: "I defy anyone to try to think it in exclusively media or communicational terms" (Jameson 1999, 55). More recent theoretical writings give communication an even more important role in global affairs. In *Empire*, Hardt and Negri (2000) write that, "communication not only expresses but also organizes the movement of globalization. It organizes the movements by multiplying and structuring interconnections through networks." As such, communication is placed at the heart of what they call "biopolitical" power. Communication "expresses the movement and controls the sense and direction of the imaginary that runs through these communicative connections; in other words, the imaginary is guided and channeled within the communicative machine" (32–33). In this context communication functions as a sort of electrical conductor between the material hardware of globalization and the symbolic processes that fill and animate these networks. Beyond mediation, communication has a constitutive role. This is how I understand Hardt and Negri's assertion that "the political synthesis of social space is fixed in the space of communication" (2000, 33).

References

Ahmad, A. 1995. The politics of literary postcoloniality. *Race and Class* 363: 1–20.

Ang, I. 1996. *Living Room wars: Rethinking Media Audiences for a Postmodern World.* London: Routledge.

Appadurai, A. 1996. *Modernity at Large: Cultural Dimensions of Globalization.* Minneapolis: University of Minnesota Press.

Archetti, E. P. 1999. *Masculinities: Football, Polo, and the Tango in Argentina.* Oxford: Berg.

Beltran, Luis Ramirez. 1978. Communication and cultural domination: U.S.-Latin America case. *Media Asia* 5: 183–92.

Bentley, J. H. 1993. *Old World Encounters: Cross-cultural Contacts and Exchanges in Pre-modern Times.* Oxford: Oxford University Press.

Berger, C. R. 1991. Communication theories and other curios. *Communication Monographs* 58: 101–13.

Bhabha, H. 1994. *The Location of Culture.* London: Routledge.

Boggs, V. W. 1991. Musical transculturation: From Afro-Cuban to Afro-Cubanization. *Popular Music and Society* 15, no. 4: 71–83.

Boyd-Barrett, O. 1977. "Media imperialism: Towards an international framework for the analysis of media systems." In J. Curran, M. Gurevitch, and J. Woollacott, eds., *Mass Communication and Society,* 116–35. London: Arnold.

———. 1997. "International communication and globalization: Contradiction and directions." In A. Mohammadi, ed., *International Communication and Globalization* 11–26. London: Sage.

———. 1998. "Media imperialism reformulated." In D. K. Thussu, ed., *Electronic Empires: Global Media and Local Resistance,* 157–76. London: Arnold.

———. 2002. "Global communication orders." In W. B. Gudykunst and B. Mody, eds., *Handbook of International and Intercultural Communication,* 325–42. 2d ed. Thousand Oaks, Calif.: Sage.

Braman, S. 2002. "A pandemonic age: The future of international communication theory and research." In W. B. Gudykunst and B. Mody, eds., *Handbook of International and Intercultural Communication,* 399–413. 2d ed. Thousand Oaks, Calif.: Sage.

Burgoon, M. 1982. *Communication Yearbook* 6, 531–54. Beverly Hills, Calif.: Sage.

Castañeda Paredes, M. 2001. "The reorganization of Spanish-language media marketing in the United States." In V. Mosco and D. Schiller, eds., *Continental Order?: Integrating North America for Cybercapitalism,* 120–35. Lanham, Md.: Rowman & Littlefield.

Cowen, T. 2003. *Creative Destruction: How Globalization Is Changing the World's Cultures.* Princeton, N.J.: Princeton University Press.

Craig, R. T. 1999. Communication theory as a field. *Communication Theory* 9, no. 2: 119–61.

Curran, J. 1990. The new revisionism in mass communication research: A reappraisal. *European Journal of Communication* 5, no. 2–3: 135–64.

Curtin, M. 1993. Beyond the vast wasteland: The policy discourse of global television and the politics of American empire. *Journal of Broadcasting and Electronic Media*, Spring.

Escobar, A. 1995. *Encountering Developing: The Making and Unmaking of the Third World*. Princeton, N.J.: Princeton University Press.

Fejes, F. 1981. Media imperialism: An assessment. *Media, Culture, and Society* 3, no. 3: 281–89.

García-Canclini, N. 1989. *Culturas híbridas: Estrategias para entrar y salir de la modernidad*. Mexico City: Grijalbo.

Gerbner, G. Mowlana, H., and Nordenstreng, K.1994. *The Global Media Debate: Its Rise, Fall, and Renewal*. Norwood, N.J.: Ablex.

Gillespie, M. 1995. *Television, Ethnicity, and Cultural Change*. London: Routledge.

Gilroy, P. 1993. *The Black Atlantic: Modernity and Double Consciousness*. Cambridge, Mass.: Harvard University Press.

Grossberg, L. 1999. Speculations and articulations of globalization. *Polygraph* 11: 11–48.

Gruzinski, S. 1999. *La pensée métisse*. Paris: Fayard.

Hall, S. 1985. Signification, representation, ideology: Althusser and the post-structuralist debates. *Critical Studies in Mass Communication* 23: 91–114.

———. [1980] 1997. "Encoding/Decoding." In A. Gray and J. McGuigan, ed., *Studying Culture: An Introductory Reader*, 90–103. London: Arnold.

Hardt, H. 1988. Comparative media research: The world according to America. *Critical Studies in Mass Communication* 5, no. 2: 129–46.

Hardt, M., and Negri, A. 2000. *Empire*. Cambridge, Mass.: Harvard University Press.

Hollinshead, K. 1998. Tourism, hybridity, and ambiguity: The relevance of Bhabha's Third Space cultures. *Journal of Leisure Research* 30, no. 1: 121–56.

Hutnyk, J. 1997. "Adorno at Womad: South Asia crossovers and the limits of hybridity-talk." In Werbner, P. and Modood, T., eds., *Debating Cultural Hybridity: Multicultural Identities and the Politics of Anti-racism*, 106–38. London: Zed.

Jameson, F. 1999. "Globalization as a theoretical issue." In F. Jameson and I. Miyoshi, eds., *Cultures of Globalization*. Durham, N.C.: Duke University Press.

Joseph, M., and Fink, J. N., eds. 1999. *Performing Hybridity*. Minneapolis: University of Minnesota Press.

Kapchan, D. A., and Strong, P. T., eds. 1999. Theorizing the hybrid. *Journal of American Folklore* 112, no. 445. Special issue.

Kaplan, L. 2000. *The Coming Anarchy*. New York: Vintage.

Kraidy, M. M. 1999. The local, the global, and the hybrid: A native ethnography of glocalization. *Critical Studies in Media Communication* 16, no. 4: 456–77.

———. 2001. "National television between localization and globalization." In Y. Kamalipour and K. Rampal, eds., *Media, Sex and Drugs in the Global Village*, 261–72. Lanham, Md.: Rowman & Littlefield.

———. 2002a. Hybridity in cultural globalization. *Communication Theory* 123: 316–39.

———. 2002b. Ferment in global media studies. *Journal of Broadcasting and Electronic Media* 46: 630–40.

———. 2003. "Globalization *Avant la Lettre?* Cultural hybridity, media power, and audience ethnography in Lebanon." In P. D. Murphy and M. M. Kraidy, eds., *Global Media Studies: Ethnographic Perspectives.* London: Routledge.

Lasswell, H. 1927. *Propaganda technique in the world war.* New York: Alfred Knopf.

Lerner, D. 1958. *The Passing of Traditional Society.* New York: Free Press.

Lippmann, W. 1922. *Public Opinion.* New York: Harcourt Brace.

Marchetti, G. 1998. Transnational cinema, hybrid identities and the films of Evans Chan. *Postmodern Culture* 8, no. 2. http://muse.jhu.edu/journals/pmc/v008/8.2marchetti.html.

Martín-Barbero, J. 1993a. *Communication, Culture, and Hegemony: From the Media to Mediations.* London: Sage.

———. 1993b. Latin America: Cultures in the communication media. *Journal of Communication* 43, no. 2: 18–30.

Mattelart, Armand. 1979. *Multinational Corporations and the Control of Culture.* Atlantic Highlands, N.J.: Humanities.

———. 1983. *Transnationals and the Third World: The Struggle for Culture.* South Hadley, Mass.: Bergin & Harvey.

———. 1994. *Mapping World Communication: War, Progress, Culture.* Minneapolis: University of Minnesota Press.

Maxwell, R. 1996. Out of kindness and into difference: The value of global market research. *Media, Culture, and Society* 18, no. 1.

McDowell, S. D. 2002. Theory and research in international communication: A historical and institutional account. In W. B. Gudykunst and B. Mody, eds., *Handbook of International and Intercultural Communication,* 295–308. 2d ed. Thousand Oaks, Calif.: Sage.

Miller, T., Govil, N., McMurria, J. and Maxwell, R. 2001. *Global Hollywood.* London: British Film Institute.

Mody, B., and Lee, A. 2002. Differing traditions of research on international media influence. In W. B. Gudykunst and B. Mody, eds., *Handbook of International and Intercultural Communication,* 381–98. 2d ed. Thousand Oaks, Calif.: Sage.

Moran, A. 1998. *Copycat TV: Globalisation, Program Formats, and Cultural Identity.* Luton, U.K.: University of Luton Press.

Moreiras, A. 1999. Hybridity and double consciousness. *Cultural Studies* 13, no. 3: 373–407.

Morris, N. 1995. Local identities and imported media: The fear of displacement in Puerto Rico. *Journal of International Communication* 2, no. 2: 7–23.

Morley, D. 1980. *The "nationwide" audience: Structure and decoding.* London: BFI.

Mosco, V., and Schiller, D. 2001. *Continental order: Integrating North America for Cybercapitalism.* Lanham, Md.: Rowman & Littlefield.

Murphy, P. D., and Kraidy, M. M. 2003a. International communication, ethnography, and the challenge of globalization. *Communication Theory* 13(3): 304-23.

Murphy, P. D., and Kraidy, M. M, eds. 2003b. *Global Media Studies: Ethnographic Perspectives.* London: Routledge.

Naficy, H. 1993. *The Making of Exile Cultures: Iranian Television in Los Angeles.* Minneapolis: University of Minnesota Press.

Nederveen Pieterse, J. 1994. Globalisation as hybridisation. *International Sociology* 9, no. 2: 161–84.

———. 2001. Hybridity, so what? The anti-hybridity backlash and the riddles of recognition. *Theory, Culture, and Society* 18, no. 2: 219–45.

Papastergiadis, N. 2000. *The Turbulence of Migration: Globalization, Deterritorialization, and Hybridity*. Cambridge: Polity.

Rogers, E. 1962. *Diffusion of Innovations*. New York: Free Press.

Said, E. 1994. *Culture and Imperialism*. New York: Knopf.

Schiller, H. 1971. *Mass Communication and American Empire*. New York: Beacon.

———. 1976. *Communication and Cultural Domination*. White Plains, N.Y.: International Arts and Sciences Press.

———. 1991. Not yet the post-imperialist era. *Critical Studies in Mass Communication* 8, no. 1: 13–28.

Schramm, W. L. 1964. *Mass Media and National Development: The Role of Information in the Developing Countries*. Stanford: Stanford University Press.

Servaes, J., and Lie, R. 2001. *Journal of International Communication*. Special issue on participatory communication research.

Singhal, A., and Rogers, E. 1999. *Entertainment–Education: A Communication Strategy for Social Change*. Mahwah, N.J.: Lawrence Erlbaum.

Thomas, N. 1996. Cold fusion cultural hybridity. *American Anthropologist* 98: 9–16.

Toumson, R. 1998. *Mythologie du métissage*. Paris: Presses Universitaires de France.

Tunstall, J. 1977. *The Media Are American*. Beverly Hills, Calif.: Sage.

Werbner, P., and Modood, T., eds. 1997. *Debating Cultural Hybridity: Multi-cultural Identities and the Politics of Anti-racism*. London: Zed.

Wilkins, K. 1999. Development discourse on gender and communication in strategies for social change. *Journal of Communication* 49, no. 1: 46–68.

Young, R. 1995. *Colonial Desire: Hybridity in Theory, Culture, and Race*. London: Routledge.

13

Transnational Genome Debates and the Return of Eugenics

Marouf Hasian Jr.

From the acceptance of social Darwinist notions at the dusk of the imperial age to the passing of eugenics legislation in 1995, China has joined a worldwide attempt at finding modern answers to a wide range of modern and ancient concerns.

—Unschuld 2000, 628

URING THE LAST HALF OF THE twentieth century, it would have been difficult to find a more disparaging term than the word "eugenics." Coming from the Greek words for "wellborn" (Larson 1995, 19), the term was coined by the British explorer and scientist Francis Galton in the late nineteenth century. The study of both "positive" and "negative" human worth was once considered a legitimate applied science that put into practice the ancient theories of those who believed in the importance of establishing human hierarchies based on hereditary value. Dikotter (1998b) has recently commented that "eugenics was a fundamental aspect of some of the most important cultural and social movements in the twentieth century" (467). Discussions of relative human betterment were used to justify a variety of social practices, including the sterilization of the supposed unfit and the segregation of the "races" (Hasian 1996; Kevles 1985; Ludmerer 1972). For a time, scientists, politicians, and laypeople openly talked about the need to pay more attention to both the quality and quantity of our human populations. Various cultural ideas about the importance of preserving particular national "characters," the prevention of "degeneration," or the encouragement of mating between those of equal social status were considered progressive goals (Pickens 1968) that rivaled the importance of preventing hereditary diseases.

In the aftermath of the Great Depression and World War II, a variety of historical events contributed to the demise of some of the public discourse surrounding eugenics. Journal articles and other essays were being written by pundits who lampooned the idea that human worth could be calibrated, or that scientists or politicians had valid ways of determining who should be considered to be "feebleminded" (Trent 1994). Hitler's rise to power brought with it the sterilization of hundreds of thousands of individuals who were considered inferior beings, and eventually the word "eugenics" came to be associated with violations of basic human rights and the abuse of scientific protocols (Kuhl 1994). U.N. resolutions were passed that attacked some of the racist rhetoric that had colonial origins. During the Cold War, observers were talking about the need to dissociate "genetics" from the abuse of hereditarian ideas. By 1963, Haller wrote a popular history of these debates and claimed that Anglo-American societies had been saved by the recognition that more cautious "scientific eugenics" (3–7) had left behind their more radical ideas. More than two decades later, Kevles (1985) wrote about how "reform" eugenics had replaced hard-line beliefs of researchers like Charles Davenport or Harry Laughlin. In most of the accounts that were written about the "pseudo" science of eugenics, the older movement—which was said to have flourished between 1880 and 1940—could now be used as a cautionary tale that could be used to explain the importance of maintaining a bright line between science and ideology, or politics and scientific inquiry.

Here I argue that the idea that "eugenics" has not been forgotten, and that the temporary demise of the eugenics "movement" did not end the influence of hereditarian beliefs or practices. The claim that modern, Western, or civilized societies have purged themselves of the "taint" of eugenics is itself a rhetorical posture that hides the continued allure of these ideologies. As I argue below, the mass-mediated representations of eugenic theories and practices are still very popular in many international cultures, and even the attacks that are made on the "old" styles of eugenics betray their "race" or "human" betterment roots. There are now a plethora of regional, national, and international debates over the ethics of amniocentesis, sterilization, genetic counseling, DNA fingerprinting, cystic fibrosis screening, abortion, intelligence tests, and germline therapy (Wertz 1997). Many of the contemporary participants in these volatile conversations end up appropriating some of the same argumentative positions that appeared in earlier genetic and hereditarian debates, but this time they are taking the "backdoor" (Duster 1990) to eugenics. Note, for example, how professor Crow discussed the matter in *Contemporary Psychology* in 1988: "Should the word *eugenics* be consigned to the wastebasket of wrongheaded and pernicious ideas? Perhaps it is so tarred that it should be. But the judicious use of genetic knowledge for the alleviation of human suffering and increase in the well being of future generations is a noble ideal, whatever it is called" (12).

The people who will be in charge of making the decisions about this "judicious use" and the standards that will used to make decisions about what constitutes "alleviation" are issues that can only be resolved when we take into account a plethora of material and symbolic realities.

This chapter provides a rhetorical analysis of some key mass-mediated representations of Chinese genomics that circulated in the Anglo-American press in the last decades of the twentieth century. I argue that a purposive sampling of scientific, political, and public commentaries on the debates over "Chinese" eugenics provides us with the discursive and iconic fragments that we need for a critical analysis of the situation.[1] In my evaluation of these artifacts, I use an ideographic type of critical analysis that looks at elite and public usages of arguments, topoi, characterizations, narratives, and other units of analysis that circulate in rhetorical cultures. For other examples of this type of work, see McGee 1980; Lucaites and Condit 1990; Condit and Lucaites 1993; and Hasian 1996. I contend that the press coverage of the disputes about the "rebirth" of the human genetics programs in China (Dickson 1998b, 303) provides us with a wealth of information on how communities in many nations feel about the study of the well-born. Editors, contributors to scientific journals, scientists, bioethicists, and other commentators help create their own self-identities even as they express their opinions on the costs or benefits of the "new" Chinese "eugenic" programs.[2] Communication scholars who look into some of the subtexts of these genomic disputes will soon find that the international media coverage of these controversies inadvertently provides us with the concomitant benefit of seeing some of the symbolic markers that are used to demarcate the lines that purportedly exist between "east" and "west," north and south, Orientalism and Occidentalism, capitalism and communism, developed and underdeveloped nations. These debates over Chinese eugenic practices supply rhetorical prisms that help reflect and refract the ways that various societies around the world think about disparate resource allocation, economic globalization, ethnic relations, sexual politics, and genomic wealth.

In order to show how eugenic arguments continue to impact the trajectory of today's genomic debates, I have divided this chapter into four major sections. In the first section I revisit some of the older eugenic and genetic arguments that circulated in Anglo-American press commentaries prior to the early 1990s. In the second section I extend this analysis by illuminating how various international communities reacted to the Chinese announcement of a new "eugenic" program. The third section looks at some Western defenses of these new Chinese genomic initiatives. The concluding section explains what these various texts and subtexts tell us about the future of eugenics in international contexts.

Popular and Elite Discussions of China and Eugenics, 1900–1990

When scholars today take up the question of Chinese eugenics, they tend to focus on contemporary debates that are taking place over the ethics or legal of the "new" Chinese Law on Maternal and Infant Health Care (1995). A longitudinal look at the discourse of the early twentieth century would reveal how many generations of eugenists—and their critics—have long been fascinated by China's approach to issues involving human genetic "betterment." For example, Wells (1907), speaking in front of an American audience of sociologists, social reformers, and immigration officials, wondered out loud if nations like China were willing to give up the religious beliefs that stood in the way of "ideal celibacy and the limitation of offspring" (707). He was convinced that in the near future, eugenics and Social Darwinism would come to the Far East, and the communities in this region would have to make choices about the continued value of "ancestor-worship" in cultures that were offered "European individual" as competing ideals (707).

Many of these early eugenic narratives portrayed "China" as a land filled with denizens who knew little about emigration, colonization, the dysgenics of warfare, or the links that existed between European population pressures and "imperialistic ambitions" (Fisher 1921, 226). Living at a time when many nativists were worried about the need for immigration restriction, Fisher was just one of the participants in conversations about the "real remedies" for the "Yellow Peril" and the "extension of birth control to the Orient" (Fisher 1921, 226). More than a decade later, Osborn (1932) toured the world to prepare for his presentation at the Third International Congress of Eugenics, convinced that "commercial invasion" and "military conquest" were going to bring modern inventions to some of the "barbaric" parts of the world (173–74). Readers of *Science* magazine were invited to consider how evidence from places like Japan, Java, and France showed the superiority of "birth selection" over "birth control."

In China, scholarly and popular interest in the eugenic arguments waxed and waned, depending on the political and cultural needs of various generations. For example, in the wake of the founding of the Republic (1912) and the May Fourth New Cultural Movement, there was interest in establishing classes in some of the social sciences, but by 1949 Sun had to report that Quantin Pan was the "only eugenist in China" (250). Westerners were constantly writing books about the need for the Chinese to take care of both the quantity and quality of their populations, but the indigenous communities in the region had their own ideas and priorities. Kiser (1947) complained that in the post–World War II years, nations like China and India needed to worry more about fertility and mortality rates, and less about "eugenics and population quality" (351). During that same year, Chen explained that eugenic arguments and population policies had to mesh with the "folkways" and "general will of the people," and that outside observers needed to understand the population ideas of thinkers like Confucius and Mo Ti (Chen 1947, 72).

After the communist takeover of China in 1949, geneticists survived by adapting their arguments about eugenics to the anti-Mendelian ideas of influential writers like Russian agronomist Trofim Lysenko. Russian technical advisers, who focused their attention on the impact of cultural and the environment on hereditarian changes, invited the Chinese to forget about capitalist books and textbooks that brought unwanted outside influences. "Geneticists had a terrible time," remembers Yang of the Chinese Academy of Sciences, because "for about two generations" the subject was "not taught at all" (quoted in Dickson 1998b, 303). This professor of genetics went on to explain that "gene" became a "bad word" that was considered a "slogan of the bourgeoisie" (303).

The ouster of the Russians and "Great Leap Forward" seemed to offer a ray of hope for those who wanted to study eugenics and genetics (Dikotter 1998a, 1999, 31), but this window of opportunity closed when the vast majority of government funds were put into large-scale industrial and agricultural production programs. Still "guided by Lysenkoist ideas," the Chinese put into place projects that brought "widespread food shortages" (Dickson 1998b, 304). Many Western observers later claimed that this is the price China paid for abandoning the true study of genetics, mixing ideology and science, and undervaluing the power of capitalism.

During the 1970s and early 1980s, population pressures were considered to be of paramount importance in China, and a one-child limit was imposed in 1979. There were numerous reports of how local officials were encouraging forced abortions and sterilization as preferred methods of birth control (Aird 1994). Organizations like the United Nations Population Fund and the International Planned Parenthood Federation had to walk the fine line between looking out for civil rights violations and helping promote population "control" in the region. Some of the formal and informal rules regarding societal reproduction that were circulating during this period were said to have skewed male-female ratios,[3] and stories were told of women being forced to terminate second pregnancies (Post 1994). In the late 1980s, Chinese officials in the province of Gansu introduced a local ordinance that prohibited the "reproduction of dull-witted, idiots or blockheads" ("China's 'Eugenics'" 1998, 707).

In the past twenty years, there has been a revival of interest in China in genetics, and geneticists like C. C. Tan (Tan Jiazhen) have helped convince government officials that China can become one of the leading nations in modern human genetics. At a recent international genetics Congress in Beijing,

Tan told his listeners that genetic investigations would help feed China's 1.2 billion population (Dickson 1998b, 304). By the last decade of the twentieth century, China had some thirty laboratories involved in genomic research, and the Chinese were considered to be some of the most vocal supporters of both the Human Genome Project (HGP) and the Human Genome Diversity Project (HGDP). The relative "isolation" of many ethnic communities within the vast border regions of China was considered "gold mines" for genetics investigations.

This revival of interest in China and genetics created a situation in which many Western observers could talk about the relative costs and rewards of projects that took into account both the quantity and quality of various populations. Was this novel interest in China just one more example of what Spivak (1999) has characterized as the "new imperialism of exploitation" (371–91), or were these programs going to help alter the material conditions of the subalterns who lived in the region? Western writers wondered whether the Chinese—who had their own histories that were vastly different from the Eurocentric stories of Nazi abuses—would embrace or reject eugenic ideals?

The International Press Reactions
to the Announcement of a "New" Chinese Eugenics

During the last decade of the twentieth century, many Anglo-American newspaper writers, scientific journalists, scientists, bioethicists, and laypeople were provided the opportunity of revisiting the question of how modern nations were going to deal with contemporary notions of eugenics. Between 1993 and 1995, Chinese officials and geneticists began talking about the need for their nation to have a healthier population and more communal ways of thinking about the right to reproduce. The Chinese minister of public health, Chen Minzhang, put up a trial balloon in December 1993 when he told reporters that his nation wanted to halt the unrestricted birth of "abnormal" children, and the government was going to order sterilizations and abortions. Minzhang told the press that there were more than 10 million disabled persons who "could have been prevented through better controls" (Tyler 1993, A8).

A reporter for the *World Tibet Network News* noted that the Chinese government was saying that there were some 50 million physically or mentally handicapped people who lived in that country, and that some officials in Gansu wanted to sterilize more than 260,000 mentally retarded residents of that northwestern province ("China to Introduce" 1993).

At first this law was openly touted as a "eugenic" health measure, but international complaints about the legislation led Chinese officials to rename the act as the Maternal and Infant Health Care Law (Mao 1997, 139). The act seemed to ban marriages between individuals who had "certain genetic diseases of a serious nature" (Post 1994, 36–37), and some language indicated the doctors were going to be required to urge all couples to abort a fetus if they detected any hereditary disease or abnormality. Supposedly these regulations simply codified existing social norms and habits throughout many regions, and indicated that all persons who wished to marry needed to have premarital medical examinations to detect serious genetic diseases, some infectious diseases, and "relevant mental disorders" (Reichman, Brezis, and Steinberg 1996, 425). One editorial writer for the *New York Times* urged Americans and others outside of China to let the Clinton administration know that it needed to let Beijing know that these legal drafts could have an adverse effect on U.S. public opinion ("Preventing" 1993, A16). Doherty (1995), a member of the Guild of Catholic Doctors, thought that only a "firm statement of western values" could effectively create the basis of dialogue that would prevent the totalitarian application of these laws (509).

At the very center of this debates was question of how to interpret the Chinese word *yousheng*, which could both refer to healthy births and describe some activities that were considered "eugenic" in the West (Renzong 1999, 30). This protean term, which had as many means as "eugenics" itself, could be tied to both "positive" and "negative" hereditary programs. The use of the term *yousheng* meant that Chinese officials had to deal with a barrage of complaints about the Maternal and Infant Health Care Law. Moreover, the possible taint of eugenics helped polarize Western geneticists (Beardsley 1997). Critics of these policies talked about the need for education, better communication, boycotts, delayed implementation (O'Brien 1996), and scientific ostracism.

From an ideographic perspective, the Chinese were said to be employing draconian measures that violated basic human "rights" and "liberties," and coercion was taking away the volition of helpless Chinese citizens. To make matters worse, Minzhang was purported to have said that the births of "inferior quality" were serious, especially among the "old revolutionary base" made up of "ethnic minorities" as well as "the poor" and those near "the frontier" (Beardsley 1997, 34). This was interpreted in the West as positive proof that China's dominant Han community was going to use these eugenic laws to help reduce the number of Tibetans, "potentially disruptive ethnic groups" ("China's 'Eugenics'" 1998, 707), or other ostracized communities. In spite of such critiques, the Chinese government refused to repudiate the 1994 ministerial statement or retract what had been said about humans of "inferior quality."

By the summer of 1998, geneticists in a number of nations, led by British scientists, were calling for a boycott of the Eighteenth International Congress of Genetics, which was going to be held in China. Beardsley (1997), a writer for *Scientific American,* claimed that "eugenics produced some of the worst horrors of the century, so geneticists get jumpy when their expertise is used to coerce. Scientists are trying to decide how to respond to a law that came into force in China in 1995 and seems unabashedly eugenic. In most of the world, choosing to have a baby is a private matter for two people" (33).

From a critical media perspective, this type of statement contains a number of textual and subtextual claims that are worthy of analysis. The author of this fragment assumes that there is some universal community that can be hailed using the Western discourse of "privacy." Second, it assumes that different cultures and nations signify the word "eugenics" in the same way. Third, it valorizes the scientists of the West, ignoring the local subalterns who are fighting for survival in a world of growing scarcity. Eugenics is treated as a bygone movement, a relic that has been left behind by modernists who know better.

Many Chinese geneticists, who were trying to negotiate their way through this political quagmire, tried to explain some of the cultural and scientific logics that went into the formation of the 1995 Maternal and Infant Health Care Law. Mao, a member of the faculty of the West China University of Medical Sciences, has been one of the most vocal participants in this controversy, and his commentaries on this situation need to be analyzed in detail. In one of the essays that he sent to the *Lancet,* Mao (1997) reminded his readers that China had "the world's oldest continuous civilization" (139). Furthermore, he observed that:

> Ironically, eugenics and many other natural and social sciences used to be criticized as [the] poison of Western imperialism in China in the early 1950s to 1970s, especially during the cultural revolution. China has paid a high price for such unscientific behaviour. In February 1995, China's population reached 1.2 billion. In 1987, the population of disabled people reached 51–64 million, which is roughly the population of the UK. Facing this reality, what are the best options for the Chinese government? (Mao 1997, 139)

Implicit in such discourse is the argument that if Western critics were going to complain about this new law, then they needed to come up with some constructive ways of dealing with existing and future population pressures. Were they going to take on the economic, political, and social responsibilities that attended this growth?

As noted above, the position that one takes regarding eugenics involves a great deal of self-identification and historical amnesia, and these Chinese observers were pointing out that both genetic and eugenic arguments were sometimes blending with traditional Chinese ideologies and practices. From a critical rhetorical perspective, one can almost feel Mao's frustration with the way that Western observers are trying to impose Western ethics on a country faced with immense social, economic, and political problems. In the hopes of persuading some of the readers of *Lancet* of the unfairness of these attacks, he (Mao 1997) goes on to claim that several "western geneticists hold that view that if any of the G7 countries had such large populations eugenic legislation would be more tolerable" (139).

The "eugenic" labeling of the Chinese Maternal and Infant Health Care Law influences more than just Western perceptions of governmental authorities— it could also influence the flow of outside invest capital into the region. In his defense of the Chinese law, Mao (1997) reminds his readers of some of the long time impact that cessation of collaboration might mean for the entire international community:

> China has a great potential to contribute huge human genetic resources to the Human Genome Diversity Project, and the Chinese geneticists have become an important force in human genetics research and practice in and outside China. . . . Constructive communication between the international scientific community and Chinese geneticists would increase awareness in China of western eugenic history, would reduce misunderstanding, and could persuade the Chinese government to consider amendment of its new law. (139)

Mao's counternarrative, filled with allusions and commentaries on Chinese culture, politics, and genetics, could be considered to be an Occidental response to the Orientalist (Said 1979) formations that undergird these rhetorical figurations. When English geneticists attack Chinese eugenic laws, they are confronting a thick discursive construct that is there in part because of their own domestic and colonial policies. Mao's defense of Chinese policies attempts to be persuasive by making appeals that involve a variety of Western concerns, including scientific fears of the lack of human biodiversity in previous studies, guilt over consumption habits, and culpability for past eugenic abuses. It also tacitly plays on Western notions of civilizing missions—perhaps Western biotechnicians and geneticists can have influence in China if they act in the right way. Responding to the vituperative challenges with the logic of cold rationality, Mao appears to be arguing that cooperation could bring a type of reformed eugenics that would satisfy many interested parties.

As a result of the controversy surrounding the so-called Chinese eugenics law, there were some changes in the "explanations" that were being handed down to all of the cities and provinces in China. In August, Renzong, the director of the program in bioethics at the Chinese Institute of Philosophy, told reporters that some of the controversial portions of the Maternal and Infant Health Care Law were being suspended, including one that allowed doctors to sterilize Chinese people with inherited disorders (Pomfret 1998, Z10). This announcement came in the wake of the Beijing genetics convention that had focused attention on the moral problematics of forced sterilization measures (Rodgers 1999, 157). At the International Genetic Federation and 1998 International Genetic Congress, there had been a special panel on eugenics, and they openly debated the relationship between genetics, eugenics, and biotechnology (Rosenthal 1998). These talks were not as widely attended as usual, but they did little to prevent the implement of China's legislation. By September of 1999, Renzong (1999) could write in the *Unesco Courier* that much of the criticism that had been leveled against the Chinese was based on misunderstandings, cultural barriers, and linguistic confusion. According to this defender of the laws, these were acts that required individual consent, and they were not founded on any forms of coercion or racism. China's laws simply allowed doctors to advice couples, but the final decision on what to do would be left in the hands of the consenting adults. While well-intentioned concern for the collective good would once in a while bring atypical abuses, the law itself should be viewed a progressive step that would allow every Chinese individual to receive genetic counseling (Renzong 1999, 30). Would these types of arguments convince the majority of Western scientists of the necessity of these laws?

Western Anxieties, Cultural Relativism, and Selective Defenses of the "New" Chinese Eugenics Program

One of the many ironies of these Chinese eugenics debates involved the ways that Western commentators tried to avoid the impression that they themselves were being coercive or unreasonable in their censure of Chinese practices. Many tried to assuage their fears and smooth over the contradictions in this situation by openly defending the goals of the Chinese, while at the same time critiquing the methods that being used to accomplish the tasks associated with improving the quality of the Chinese population. After all, weren't there some acceptable variants of eugenics that would be used to improve public health, maternal well-being, and pronatalism?

Outside observers often tried to give the impression that they were being objective and egalitarian in their critique of China's genetic policies, but even defenders of this nation's sovereignty often provided conflicting and ambiguous comments on how this could be accomplished. For example, one editorial writer for the *Lancet* opined that it was "perilous to impose western morality on China" ("Western Eyes" 1995, 131).[4] Three years later, an essayist for *Nature* admonished naysayers to remember that the Chinese people had had to deal with communist regimes, widespread poverty, and "technological backwardness" ("Opportunity" 1998, 109).

One of the most popular approaches used in these partial defenses of the Chinese Maternal and Infant Health Care Law involved an acknowledgment of the special nature of that country's population conundrums. Drake, an employee of the National Institute of Environmental Health Sciences, remarked that few "Westerners have an appreciation of the magnitude of the population problem China is trying to come to grips with" (quoted in Beardsley 1997, 33–34). Reichman, Brezis, and Steinberg (1996), who complained about "China's gross violation of medical ethics and human rights," had to reluctantly concede that "China's burgeoning population is unquestionably detrimental to its well-being, and a legitimate goal is fewer but healthier babies" (426). Such contradictory remarks provide us with several reminders that there are a great many competing varieties of eugenic arguments that are often simultaneously circulating in the public sphere, which meant that the Chinese had to deal with commentaries on both the "old" and "new" forms of eugenic attacks and defenses.

Another relativist argument that was deployed in defense of these Chinese regulations highlighted the popularity of eugenics among many of the professionals living in China.[5] In 1998, a survey was released to the mainstream Anglo-American presses that showed that there was overwhelming support for the use of eugenics "to improve public health" (Coghlan 1998, 18; Rodgers 1999, 161). Ninety-three percent of Chinese geneticists agreed with the statement that people "at high risk for serious disorders should not have children unless they use prenatal diagnosis and selective abortion" (Wertz 1999, 47). Other survey data showed that genetic service providers in Cuba, Mexico, and Greece had "all felt that an important goal of genetics was to prevent the spread of genetic diseases" (Dickson 1998a, 1096). To counter claims that Tibetan nationalists or other ethnic groups were being targeted by eugenic laws, some journalists noted that Chinese authorities were using family planning in ways that "applied more strictly to the Han majority" ("China's 'Eugenics'" 1998, 707).

Some observers were even willing to acknowledge that the Chinese Maternal and Infant Health Care Law might be an improvement over conditions in the status quo. Haynes, a professor at York University in Toronto, told one reporter that in a country where millions of female children vanish and many children with developmental abnormalities are left to die, the new legislation might be an improvement because of the health care provisions (quoted in Beardsley 1997, 33). Ashman (1998), writing from London, claimed that the children born under China's new law would be "wanted, planned and cherished," and that they would be unusually well provided for (58). After having a conversation with one Chinese woman, she was convinced that the "ordinary Chinese" accepted a "policy contributes to the common good, in spite of the way in which it seems to promote the practice of eugenics" (58). In sum, this ostensible debate about China becomes the opportunity to converse about eugenics and majoritarianism, national autonomy, and even the potential benefits of such policies in general ("Opportunity" 1998, 109).

Conclusion: Transnational Genomic
Debates and the Future of Chinese Eugenic Discourse

Even though many scientists and other researchers have tried to distance themselves from the taint of Galton's "eugenics," they nevertheless must cope with the penumbral shadows following their core beliefs on the importance of heredity and genetic influences. This rhetorical analysis of some of the fragments that circulate in newspaper articles, popular magazines, scientific journals, and books on these subjects illustrates how eugenic ideologies have not disappeared, and how they have resurfaced in new forms to fit modernist and postmodernist circumstances. For example, during these mass-mediated debates that focused on the Chinese Maternal and Infant Health Care Law, both sides in the dispute were intentionally or unintentionally using some standard eugenic terms, characterizations, and narratives in their debates with their opponents. For example, some of the critics of Chinese policies were using the arguments of the "new" reform eugenicists—that appeared in the post–World War II years—to critique the positions that resembled the claims of the "old" eugenists who lived between 1880 and the 1930s.

These debates tell us a great deal about some of the discursive trends that are taking place in the early part of the twenty-first century, because we can now witness how Chinese geneticists feel comfortable talking about the needs of the collective, the lack of coercion, the need for counseling, and the purported voluntariness of their programs. Many of their commentaries seem to provide a plethora of rationales for evaluating the quality of China's genomic makeup.

In spite of the attacks that are still being made on some of China's legal policies during the last decades of the past century, it appears that this will be a nation that will be a major player in future genomic studies. Yang (2001), director of the Beijing Genomics Institute (BGI), opined that "now everyone in China knows what they human genome is," and they are "proud to be part of this international effort" (quoted in Cyranoski 2001, 10). While some "Western geneticists" remain "uneasy about China's flirtation with eugenics," the Chinese seem to be treasuring the importance of their "genetic resources" ("Politics" 2001, 11). More than fifty genomic programs dot this region's landscapes, and hundreds of Chinese scientists are flocking to well-financed centers, like the Chinese National Human Genome Center (CHGC), which has branches in Beijing and Shanghai. There now appears to be strong governmental support for large-scale studies of protein structures, population studies that try to track down the causes of genetic diseases, and stem cell research. Mao's (1997) commentaries on the importance of the Chinese contributions to the study of the human genome may have been prescient.

Yet these giant leaps forward will always be accompanied by the ideological baggage of past eugenic abuses. The elite supporters of the HGP and regional diversity projects may be able to temporarily dissociate themselves from the legal applications of genomic research, but this may not alter the long-term perceptions of the linkages that can be made between the two—and not all of the critics who can make these associations will be living in the West. Cyranoski (2001) reports that "there are obstacles to progress":

> Some Chinese people are unwilling to take part in studies for fear that discovery of a genetic disease could lead to discrimination. And in the longer term, China's one-child policy, and the increasingly population mobility being promoted by the country's economic development, will pare down the number of large pedigrees and lead to genetic mixing between populations. (12)

These public concerns remind us of the need to take into account both elite and vernacular views of genomics. By studying the arguments, characterizations, narratives, and other discursive units of analysis that are used in these debates, communication scholars can keep an eye on the recurring and future abuses of activities that may be justified as necessitous acts in the name of "eugenics." Regardless of whether we are critiquing eugenic sterilization, the use of pedigree charts, the collection of blood in the "Third World," or the acceptance of gene patents, critics need to be engaged in critiques of both emancipation and domination—where we need to be self-reflective and aware of the uses and uses of all forms of scientific and technological arguments—regardless of whether these ideologies are presented to us in the name of "coercion" or "choice." Reichman, Brezis, and Steinberg (1996) are on point when they mention the talk about the need to critique such issues, but it is not only "the leading representatives of the medical community" (426) who need to be involved in debates about biotechnical advances, genetics, and eugenics. They may be right that "silence" may be the "equivalent of consent," but this thick ideological structure cannot be blamed solely on some distant Chinese activities.

Simply changing the label that appears on a law may help with the public relations dimensions of policy proposals, but they don't erase the contested nature of these activities. Nor do they obviate the need for constant vigilance when we a plethora of communities defending laws that rise to the surface in times of resource scarcity. "In a society that came to view its members as just so many cells or molecules to be manufactured or rearranged at will," noted Tribe (1973), "one wonders how easy it will be to recall what all the shouting about 'human rights' was supposed to mean" (649). Obviously we need to find ways of improving our understanding of human genetics, as well as enhancing our intercultural skills, without revisiting the tragedies of the past through the transmigration of enticing ideologies. When the next congress of the International Genetics Federation meets, we may have even more information about the revived popularity of international eugenics ("China's 'Eugenic'" 1998, 707).

Notes

1. In preparation for this chapter, I used a purposive sample of some 50 out of 100 major articles on Chinese eugenics that appeared in newspapers, popular magazines, and scientific journals between 1993 and 2001. I used the following databases: Articles First, Humanities Index, Ingenta, JSTOR, Legal Periodicals Index, Lexis-Nexis, and Medline. These databases provided a wealth of information on national and international science publications, newspaper clippings, international protocols, indigenous statements, and organizational evaluations of various genomic projects.

2. For a copy of these laws, see "The New Chinese Law" (1995). At first the law openly connected to eugenics, but it would later be renamed the Maternal and Infant Health Care law.

3. Some commentators argue that male children are preferred because of the perception that they can contribute to agricultural labor (Reichman, Brezis, and Steinberg 1996, 426).

4. Yet some representatives of foreign biotech companies—who are themselves involved in collecting biodiverse materials in the name of population genetics—argued that communities need to employ "Western-style ethical safeguards" (Beardsley 1997, 33). No wonder that some Chinese geneticists have expressed worries about becoming little "more than 'sample vendors' for their foreign partners" ("Politics" 2001, 11).

5. For an attack on this "relativist perspective," see Clarke 1995. He argued that those who tried to avoid the "charge of ethnocentrism" might as well avoid talking about such issues as freedom of speech, torture, or the death penalty (508).

References

Aird, J. S. 1994. The force be with you. *Far Eastern Economic Review*, January, 21.
Ashman, D. 1998. The Chinese way. *New Scientist*, November 14, 58.
Beardsley, T. 1997. China syndrome. *Scientific American*, March, 33–34.
Chen, T. 1947. Population policy. *American Journal of Sociology* 52: 72–77.

China to introduce eugenics law. 1993. World Tibet Network News, December 22. www.tibet.ca/wtnarchive/1993/12/22_1.html. Accessed December 17, 2001.

China's "eugenics" law still disturbing despite relabelling [*sic*]. 1998. *Nature*, August 20, 707.

Clarke, A. 1995. Eugenics in China. *Lancet*, August 19, 508.

Coghlan, A. 1998. Perfect people's republic. *New Scientist*, October 24, 18.

Condit, C. M., and Lucaites, J. L. 1993. *Crafting equality: America's Anglo-African word.* Chicago: University of Chicago Press.

Crow, J. F. 1988. Eugenics: Must it be a dirty word? *Contemporary Psychology* 33: 10–12.

Cyranoski, D. 2001. A great leap forward. *Nature*, March 1, 10–12.

Dickson, D. 1998a. Survey: Some countries side with China on genetic issues. *Nature Medicine* 4 (October): 1096.

———. 1998b. Back on track: The rebirth of human genetics in China. *Nature*, November 26, 303–6.

Dikotter, F. 1998a. *Imperfect Conceptions: Medical knowledge, birth defects, and eugenics in China.* New York: Columbia University Press.

———. 1998b. Review of race culture: Recent perspectives on the history of Eugenics. *American Historical Review* 103: 467–78.

———. 1999. Is China's law eugenic? "The legislation imposes decisions." *Unesco Courier* 52, no. 9: 31.

Doherty, P. 1995. Eugenics in China. *Lancet*, August 19, 509.

Duster, T. 1990. *Backdoor to eugenics.* New York: Routledge.

Fisher, I. 1921. Impending problems of eugenics. *Scientific Monthly* 13: 214–31.

Haller, M. 1963. *Eugenics: Hereditarian attitudes in American thought.* New Brunswick, N.J.: Rutgers University Press.

Hasian, M. A., Jr. 1996. *The rhetoric of eugenics in Anglo-American thought.* Athens: University of Georgia Press.

Kevles, D. J. 1985. *In the name of eugenics: Genetics and the uses of human heredity.* New York: Knopf.

Kiser, C. V. 1947. Population in modern China. *Social Forces* 25: 349–51.

Kuhl, S. 1994. *The Nazi connection.* Oxford: Oxford University Press.

Larson, E. J. 1995. *Sex, race, and science: Eugenics in the Deep South.* Baltimore, Md.: Johns Hopkins University Press.

Lucaites, J. L., and Condit, C. M. 1990. Reconstructing <equality>: Culturetypal and counter-cultural rhetorics. *Communication Monographs* 57: 5–24.

Ludmerer, K. 1972. *Genetics and American society: A historical appraisal.* Baltimore, Md.: John Hopkins University Press.

Mao X. 1997. Chinese eugenic legislation. *Lancet*, January 11, 139.

McGee, M. C. 1980. The "ideograph": A link between rhetoric and ideology. *Quarterly Journal of Speech* 66: 1–16.

The new Chinese law on maternal and infant health care. 1995. *Population and Development Review* 21: 698–702.

O'Brien, C. 1996. China urged to delay "eugenics" law. *Nature*, September 19, 131.

Opportunity for depth in Chinese eugenics debate. 1998. *Nature*, March 12, 109.

Osborn, H. F. 1932. Birth selection versus birth control. *Science* 76: 173–79.

Pickens, D. K. 1968. *Eugenics and the Progressives.* Nashville: Vanderbilt University Press.

Politics, ethics, and collaborations. 2001, March 1. *Nature,* 410, 11.

Pomfret, J. 1998. China clarifies its law on sterilization. *Washington Post Foreign Service,* August 18, Z10.

Post, T. 1994. Quality not quantity. *Newsweek* 124 (November): 36–37.

Preventing "inferior" people in China. 1993. *New York Times,* December 27, A16.

Reichman, J. M., Brezis, M., and Steinberg, A. 1996. China's eugenics law on maternal and infant health care. *Annals of Internal Medicine,* September 1, 425–26.

Renzong, Q. 1999. Is China's law eugenic? "A concern for collective good." *Unesco Courier* 52, no. 9: 30.

Rodgers, G. 1999. Ying and yang: The eugenic policies of the United States and China: Is the analysis that black and white? *Houston Journal of International Law* 22: 129–68.

Rosenthal, E. 1998. Scientists debate China's law on sterilizing the carriers of genetic defects. *New York Times,* August 16, A14.

Said, E. W. 1979. *Orientalism.* New York: Vintage.

Spivak, G. C. 1999. *A critique of postcolonial reason.* Cambridge, Mass.: Harvard University Press 1999.

Sun, P.-W. 1949. Sociology in China. *Social Forces* 27: 247–51.

Trent, J. W., Jr. 1994. *Inventing the feeble mind: A history of mental retardation in the United States.* Berkeley: University of California Press.

Tribe, L. H. 1973. Technology assessment and the fourth discontinuity: The limits of instrumental rationality. *Southern California Law Review* 46: 617–60.

Tyler, P. E. 1993. China weighs using sterilization and abortions to stop "abnormal" births. *New York Times,* December 22, A8.

Unschuld, P. U. 2000. Review of *Imperfect conceptions. Bulletin of the History of Medicine* 74: 627–29.

Wells, D. C. 1907. Social Darwinism. *American Journal of Sociology* 12: 695–716.

Wertz, D. C. 1997. Society and the not-so-new genetics: What are afraid of? Some future predictions from a social scientist. *Journal of Contemporary Health Law and Policy* 13: 299–346.

———. 1999. Chinese genetics and ethics. *Nature Medicine* 5, no. 3: 247.

Western eyes on China's eugenics law. 1995. *Lancet,* July 15, 131.

14

Islamism and the Politics of Eurocentrism

S. Sayyid

A STORY IS TOLD ABOUT THE TIME when Kissinger met Mao Zedong and asked him, "What do you think is the significance of the French Revolution?" Mao replied that it was too early to tell. Such caution, however, has been lacking in regard to Islamism. Almost from its inception, Islamism was seen as a strange sort of fad that would imminently disappear. Commentaries regularly declare that Islamism and its cognates have come to an end. These arguments for the decline of political Islam are quickly cast aside when "Islamic fundamentalism" hits the headlines. Prior to the September 11, 2001, attacks on the Pentagon and the World Trade Center, a number of commentators pointed to the end of Islamism. Because of the inability to treat Islamism as something more than a set of pathological reactions to developments in the world, Islamism as an object of analysis remains obscure and beholden to a number of recurring tropes: Islamism as an essential feature of Islam, Islamism as a form of fascism, Islamism as a form of resentment, Islamism as a form of fundamentalism, Islamism as a form of primitivism, Islamism as a form of pathology, and so on.

In this chapter I place Islamism within the context of the current world order. In the first part of this chapter, I look at how many of the popular conceptions of Islamism circulate in popular, journalistic, and public policy narratives. In the second half of the chapter I examine the extent to which the discourse of Eurocentrism gets in the way of an understanding of Islamism. In other words, this chapter is an investigation and an elaboration into the phenomenon of Islamism and its relationship to Eurocentrism.

The Politics of Emptiness: Islamism and the West

Rarely is Islamism presented as a distinct political movement with all the ambiguities and contradictions of other political movements. This is partly a function of the way in which the end of the Cold War has led to a general depoliticization. With the unraveling of the communist project of transnational radical transformation, politics has been reduced to liberalism—which, it can be argued, is not a politics at all, but rather the expansion of an economic logic from the market to the state. The effect has been to produce a definition of politics in which political activity becomes a branch of economic rational calculation. At the same time politics is viewed as what Western plutocracies do. Therefore, by definition, Islamism with its projects of refounding an Islamic order within Muslim communities is seen to be engaging an antipolitics, a politics that is not about the art of the possible but of trying to make the impossible possible. By the political I mean the processes by which social order is instituted. The political is simply a condition that arises whenever it is possible to make a distinction between friend and enemy, and this distinction is a public one (Schmitt 1996; Derrida 1999). Any sphere of social life can become politicized, and it can be politicized when there are antagonisms.

Strangely, the political nature of Islamism is represented as its penchant for violence and fanaticism, thus demarcating Islamism as the negation of politics. This negation of politics finds expression in the descriptions of Islamism as a form of emptiness. This emptiness takes two main forms: practical and conceptual.

It is argued that the practical emptiness of Islamism is based on the evidence of the real world. Events in various parts of the Muslim world, and the disillusionment that Muslims feel with this project, demonstrate the hollowness of Islamism. It is argued that the failure of Islamist movements to take state power is an illustration of this hollowness. Another example is the disappointment with Islamist movements that have exercised state power; for example, the experiences of the Taliban in Afghanistan, the Refah party in Turkey, and the Islamic republic of Iran. There is also the failure of Islamist groups to make headway in Tunisia and Morocco, the hegemony of the "moderates" in post-Khomeini Iran, and the continuing "popular" support enjoyed by the moderate regimes of *dar-ul-Islam* (Babeair 1990, 124). These general accounts assume that the Islamist rejection of consumerism is something that the ordinary people of the Muslim world do not want. Rather, it is argued, Muslims, just like the people of the Western plutocracies, want prosperity. Thus the Islamist project is unable to provide answers to what may be called the "bread-and-butter" issues, and the majority of Muslims are unable to accept that it has much to say about how to improve their lives. These arguments are based on the characterization of the Islamist agenda as being dominated by the impossibility of adhering to Islam outside the borders of an Islamic state; the necessity of taking part in jihad against infidels and corrupt Muslims; the equation of modern Muslim societies with *Jahiliyya* and the description of most Muslim leaders as *kufr* (i.e., unbelievers). What Islamists want to establish is not a prosperous society but an Islamic moral order.

It is often argued that Islamism does not offer a clear, consistent pattern of government. This conclusion is often reached either by comparing Maududi, Qutb, and Khomeini and finding not only that they do not agree with each other but that they also contradict each other, or by pointing out the many differences between political parties such as HizbAllah and the Muslim Brotherhood. Islamists are often dismissed as being peculiarly prone to disagreements, having vague public policies, and focusing on trivial issues (Babeair 1990, 133). These inconsistencies are considered to weaken the appeal of Islamism, and they can also be found in the policies of Islamist regimes, for example, the Iranian alliance with Baathist Syria during its war with Iraq, in spite of Syria's anti-Islamist and prosecularist policies (Ahady 1992, 240).

The conceptual emptiness of Islamism is seen, it is argued, in its insistence on terrorism and violence and its inability to provide a credible socioeconomic alternative to global capitalism (Ahady 1992, 239). Since October 1917, the idea has been that the only true conflict is one in which there is competition over the organization of the economy; everything else is secondary. This economism, which has been central to Marxism traditionally, is not restricted to Marxism or even to leftist political thinking in general. Hayek (1994), for example, shares economism—free markets will guarantee the good society. Economism has penetrated international relations literature through both Marxist theories and realpolitik, where material interests are often read as economic interests/resources. Attempts by Islamists to deal with these issues have involved articulating Islamic economics by consolidating Qur'anic injunctions and hadith as a comprehensive economic system. Various attempts to devise an "Islamic economics" have not provided a radical break from existing models of economic management organization. Another approach has been to reduce economics to a set of ethical questions rather than trying to "invent" Islamic economics. Inflation, for example, is presented as the work of greedy merchants, and so on. Economic distortions, to cite another example, are considered to be due to ethical misconduct, which can be corrected by following the right behavior as instructed in Islamic canonical texts.

This insistence on the conceptual emptiness of Islamism, as manifested in the meagerness of its economic program, implies that the challenge of Islamism is not really serious. Since Islamism does not challenge the capitalist structure of the world in the way that the communist discourse did, it can be reduced to a reaction to globalization rather than a serious contestation of the global capitalist order. In certain quarters it has been suggested that the "Islamic threat" has taken the place of communism. Of course some people from the left (e.g., Halliday 1996) have pooh-poohed this idea. They have sought to demonstrate Muslim states' inability to threaten the North Atlantic plutocracies with mutually assured destruction (despite the scare stories about an Islamic nuclear bomb). Indeed, the members of the Organization of Islamic Countries do not have the economic resources to threaten the Western plutocracies. There are two reasons for this. First, with the possible exception of Malaysia or Indonesia, no OIC member state has an economy capable of competing with the Pacific newly industrializing countries, never mind the more established North Atlantic economies. Second, and more importantly, among Muslims most committed to radical revision of the global order there is no clear blueprint for economic transformation. As Khomeini is supposed to have said, "We did not make the revolution for the price of watermelons." This is considered a major lacuna among Marxist commentators who see no real alternative opposition to global order in the absence of an economic blueprint. This allows them to dismiss the "Islamic resurgence" as just another example of "indigenizing culturalism." The idea that genuine conflict must include a socioeconomic element, however, is a product of the seventy-year struggle with the Soviet Union. Intense international conflict has occurred without a conflict about models of economic management: the revolutionary wars, the Napoleonic Wars, and World War I, to name just three. At stake in these conflicts were not different models of economic management. Unless one maintains an economistic framework, it is difficult to sustain the view that geopolitical conflict should only be significant if rival economic models are at stake.

From Revolution to Salvation

Oliver Roy (1994) has argued that political Islam has been checked because of its inability to forge an alternative to the dominant global order. For Roy, the defining feature of the Islamist political imagination is that "politics can only be founded upon acts of individual virtue" (21). Roy distinguishes between Islamization from the top (which he confusingly calls Islamism) and Islamization from the bottom (which he labels neofundamentalism). Islamism, for Roy, is represented by political activism dedicated to capturing the state and transforming society. This revolutionary path, exemplified by the Iranian revolution, was, according to Roy, a failure (25). Although he seems uncertain about the effect of Islamism (in his preface it has not altered the landscape; however, on page 25, it has profoundly marked the landscape, which begs the question,

What kind of mark is profound enough to mark without an alteration?), he suggests that the increasing influence of Saudi money has tipped the balance away from the revolutionary path to the ultra Wahabist tendencies of personal salvation. He argues that as Islamism has spread among the Muslim masses, and as it has become more popular, it has become less political (26). "The essential premise of the Islamist movement is that the political model it proposes presupposes the virtue of individuals, but this virtue can only be acquired if the society is truly Islamic. All the rest is plot, sin or illusion" (27).

Roy's critique has been influential, and the distinction he makes between Islamism as a political project and Islamism as a project of personal salvation is useful. However, the difficulty with his critique is that his conception of political struggle is state-centric. It may be more helpful to use a distinction introduced by Antonio Gramsci that distinguishes between political movements that aim to seize state power and then transform society and those movements that seek to win influence over civil society before attempting to seize state power. One could easily argue that the difference between the revolutionary and what Roy considers to be salvationary are differences in methodology rather than fundamental differences in aims. At stake is the nature of Islamism.

The reason for understanding Islamism as a discourse rather than just an ideology is precisely because of its amorphous nature. There are features of Islamism, I would argue, that make it consistent with a discourse rather a specific ideology. First, a discourse has many points of enunciation; it is not articulated from one particular center, hence the plurality of sites from which Islamism is articulated. Second, a discourse consists of a diverse number of statements, just as Islamism is not reducible to the statements from purely political parties; it is constituted by a variety of discourses. Third, these statements have a nonrandom and systematic relationship with each other. Fourth, Islamism's specificity arises when its constitutive elements are organized in terms of a frontier, which excludes elements that are considered to have an antagonistic relationship with elements internal to Islamism. In other words, Islamism becomes about differentiating itself from the discourse of Kemalism (Sayyid 1997). For these reasons, Islamism cannot be seen simply as an ideology. Its discursive character includes both linguistic and extra-linguistic elements. Its discursive character also means that it is not located within one specific domain of society (e.g., the field of public affairs). Thus Islamism's reach is as much cultural as any other narrowly conceived idea of politics.

This has created a number of difficulties for a more politically oriented project that wishes to center Islam within public affairs, since Islamists have not been as successful as one would assume in transforming the cultural aspects of Islamism into support for their specific political agendas. The increasingly overt assertion of Muslim subjectivity—in the form of dress or greater identification with the vocabulary of Islam—has not translated into overwhelming popular support for Islamist political projects. In communities where the overwhelming majority of the population considers itself Muslim, a few Islamists have been able to demonstrate that they enjoy popular support commensurate with a number of Muslims within those regions. There are a variety of reasons for this: there is no doubt that the Islamist political parties have been subject to levels of repression, both overt and covert, which have certainly been effective in terms of restricting their popular base. This repression has been supported by a convergence of interests of international great powers, who, for a variety of reasons, see in Islamism a challenge either to their own sovereignty and integrity or to the international order itself. This, however, is not the only explanation. It is still a valid question to ask why Islamist projects have been less successful in establishing themselves more securely within the Muslim world. Even where they have been successful in gaining some kind of power, their ability to "Islamize" these societies has been heavily contested and remains precarious. Even where Islamist political projects have taken control of state power they have not been able to "naturalize" their rule. The inability of an Islamist political hegemony has meant that Islamist regimes must rely on overt coercion as a means of sustaining their hold on power, since what Gramsci called their "intellectual and moral leadership" has not been sufficient. They have not been able to disorganize dissent to the extent that an alternative to an Islamist regime becomes largely unthinkable.

Most Islamist regimes promise to implement a social order that by definition most Muslims should accept, an order based on Islamic precepts. Although most Muslims argue that an Islamic government is the best form of government, when they have been offered practical attempts to establish this ideal form of government, they have tended to be hesitant, if not critical. Thus the discourse of Islamism is divided between a cultural and a narrowly conceived political dimension. This would seem to endorse Roy's conclusion that political manifestations of Islamism have been checked. The failure or success of Islamism depends, however, on what criteria we use to make such judgments, and this, of course, depends on what exactly we consider Islamism to be. Previously I suggested understanding Islamism in terms of a discourse. In the next section of the chapter I will place Islamism in its context before examining whether or not it has failed.

The current world order is characterized by three main features. First, there is the process of globalization, which is the undermining of the Westphalian template for international order. The causes of this undermining are varied and range from the collapse of the Soviet Union and the end of bipolarity to the technological destruction of distances, to the organization of production and consumption on a planetary scale. Second, there is the process of the decentering of the West and ongoing weakening of the hegemonic role of Western cultural formation. In short, the idea that "the West is the best" is increasingly being abandoned. Third, there is the project of Eurocentrism, a multidimensional attempt to restore Western cultural practices as universal. A manifestation of such a project can be seen in the American-led crusade—the so-called war on terrorism. It is this vortex, produced by these processes, that ensnares the Muslim *Ummah* and produces the conditions of possibility of Islamism. Too often Islamism is presented as a reaction to globalization (see, for example, Benjamin Barber's differentiation between McWorld and jihad). Closer examination of the various Islamist projects reveals the way in which they depend on globalization: the possibility of Islamism is partly enabled by globalization. One of the most apt examples of this is provided by al Qaeda, which is clearly a deterritorialized political agent whose membership is transnational and transethnic, and whose operations depend on global communication technologies. I would like to suggest that it is more useful to see Islamism as the other of Eurocentrism rather than a reaction to modernization or globalization. To make good my claim, in the next part of this chapter, I will sketch out what I understand by Eurocentrism before addressing its relationship with Islamism.

Eurocentrism/Islamism

A common way of deploying Eurocentrism is through polemics. Those who consider themselves to be subjects of Eurocentrism seem to think that by labeling something Eurocentric we can rule it out of court, rather like accusing someone of being sexist, fundamentalist, or racist. Champions of Eurocentrism often give the impression that they don't know what all the fuss is about, or that Eurocentrism is harmless and inevitable. Whether Eurocentrism is hurled as a term of abuse or worn as a badge of pride, it appears as a cognate of European or Western. I want to try out a conceptual understanding of Eurocentrism. One way of reading the twentieth century is as a period in which the very idea of the West has been subject to intense contestation. It should be clear here that the West does not refer to a geographical entity. Rather, it is an ideological entity; it is not a place but a project (Glissant 1989; Hall 1992). It signifies a political-cultural formation predicated around a set of uneven power relations in which an essentialized West exerts its superiority over an essentialized rest. The wars of 1914 and 1945, the Holocaust, decolonization (however incomplete), and the emergence of post-Western political movements had the effect of putting the claims of Western superiority, and the assumption that Western values incarnate universal values, into question

(Sayyid 1997). Western hegemony was based on the convergence of universal values and Western values. It is the dis-articulation of this convergence that lays the ground for a challenge to Western global hegemony. It is this decentering of the West that the strategy of Eurocentrism attempts to remedy. In other words, Eurocentrism can be understood as the "discourse that emerges in the context of the decentering of the West" (Sayyid 1997, 128). Thus Eurocentrism is a project that seeks to close the gap between the universal and the Western.

The conflation between the universal and the Western came as a result of a complex set of processes beginning with the European conquest of the Western Hemisphere (Blaut 1993; Frank 1998). This profoundly transformed the world balance of power and made possible the era of European global domination. This global domination was not purely economic or military, but it had a cultural aspect. The narratives that were used to account for Europe's ascendancy became constitutive of a world order in which Europe's superiority was considered to be the product of the intrinsic attributes of Europe (be they geographical or cultural). The establishment of a Western hegemony meant the destiny of the West came to be represented as the history of the world. Until fairly recently, many people believed that not only was it possible that with time humans would discover all the correct answers to the problems humanity confronted, but also that the societies located on the Western edge of the Asian landmass were the ones to do so. The royal road to the good life was the route pioneered by the West. Modernization became westernization when modernity was given a concrete form by drawing on European cultural practices. The modern man was someone who dressed like a European, ate like a European (with a knife and fork), and lived like a European. Societies and cultures that followed the Western lead could have all the things that a life in the West entailed. The destiny of the world was westernization. The notion that the "West is best" was also held by many people considered to be outside the pale of Western civilization.

Among Muslims, Mustafa Kemal was the most prominent political figure who bought the ideology of "the West is the best." Under his leadership this ideology was put into practice in the rump of the Ottoman Empire. In 1924, Kemal and his supporters launched a series of reforms that included the abolition of the caliphate, the replacement of Arabic script, and the banning of the hijab and the fez (on the grounds of being uncivilized). Kemal had many admirers and imitators throughout the Muslim world. While some of these fans were explicit in their admiration, others, while not mentioning Mustafa Kemal, were still heavily influenced by what he had done. The Muslim world that emerged in the wake of the European empires, allowing for different local histories and experiences, was at heart based on the discourse of Kemal and faith in the superiority of Western cultural practices.

There was this belief that somehow over time (with modernization) Muslims would disappear. The modern world was going to be a world without Muslims, and with Islam only as a memory or a museum piece. This faith in Western supremacy began to be undermined by a number of developments (e.g., decolonization, the Holocaust). The effects of these developments are often confusingly abbreviated as the postmodern condition, in which the West has been knocked off its central perch. It is this unraveling of the universal and the Western that provides the context for the emergence of Islamism. At the same time, as Islamism grows in strength, it hastens the delinking between the universal and the Western. It is no coincidence that the crisis of Western identity is represented by the presence of Islam. Islam is one of the key forces in contrast to which Western identity was first forged, and it still seems to represent the past of Western history. Its rejection of secularism, its attempt to articulate a culture centered on notions of the divine, its supposed intolerance, and its supposed fanaticism serve to suggest how Islam operates as a mirror of the West's own past. Hence its continued presence has a haunting quality to it: the ghost of the god that the West killed.

Islamists have successfully and ostentatiously inserted a Muslim identity in the contemporary world. The opponents of Islamism see it as a reactionary force determined to turn back the clock of history. In these narratives, naturally enough, the West is the star, and the script seems to insist that the rest of humanity should play bit parts. (In most narratives, for example, Islamicate civilization is reduced to the role of postal workers carrying the heritage of classical Roman-Greek civilization to the Renaissance). The discourse of Western supremacy (Westernese) would have us believe that this script is transcendentally sanctioned (History, Science, and Reason are the authors of this script). Many in the Islamicate world, including most of the ruling elites, accept this. For them the age of the West never ended. They are still trying to westernize their reluctant societies. For they continue to see in westernization the essence of modernization. These true believers must be disconcerted by the way in which everybody around them seems to have lost faith in westernization—even Westerners don't believe that the West is the best anymore. This loss of faith in westernization has produced the space that allowed Islamism to not only emerge but to become the most significant opposition to the current order in Muslim societies. It is this loss of faith in westernization that the "westoxicated" elite have tried to conceal with cynicism and repression.

Islamism does not depend on the language of political protest that has been with us for the past 200 years. It does not promise a faster route to westernization. In its most radical form it simply stakes out its own path toward the good life, with its own notions of good and evil. The unraveling of the link between the universal and the Western has created a space where it is possible for different cultural complexes to find different political vocabularies.

Many Islamist movements have borne the brunt of westoxicated elites' attempt to hold on to its monopoly of power. The measures used against the Islamists have ranged from campaigns of extermination initiated by the Baathists regimes and the Algerian junta, to the dirty wars and the use of paralegal violence, and to the legislative prohibitions and smear campaigns, used by so-called moderate regimes such as that of Mubarak in Egypt. Some of the difficulties encountered by Islamists have been common to other historical attempts at transnational reform. In particular, the Islamists face three main challenges to their ambitions to institutionalize a new order. First, in most Muslim societies a large section of the population remains committed to westernization. For various reasons, Islamists have not been as successful in winning over this group. This section of the population believes itself to be secularist, liberal, and democratic, and it certainly presents itself in these terms to the Western audiences. Despite their much proclaimed love of liberalism and democracy, however, many of these people have been willing to support most illiberal and antidemocratic measures taken by state machinery against Islamists.

Second, the current divisions of the Muslim world are sanctioned and manipulated by an international order enforced by the new concert of mainly European powers based around the leadership of the United States (G8), constituting what Martin Shaw (2001) has described as a "conglomerate global state." It is the main defender of the current world order, which includes the current distribution of Islamicate world into rival and often contending nation-state blocs. As such, most Islamist groups are forced into making accommodations to the nation-state, with the consequence that nationalism begins to penetrate their discourse (e.g., the parties in Kuwait, who claim to be Islamist, are unwilling to allow non-Kuwaiti Muslims to become members). This nationalization of Islamism means that Islamist groups are prone to being isolated, and are often forced into political positions that undermine their Islamist objectives (e.g., their pandering to policies of ethnic and cultural homogenization even when dealing with Muslim minority ethnic groups).

Third, current global order is dominated by discourse of capitalism, which privileges the subjectivity of a sovereign consumer. In this way, all values and convictions become matters for individual choice and consumption. Islamists, despite the energy spent on devising "Islamic" economics, have largely failed to counter the discourse of global capital. Their attacks have been based on questions of moral regulation and rectitude rather than transcending the terms of the global capitalism. In this important sense, they have not yet articulated a counterhegemonic project to global capital.

In this environment, Islamism proper—an attempt to articulate a political order centered on Islam—has only been successful in Iran, and to some extent

Sudan and Afghanistan. In general, the power of the modern postcolonial state is formidable and unrelenting. The international discourse of terrorism, articulated by the United States and subsequently used by authoritarian regimes, has become hegemonic to the extent that the category of freedom fighter has almost disappeared. Moreover, challenges to state authority are considered terrorism, which has the effect of delegitimating any resistance to repressive regimes. Unrepresentative regimes have successfully articulated Islamist opposition as terrorism, thus creating the excuse for "dirty wars" against Islamists. Even Islamists who have tried the electoral route have been forced on the defensive by being branded as "terrorists," with the ruling elites of the Islamicate world declaring them a national security threat, a threat that justifies the state using extra-constitutional means including violence to combat it. Currently the electoral as well as the revolutionary route to an Islamic state seems to have been diverted or blocked by the westoxicated elites' use of death squads and torture centers.

Despite the current strategic difficulties faced by Islamists, most Muslim communities are becoming increasingly Islamized. More and more Muslims are beginning to adhere with greater conviction and regularity to Islamic norms and values. In many ways, this can be seen as the conceptual analog to the sovereign consumer of free market fundamentalism: once we have a society full of good Muslims, then we shall have an Islamic order. Such an approach is locked into a methodological and epistemological position in which the individual is the basic building block of social order. By making the individual sovereign, this salvationist strategy risks turning Islam into matter of private ethics with little or no impact on public affairs. The sovereignty of the individual hollows out the idea of society. The logical conclusion to such a strategy would be Muslims without the *Ummah*—a world of individual pious Muslims enclosed in their private spheres, where public spaces remain Islam-free zones. In Islamicate societies this Islamization is encouraged as a vaccine against Islamism (even secularist Iraq decided to add "Allah Akbur" to its flag in wake of the second Gulf War). Islamization from below has heightened the difference between the westoxicated elite and the Islamized section of society. In this way, even gradual Islamization risks eroding the legitimacy of the existing regimes.

The problems that beset the Islamicate world will not be solved by a slavish imitation of the Western template. At the same time, there is no reason to assume that the qualities most people want in their ideal society cannot be generated by Islamic cultural formations. Values with universal significance are not the monopoly of the West. The greatest trick the West has played is to convince the world that only Western culture knows what is good and what is evil, and only by following the lead of the West can other societies partake of universal values. It is time to recognize this trick for what it is. We Muslims can have a good life, a good society, and good governance without trying to force our history, our traditions and our culture into a pale imitation of the Western historical development. The ways things happened in the West (Renaissance, Reformation, Counter-Reformation, Enlightenment, modernity) are part of a contingent and political sequence; they are not a necessary or logical development to be imposed on Muslim societies with very different starting points and very different locations in the current world order.

The clash between Eurocentrism and Islamism increasingly dominates considerations of international relations and domestic security policies. To the extent that the "war on terror" has an overarching political logic, other than an attempt by the American imperium to discipline the world, it is to ward off the challenge of Islamism. Time will no doubt demonstrate that the challenge of Islamism is not something that can be defeated by a crusade against terrorism. The power of Islamism derives from its critique of the assumption that the royal road to a better future is pioneered by the West. Ultimately, the success or failure of the "war on terrorism" will depend on the extent to which the project of Eurocentrism is able to close the gap between Western cultural formations and universal values, that is, the extent to which Eurocentrism is able to present as universal, inevitable, and natural its own contingent destiny. In the absence of hegemony that closes the gap between the universal and Western, more and more Western resources will go into regulating and coercing compliance to Western values. The very fact that the American imperium has to resort to large-scale armed violence and demonize many Muslims shows the limits of the project of Eurocentrism. It remains to be seen whether these limits are temporary or not.

The very condition of possibility of Islamism is the decentering of the West (Sayyid 1997). Thus it is possible for Muslims to imagine a project of transformation without having to route that project through the Western cultural heritage. Islamists believe that it is possible to think of a better way of life by drawing on the resources of Islamicate cultural formations. This project for the future reconstruction of social relations puts into question the notion that only Western cultural resources are useful for building a future.

The argument that Islamists have been checked in their drive for state power depends on treating the Islamists as narrowly conceived political movements reacting to the conditions found in Islamic societies. Such arguments do not take into account that Islamists operate in global context and their emergence is not simply related to local situations (though it would be foolish to deny that local factors have their part to play in the variety of forms that Islamism has taken). Islamism challenges not just the various Kemalist regimes that hold sway in the Islamicate world. Nor is it simply an angry reaction to the currant world order. More significantly, Islamism is a challenge to the project of Eurocentrism. Islamists hint at the possibility that the universal can be generated from histories and cultures other than the official version of Western history and culture. The existence of Islamism points toward a plural world order in opposition to Eurocentrism, which seeks to continue to organize the world in terms of "the West and the rest."

References

Ahady, A. 1992. The decline of Islamic fundamentalism. *Journal of Asian and African Studies* 27: 3–4.

Amin, S. 1989. *Eurocentrism*. London: Zed.

Babeair, A. 1990. Contemporary Islamic revivalism: A movement or a moment? *Journal of Arab Affairs* 9, no. 2: 122–46.

Barber, B. R. 1996. *Jihad vs. McWorld*. New York: Ballantine.

Blaut, J. M. 1993. *The colonizer's model of the world: Geographical diffusionism and Eurocentric history*. London: Guilford.

Derrida, J. 1999. *The politics of friendship*. London: Verso.

Frank, A. 1998. *Reorient: Global economy in the Asian age*. Berkeley: University of California Press.

Geyer, M., and Bright, C. 1995. "World history in a global age." *American Historical Review* 100, no. 4: 1034–60.

Glissant, E. 1989. *Caribbean discourse*. Charlottesville: University of Virginia Press.

Hall, S. 1992. "The West and the rest: Discourse and power." In S. Hall and B. Gieben, eds., *The formation of modernity*. Cambridge: Polity.

Halliday, F. 1996. *Islam and the myth of confrontation*. London: I. B. Tauris.

Hayek, F. A. [1944] 1994. *The road to serfdom*. 50th anniversary ed. Chicago: University of Chicago Press.

Hesse, B. 1999. "Reviewing the western spectacle: Reflexive globalisation through the black diaspora." In A. Brah, M. J. Hickman, and Macan Ghaill, eds., *Global futures: Migration, environment and globalisation*. London: Macmillan.

———. 2002. "Forgotten like a bad dream: Atlantic slavery and the ethics of post-colonial memory." In D. T. Goldberg and A. Quayson, eds., *Relocating postcolonialism*. Oxford: Blackwell.

Huntingdon, S. P. 1996. *The clash of civilizations and the remaking of world order*. New York: Simon & Schuster.

Husserl, E. 1970. *The crisis of European sciences and transcendental phenomenology: An introduction to phenomenological philosophy*. Translated by D. Carr. Evanston, Ill.: Northwestern University Press.

Roy, O. 1994. *The failure of political Islam*. London: I. B. Tauris

Said, E. W. 1985. *Orientalism*. London: Routledge & Kegan Paul.

Sayyid, S. 1997. *A Fundamental fear: Eurocentrism and the emergence of Islamism*. London: Zed.

Schmitt, C. [1932] 1996. *The concept of the political.* Translated by George Schwab. Chicago: University of Chicago Press.

Shaw, M. 2001. *Theory of a global state.* Cambridge: Cambridge University Press.

Shohat, E., and Stam, R. 1994. *Unthinking Eurocentrism: Multiculturalism and the media.* London: Routledge.

Slater, D. 1994. "Exploring other zones of the postmodern: Problems of ethnocentrism and difference across the north-south divide." In A. Rattansi and S. Westwood, eds., *Racism, modernity, and identity: On the western front.* Cambridge: Polity.

Index

About the Editor and Contributors

Amin Alhassan holds a Ph.D. in communication from Concordia University, Montreal, an M.A. in mass communication from University of Tampere, Finland, and a diploma in journalism from the Ghana Institute of Journalism in Accra. He is currently a part-time faculty in the graduate program in communication at McGill University, Montreal. Previously he worked for five years as a journalist with the Ghana News Agency and later with the Ghana Broadcasting Corporation in Accra.

Heidi Marie Brush is a doctoral candidate at the Institute of Communications Research at the University of Illinois, Urbana-Champaign. Her research interests address the intersection of technologies/politics/economies in the eruption of netwar through, across, and against globalizing networks.

François Debrix is assistant professor of international relations at Florida International University in Miami. He is the author of *Re-Envisioning Peacekeeping: The United Nations and the Mobilization of Ideology* (1999), the editor of *Language, Agency, and Politics in a Constructed World* (2003), and the coeditor (with Cynthia Weber) of *Rituals of Mediation: International Politics and Social Meaning* (2003). His research in the domains of critical world order studies, international relations and political theories, media studies, and postmodern analysis of popular culture has been published in journals like *Alternatives*, *Philosophy and Social Criticism*, *Strategies*, *Third World Quarterly*, *Geopolitics*, and *Postmodern Culture*. He has translated several of Jean Baudrillard's recent essays for the journal *C-Theory: Technology, Theory, and Culture*.

John D. H. Downing is the director of the Center for Global Media Studies, Southern Illinois University. Downing's major work focuses on international communication, studies of racism, ethnicity and media, and alternative media and social movements. His books include *Film and Politics in the Third World* (editor); *Radical Media: Rebellious Communication and Social Movements*; *Questioning the Media: A Critical Introduction*, 2d ed. (coeditor); *Internationalizing Media Theory*. Among his numerous articles are a series of essays on Soviet and post-Soviet media (published in *Soviet Studies, Space Policy*, the *European Journal of Communication*, and the *Electronic Journal of Communication*); further studies of alternative media (*Media, Culture, and Society; Journal of Communication*). His current research focuses on comparative analysis of ethnicity, racism, and media, and alternative media globally.

John Nguyet Erni is associate professor of media and cultural studies in the Department of English and Communication, City University of Hong Kong. His areas of research and teaching include gender and sexual politics, media studies, youth consumption studies in Asia, and critical public health studies. He was a recipient of the Rockefeller Humanities Research Fellowship in 1999, which enabled him to work at Columbia University's School of Public Health in the Program on Gender, Sexuality, Health, and Human Rights. His books include *Unstable Frontiers: Technomedicine and the Cultural Politics of "Curing" AIDS* (1994), *Internationalizing Cultural Studies* (coedited with Ackbar Abbas), and *Asian Media Studies: The Politics of Subjectivities* (coedited with Chua Siew Keng) (forthcoming). He was also editor of a special issue entitled "Becoming (Postcolonial) Hong Kong" for *Cultural Studies* (2001).

Michael Robert Evans is assistant professor at the Indiana University School of Journalism. His research focuses on indigenous media; he has conducted ethnographic research with the Inuit of the eastern Canadian Arctic, the Mohawk of upstate New York and Ontario, and the Aborigines of the Australian Outback. He is particularly interested in indigenous media performance and indigenous journalistic practices.

Marouf Hasian Jr. is professor of communication in the Department of Communication at the University of Utah. His areas of interest include postcolonial studies, law and rhetoric, and critical memory studies. He is the author of numerous scholarly journal articles. His books include *The Rhetoric of Eugenics in Anglo-American Thought* (1996) and *Legal Memories and Cultural Amnesias in Anglo-American Rhetorical Culture* (2000).

Clifford A. Jones (J.D., M.Phil., Ph.D.) teaches at the University of Florida's Levin College of Law. He is a former Fulbright scholar to Germany and a visiting fellow at Oxford University's program in comparative media law and policy. His teaching and research interests include European Community, international, and media and Internet law.

Marwan M. Kraidy teaches global communication and transcultural processes in the Division of International Communication, School of International Service, American University, in Washington, D.C. His publications include articles in *Critical Studies in Mass Communication, Communication Theory, Media, Culture and Society, Journal of Transnational Broadcasting Studies, Journal of Broadcasting and Electronic Media, Journalism and Mass Communication Quarterly, Journal of International Communication* and *Global Media Journal,* in addition to several book chapters on international communication, globalization and culture, and Middle Eastern media. He is coeditor of *Global Media Studies: Ethnographic Perspectives* (2003), and is currently completing a a book-length critical examination of cultural hybridity in international communication.

John Nerone is research professor of communications at the University of Illinois at Urbana-Champaign. He has written extensively on the history of the media and normative press theory, including *Last Rights: Revisiting Four Theories of the Press* (1995), which he coauthored and edited, *Violence against the Press: Policing the Public Sphere in U.S. History* (1994), and, with Kevin Barnhurst, *The Form of News: A History* (2001). He is at work on a textbook history of the media and public life in the United States.

Rick Rockwell is associate professor of journalism at the American University, Washington, D.C. He is the coauthor of a forthcoming book, *Media Power in Central America.* Previously he was a journalist covering Mexico and Central America for the Associated Press, PBS, and other media outlets.

S. Sayyid is research fellow at the University of Leeds. His book, *A Fundamental Fear: Eurocentrism and the Emergence of Islamism* (1997), is in its second edition (2003). He has written widely on postcolonialism and globalization.

Mehdi Semati is assistant professor of communication at Eastern Illinois University. His writings on cultural studies, media and transnationalism, culture and international relations, pedagogy of international communication, and terrorism imagery and press coverage have appeared as book chapters and articles in journals such as *Journal of International Communication, Critical Studies in Mass Communication, Journal of Popular Film and Television, Transnational Broadcasting Studies,* and *Television and New Media.* He coedited a book (with N. Chitty and R. Rush) entitled *Studies in Terrorism: Media Scholarship and the Enigma of Terror* (2003).

Sujatha Sosale teaches in the School of Journalism and Mass Communication, the University of Iowa. Her research interests include cultural approaches to communication, development, and social change; the global cultural economy; and media technology and society. Currently she is completing a book on communication, democracy, and development.

McKenzie Wark teaches media and cultural studies at the New School University in New York. He is the author of *Virtual Geography* (1994); *The Virtual Republic* (1997); *Celebrities, Cultures and Cyberspace* (1999); and *Dispositions* (2002) and is coauthor of *Speed Factory* (2002).